COMMUNICATING WITH
COMPETENCY

Lawrence B. Rosenfeld
University of North Carolina, Chapel Hill

Roy M. Berko
Lorain County Community College

SCOTT, FORESMAN/LITTLE, BROWN HIGHER EDUCATION
A Division of Scott, Foresman and Company
Glenview, Illinois   London, England

ISBN 0-673-18706-3

PREFACE

We wrote this textbook with one question continuously in mind: *How can this information be useful?* If we have learned anything from our students during our combined fifty-five years of teaching it is that **usefulness is an important goal**—perhaps the most important goal when working with students beginning their study of communication. So our goal is to provide information that directly applies to your development of communication skills and to help you develop communication skills that demonstrate the relevance of the information we present.

Knowledge without application may be useful under some circumstances, but not when the goal is to become a competent communicator. And application without knowledge assumes a robot-like view of humanity—humans as "behavior machines"—an attitude that is both incorrect and sterile.

Communication competencies are **life-necessary** *competencies.* If you doubt this, consider that how well you communicate determines the extent to which you achieve your personal, occupational, and relational goals. Success on and off the job depends on being able to listen effectively, express thoughts clearly and concisely, and build and maintain personal relationships—whether with one other person, in a small group, or in a public setting. Day after day, you need to communicate competently to ensure yourself the richest and fullest life possible. And that brings us to the primary objective of this textbook: **to provide you with the information, skills, and motivation to become a competent communicator.**

Objectives

To communicate competently, you must first know what communication behaviors are likely to help you achieve success in a particular situation. This requires that you understand yourself, the situations in which you interact with others, and the communication behaviors that are available to you. This textbook will teach you to assess your strengths and weaknesses as a communicator and to analyze the situations in which you communicate with others. Then, based on your new knowledge, you will learn which behaviors are necessary to become a successful communicator.

Second, you must possess the skills to communicate successfully. *Knowing how* to communicate does not equal *being able* to communicate. You need to develop new skills and perfect those you have. This textbook gives you numerous opportunities to practice the skills that enhance your ability to communicate competently.

Third, you need to be motivated to communicate competently. We hope that this textbook—its examples, its practical orientation, and its way of presenting information and activities—will help you realize how important it is to be a competent communicator and will therefore motivate you to gain the necessary understanding and skills.

Special Features

Many special features have been built into *Communicating with Competency* to help you increase your understanding, skills, and motivation.

First, the communication competencies presented in each chapter have been carefully selected and sequenced. They have been tested and taught by researchers and teachers interested in communication and represent our most current understanding of what it means to communicate with competency.

Second, this textbook is written *to* you and *about* you:

▶ Examples are drawn from everyday life.
▶ Technical language is avoided, but when specialized terms must be used, they are defined simply and immediately. In addition, to ease your study, a glossary of key terms is included at the end of the book.
▶ References to research papers, names, and dates have been kept to a minimum to avoid distracting you as you read and apply the material in each chapter.
▶ Carefully devised Knowledge Checkups and Skill Checkups have been systematically placed throughout each chapter. These activities—ranging from brief tests aimed at enhancing your self-understanding to more complicated tasks involving the observation of human behavior or the direct application of specific communication skills—have been designed to be quickly accomplished, tightly focused and *doable*. They are an integral part of the learning process and should be neither skipped nor viewed as ancillary.
▶ Chapter-ending Communication Competency Checkups present thought-provoking problems that help you review each chapter's content and apply it to a realistic situation, such as advising a family member on how to deal with a conflict or helping a friend cope with public speaking anxiety.
▶ A thorough subject index is provided at the end of the book to help you locate topics quickly and easily. Plus, sources for further investigation are presented at the end of each chapter to help you find more information on particular topics.

Organization

The material in *Communicating with Competency* is organized to enhance your understanding and development of communication competencies. The first three chapters present the background you need to begin your study on communication. You will be introduced to some basic definitions and components of communication competency, you will begin to assess your strengths and weaknesses as a communicator, and you will learn effective ways of using verbal and nonverbal communication.

Because who you are provides the foundation for how you communicate, the next two chapters focus on you as a communicator. These chapters explore how your view of yourself and your perceptions of the world affect your communication. They are followed by an entire chapter on listening, an especially important competency that comes into play in virtually every communication situation, from one-on-one and small-group discussions to public speeches.

The remaining chapters examine communication on three different levels. Chapters 7, 8, and 9 present the knowledge and skills required to communicate competently in one-on-one settings, the first level of communication. You will learn about the goals, structures, and rules of relationships, and how competent communication can help you develop strong relationships and deal with conflict.

The next two chapters focus on communication competencies associated primarily with the second level of communication, the small group setting. How groups develop and work, obstacles to effective group interaction and methods for overcoming them, and the communication roles group members enact, such as leadership, are covered in these chapters.

The final five chapters focus on communication competencies at the third level of communication, the public setting. Beginning with an assessment of yourself, the audience, and the situation, and proceeding through the final evaluation of your speech and recommendations for improvement, these chapters provide a step-by-step system for developing and delivering an effective public speech.

A Note to the Instructor

An instructor's manual is available to enhance the effectiveness of *Communicating with Competency*. It includes several alternative approaches to teaching your course and using this book, a bibliography of readily available supplementary media sources, discussion questions for each of the Knowledge and Skill Checkups to enhance their application in your classroom, and a test bank with interesting and provocative questions in a variety of formats.

Communication: 1940–1989, a special edition of *TIME* magazine that offers a historical look at *TIME*'s coverage of major events illustrating the power of communication in 20th century society, is also shrinkwrapped with the text.

Acknowledgments

This book is the result of a team effort—not just the team whose names are on the cover, but a much larger team. We want to thank those who provided us with critiques and suggestions:

Rudolph E. Busby, San Francisco State University
Ann Cunningham, Bergen Community College
Mary C. Forestieri, Lane Community College
Carolyn Hanson, Richland College
Lawrence W. Hugenberg, Youngstown State University
Robin Pulver, Sanford County Community College
Stephanie L. Shaefer, George Mason University
Walter Terris, San Francisco State University

We also want to thank Barbara Muller, the Scott, Foresman/Little, Brown editor who initiated the process that resulted in this book, and Vikki Barrett, who saw the project through to completion: the encouragement, help, and good humor of both made this an enjoyable experience.

Cynthia Fostle, our developmental editor, did for us what we often do for others: took a red pencil and pushed and pulled a better book out of the one we wrote. We appreciate the extraordinary effort!

Finally, we dedicate this text to our families and students, who provided the context in which many of the ideas presented here were developed, tested, and honed to their present form.

Lawrence B. Rosenfeld
Roy M. Berko

Communication: 1940–1989

Edited by:

James Gaudino, Executive Director of the Speech Communication Association
Gustav Friedrich, University of Oklahoma-Norman
J. Jeffery Auer, Indiana University-Bloomington
Carolyn Calloway-Thomas, Indiana University-Bloomington
Patti Gillespie, University of Maryland
Robert C. Jeffrey, University of Texas at Austin
Mark Knapp, University of Texas at Austin
Jerry Miller, Michigan State University

This exciting new magazine piece, shrinkwrapped into each purchased copy of *Communicating with Competency* is a joint production of *TIME* and Scott, Foresman/Little, Brown. Compiled and edited by members of the Speech Communication Association, *Communication: 1940–1989* contains articles and excerpts relating to communication topics from past issues of *TIME*. It also includes a "You Are There" feature that illustrates the power of the spoken word. Spanning almost fifty years, *Communication: 1940–1989* offers students a unique glimpse of communication in the 20th century.

CONTENTS

CHAPTER 1

▶ *Foundations for Communication Competency*

COMMUNICATION COMPETENCIES   2

Defining Communication   3
    The Elements of Communication   3
    The Characteristics of Communication   4
    Human Communication: A Summary   6
The Components of Communication Competency   7
    Knowledge   8
    Skills   8
    Motivation   11
The Functions of Communication Competency   12
The Qualities of Competent Communicators   13
    Competent Communicators Are Appropriate   13
    Competent Communicators Are Effective   14
    Competent Communicators Are Adaptable   14
    Competent Communicators Recognize Roadblocks to Effective
        Communication   14
    Competent Communicators Recognize That Competency Is a
        Matter of Degree   16
    Competent Communicators Are Ethical   16
You as a Communicator   17

COMMUNICATION COMPETENCY CHECKUP   18

Note   18
For Further Investigation   19

CHAPTER 2

▶ *Verbal Communication*

COMMUNICATION COMPETENCIES   20

The Importance of Verbal Communication   21
Language and Meaning   22
    Abstract and Concrete Symbols   23
    Denotion and Connotation   26

Barriers to Successful Communication: Our Imperfect Language   29
    Polarization   29
    Indiscrimination   31
    Fact-Inference Confusion   32
    Allness   34
    Static Evaluation   34
    Bypassing   35
Using Language Effectively   36
    Unclear Language   36
    Language that Affects Impressions   40
COMMUNICATION COMPETENCY CHECKUP   46
Notes   46
For Further Investigation   47

CHAPTER 3

▶ *Nonverbal Communication*

COMMUNICATION COMPETENCIES   48
Functions of Nonverbal Communication   49
Physical Appearance   51
    Body Shape   51
    Body Image   52
    Clothing and Other Artifacts   54
Face and Eyes   56
Contexts of Interaction   59
    Physical Context   59
    Psychological Context   60
Touch   64
    Uses of Touch   65
    Expectations for Touch   66
Voice   68
Body Movements   72
    Types of Body Movements   72
    Uses of Body Movements   74
Nonverbal Clues to Deception   76
Feeling = Behavior = Feeling   77
COMMUNICATION COMPETENCY CHECKUP   78
Notes   79
For Further Investigation   80

CHAPTER 4

▶ *Conceiving the Self*

COMMUNICATION COMPETENCIES   82

Who You Are: Your Self-Concept   83
　　　The Person You Are   84
　　　The Person You Wish You Were   93
　　　The Person You Present to Others   94

How You Feel about Yourself: Your Self-Esteem   97
　　　Improving Your Self-Esteem   99

COMMUNICATION COMPETENCY CHECKUP   103

Notes   104
For Further Investigation   104

CHAPTER 5

▶ *The Self and Others*

COMMUNICATION COMPETENCIES   106

Perception   107
　　　Selective Perception   107
　　　Selective Organization   108
　　　Selective Interpretation   111
　　　The Self-Fulfilling Prophecy   113

Increasing Perceptual Accuracy   114
　　　Stretch Yourself   114
　　　Remain Open-Minded   117
　　　Increase Empathy   118

Stress and Communication   120
　　　Communication Indicators of Stress   120

Communication Anxiety   122
　　　Communication Anxiety and You   124
　　　Causes of Communication Anxiety   125
　　　The Effects of Communication Anxiety   125
　　　Dealing with Communication Anxiety   126

COMMUNICATION COMPETENCY CHECKUP   127

Notes   128
For Further Investigation   128

CHAPTER 6

▶ *Effective Listening*

COMMUNICATION COMPETENCIES   130

Investigating Your Listening Patterns   131
    What Is Listening?   133
    The Stages of Listening   133
    The Levels of Listening   134
    The Reasons for Listening   136

Barriers to Effective Listening   137
    Nonlistening Cues   138

Making Listening Work for You   142
    Focusing Attention   142
    Organizing Material   144
    Providing Feedback   146

Developing Empathic Listening Skills   147
    Empathic Response Style   150
    Recommendation Response Style   150
    Asking for Information Response Style   150
    Critical Response Style   151

COMMUNICATION COMPETENCY CHECKUP   152

Notes   153
For Further Investigation   153

CHAPTER 7

▶ *Interpersonal Processes*

COMMUNICATION COMPETENCIES   154

Dimensions of Relationship Processes   154

The Framework for Interaction   157
    Goals   157
    Structure   158
    Rules   164

Qualities and Resources of Relationships   166
    Commitment   166
    Intimacy   168
    Resources   169

COMMUNICATION COMPETENCY CHECKUP   170

Notes   171
For Further Investigation   171

CHAPTER 8

▶ *Interpersonal Relationships*

COMMUNICATION COMPETENCIES   172

Relational Development: Beginning, Maintaining, and Ending
    Relationships   173
        Beginning a Relationship   173
        Maintaining a Relationship   180
        Ending a Relationship   190

Increasing Relational Satisfaction   192

COMMUNICATION COMPETENCY CHECKUP   193

Notes   194
For Further Investigation   195

CHAPTER 9

▶ *Managing Relationship Discord*

COMMUNICATION COMPETENCIES   196

Conflict and Conflict Situations   197
    A Definition of Conflict   198

Perceptions of Conflict   200
    Family   201
    Educational Institutions   202
    Television   202

Consequences of Conflict   202
    Effects on Work   203
    Effects on Relationships   203
    Personal Effects   204

Approaches to Conflict   205
    Conflict Strategies   205
    Conflict Styles   211

Managing Relationship Discord   218
    Win-Lose Conflict Management   219
    Lose-Lose Conflict Management   220
    Usual Outcomes of Win-Lose and Lose-Lose Conflicts   220
    Win-Win Conflict Management   221

Assessing Conflict Processes and Outcomes   224

COMMUNICATION COMPETENCY CHECKUP   227

Notes   228
For Further Investigation   228

CHAPTER 10

▶ *Communication in Small Groups*

COMMUNICATION COMPETENCIES   230

The Importance of Small Groups   231
What Is a Small Group?   232
Why Do You Join Specific Groups?   233
    Sources of Attraction   233
    High Attraction   236
Group Development   237
    The Orientation Phase   237
    The Conflict Phase   238
    The Balance, or High Work, Phase   239
    The Disintegration Phase   239
Group Problem Solving   241
    Preconditions for Problem Solving   241
    Steps in the Problem-Solving Process   243
    Overcoming Obstacles to Effective
      Problem Solving   250

COMMUNICATION COMPETENCY CHECKUP   255

Notes   256
For Further Investigation   257

CHAPTER 11

▶ *Influence and Participation in Small Groups*

COMMUNICATION COMPETENCIES   258

Norms and Conformity   259
Group Roles   261
    How Roles Are Determined   261
    Specific Roles   265
    Problems with Roles   269
Power and the Potential for Leadership   270
    Power Bases   272
    Choosing Your Power Base   276
Leadership   277
    Approaches to Leadership   277

COMMUNICATION COMPETENCY CHECKUP   285

Notes   285
For Further Investigation   286

CHAPTER 12

▶ *Public Speaking: The Groundwork*

COMMUNICATION COMPETENCIES   288

Public Speaking and You   289
  The Five-P Process for Speeches   289
  The Benefits of Learning Public Speaking   291
Gathering Information: Assessing the Situation   292
  Assessing Yourself   292
  Assessing the Audience   295
  Assessing the Setting   300
Using the Information: Selecting a Topic and Developing a Purpose   301
  Selecting a Topic   301
  Narrowing Your Topic   303
  Developing a Statement of Purpose   304
COMMUNICATION COMPETENCY CHECKUP   308

Notes   309
For Further Investigation   309

CHAPTER 13

▶ *Public Speaking: Information Strategies*

COMMUNICATION COMPETENCIES   310

Prepreparation   311
Audience-Centered and Speech-Centered Communications   312
Informational Support   312
  Speaker Credibility   313
  Logical Appeals   318
  Emotional Appeals   323
Resources for Logical and Emotional Appeals   326
  Conducting Interviews   326
  Library Resources   328
Ethics and Public Speaking   330
COMMUNICATION COMPETENCY CHECKUP   332

For Further Investigation   333

CHAPTER 14

▶ *Public Speaking: Developing the Speech*

COMMUNICATION COMPETENCIES   334
The Parts of a Speech   335

Gaining the Audience's Attention   336
    Tell a Joke   337
    Tell a Story   337
    Pose a Question   337
    Give a Highly Dramatic Piece of Information   338
    Use a Quote   338
    Make a Reference to the Occasion or the Audience   338

Providing Necessary Background   339

Stating Your Purpose   340

Discussing Your Information   341
    Topical Arrangement   341
    Sequence Arrangement   341
    Spatial Arrangement   342
    Causal Arrangement   342
    Problem-Solution Arrangement   343
    Comparison and/or Contrast Arrangements   344

Summarizing Your Information   346

Driving Home Your Point   348

Analyzing a Model Speech   348
    Self-Knowledge and Student Mental Health: A Case for Both   348

COMMUNICATION COMPETENCY CHECKUP   356

Note   356
For Further Investigation   357

CHAPTER 15

▶ *Public Speaking: Methods of Presentation*

COMMUNICATION COMPETENCIES   358

How Do You Prepare?   359

To Prepare or Not to Prepare   359
    The Impromptu Speech   360
    The Extemporaneous Speech   362
    The Manuscript Speech   367
    Guideposts for the Audience   369

Auxiliary Materials   371
    Types of Auxiliary Materials   371
    Guidelines for Selecting Auxiliary Materials   375

Managing the Speaking Event   377
    Before the Speech   377
    After the Speech   378

COMMUNICATION COMPETENCY CHECKUP   380

Note   381
For Further Investigation   381

CHAPTER 16

▶ *Public Speaking: Presenting the Speech*

COMMUNICATION COMPETENCIES   382

Speechophobia   383
        Dealing with Speechophobia   384
        Preparation   385

Delivery   388
        Verbal Presentation   389
        Nonverbal Presentation   392

Postperformance Evaluation   394

COMMUNICATION COMPETENCY CHECKUP   396

Notes   397
For Further Investigation   397

GLOSSARY   398

INDEX   410

CHAPTER 1

▶ *Foundations For Communication Competency*

This chapter defines what communication is and explains the characteristics of competent communication. It also provides the background you need to understand and apply the material presented in the rest of this book. Subsequent chapters focus on both presenting principles of effective communication and developing your communication competencies. Specifically, in this chapter, you will learn to do the following:

▶ *Define the characteristics of communication.*
▶ *Understand the components of communication competency.*
▶ *Understand the functions of competent communication.*
▶ *Define the qualities of a competent communicator.*

When you say that communiation has taken place, what do you mean? How would you define *communication*, and what would you list as its important characteristics? Would you care how many people were involved? Would it matter where the activity took place? Is it important to accomplish some specific goal? Does it matter, as part of your definition, whether the participants are face to face or communicating through some electronic medium? Does it matter whether the messages are spoken or communicated without words? Is it important to consider what roles the participants assume—for example, whether one is a sender and the other a receiver?

DEFINING COMMUNICATION

Communication is a distinctly human process composed of six key elements that combine a number of unique characteristics.

Although we may say that computers "talk" to other computers and that thermostats "communicate" electronically to switch on air conditioners, communication for our purposes is a human process, not a mechanical one. What do humans do that constitutes communication?

The Elements of Communication

Communication, the process of sending and receiving messages, includes six elements: senders, receivers, messages, a context, purposes, and feedback. Communication can be likened to an archer, armed with bow and arrow, staring at a not-too-distant target. See Figure 1.1 on page 4. The archer is the **sender** (the person who devises the message), the arrow is the **message** (the information the sender devises for the receiver), and the target is the **receiver** (the person who takes in the message).

The archer is well aware that particular arrows suit particular targets in particular instances (for example, the arrow must match the wind condition). So, with the distance, type of target, and a bull's-eye in mind, the archer selects a specific arrow. The particular instance makes up the **context** (the characteristics of the situation in which the communication takes place, such as the physical environment and the other people present), and hitting the bull's-eye is the **purpose** (the goal of the communication).

The arrow flies off and the result is noted. Observing whether the bull's-eye is hit provides the feedback necessary for the archer to note success or failure. **Feedback** in communication is the process of obtaining information about the effect of a message.

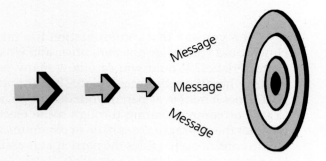

▶ **FIGURE 1.1**   The Elements of Communication

The Characteristics of Communication

Communicating with other human beings—especially in face-to-face situations—differs from our archery example because human communication has some unique characteristics. Archers' targets cannot run, hide, duck, fake a reaction, lie, manipulate, or scream when hit. People can! Likening human communication to archery means viewing communication as predominantly a one-way phenomenon. This, however, is an extremely limiting view. Adding feedback to the process still does not match the reality of all communication experiences. Trading in the archer metaphor, consider the following dialogue:

Laura: Kara, hand me the sheet of paper on the desk. *(Kara hands Laura a sheet of paper.)* Not that one, the yellow one.

Kara: *(Kara puts her hand on a yellow sheet of paper.)* This one?

Laura: Not that one, the yellow one with the flowers in the margin. *(Kara hands Laura the desired paper.)* Thank you.

Laura and Kara have participated in an interaction in which, *presumably*, one served as the sender, the other as the receiver, and they switched roles several times until the desired outcome was achieved. In other words, based on the feedback, Laura and Kara made adjustments in the cooperative pursuit of accomplishing their joint goal. In the process, they demonstrated four key characteristics of human communication:

1. Messages are simultaneously sent and received.
2. Messages cannot be erased or taken back.
3. Communicators respond to messages proactively—that is, they respond based on their unique backgrounds.
4. The meaning of any message depends on the situation.

Messages Are Simultaneously Sent and Received

The work *presumably* is used in the previous paragraph to indicate that the communication process doesn't mechanically alternate between sender and receiver. In reality, as Laura was making her initial request, she was simultaneously functioning as a receiver by watching Kara's reactions. She functioned as a sender and a receiver at the same time. Kara, while functioning initially as a receiver, was simultaneously functioning as a sender by giving Laura feedback.

Messages Cannot Be Erased

Notice that each message in Kara's and Laura's conversation is built on what preceded it. Messages cannot be erased, but they can be modified and adjusted with subsequent messages. Laura continued to deal with Kara's lack of understanding by modifying her directions until she accomplished her goal. She did this by clarifying.

Suppose that, in the heat of an argument with a friend, you blurt out the one insult that you know will most hurt the other person. And, as soon as you complete the offending message, you want to plead, "I take it back, I didn't mean it!" However, there is no such thing as "taking it back." You and your partner may choose to behave as if the message were erased, but, in reality, you both know that it exists and continues to exist.

Communication Is Proactive

Kara and Laura's dialogue shows that communication is a **proactive process**— that is, you respond to any message based on your total history. If Kara had not understood English, or recognized the color yellow, or had not cared to cooperate, then her reaction would have been different. Kara's reaction to Laura's request indicated that she was not merely a passive recipient of Laura's messages: she selected what to hear, amplified and ignored portions to suit her taste, and remembered what she considered relevant based on her past experiences.

Meaning Depends on Context

The meaning of a given act of communication cannot be separated from its context. The context has three aspects: the people who are interacting, their physical surroundings, and their social relationships.

The context depends on the people communicating. If Kara is only five years old, Laura will probably adapt her message to that age level, perhaps by using simpler language. If Laura had said, in describing the yellow-toned sheets of paper, "Hand me the canary paper," a five-year-old Kara might have looked for paper in the shape of a bird, based on her literal translation of the word *canary*.

The number of people present also affects how a message is interpreted. For example, if Laura and Kara are surrounded by other people and Laura whispers her request, Kara might assume that the message is meant to be secret. Or if several people in the group are named Kara, the message may be mistakenly ignored by the one Kara for whom it is intended.

Where you are also affects the meanings you attribute to the messages you received. For example, if Kara and Laura are at home, Kara will probably assume Laura wants the paper to write on; however, if they are in a stationery store, she might assume that Laura wants to look at the paper to consider buying it.

Different social situations have different rules, and communication messages are interpreted based on the rules. For example, if Kara and Laura are taking a test and one of the rules is "No talking," Kara might interpret Laura's request as an invitation to cheat. If they are in a classroom working together on a project, Kara might interpret the request as part of the normal process of sharing.

Some acts of communication derive their meaning totally from the context. For example, if taken literally, the message "Hi, how are you?" is an inquiry about the state of your health. You know, however, that within the context of passing an acquaintance on the street, it means "Hello," or "I see you're around." It is not really asking for a health-related response. In fact, if you actually describe how you feel, you may startle the other person. In a physician's office, however, the same message would have a totally different meaning. In this context, your doctor would think you were strange if you gave anything but a detailed, health-related response.

Human Communication: A Summary

Human communication is an event that involves sending and receiving messages within a context. The event is purposeful even if the purpose is not as clear-cut as hitting a bull's-eye. Responses to messages are proactive. The number of participants in the activity may vary. Communication events also are characterized by feedback, the simultaneous sending and receiving of messages, and the nonerasability of messages once they are uttered.

KNOWLEDGE CHECKUP 1.1

Recognizing the Elements and Characteristics of Human Communication

Throughout this text you will be asked to complete a variety of self-evaluations. Keep two things in mind as you respond to each. First, the value of the results depends on the honesty of your responses. Second, the results are pieces of information that will help you understand yourself and assess your knowledge. They should alert you to the additional information and skills you need to become a more competent communicator.

Read the following dialogue and identify the elements and characteristics of human communication:

> *(Roberto and Sylvia are standing in line at a movie theater, waiting to purchase tickets.)*
>
> **Roberto:** I'm really glad we got the chance to get out of the house tonight. The kids were driving me crazy.
>
> **Sylvia:** After spending all day at the hospital examining children, I was more than ready to relax.
>
> **Roberto:** Just because you're an intern on thirty-six hour shifts doesn't make you any more tired than I am!
>
> **Sylvia:** Don't let your male chauvinist attitude about my being a doctor get in the way of our seeing the movie!
>
> **Roberto:** Don't give me that male chauvinist garbage! That's just your easy answer! I'll see you at home!

1. Who is the sender?

2. Who is the receiver?

3. Describe the effects of the context on the creation and interpretation of each person's message.

4. What purposes can their messages serve for them?

5. Describe the feedback in the dialogue.

6. What possible effect might the nonerasability of language have on this conversation?

7. Given the proactive nature of human communication, what assumptions can you make about Roberto and Sylvia?

8. What recommendations would you make to Roberto and Sylvia to help them communicate more competently with each other?

THE COMPONENTS OF COMMUNICATION COMPETENCY

Communication competency, the ability to achieve your communication goals, has three components: knowledge, skills, and motivation. To reach competency, first you need to understand the situation, yourself, and the skills it takes to be effective. Second, you need to harness your knowledge and put the skills to use;

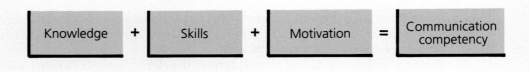

▶ **FIGURE 1.2** The Components of Communication Competency

doing so takes practice and experience with the appropriate behaviors. Third, you must be motivated to communicate competently: Knowing what to do and developing the appropriate skills aren't enough—you have to want to put them to use.

Knowledge

Once you decide to communicate, you must analyze the who, what, and where of the situation. Who are the participants? What are your objectives for the interaction? Where is the communication taking place? To answer these questions you must know who you are, how the other person perceives you and the world, how anxiety-arousing the situation is for you and for the other person, how closely you need to listen, your relationship with the other person, and the various means available for presenting your ideas. For example, assume you are invited to address nurses who work in the local hospital. Your objective is to tell them about the six elements of the communication process to make them more aware of the importance of analyzing each communication situation before speaking. You are told that a small room is available for your talk.

What you know about the topic will determine, in part, what you choose to say. What you think the nurses know about the topic will affect the content of your talk. The room where you will give your talk will affect how loudly you decide to speak and the kinds of visual aids you present. Your relationship with the nurses will further affect the choices you will make. For instance, if they don't know you, you might speak and dress more formally than you would if you knew them already.

Knowing who, what, and where forms the basis for deciding what skills are necessary to communicate competently. *Knowing* what skills are necessary to perform is not the same as being able to *perform* them. Knowledge and skills are separate aspects of communication competency, although the skills you employ will be based on your knowledge of what the situation requires.

Skills

How competent do you think you are in using communication skills? The following Knowledge Checkup will help you determine what skills you already have and what skills need further development.

KNOWLEDGE CHECKUP 1.2

How Competently Do You Communicate?

Following is a list of communication skills.[1] Indicate how often you use each skill and how satisfied you are with your ability. Use the following scale to indicate how *often* you use each skill:

5 = all or most of the time (91–100 percent of the time)
4 = often (71–90 percent)
3 = sometimes (31–70 percent)
2 = rarely (11–30 percent)
1 = never or almost never (0–10 percent)

Use the following scale to indicate how satisfied you are with your use of each skill:

5 = very satisfied
4 = somewhat satisfied
3 = neither satisfied nor dissatisfied
2 = somewhat dissatisfied
1 = very dissatisfied

	How Often	How Satisfied
1. I listen effectively.	_____	_____
2. I use appropriate words for the situation.	_____	_____
3. I use appropriate pronunciation for the situation.	_____	_____
4. I use appropriate grammar for the situation.	_____	_____
5. I use effective eye contact.	_____	_____
6. I speak at a rate that is neither too slow nor too fast.	_____	_____
7. I speak fluently (avoiding "uh," "like, uh," "you know," awkward pauses, and silences).	_____	_____
8. My movements, such as gestures, enhance what I say.	_____	_____
9. I give appropriate spoken and unspoken feedback.	_____	_____
10. I use vocal variety when I speak (rather than speaking in a monotone voice).	_____	_____
11. I speak neither too loudly nor too softly.	_____	_____
12. I use appropriate facial expressions.	_____	_____
13. I understand a speaker's main ideas.	_____	_____

	How Often	How Satisfied
14. I understand a speaker's feelings.	_____	_____
15. I distinguish facts from opinions.	_____	_____
16. I distinguish between speaking to give someone information and speaking to persuade someone to think, feel, or act a particular way.	_____	_____
17. I recognize when a listener does not understand my message.	_____	_____
18. I express ideas clearly and concisely.	_____	_____
19. I express and defend my point of view.	_____	_____
20. I organize messages so others can understand them.	_____	_____
21. I use questions and other forms of feedback to obtain and clarify messages.	_____	_____
22. I respond to questions and other forms of feedback to provide clarification.	_____	_____
23. I give understandable directions and instructions.	_____	_____
24. I summarize messages in my own words and/or by taking notes.	_____	_____
25. I describe another's viewpoint.	_____	_____
26. I describe differences of opinion.	_____	_____
27. I express my feelings and opinions to others.	_____	_____
28. I initiate and maintain conversations.	_____	_____
29. I recognize and control my anxiety in communication situations.	_____	_____
30. I involve the other person in what I am saying.	_____	_____
Total	_____	_____

Scale:
Compare your totals with the following ranges:

How Often
135–150 = Communicate skillfully all or most of the time
105–134 = Often communicate skillfully
75–104 = Sometimes communicate skillfully
45–74 = Rarely communicate skillfully
30–44 = Never or almost never communicate skillfully

How Satisfied
135–150 = Very satisfied with my communication skills
105–134 = Somewhat satisfied with my communication skills
75–104 = Neither satisfied nor dissatisfied with my communication skills
45–74 = Somewhat dissatisfied with my communication skills
30–44 = Very dissatisfied with my communication skills

Each item in the self-analysis you just completed describes a skill that is a component of communication competence. Your effective performance of these behaviors increases your potential for being a competent communicator.

Don't be discouraged if you scored lower than you would have liked. The purpose of this text and of your communication course is to help you develop the knowledge and skills you need to improve your competency as a communicator. And even if you scored close to 150 on both parts of the self-quiz, you will find that there is still much to learn and put into practice!

Motivation

To be a competent communicator, you must want to communicate competently. You might be motivated by such possibilities as forming a new relationship, gaining desired information, influencing someone's behavior, engaging in joint decision making, or solving a problem.

In addition to potential benefits, every communication encounter has potential drawbacks. To communicate competently, you must be motivated to overcome such drawbacks. For example, you may have learned from past experiences to fear certain communication situations. Talking with a friend may pose no problem, but talking with an authority figure, such as a professor, may cause you to fidget and show other signs of nervousness. To compensate for negative feelings, you must be strongly motivated to take the necessary action to communicate.

The amount of confidence you have in your ability to communicate will probably determine the strength of your motivation to communicate. If, for example, you think of yourself as shy, you are unlikely to initiate conversations with strangers. The reward for interacting might be clear to you, but your self-perceived lack of social skills decreases your motivation.

Look at those items in Knowledge Checkup 1.2 for which you indicated low satisfaction (ratings of 1 or 2). Now examine the *how often* scores for those items. You may find that the skills with which you are most dissatisfied are the same ones you avoid using. You may be saying to yourself, "If I haven't developed that skill enough, I'm not going to risk using it."

By studying the information presented in this text, you will begin to understand the components of competent communication. And by performing the activities, you will develop the necessary skills. This combination should increase your motivation to communicate and to communicate competently.

THE FUNCTIONS OF COMMUNICATION COMPETENCY

Each time you communicate, you have a purpose, and you are most likely to accomplish your purpose if you communicate competently. For example, if your goal is to gain information, you will increase your likelihood of success if you do a good job of listening, asking questions, and summarizing information. If your goal is to form a relationship, the degree to which you are knowledgeable, skillful, and motivated to initiate conversations and express your opinions and feelings will influence your success.

Communication has numerous functions:

1. to establish human contact,
2. to exchange information,
3. to share and change attitudes and behaviors,
4. to reduce uncertainty in your life,
5. to understand yourself and the world around you, and
6. to achieve your occupational goals.

These functions are not separate. All six may occur in any communication interaction.

Think back to your first day on campus. You needed to know where your classes met, where the bookstore was located, and how to register for courses. How did you find these things out? You probably asked questions, read your college guidebook, followed maps, and, through trial and error, stumbled onto some useful information. By communicating competently, you discovered the people, places, and things that made up your world, and you reduced your uncertainty as you learned about your environment.

Suppose that you are thinking about taking a particular professor's class. You have heard through the grapevine that she has an exciting class and is a tough grader. You need to test the accuracy of your discovery before taking the plunge and signing up. So you find people who have actually been in her class and make statements such as, "I heard that Professor X is an easy grader," and watch and listen to how they respond. Through this process, you hope to separate facts about Professor X from opinions that may not have been based on actual experience. By communicating competently, you can test the accuracy of your initial discoveries about what your world is like and, if those discoveries relate to courses in your major area of study, you can achieve your academic goals more effectively.

By communicating competently you can share your understanding of the world in an effort to get others to see things the way you do. For example, if you believe that it is good to have a weekend to study before a test and you can persuade your classmates and your professor to see the situation in the same way, you have a chance at getting the test moved from Friday to Monday. There is probably nothing more comfortable than being surrounded by people who share your attitudes and opinions. And your ability to communicate competently can increase your likelihood of achieving such harmony.

THE QUALITIES OF COMPETENT COMMUNICATORS

Competent communicators have six qualities in common:

1. Competent communicators are appropriate—they follow the rules.

2. Competent communicators are effective—they communicate in ways that help them achieve their goals.

3. Competent communicators are adaptable—they adjust their communication to the situation.

4. Competent communicators recognize roadblocks to effective communication—they note potential obstacles and work to overcome them.

5. Competent communicators understand that competency is a matter of degree—they realize that a given act of communication is rarely completely competent or incompetent, but probably somewhere between these two extremes.

6. Competent communicators are ethical—they adhere to standards of right and wrong based on their culture, personal views, and circumstances.

Competent Communicators Are Appropriate

For communication to be appropriate, a speaker must recognize and follow the rules that guide interaction in a particular circumstance. A person who fails to follow the rules is often perceived as abrasive or bizarre, and may be treated as an outcast. Of course, because different situations call for different rules, what may be appropriate in one situation may be inappropriate in another. For example, a rule in a family may be "No foul language." Thus, if you tripped over a bicycle when your family was around, it would be inappropriate to cry out a four-letter obscenity. In contrast, if the same thing happened with a group of friends, your cry might not break any rules and would therefore be acceptable. Similarly, a male job hunter may be refused employment in a clothing store for middle-class businessmen if he comes to an interview wearing jeans and an earring, but a store aimed at up-scale, fashion-conscious teens may be very pleased to hire him.

Competent Communicators Are Effective

Effective communicators set goals related to their needs, wants, and desires and communicate in ways that help them achieve those goals. For example, if you want to persuade a personnel director to hire you, you will tell her about all the experience and education that qualify you for the position.

Competent communicators create appropriate and effective messages for the contexts in which they find themselves. In Knowledge Checkup 1.2, questions 2, 3, 4, 5, 6, 7, 8, 10, 11, 12, 16, 18, 20, and 30 highlight these characteristics of competent communication. How satisfied are you with your ability to create appropriate and effective messages?

Competent Communicators Are Adaptable

Adaptable communicators recognize the requirements of a situation and adjust their communication to accomplish their goals. For example, a professor presenting a talk on competent communication would use one set of examples when speaking to a group of doctors and a different set of examples when addressing members of the business community.

Adaptation has three components. The first two—recognizing the requirements of a situation and adapting your communication behavior to suit a setting—have already been discussed. The third component of adaptation is realizing that your values affect the way you adapt.

You may strongly believe that people should accept you as you are. But if you are inflexible in such beliefs, you will limit the number of contexts in which you can communicate competently. As long as you stay in situations that do not require adaptation, everything will be fine. But outside those situations— whether you are searching for a job, attempting to influence others, or meeting a friend's parents—your unwillingness to adapt will make it more difficult to accomplish your goals.

As illustrated in Knowledge Checkup 1.2, competent communicators have a large repertoire of behaviors available to them. They learn to pick and choose appropriate techniques based on the situation (including its participants) and their intentions for the interaction. Especially important for competency are **flexibility skills,** skills that enhance your versatility and resourcefulness. These include **empathy**—seeing things from another person's point of view; **role taking**—engaging in behaviors that fit a situation and do not conflict with your sense of self; and **problem solving**—analyzing a problem and generating appropriate solutions.

Competent Communicators Recognize Roadblocks to Effective Communication

A **roadblock,** an obstacle that keeps you from accomplishing your communication goal, may take one of five forms: cultural, environmental, personal, relational, or language.

Cultural roadblocks are the results of people's differences in background and experience. You have been taught rules for communicating within your family, in school, and in society at large. When your rules and someone else's rules clash, there is a cultural roadblock. For example, you may believe that women should stay home and take care of children, whereas the person with whom you are talking may believe that both men and women have equal responsibility for child care. Consider the problems that could arise if you were discussing dual-career marriages. You and your friend might not correctly interpret each other's comments if you failed to recognize your different beliefs.

Environmental roadblocks occur when something in the physical environment impairs your ability to send or receive messages. For example, loud, piped-in music may make it difficult to hear what your friend is saying, even if he or she is standing close to you.

Personal roadblocks stem from your likes and dislikes, what you think is important or unimportant, what you do and do not want. When your personal attitudes, values, and beliefs get in the way of your listening, they become personal roadblocks. Have you ever noticed that the person who is speaking to you may matter as much as what is said? Do certain conversations bore you? Do certain topics set your thoughts off on a tangent? Do certain words trigger embarrassment or anger? Do you feel you have too many things on your mind to concentrate on communicating? If you answered yes to any of these questions, your personal roadblocks have created barriers to effective communication.

Relational roadblocks may result from differences in status and power, differences in the way people define their roles in a relationship, and differences in the way people perceive their relationships. The titles *boss, parent, professor, police officer, judge,* and *president* all connote status and power. Unless you are one boss talking to another boss, or one parent talking to another parent, status differences exist. There may even be a status difference between two bosses or two parents. Status differences may designate who has the right to initiate conversations, give directions, make decisions, and reward or punish.

Each person in a relationship may define his or her own role differently. For example, a student who defines a teacher's role as *guide* in a class where the teacher defines his role as *lecturer* will encounter relational roadblocks—the student will ask questions and seek information, while the instructor will want the student to be quiet and take notes.

Finally, individual participants may define their relationship differently. For example, in the case of two persons who are dating, one individual may see the relationship as a friendship, while the other may consider the relationship to be more intimate. Their different definitions affect any discussion of the relationship, such as future plans. Conflict is likely to occur.

The different meanings people give to words and the way they organize those words create **language roadblocks.** Meaning is not inherent in a word but in the person who interprets the word. What does the word *gross* mean to you? To a shipper it means 144 of an item. To a teenager it may mean obnoxious or offensive. To a surveyor it may mean imprecise. And to a person trying to be insulting, it may mean that someone's language is foul or that someone is unattractive.

Grammatical structure can either help or hinder you in communicating ideas. Say the following two sentences aloud:

What's the latest, dope?
What's the latest dope?

In the first question, by pausing at the comma, you insult the other person while asking for information. In the second question, by not pausing, you merely ask for information.

Competent Communicators Recognize That Competency Is a Matter of Degree

Competency is not something you either have or do not have; it comes in degrees. Each component of competency can be thought of as occurring "more" or "less." For example, *effectiveness* refers to communicating in ways that help you achieve your goals. If you always achieve your goals, your behavior may be considered completely effective. If you never achieve your goals, your behavior may be considered completely ineffective. Between these extremes are degrees of effectiveness, such as achieving your goals some of the time.

This notion of degree holds true for being appropriate, being adaptive, and being aware of roadblocks to effective communication. As a communicator, you need to recognize that you are not going to be competent all of the time. By increasing your knowledge of the communication process, and by learning and practicing communication skills, however, you will increase the number of instances in which you communicate competently.

Competent Communicators Are Ethical

Ethics are rules for conduct that distinguish right from wrong. Competent communicators are ethical—that is, they adhere to their standards of right and wrong. Your definition of what is right or wrong, what is ethical or unethical, depends on at least three considerations. The first is the culture in which you were raised. Your culture has taught you what your standards should be. For example, the Judeo-Christian code of ethics considers lying wrong.

Second, who you are and how you have interpreted "should" messages from your family, school, religion, friends, television, and movies also determine your personal code of what is right and wrong. If you have been taught that plagiarizing is wrong, you won't do it no matter how desperate you are for a good grade on a speech. But if you have been taught that you should always get high grades, you may not think of cheating as right or wrong, but only as another means of obtaining your goal.

If all you had to work with were cultural and personal "shoulds," it would be relatively easy to make ethical choices. However, a third consideration, the situation in which you find yourself, complicates matters. For example, if a job interviewer asks whether you have ever been fired, should you admit that you were once dismissed from a position? One "should" message tells you to get a good job, while another says not to lie. If you believe that you won't get the job if you tell the truth, what will you tell the interviewer?

Because the range of variables that influence an individual's ethics is so wide, there are very few absolutes when it comes to communicating ethically. Perhaps the only one may be, don't purposely hurt or limit another person's choices.

YOU AS A COMMUNICATOR

Communication competency refers to both particular behaviors and overall impressions. You may be perceived as competent in a particular situation or at performing particular skills. For example, you may communicate well with your friends (a particular situation) and you may also have been told by one of your instructors that you are a good listener (a particular skill). This does not automatically mean that you are equally competent in other situations or equally skilled in other areas of communication.

Your overall impression of your own or someone else's communication is based on three factors: observation of behaviors, judgment of the appropriateness of the behaviors, and past shared experiences. These factors must be dealt with simultaneously. No single behavior, judgment, or aspect of the history of an interaction by itself creates the overall impression. Rather, the combination of all the behaviors, judgments, and history leads to the conclusion that someone is a competent communicator.

Take another look at your answers to Knowledge Checkup 1.2. Now that you have a general understanding of the defining characteristics of the communication process, the importance of communicating competently, and the qualities of competent communicators, see if there are any answers you would like to change. What are your strengths? What are your weaknesses? What goals will you set for your knowledge, skills, and motivation as a communicator?

As you progress through this book, you will gain the understanding and skills you need to communicate appropriately and effectively. As your understanding and skills increase from reading the text and completing the examples in this book, so will your chances of being perceived as a competent communicator.

COMMUNICATION COMPETENCY CHECKUP

Look at yourself in the mirror and picture yourself as the competent communicator you hope to be after reading this text and performing the activities in each chapter. You can begin by reflecting on your communication strengths and weaknesses and reviewing the material in this chapter.

1. Describe your communication strengths and weaknesses using the results of Knowledge Checkup 1.2. Based on your description and the information in this chapter, formulate goals for increasing your effectiveness as a communicator.

2. Define *communication*.

3. Explain each component of competent communication and illustrate each with personal examples.

NOTE

1. These communication skills were determined by a task force of the Speech Communication Association (SCA), and endorsed by the organization's Educational Policies Board, to be minimal competencies for communicators. They were stated as an SCA guideline in "Speaking and Listening Competencies for High School Graduates." The full report on these competencies appears in "The Basics in Speaking and Listening for High School Graduates: What Should be Assessed?" by Ronald E. Bassett, Nilwon Whittington, and Ann Staton-Spicer, in *Communication Education* 27 (1978): 293–303.

FOR FURTHER INVESTIGATION

Backlund, Philip. "Essential Speaking and Listening Skills for Elementary Students." *Communication Education* 34 (1985): 185–95.

Bassett, Ronald E., Nilwon Whittington, and Ann Staton-Spicer. "The Basics in Speaking and Listening for High School Graduates." *Communication Education* 27 (1978): 293–303.

Berlo, David K. *The Process of Communication: An Introduction to Theory and Practice.* New York: Holt, Rinehart and Winston, 1960.

Dance, Frank E. X. "The 'Concept' of Communication." *Journal of Communication* 20 (1970): 201–10.

Dance, Frank E. X., and Carl E. Larson. *The Functions of Communication: A Theoretical Approach.* New York: Holt, Rinehart and Winston, 1976.

Farb, Peter. *Word Play.* New York: Bantam, 1974.

Miller, Gerald R. "On Defining Communication: Another Stab." *Journal of Communication* 16 (1966): 88–98.

Muchmore, John, and Kathleen Galvin. "A Report of the Task Force on Career Competencies in Oral Communication Skills for Community College Students Seeking Immediate Entry into the Work Force." *Communication Education* 32 (1983): 207–20.

Rubin, Rebecca B. "Assessing Speaking and Listening Competence at the College Level: The Communication Competency Assessment Instrument." *Communication Education* 31 (1982): 19–32.

Spitzberg, Brian, and William Cupach. *Interpersonal Communication Competence.* Beverly Hills, CA: Sage, 1984.

Watzlawick, Paul, Janet H. Beavin, and Don D. Jackson. *Pragmatics of Human Communication: A Study of Interactional Patterns, Pathologies, and Paradoxes.* New York: Norton, 1967.

CHAPTER 2

► # *Verbal Communication*

This chapter on verbal communication will help you to practice and develop communication competencies that fall into three broad categories: (1) communication codes, which include using words and grammar appropriate to a particular situation; (2) basic speech communication skills, which include expressing ideas clearly and concisely; and (3) human relations, which include expressing feelings clearly to others and performing social rituals. Specifically, the competencies you will gain will enable you to do the following:

► *Understand the relationship between language and meaning.*
► *Distinguish between abstract and concrete language, denotative and connotative meaning, and private and shared language.*
► *Identify and overcome barriers to verbal interaction caused by language problems.*
► *Improve your use of language to ensure clear communication.*
► *Recognize and avoid sexist and racist language.*
► *Develop skills in using powerful language.*

*R*ead the following two descriptions of the same event:

> The sun and moon hung in the sky opposite each other—not quite day, not quite night. This battle for control of the evening sky was out of my control. My part in the spectacle was well defined: witness.

> I watched as the evening sky grew dark.

These descriptions of the shift from evening to night were composed by two different persons. What can you tell about each individual? Do they see the world in the same way? Do their language differences reflect differences in who they are?

THE IMPORTANCE OF VERBAL COMMUNICATION

Before you went to school you accomplished the most complex feat you will ever accomplish: you mastered the basics of **verbal language**, the ability to communicate using words. You discovered how to use words in the way the people around you use them. You learned to create sentences that fit the rules for how sentences should be created in your culture—you said "put the pen on the table" and not "the pen on the table put," and you used words to mean what others in your culture generally share as their meaning—you said "dog" and not "bird" when you pointed to a four-legged, furry animal that barked.

By age four you had learned enough vocabulary to survive for the rest of your life. You learned meanings for words like *love*, *good*, and *right* that were too subtle for dictionaries to explain fully. You learned rules for combining words that are so complex that researchers and philosophers have yet to spell them out in a comprehensible way. Did you ever stop to think about how you were able to put together sentences that you never heard and understand statements that were new to you? You knew how to use language to satisfy your need to understand your world, to express yourself, and to form relationships—all by the age of four, all without the aid of formal schooling!

Verbal language is a useful tool. You use it to organize information you gather about the world; to relate to people and events you experience; to regulate your own behavior, as when you talk to yourself while choosing a course of action; and to regulate the behavior of others, as when you try to persuade your friends to see one movie instead of another. Consider what it would be like to lose your ability to communicate verbally for a day. How would you make sense out of new information if you couldn't use words to place the information into categories? How would you keep track of where you should be if you couldn't use words to remind yourself? How would you interact with others? The day would be difficult, frustrating, and probably not as productive as it could be—for you as well as for those you encountered.

Language is your primary tool for survival. Understanding obstacles to its use and developing ways to overcome them help you communicate more effectively. But there is still another reason for studying verbal communication: your language reflects who you are. What differences do you presume between the person who communicated the first description at the beginning of the chapter and the one who communicated the second? Does the first person seem sensitive and poetic, and the second straightforward and unimaginative? Does the first person see things the second person ignores, or does the second person get to the point?

Your language both reflects and affects what you perceive. Anthropologist Edward Sapir argued more than sixty years ago that we are prisoners of our language, that what we experience is largely due to the language habits of our community. The **Sapir-Whorf hypothesis** states that the language we use guides how we see and interpret the environment and shapes our ideas. To understand a person's verbal communication is to understand how that person sees the world, how that person thinks.

Many examples support the Sapir-Whorf hypothesis. For one, Eskimos have no single word for snow but a great many discrete words for different kinds of snow. The Masai of Africa have seventeen terms for cattle. Arabic has over 6,000 words for what most Americans call a camel. And Americans have a wide vocabulary for distinguishing types and models of cars. This reflects the importance of snow for Eskimos, cattle for the Masai, camels for Arabs, and cars for Americans. The point isn't that Americans *cannot* see the distinctions in snow that Eskimos see, but that they *do not* see them because such subtleties about snow aren't important to them. The vocabulary you use reflects your interests and concerns, the way you look at the world, and the distinctions among objects, people, and events that are important to you.

Grammar, too, serves as evidence for the Sapir-Whorf hypothesis. How you think about something is reflected in and affected by the grammar you use. The English, for example, use primarily inductive reasoning (beginning with particulars and building to the general), whereas the French use primarily deductive reasoning (beginning with the general and moving to the specific). The grammar of each language community reflects the thinking process: in English, for example, you would say *the white wine* (the specific, *white*, comes first and the general, *wine*, follows), while in French you would say *le vin blanc* (the general, *wine*, comes first, and the specific, *white*, follows).[1] As with differences in vocabulary, differences in grammar do not necessarily reflect inabilities to think differently, but rather preferences for what is important to a particular language community.

LANGUAGE AND MEANING

Language is **symbolic**: that is, words have no meaning in themselves but are arbitrary letter combinations that stand for or represent something. The word *pizza* is not edible and the word *water* is not drinkable. There is nothing pizza-like about the word *pizza*, and nothing liquid-like about the word *water*. If there were a logical connection between a symbol and what it symbolized, wouldn't it seem silly for the word *big* to have fewer letters than the word *small*? Why would *ten*, *dix*, and *diez* all mean the same thing (and how come not one of the three has ten letters?)?

The relationship between a symbol and what it symbolizes is arbitrary, agreed upon by the people who use the symbol. Learning a language is, in part, learning the rules for how meanings and symbols are connected.

If the connection between a symbol and the object, idea, or event that it refers to were simple, communicating would be rather easy. Every time you said the word *car* it would mean the same thing to you as it meant to the person with whom you were talking. But because the relationship between a word and what it symbolizes is arbitrary, *meanings are in people, not in words*. No meaning is inherent in any symbol: the meaning is in the persons using the symbol. People attach a specific, personal meaning to every word they use. For example, for you, the word *car* may mean a 1985 Ford Thunderbird, even though the word *car* could refer to many different automobiles. For someone else, *car* might mean a different specific automobile, such as the one she owns, or all autos of a particular make, such as Chrysler. And if the person is from a nonmotorized culture, the word *car* might be a funny-sounding word without meaning.

The meaning you attribute to a symbol—which reflects something about who you are—differs according to how concrete or abstract the symbol is, its denotations and connotations, and whether the language is private or shared.

Abstract and Concrete Symbols

Symbols differ in the degree to which what they refer to is concrete or abstract. **Concrete symbols** are highly specific and refer to one thing. **Abstract symbols**, on the other hand, are general and may refer to many things. For example, consider a car that has been named *The Toy* by its owner. The name *The Toy* is a concrete symbol because it refers to one particular car—a reality that can be verified. As we move from this concrete symbol to more abstract ones, we move from the reality of the particular car to more general concepts. A useful model of this movement from concrete to abstract is the ladder of abstraction, with its first rung being the most concrete and its final rung being the most abstract. A progression for *The Toy* from most concrete to most abstract, from the first rung to the last rung on the ladder of abstraction, is as follows:

The symbol that stands for the particular object—the name that refers to the particular object, *The Toy*—is the most concrete level of language possible. It appears on Rung 1.

A description of the physical characteristics of the object is also concrete, but not as concrete as the symbol for the particular object, so it appears on Rung 2.

Sports car may seem fairly concrete, but it is still a broad category that encompasses a variety of makes, types, sizes, shapes, and colors.

Car is more abstract because this category expands to include two-seater sports cars, limousines, station wagons, and experimental three-wheeled designs.

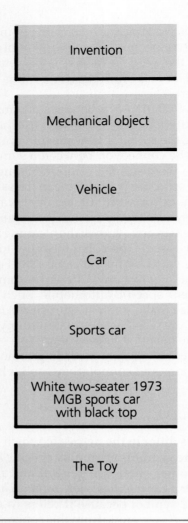

▶ **FIGURE 2.1** Ladder of Abstraction

Vehicle is still more abstract because this term may refer to planes, trains, buses, tanks, and boats in addition to cars.

A *mechanical object* is highly abstract because it could include washers and dryers, can openers, and clocks, as well as cars and other vehicles.

Finally, the category *invention* is the most abstract term when contrasted with the label *The Toy* because it includes everything created through people's imaginations. Thus it occupies the highest rung on the ladder of abstraction.

The more abstract a symbol is, the greater the probability that different people attach different meanings to it. A speaker who tells his audience "It's important to have many friends" may run into trouble with listeners' interpretations of *many* and *friends* because both words are abstract. *Many* could mean three to some people and twenty to others, and *friend* could mean anything from a passing acquaintance to an intimate confidante. The speaker may have something particular in mind, but so will each audience member, and the differences among them may be great.

People's tendency to assign different meanings to the same symbol is only one problem with abstract language. People also use the same abstract word to mean different things on different occasions. You might use the abstract word *love* to refer to one set of feelings when talking about the person with whom you are romantically involved and another set when talking about a good friend. A problem could arise if a listener is unaware that *love* is being used to refer to two different feelings, one, deep emotional commitment (referring to your romantic partner) and the other, friendship (referring to your friend). One way to resolve this problem is to use less abstract symbols.

As you move up the ladder of abstraction, more and more meanings may be attributed to the symbols you use. But to communicate clearly, both you and other people must have similar notions of what your symbols refer to. Thus, the less abstract your language is, the higher the probability that you and your listeners will agree on meaning. Telling the doctor "I don't feel well" is not as useful as giving a detailed, concrete description of where, when, and for how long you have had pain.

Knowledge Checkup 2.1 will help you construct a ladder of abstraction and compare more and less abstract words and descriptions for the same object.

KNOWLEDGE CHECKUP 2.1

Constructing a Ladder of Abstraction

Select the name of your pet, the address of your house or apartment, or the name of an article of clothing you are wearing and place it on the bottom rung of the ladder of abstraction. Complete each step of the ladder with one or more words until you are at the most abstract level.

_____ Most abstract level
_____
_____
_____
_____ Most concrete level

1. What happens to meaning as you move up the ladder of abstraction? What happens when you move down the ladder?

2. How can the ladder of abstraction help you communicate more clearly?

Denotation and Connotation

The meaning of a symbol is affected not only by its level of abstraction but also by its denotation and connotation. Denotation refers to the usual associations that members of a particular language community have for a symbol. **Connotation** refers to the secondary associations for the symbol that are more personal and may not be shared by every member of the language community. For example, a denotation for *home* may be *shelter*, while connotations could include *warmth*, *pleasant retreat*, *place back in the city*, or *where my folks live*.

Denotations

An examination of any dictionary will confirm that most words have several denotations. The most commonly used 500 words in English have approximately 14,000 definitions. Of course, the more denotations a word has, the more ambiguous it is.

The word *car*, used earlier in the ladder of abstraction, has several denotations in addition to *an automobile*. It refers to a vehicle running on rails (such as a train car or a streetcar), the part of an elevator that carries passengers, and the box floated in water to preserve live fish, lobsters, and clams. If you're speaking with someone Scottish, you can add *sinister* to the list of denotations of *car*.

Connotations

The connotations of the word *car* refer to the attitudes or feelings people have for a symbol or what it symbolizes. What are your connotations for the word *car*? Is it something good or bad? Fast or slow? A plaything or a workhorse? Necessary or frivolous? If you have had good experiences with cars—no accidents and few repairs—you are likely to have positive associations with the symbol. Problems with cars in the past are likely to give rise to negative connotations. There can be as many connotations as there are people who use the word, whereas the number of denotations is limited.

The following words refer to the same thing, but their connotations may be different. How do you feel about each word? What are your connotations?

work, job, occupation, calling, trade, profession, task, employment, function

The connotations you have for a word are more likely to determine your response than are the denotations, probably because you learned the connotative meanings for many words before you learned their denotations. For example, in your family you may have learned that *bills* are an annoyance before you ever understood what bills were. The process of reacting first and learning the denotation second is a hard habit to break.

One device used for measuring connotative meaning—the attitudes and feelings you have toward a concept or term—is called the **semantic differential**, a tool that measures a person's reactions to an object or concept by marking spaces between a pair of adjectives, one positive and one negative, with each space representing an attitude position. For example, rate the concept *my college education* on the following scales by circling the number that best reflects your feelings. The endpoints 1 and 7 are defined by the adjectives. The numbers between them represent less extreme positions. On the first scale, 1 = bad, 2 = somewhat bad, 3 = slightly bad, 4 = neither good nor bad, 5 = slightly good, 6 = somewhat good, and 7 = good.

bad	1	2	3	4	5	6	7	good
not satisfying	1	2	3	4	5	6	7	satisfying
boring	1	2	3	4	5	6	7	exciting
tense	1	2	3	4	5	6	7	relaxed

You can get a sense of whether your connotations for the concept *my college education* are positive or negative simply by adding your responses to the four scales and comparing your sum with the highest score possible, 28, and the lowest score possible, 4. If your sum is close to 28, your connotations are positive. On the other hand, if your score is close to 4, your connotations are negative.

Private and Shared Language

Private language refers to language whose meanings are agreed upon by one segment of a larger language community; **shared language** refers to language whose meanings are agreed upon by all members of the language community. Private language may consist of both specialized words and specialized meanings for common words. For example, *input* and *output* may not mean much to people unfamiliar with computers; *ollies* may defy definition by anyone who doesn't ride a skateboard; *vertebral subluxation* may confuse those outside the chiropractic profession; and, although you have probably suffered from *cephalagia*, only your doctor would call a headache by this name.

Specialized words, often called *jargon*, have two purposes. First, they serve as shorthand for those familiar with them. *The third cervical vertebra* can be shortened to the specialized symbol C3 to save chiropractors time when talking to each other and to patients familiar with their vocabulary. Specialized words also help identify those who use them as members of the same group. With the right vocabulary, you can sound like a lawyer, doctor, teacher, mechanic, or plumber because each profession has its own language. Who would say the following (and what does it mean):

That the sense of smell was used by these cattle was established because of the marked audible variation in inhalation intensity as the animals grazed.

The sentence, which means "We knew the cattle used their sense of smell while grazing because we heard them sniffing," is from the book *Ethology of Free Ranging Domestic Animals*. The sentence won an Obscure Prose in Scientific Literature Award from the *Veterinary Record*. The meaning of each word is clear, but the joint meaning of the words would make sense only to someone specializing in cattle care.

In addition to using specialized words, specialized language may use common words in special ways. What meanings would you assign to the following words and phrases in classified advertisements to sell houses:

Owner will sacrifice.
Must sell.
Cozy, intimate.
Secluded.

The first two probably mean "for sale," the third probably means "very small," and the fourth probably means "very far from the nearest city." Although the common meanings of these words are clear, their specialized meanings in this context may not be so obvious.

What meaning would you assign to the following sentences, knowing that the speaker is a typical teenager living at home:

My room is clean.
I have nothing to wear.
Everybody's wearing it.

The first probably means "The mess you saw earlier has been stuffed into my closet." The second probably means "The particular shirt I want to wear isn't here." And the third probably means "The person I've chosen to set the standards for what I should wear was wearing it yesterday."

Problems arise when either specialized words or specialized usages come into play. When you encounter a specialized word, you know that whatever it means to you—if anything—it probably does not mean the same thing to the other person. Specialized usage, however, can go undetected unless other information is available. The statement "My room is clean" seems clear enough, but it will probably remain incorrectly interpreted until a closet door is opened!

Shared language—words that have similar meanings for those who are communicating—is the basis for effective communication. Problems occur when language is too abstract, when connotations differ widely, or when language is private and you happen to be the outsider. Under these circumstances, the meanings attributed to the words and phrases could be different enough to render communication ineffective.

Knowledge Checkup 2.2 provides you with the opportunity to grapple with the meanings of words from a private language.

KNOWLEDGE CHECKUP 2.2

Specialized Vocabulary

Define the following words or phrases:

1. *nosocomial infection*

2. *goober*

3. *hey*

4. *scarf*

5. *scope*

If you are unfortunate enough to suffer from a *nosocomial infection*, you have an infection caused by germs that are in a hospital. If you are in a hospital, you may get *goobers* to eat, so you'd better like peanuts. People will probably go by all day and say *hey* to you, which is hello or good-bye, depending upon whether they are coming or going. And you will *scarf* (eat) up your dinner while you *scope* out the patient in the next bed by looking intently at him or her.

BARRIERS TO SUCCESSFUL COMMUNICATION: OUR IMPERFECT LANGUAGE

Barriers to successful communication are inherent in language. Language is a tool created by people and, like any tool, it has limitations. Among the most common barriers to successful communication are polarization, indiscrimination, fact-inference confusion, allness, static evaluation, and bypassing.

Polarization

Polarization is the tendency to describe people, ideas, and events in either-or terms. When you use polarized language, an idea is either ridiculous or wonderful, a new acquaintance is either friendly or aloof, and a movie is either the best you've seen or the worst. The problem stems not simply from your wanting to make events seem more dramatic, but from the English language. Our language tends to consist of well-defined extremes and offers few words to describe the points in between. Time how long you need to write the opposite of each of the following words:

hot   _____

short   _____

tense   _____

legal   _____

You probably need only a few seconds to come up with the four opposites: *cold*, *tall*, *relaxed*, and *illegal*. But now see how long it takes you to come up with the midpoint for each pair.

If you were able to identify true midpoints at all, it probably took you a lot longer than it did to think of opposites. And you may have noticed that some of your midpoints, which may be one word or whole phrases, are not specific to a particular pair of opposites. *Average*, *OK*, *usual*, *normal*, and *neither-nor* constructions (neither hot nor cold, neither short nor tall) are cited as typical midpoints for most pairs. What was your midpoint for *legal* and *illegal*? A midpoint exists or we wouldn't need courts.

A problem with many word pairs is that there is no real midpoint to refer to. For example, if you're not happy, you're sad—and any response that falls between the two extremes is usually interpreted as sad. If, in response to your question "How are you?" someone said "OK," "average," "usual," or "neither terrific nor terrible," you would probably think he or she was not doing well.

Although there are instances when either-or language is appropriate—either you are reading this book or you're not, either you had lunch yesterday or you didn't—such language still denies that there are degrees of virtually everything. You might be reading this book but not concentrating, which is different from reading intently, just as an apple and a cup of coffee for lunch is different from a three-course meal. There are degrees of reading and degrees of eating lunch.

Our language's tendency to polarize the world can have drastic results. For example, if you call yourself a healthy person and you get ill (which is not unusual), you may begin to call yourself unhealthy because our language lacks a midpoint between the two. Such a change in labels could affect your behavior. For instance, you might avoid skiing because you fear that going out in cold weather will make you sick.

To avoid the problems of polarization, *be aware that the world comes in shades between the colorful extremes of our language*. People and events are rarely one thing or another. Be aware that reality is often the middle ground, somewhere between the dramas of the polarized extremes.

By increasing your vocabulary to include midpoints, you can avoid limiting yourself to polarized opposites. The following Skill Checkup is designed to give you practice in communicating midpoints.

SKILL CHECKUP 2.1

Finding Midpoints Between Extremes

Describe the midpoint for each of the following pairs of words.

1. honest _____ dishonest

2. graceful _____ clumsy

3. big _____ little

4. smart _____ stupid

Indiscrimination

No two people, ideas, events, or processes are identical. However, to deal with the world as if everything were unique would be an overwhelming task. Our language helps us to categorize things that are similar by providing general nouns, such as *house* (when no two houses are the same) and *cat* (when no two cats are the same). Difficulties arise when we focus only on the similarities between things, because then we lose or ignore the differences. The problem is one of **indiscrimination**, the failure to see things as unique and individual.

Stereotypes, oversimplified images of things or people, whether related to gender, age, race, or some other feature, are examples of the process of indiscrimination. Stereotypes are based on similarities, whether positive or negative, and once an individual is placed in a general category, all the presumed similarities are attributed to him or her. Stereotypes are quick ways to organize information about people. If stereotypes are incorrect, the qualities that make the person unique are lost. For example, a seventy-five-year-old person may have nothing in common with other seventy-five-year-olds except for age. The category "old person," however, includes a host of presumed similarities among the people so labeled, such as inflexibility and loss of memory.

Another problem with indiscrimination is that once a person, idea, or event is categorized, the tendency is to keep it pigeonholed. New information m~ ignored or denied to keep the classification intact. The goal is to ke~ neat, and well organized, even though life is often comple~

The process of indiscrimination is one reason why important to relationships. We use the first pieces of inf categorize the other person—for example, by race, height subsequent information to fill out the categories rather t Our first impression thus tends to stick.

To avoid the problem of indiscrimination, *be aware that no two people, ideas, objects, events, or processes are identical, even if they share the same category—or are called by the same name—because of some similarities*. Keep in mind that differences are as important as similarities, and that there is always more to know about everything. Avoid hardening of the categories.

SKILL CHECKUP 2.2

Communicating Differences

1. List five characteristics that individuals who share the title *teacher* have in common.

2. List five characteristics that differentiate one teacher from another.

3. Describe two teachers you know.

4. What is useful about nouns such as *teacher*?

5. What problems occur when nouns such as *teacher* are used?

Fact-Inference Confusion

Facts are statements based on observations; they relate directly to what you see, hear, touch, taste, or smell.[2] **Inferences** are conclusions that are suggested by observations but not based on them. For example, the statement "John is six feet tall" can be verified by measuring John's height in stocking feet: it is a fact. The statement "John is handsome," however, is an inference. Several facts may be put together and the conclusion drawn that John is handsome, but there is no direct observation of the conclusion "handsome."

Fact-inference confusion, the tendency to respond to something as if it is observed when, in reality, it is merely a conclusion, occurs because our language makes no grammatical distinction between facts and inferences. The two statements, "John is six feet tall" and "John is handsome," are grammatical equivalents. The tendency, then, is to interpret inferences as facts, so that "John is handsome" has the same truth value as "John has blue eyes."

Problems occur when you state inferences as if they are facts, because while you and others may agree on the truth of facts, there is no guarantee of agreement on the truth of inferences. You may state an inference as a fact and expect others to treat it as such, but you may run into misunderstandings if you fail to recognize that the inference is really a subjective opinion. For example, "John is handsome" may seem like a fact to you, given that John is six feet tall and has blue eyes and blond hair, and that these are your criteria for handsomeness. However, someone else, while agreeing with the facts of John's physical traits (six feet tall, blue eyes, blond hair), may consider brown eyes and black hair the necessary criteria for handsomeness. Thus, for this person, John is not handsome.

Knowledge Checkup 2.3 will provide you with some experience distinguishing facts from inferences.

KNOWLEDGE CHECKUP 2.3

Distinguishing Facts from Inferences[3]

Read the following story, assuming that all the information is accurate and true. Then, for each statement, indicate **T** (true), **F** (false), or **?** (don't know).

> A husband and wife had their small house thoroughly redecorated and painted—walls, windows, woodwork. At 5:00 P.M. the decorators left. The husband and wife cleaned up the house, locked the silverware cabinet, and went to bed. The next morning, they found a window open, the cabinet unlocked, and all the silverware missing. The police subsequently found a set of fingerprints on the windowsill and sent them to headquarters for identification. Headquarters reported that the fingerprints on the windowsill matched those of a notorious criminal named Joe Bender.

1. The silverware was stolen.	**T**	**F**	**?**
2. Joe Bender stole the silverware.	**T**	**F**	**?**
3. Yesterday, at some moment between the time the house was painted and now, Joe Bender was in or around the room.	**T**	**F**	**?**
4. The decorators left at 5:00 P.M.	**T**	**F**	**?**
5. The husband and the wife went to bed before cleaning up the house.	**T**	**F**	**?**

Key

1. **?** We do not know the silverware was stolen. All we know is that it was missing.
2. **?** We do not know that Joe Bender stole the silverware.
3. **?** We do not know when Joe Bender was in or around the room. All we know is that his fingerprints were on the windowsill.
4. **T** The story specifies that "At 5:00 P.M. the decorators left."

5. F The story specifies that "The man and wife cleaned up the house, locked the silverware cabinet, and went to bed."

Statements 1, 2, and 3 are inferences because they are not based on observations, but only suggested by them. Statements 4 and 5 are facts because they are based on observation.

Be aware that factual statements can be made only after an observation and are limited to what is observed, whereas inferences can be made anytime and go beyond what is observed. Also, although facts have a high degree of certainty, inferences vary in their probability—some being highly probable and others being highly improbable. Recognize facts and inferences for what they are and avoid confusing them. When confronted with an inference, ask yourself, "What is the probability that this inference is true?" An inference should spark questions and a search for the facts, if any, that support it.

Allness

Allness is the assumption that when you say something, you've said all there is on the subject. John Saxe's poem about six blind men and an elephant is an excellent illustration of this concept. Never having felt an elephant before, each blind man examines a small part and, based on the little information gathered, attempts to describe the entire beast. The first blind man touches the elephant's side and describes it as a wall; the second touches the tusk and describes it as a spear; the third touches the trunk and likens the elephant to a snake; the fourth touches the knee and describes the elephant as a tree; the fifth touches the ear and says the elephant is like a fan; and the sixth touches the tail and likens the elephant to a rope. Each is right and each is wrong.

The point to the poem is that we are all similar to the blind men when it comes to describing anything in the world. We see only a small part of something and, based on insufficient information, assume we can describe all of it. Whether it's another person, an idea, or an event, we know very little in comparison to what can be known. What you say about something is what you choose to say at the moment, or all you know about it at the moment, and not all there is to know. Our language, however, does not reflect this.

Be aware that whatever you or someone else says about something, there is more that can be said. Keep an open mind and realize that our finite language is being used to describe infinitely complex things.

Static Evaluation

Everything in the world is continuously changing, continuously in process, but our language tends to remain static. The result is called **static evaluation**, the inability of our language to account for constant change. When you meet a person for the second time you act as if she or he is the same person, but in reality that person has changed, just as you have changed. Since the first meeting each of you has gotten older and has had experiences that have changed you. Although changes may be minor, they exist. Our language rarely takes these changes into account. Statements are fixed in time, whether past, present, or future, even when the subject of the statement changes.

The permanent record in education is testimony to the problem of static evaluation. If a student is evaluated negatively by one teacher, subsequent teachers who read the evaluation may take it for the current reality. The former teacher's point of view becomes imposed on new situations and the student has an uphill battle to persuade others that he or she has changed. To confront this problem, one college instituted a forgiveness policy that allows seniors who received D's or F's as freshmen to have the poor grades removed from their records if their junior- and senior-level grades are all A's and B's.

Be aware that everything that is said applies to a particular time. A new perspective, or at least a healthy skepticism of the old perspective, is necessary to keep up with changes. When you communicate, let others know the time frame for what you're saying and ask others for their time frames. Skill Checkup 2.3 will help you eliminate static evaluation in your communication.

●KILL CHECKUP 2.3

Eliminating Static Evaluation

Combating the problem of static evaluation requires dating your communication—specifying the time frame for a particular message. Rewrite the following two statements to eliminate their static evaluations, making up the details that you need. For example, "John is a thief" could be recast as "John stole a piece of candy from a supermarket in Iowa City on March 28, 1989."

1. Margaret is a great student.

2. Bob likes to fish.

Bypassing

At one time or another, you've probably told someone how to locate a particular address only to find out later that your directions didn't work, that the person was unable to find the right street. You thought you were clear, and you probably were—for *you*. Most people speak until their message is perfectly clear to themselves, which does not mean that it is clear to the other person! Those speakers are likely to be bypassing. **Bypassing** occurs when you assume incorrectly that your meaning for your words is the same as another person's. But, as you learned earlier, different people assign different meanings to the same words because meaning is in people, not in words.

To avoid the problem of bypassing, *don't assume that meaning is shared merely because the other person nods encouragingly and seems to understand.* Ask questions when you are unsure whether your meaning and another's are the same.

USING LANGUAGE EFFECTIVELY

Barriers to successful communication may begin with the limitations inherent in our language, but they do not end there. The way we use language—the words we select and the way we put them together—poses more problems. Among the most common communication problems are the use of unclear language and the use of language that creates negative impressions. If you are aware of the problems you face when selecting words to communicate, you increase your chances of communicating effectively.

Unclear Language

Given the arbitrary relationship between symbols and their referents, different words may refer to essentially the same thing. A glance at *Roget's International Thesaurus* proves that every idea can be expressed in many different ways. Each way, however, presents a slightly different slant, much like our earlier list of synonyms for the word *work*. The most widespread examples of unclear language include relative words, euphemisms, clichés, emotive words, distortions, and oxymorons.

Relative Words

Relative words gain their meaning by comparison. Unless the point of comparison is specified, relative words lack clarity. For example, consider the following questions: Is your car fast? Are you smart? Are you tall? Is your school a good one? It's impossible to define *fast, smart, tall,* and *good* without knowing the basis for comparison: Fast compared to a new Jaguar? Smart compared to Albert Einstein? Tall compared to professional basketball player Michael Jordan? Good compared to Harvard?

Whenever you evaluate something without indicating your criteria, the meaning for your words is likely to differ from another person's meaning. An easy class for you may not be easy for someone else, and a good restaurant for you may not please your friends. To what other classes are you comparing the class? What is your basis for comparison? Is it the amount of homework? How lively the class meetings are? How strict the grading is? With what other

> ### Overcoming Language-based Barriers to Communication
>
> To overcome problems inherent in our language you must be aware of six barriers to communication:
>
> **1. Polarization,** the tendency to use either-or terms, can be overcome by recognizing the gradations between the extremes and increasing your vocabulary to include these midpoints.
>
> **2. Indiscrimination,** the tendency to focus on similarities and ignore differences, can be overcome by realizing that no two people, ideas, objects, events, or processes are identical even if you can refer to them by the same words. Remember that differences always exist.
>
> **3. Fact-inference confusion,** the tendency to respond to something as if it is observed when, in reality, it is merely a conclusion, can be overcome by realizing that facts are based on observations and that inferences are only suggested by observations. Be aware that inferences are subjective opinions open to debate.
>
> **4. Allness,** the assumption that what is said about something is all there is to say, can be overcome by realizing that more can always be said about everything. All statements are limited by current knowledge.
>
> **5. Static evaluation,** the tendency to ignore changes and assume that things stay the same, can be overcome by dating your messages.
>
> **6. Bypassing,** incorrectly assuming that the other person understands your message the way you understand it, can be overcome by asking questions to check others' comprehension of your comments.

restaurants are you comparing the restaurant? What is your basis for comparison? Is it the prices? The way the food is prepared? The amount served?

Euphemisms

Euphemisms are inoffensive language substituted for possibly offensive language. The goal of a euphemism is to soften the blow of what you have to say. Unfortunately, softening often leads to an unwanted side effect: lack of clarity.

How can you tell a friend his sweater is ugly? Telling him outright may be too blunt, but what happens when you use the words *unique, interesting,* or *makes a fashion statement?* And how do you respond to a friend who asks how you like her new furniture when you hate it? Do you call it *original*? How about *tasteful*? Or do you change the subject?

The Pentagon has created several memorable euphemisms. For example, combat is *violence processing* and civilian casualties are *collateral damage*. Educational institutions have their own fair share of euphemisms. For example, the term *remedial English* has been replaced with *developmental English*, the *remedial reading room* has become the *skill-development center*, and *pay raises* have become *salary adjustments*.

Although politeness and attempts to help people feel better about themselves are laudable, when a euphemism distorts meaning, it needs to be replaced with more accurate, blunter language. If you use "I" language to assume responsibility for your opinions, you can say what is on your mind without resorting to unclear language. For example, you may tell the friend whose sweater you find ugly, "I like sweaters that are less colorful." Such a statement lets him know that you don't like the sweater and why, and that the opinion is *yours*.

Clichés

Clichés are trite expressions that convey a common or popular thought. They lack originality and impact because of overuse. When what are now clichés first began being used, they had particular meanings based on what they were actually describing. In time, the original meaning disappeared and only the sentiment was left. For example, "put to the acid test" dates back to a time when gold was in wide circulation and users questioned whether they had the genuine ore. Nitric acid was applied, and if the sample was false, the acid decomposed it. Do you know the original meaning of the phrase "have an ax to grind"? According to one story, a man approached a boy and persuaded him, by flattery, to sharpen his ax. The boy sharpened the ax but received no thanks. From that point on, whenever the boy saw someone flattering someone else, he wondered whether the flatterer had an ax to grind, that is, some hidden purpose in mind.

Although the meaning of a particular cliché may be clear to the person using it, others may not understand its point. For example, although the meanings of "play it by ear" and "stiff upper lip" may be clear to you, how would a person learning English as a second language interpret those phrases? To avoid possible misunderstanding when speaking with people whose background is different from your own and who may thus be unfamiliar with some of your phraseology, avoid clichés altogether.

Emotive Words

Emotive words seem to be descriptive but actually communicate an attitude toward something or someone. Depending on your likes or dislikes, you select the words that communicate your attitude. Clarity is sacrificed when the word is used as a description rather than an expression of a point of view. For example, a 1956 Chevrolet may be called a "car" (neutral attitude), a "jalopy" (negative attitude), or a "classic" (positive attitude). The description "1956 Chevrolet" is **nonemotive**, that is, it does not communicate an attitude toward the object.

Someone who saves money may be called "thrifty" (positive) or a "tightwad" (negative). A small house may be called "cozy" (positive) or "claustrophobic" (negative). Such emotive words *seem* to describe something, but what they describe is less important than the speaker's attitude.

Listen for emotive words and separate them from what the speaker is describing. The clearest meaning occurs when what is described and how the speaker feels about it are both known.

Distortions

Communication is least clear when language is used to distort meaning. Attempts to exaggerate (or to minimize) the value, importance, or worth of something usually involve distorted language.

Advertisers use phrases such as "gives you more" without explaining more of what. They tell you "you can be sure" without mentioning what you can be sure of. They describe drinks as "the real thing" and cigarettes as having "real taste" without defining the word *real*. And they describe products as "new" and "improved" without explaining what's new or how they're improved.

Qualifiers may be used to make a claim more accurate, but questions remain about the meaning. For example, a dishwashing product may leave dishes *virtually* spotless, but what does a "virtually spotless" dish look like? Other qualifiers that may distort meaning include *up to* ("up to ten days' relief"), *as much as* ("as much as a full day's supply"), *like* ("feels like real wool"), *fights* ("fights cavities"), and *helps* ("helps prevent tooth decay"). The hope is that the qualifier will be forgotten and the **residual message**, the information you remember, will be that the dishes will be spotless, relief will last ten days, the supply will last a full day, the product is real wool, the toothpaste stops cavities, and the toothpaste prevents tooth decay. Do not ignore exaggerations or qualifiers when assessing the meaning of messages you receive; also, avoid using distortions in your own messages.

Oxymorons

Oxymorons are self-contradictory phrases. For example, how can there be a "cruel kindness" or something that's "almost unique"? Have you ever heard a book described as an "instant classic," a trip described as a "working vacation," a milk substitute called a "nondairy creamer," a person described as being "vaguely aware," and a guess at your car's repair cost called an "exact estimate"? Each phrase contains two words that contradict each other, resulting in a lack of clarity. Oxymorons confuse rather than clarify, so rather than assume what a speaker means, ask questions. Substitute more precise language for oxymorons in your own language. For example, "creamer substitute" is more precise than "nondairy creamer."

KNOWLEDGE CHECKUP 2.4

Recognizing Unclear Language

Read the following paragraph from a hypothetical teacher evaluation. Identify the uses of relative words, euphemisms, clichés, emotive words, distortions, and oxymorons.

> I am very pleased to evaluate the instructor who is being considered for a full-time position. It is my opinion that his approach to teaching is quite interesting. Although some might claim that he has an ax to grind in the classroom, I find his teaching style clean as a whistle. His lectures are spontaneously planned, giving them a quality that is virtually unmatchable. The acid test of whether he should be hired is that he is a grade-A teacher.

The unclear language you should have spotted is as follows:

> I am very pleased to evaluate the instructor who is being considered for a full-time position. It is my opinion that his approach to teaching is quite *interesting* (relative term—interesting compared to what?). Although some might claim that he has *an ax to grind* (cliché) in the classroom, I find his teaching style *clean as a whistle* (cliché). His lectures are *spontaneously planned* (oxymoron—how can a lecture be both spontaneous and planned?), giving them a quality that is *virtually unmatchable* (distortion—what is a virtually unmatchable quality?). The *acid test* (cliché) of whether he should be hired is that he is a *grade-A* (emotive word) teacher.

Language that Affects Impressions

Because others take what you say as a reflection of who you are, they form impressions of you based on your language. Language that is nonsexist, nonracist, and powerful leads to a positive impression, whereas sexist, racist, and powerless language leads to a negative impression.

Sexist Language

Sexist language expresses stereotyped sexual attitudes or the superiority of one gender over another. The prejudice against women dates back to when "God created Adam lord of all creatures." Whether the creation story is taken literally or not, the point is clear: men are the presumed lords.

Words used to describe males—*independent, logical, aggressive, confident, strong*—often have positive connotations, whereas those used to describe

Ensuring Clear Communication

To ensure that your language is clear, you must be aware of six common problems that occur when selecting the words you use.

1. Relative words, words that gain their meaning by comparison, can be made clearer by specifying the basis for the comparison.

2. Euphemisms, inoffensive language substituted for offensive language, needs to be replaced by more accurate, blunter language when it distorts meaning. Using "I" language should reduce the probability of getting a defensive reaction.

3. Clichés, trite expressions that have lost their impact through overuse, should be avoided when speaking with someone with a different background from yours who may not understand.

4. Emotive words, words that appear to describe something but actually convey an attitude, need to be separated from what is being described. Emotive words tell you how a speaker feels about what is being described and not the characteristics of the object.

5. Distortions, unclear qualifiers such as exaggerations, need to be taken into account when assessing the meaning of a message. Ignoring a qualifier or an exaggeration will result in a residual message that is not the same as the message communicated by the speaker.

6. Oxymorons, self-contradictory phrases, can be clarified by questioning the speaker as to her or his intent.

females—*dependent, illogical, gullible, timid, weak*—often have negative connotations. Men and women are too often viewed as opposites.[4]

In addition, the word *man* is used generically to refer to people in general, as in *mankind.* Sexist language implies that the world is made up of superior, important men and inferior, unimportant women.

Contrast the different descriptions of the same behavior in men and women:

He's curious; she's nosy.
He's a bachelor; she's a spinster.
He's suffering a midlife crisis; she's menopausal.
He's firm; she's stubborn.
He's ambitious; she's clawing.
He's versatile; she's scattered.
He's concerned; she's anxious.

In contrast, nonsexist language either makes no reference to gender or does not imply superiority of one gender over another. For example, references to people in general include women and men, so the word *mankind* is inappropriate. Words such as *humanity, people,* and *humankind* are both more accurate and nonsexist.

Nonsexist Communication

You can eliminate sexist language in two ways. The first calls for circumventing the problem by eliminating gender-specific terms or substituting neutral terms. For example, using the plural *they* eliminates the necessity for *he, she, she and he,* or *he and she.* Eliminate derogatory terms, such as *chick* and *the weaker sex.* When no gender reference is appropriate, substitute neutral terms to solve the sexism problem. For example, given that both men and women work for the postal system, substitute *letter carrier* for *mailman.* Of course, some terms refer to things that could not possibly have gender; make those terms gender-neutral. For example, a *manhole* is a *sewer lid* and something *man-made* is *synthetic.*

The second method for eliminating sexism is to mark gender clearly—to heighten awareness of whether the reference is to a female or a male. For example, rather than substitute *letter carrier* for *mailman,* use the terms *mailman* and *mailwoman* to specify whether the letter carrier is a man or a woman. Other examples include the following:

Saleswoman and *salesman* (rather than *salesperson*)
Congresswoman and *congressman* (rather than *congressperson* or *member of congress*)
Chairman and *chairwoman* (rather than *chair* or *chairperson*)
Policeman and *policewoman* (rather than *police officer*)

Inherent in this second approach is the notion that there is nothing sacred about putting *he* before *she.* Use both orders interchangeably—she and he, her and him, and hers and his. Adding *she, her,* and *hers* after *he, him,* and *his,* without changing the order, continues to imply that males are the important gender and should come first.

SKILL CHECKUP 2.4

Eliminating Sexist Language[5]

Rewrite the following sentences to make them gender-neutral.

1. The average student is worried about his grades.

2. Ask the student to hand in his work as soon as he is finished.

3. Writers become so involved in their work that they neglect their wives and children.

4. The class interviewed Chief Justice Rehnquist and Mrs. O'Connor.

5. I'll have my girl type the letter and get it out to you.

Rewritten, gender-neutral sentences:

1. "The average student is worried about grades" eliminates the *his* form altogether.
2. "Ask students to hand in their work as soon as they are finished" uses the plural to eliminate the singular *he*.
3. Writers become so involved in their work that they neglect their families" eliminates the assumption that writers are men.
4. Either "The class interviewed Chief Justice Rehnquist and Justice O'Connor" or "The class interviewed Mr. Rehnquist and Ms. O'Connor" treats both the male and the female justices in parallel manner.
5. "I'll have my secretary type the letter and get it out to you" eliminates the stereotyped image of secretaries as women and avoids language that is patronizing.

Racist Language

Racist language expresses stereotyped racial attitudes or the superiority of one race over another. Whereas sexist language in the United States divides the world into superior males and inferior females, racist language usually divides the world into superior whites and other inferior racial groups. All the same sexist assertions about women have been made for so-called inferior racial groups. For example, _____ (fill in any group) are less intelligent and more childlike and emotional than _____ . As with the word *male*, connotations of the word *white* are positive—clean, pure, innocent, and bright—and connotations of the word *black* are negative—dirty, dark, decaying, and sinister.

Racist language reflects indiscrimination; that is, it fails to make important distinctions among people who may have only one characteristic in common. Members of a racial group may differ more from each other than they do from members of other racial groups. For example, the primary distinction between whites and blacks is skin color (although there are many whites with dark skin and many blacks with light skin), and this one difference does not counter the host of similarities that make both blacks and whites *people*.

Remarks that encompass entire groups of people should be eliminated from your communications. Avoid abstractions and be concrete: refer to your own experience and to the particular limitations of your own experience.

> ## Creating a Positive Impression
>
> To ensure that your messages create a positive impression, be aware of and eliminate sexist, racist, and powerless language.
>
> **1. Sexist language,** language that expresses stereotyped sexual attitudes or the superiority of one gender, can be eliminated two ways: substitute neutral terms for the gender-specific ones, or mark gender clearly.
>
> **2. Racist language,** language that expresses stereotypical racial attitudes or the superiority of one race, can be eliminated by using concrete language.
>
> **3. Powerless language,** language that modifies what is said and detracts from the certainty of a statement, can be controlled by listening for hedges, qualifiers, hesitations, tag questions, and disclaimers and avoiding them. Use straightforward language.

Powerful and Powerless Language

Powerful language creates an impression of strength, capability, and control. Several language habits contribute to perceptions of powerlessness and should thus be used sparingly.

Hedges—words that limit your responsibility for what you say—and **qualifiers**—words that modify what you say—detract from the certainty of a statement. For example, "kinda," "I think," and "I guess" indicate that you are unsure of yourself. Consider the degree of assertiveness in "I guess I'll leave work today at 5:00" versus "I'll leave at 5:00."

Hesitations also indicate uncertainty. Whether you add "um," "uh," or "well" to your speech, you create the perception that you are uncertain about your topic. Compare "I . . . well . . . er . . . want you to know that . . . well . . . I'll be leaving today at . . . uh . . . 5:00" to "I want you to know I'll be leaving at 5:00."

Tag questions, unnecessary questions added to statements, indicate you are unsure of what you're saying or are unwilling to take a stand. For example, "right?" or "OK?" at the end of a statement requests approval or agreement. Note the difference between "I'm leaving today at 5:00, right?" versus "I'm leaving today at 5:00."

Disclaimers, expressions that excuse what you're saying or ask another person to bear with you while you make a point, indicate uncertainty and communicate subservience to the other person. For example, compare "I probably shouldn't say this, but I'm leaving at 5:00" or "If you'll just let me tell you one more thing, I want to say I'm leaving at 5:00" to "I'm leaving at 5:00."

If your language is powerless, you will be perceived as incompetent and passive as opposed to competent and dynamic. You will not be considered as attractive as someone who uses powerful language. And because you will be perceived as less competent, dynamic, and attractive, you will not be as persuasive as someone who uses powerful speech.

To be perceived as powerful, eliminate—as much as possible—the use of hedges, qualifiers, hesitations, tag questions, and disclaimers. The following Skill Checkup will help you eliminate powerless language from your messages.

SKILL CHECKUP 2.5

Eliminating Powerless Language

Rewrite the following paragraph by substituting powerful language for powerless language.

I was thinking that, uh, maybe you'd like to go out this weekend, you know? I know I'm not asking this the way it should be asked, but I thought that, well, you'd possibly like to go out with me, right?

The most powerful way this could be rewritten is as follows:

I would like you to go out with me this weekend. This straightforward statement eliminates the hedges ("I was thinking" and "I thought"), qualifiers ("maybe" and "possibly"), hesitations ("uh" and "well"), tag questions ("you know?" and "right?"), and the disclaimer ("I know I'm not asking this the right way"). Also, it increases perceptions of power by changing the question, "Would you like to go out with me this weekend?" to a statement.

To communicate effectively, you must understand how words, what they symbolize, and the thoughts they stimulate relate to each other—how meaning and language are connected. You must also understand barriers to successful communication and gain appropriate skills to overcome those barriers. Language may have problems that reflect its imperfection, and you may not always put this imperfect tool to the best use, but effective verbal communication can be a reality. By combining your understanding and skill with your motivation, you can become a competent communicator.

Sometimes students and teachers do not communicate effectively. This student and this teacher have a problem: the teacher has presented a definition of *communication* that is meaningless to the student.

1. Describe, from the student's point of view, the relationship between the word *communication* and what it refers to (note the student's thought, "Huh?"). Do a second description from the teacher's point of view. Can you define the problem identified in this cartoon by comparing your two descriptions?

2. Analyze the teacher's language in terms of abstractness versus concreteness. What are the denotations and connotations of the teacher's words? Is the language private or shared?

3. Language is an imperfect tool and, as this teacher demonstrates, can be used imperfectly. What problems of verbal interaction does this cartoon highlight?

4. If the teacher hired you as a consultant to help prepare the lesson on communication, what advice would you offer? What does the teacher need to understand about language in terms of (a) the relationship between language and meaning, and (b) barriers to verbal interaction? What specific skills does the teacher need to develop in order to overcome barriers to verbal interaction?

NOTES

1. For a discussion of the issues raised in this section, see: Sarah Trenholm, "The Problem of Signification," in *Human Communication Theory* (Englewood Cliffs, NJ: Prentice-Hall, 1986), pp. 68–96.

2. Joseph A. DeVito, *The Communication Handbook: A Dictionary* (New York: Harper and Row, 1986), pp. 112–13.

3. This test is adapted from: Sanford I. Berman, *Why Do We Jump to Conclusions?* (San Francisco: International Society for General Semantics, 1969), pp. 2, 4–5.

4. See: B. Bate, *Communication and the Sexes* (New York: Harper and Row, 1988), and Judy C. Pearson, *Gender and Communication* (Dubuque, IA: Wm. C. Brown, 1985).

5. Adapted from: *Guidelines for Nonsexist Use of Language in NCTE Publications*, rev. ed. (Urbana, IL: National Council of Teachers of English, 1985).

FOR FURTHER INVESTIGATION

Ananis, Michael. "Teenspeak: A Rudimentary Guide to a Secret Language." *Review* [Eastern Airlines in-flight magazine] (April 1987): 44–49.

Andrews, Lori B. "Exhibit A: Language." *Psychology Today* (February 1984): 28–33.

Bate, B. *Communication and the Sexes*. New York: Harper and Row, 1988.

Berryman, Cynthia L., and James R. Wilcox. "Attitudes Toward Male and Female Speech: Experiments on the Effects of Sex-Typical Language." *Western Journal of Speech Communication* 44 (1980): 50–59.

Bradac, James J., and Anthony Mulac. "A Molecular View of Powerful and Powerless Speech Styles: Attributional Consequences of Specific Language Features and Communicator Intentions." *Communication Monographs* 51 (1984): 307–19.

Dance, Frank E. X., and Carl E. Larson. *The Functions of Human Communication: A Theoretical Approach*. New York: Holt, Rinehart and Winston, 1976.

DeVito, Joseph. *Language: Concepts and Processes*. Englewood Cliffs, NJ: Prentice-Hall, 1976.

Froman, Robert. "How to Say What You Mean." *Etc.* 43 (1986): 393–402.

Guidelines for Nonsexist Use of Language in NCTE Publications, rev. ed. Urbana, IL: National Council of Teachers of English, 1985.

Haney, William V. Communication and Interpersonal Behavior, 5th ed. Homewood, IL: Irwin, 1986.

Hardy, William G., ed. *Language, Thought, and Experience*. Baltimore: University Park Press, 1978.

Hayakawa, S. I. *Language in Thought and Action*, 4th ed. New York: Harcourt Brace Jovanovich, 1978.

Johnson, Craig E. "An Introduction to Powerful and Powerless Talk in the Classroom." *Communication Education* 36 (1987): 167–72.

Miller, Casey, and Kate Swift. *Words and Women*. New York: Anchor Press, 1976.

Mulac, Anthony, John M. Wiemann, Sally J. Widenmann, and Toni W. Gibson. "Male/Female Language Differences and Effects in Same-Sex and Mixed-Sex Dyads: The Gender-Linked Language Effect." *Communication Monographs* 55 (1988): 315–35.

Pearson, Judy C. *Gender and Communication*. Dubuque, IA: Wm. C. Brown, 1985.

Rothwell, J. Dan. *Telling It Like It Isn't*. Englewood Cliffs, NJ: Prentice-Hall, 1982.

Sapir, Edward. *Language: An Introduction to the Study of Speech*. New York: Harcourt, Brace and World, 1921.

Trenholm, Sarah. "The Problem of Signification." In *Communication Theory*, pp. 68–96. Englewood Cliffs, NJ: Prentice-Hall, 1986.

Wood, Barbara. *Children and Communication: Verbal and Nonverbal Language Development*, 2d ed. Englewood Cliffs, NJ: Prentice-Hall, 1981.

CHAPTER 3

▶ *Nonverbal Communication*

*This chapter on nonverbal communication will help you practice and develop communication competencies in two broad areas: (1) **communication codes,** which include using appropriate nonverbal signs and effective vocal cues, and (2) **human relations,** which include describing another's emotions, expressing feelings to others, and performing social rituals. Specifically, the competencies you will gain will enable you to do the following:*

▶ *Describe the nonverbal behaviors important in assessing strangers.*

▶ *Recognize the stereotypes associated with physical appearance, including body type, physical attraction, clothing, and jewelry.*

▶ *Control and interpret facial movements and eye behavior.*

▶ *Assess the effects of physical and psychological contexts on the interpretation of nonverbal cues.*

▶ *Describe the importance and uses of touch.*

▶ *Use vocal cues to express emotions and regulate social interactions.*

▶ *Describe the types and uses of body movements, and learn to mirror body movements of others to increase their perceptions of similarity to you.*

▶ *Recognize nonverbal messages that indicate deception.*

▶ *Use nonverbal behaviors to affect how you feel.*

*L*ike a detective, you try to make sense out of the information that bombards you. Unlike a detective, however, your goal is rarely to solve a crime. More often, your goal is to size up strangers, to gather enough data to predict someone's behavior, and to determine whether someone might make a good acquaintance, friend, business partner, or teacher—or perhaps a worthy adversary.

Picture yourself being introduced to someone. Before a word is spoken, a great deal of information is exchanged. Which of the person's actions and characteristics do you focus upon? Do you note the person's body shape, whether she or he is fat or thin, muscular or flabby, short or tall? Do you examine what the person is wearing? Do you care whether the clothes are clean or dirty, in or out of style? Do you look for a wedding band or college ring and notice other jewelry?

When you're close enough to see the other person's face and make eye contact, do you consider how the other person looks at you, how long eye contact is sustained? Does it matter whether the person is smiling, frowning, or looking bored or puzzled? Are you aware of the distance between you and the other person? Does it matter how close you can get before the other person backs up or breaks eye contact? Do you care what the person's voice sounds like, whether it's nasal, throaty, or resonant? Do you notice how the person moves and whether she or he engages in preening behavior, such as hair smoothing? Do you pay attention to whether the person touches you, or how she or he responds to your touch?

And what would you like another person to notice about you? Should a person notice your shape and height, what you're wearing, whether you maintain eye contact or use facial expressions, how close or far away you stand, your voice, and whether you're willing to touch and be touched?

These questions suggest the many forms of nonverbal communication that will be discussed in this chapter. **Nonverbal communication** includes those actions and attributes of people *other than words* that convey meaning.

FUNCTIONS OF NONVERBAL COMMUNICATION

You base first impressions almost entirely upon nonverbal information. The importance of nonverbal behavior, however, does not stop with first impressions. Rather, nonverbal communication is always an important part of the total communication process, which includes both verbal and nonverbal messages.

Emotions and feelings are more accurately and easily communicated nonverbally than with words. Also, because nonverbal behaviors are not easily controlled consciously, they often reveal more than words do about how you and others react.

When you use nonverbal behaviors to regulate your interaction with other people, you run less risk of rebuke or embarrassment than you might if you used words. For example, raising your eyebrows and looking directly into a speaker's eyes signals your desire to say something. Because you have not overtly interrupted by saying "I have something to say," you are not likely to be told "Wait until I am through!" Moreover, if the speaker stops and angrily demands whether you want to say something, you can either deny your intention to interrupt or mention that you would like to say something later. Frequently, your nonverbal signal will be countered with a nonverbal signal from the speaker—a slightly raised hand, perhaps, indicating that you should wait a moment—so the speaker's train of spoken ideas remains uninterrupted.

Embarrassing situations can often be alleviated if you communicate your intentions nonverbally instead of verbally. For example, you may find leave-taking difficult because saying good-bye will interrupt the flow of conversation and draw attention to you. Moving toward the door or putting on your coat, however, can signal your intention to exit in a subtle, unobtrusive way.

Sometimes nonverbal communication works in conjunction with verbal communication. You may use nonverbal communication to elaborate your words, as when you point south while saying "The post office is south of here." You may also use it to accentuate your words, as when you pause before making a point in order to emphasize the thought's importance. Nonverbal communication may also complement spoken words. For example, pounding your fist on the lectern during a public address adds impact to your words. A complementing nonverbal message, in contrast to an accenting one, enhances the meaning of the spoken words by adding information. In this case, your fist-pounding adds the message "I mean what I'm saying!"

Besides working in conjunction with spoken words, nonverbal communication can substitute for spoken words. For example, rubbing your stomach and licking your lips while looking at a pie substitutes for saying "I want a slice."

Finally, others' nonverbal behaviors may indicate how you should interpret the verbal messages you receive. Consider the difference between someone saying "I think I understand your directions to Mario's Restaurant" in a confident tone of voice and someone saying the same thing in a hesitant tone, accompanied by head-scratching and raised eyebrows. In the first situation you might feel pleased with your direction-giving; in the second one you might consider how to restate your message to make it clearer.

Just as nonverbal communication has many uses—forming first impressions, expressing feelings and emotions, regulating interaction, and repeating, accenting, complementing, substituting, and helping in the interpretation of spoken words—it takes many forms. People communicate nonverbally through physical appearance, face and eyes, context of communication, touch, voice, and body movements.

PHYSICAL APPEARANCE

Your physical appearance includes everything that's visible to others, from the top of your head to the bottom of your feet, including your body shape and the clothing you wear. How much importance do you place on your own physical appearance? How much importance do you place on the physical appearance of others?

Body Shape

If you are like most people, one of the first pieces of data you use to size up another person is body shape, whether the person is **ectomorphic**—thin and frail-looking; **mesomorphic**—muscular and well-proportioned; or **endomorphic**—fat and round. Each body shape encourages different stereotypes: "Thin people are so *tense*"; "Fat people are very *lazy*"; and "Muscular people are so *confident*." Knowledge Checkup 3.1 will provide you with the opportunity to assess how well the stereotyped personality characteristics predict your own body type.

KNOWLEDGE CHECKUP 3.1

Body Shape Self-Analysis[1]

Complete the sentences by choosing from the words provided.

1. Most of the time I feel _____ , _____ ,

and _____ .

calm	relaxed	complacent	anxious	cheerful
confident	energetic	impetuous	shy	thoughtful

2. When I work or study, I seem to be _____ ,

_____ , and _____ .

efficient	enthusiastic	reflective	meticulous	precise
serious	competitive	sluggish	cooperative	placid

3. Socially, I seem to be _____ , _____ ,

and _____ .

outgoing	considerate	talkative	cool	tolerant
warm	sympathetic	awkward	assertive	kind

Do you see yourself as an ectomorph, a mesomorph, or an endomorph? Here are the personality traits stereotypically associated with each body type. Circle the ones you selected.

Ectomorph	Mesomorph	Endomorph
anxious	assertive	calm
awkward	cheerful	complacent
considerate	competitive	cooperative
cool	confident	kind
meticulous	efficient	placid
precise	energetic	relaxed
reflective	enthusiastic	sluggish
serious	impetuous	sympathetic
shy	outgoing	tolerant
thoughtful	talkative	warm

Did you circle a majority of adjectives in any one list? How do the adjectives you circled suit your body type? Like any stereotype, the generalization may not apply to a particular example—in this case, you.

The consequences of being tall or short are well documented. Tall people have a distinct advantage over their shorter peers. For example, men 6′2″ and taller receive starting salaries about 12 percent higher than those under 6′; short actors often get the "short end of the stick" by being cast as buffoons, archvillains, or "small tough guys." Many jobs, from flight attendant to police officer, require a certain minimum height.

Body Image

How you *feel* about your appearance has greater influence on your interaction with other people than how you actually look. If you are uncomfortable with your appearance, you are likely to avoid interaction with others or at least assume that you deserve negative reactions. Teenagers suffering from acne may confine themselves to the house on weekends or assume that dating is out of the question, just as adults who put on a few pounds may skip a party, wanting to lose weight before appearing "in public."

Knowledge Checkup 3.2 will help you learn how you perceive your own appearance.

KNOWLEDGE CHECKUP 3.2

Assessing Your Body Image

Use the scales to rate the following of your body components: height, weight, hair, eyes, ears, nose, mouth, teeth, chin, complexion, overall facial attractiveness, shoulders, chest/breasts, arms, hands, stomach, hips, legs, feet, general muscle tone, and overall body appearance. Use all five scales to rate each body component.

beautiful	1	2	3	4	5	6	7	ugly
hard	1	2	3	4	5	6	7	soft
strong	1	2	3	4	5	6	7	weak
pleasant	1	2	3	4	5	6	7	unpleasant
appealing	1	2	3	4	5	6	7	unappealing

The more physically attractive you perceive yourself to be, the more positive your self-concept is. This explains why physically attractive people tend to be more independent and more resistant to pressure to conform than are less attractive people. Attractive females are generally more confident, and attractive males are generally more assertive and less critical than their less attractive peers.

Also, if others perceive you as physically attractive, they are more likely to evaluate you positively. Attractive people are thought to be kinder, stronger, sexier, and more interesting, poised, modest, sociable, and outgoing than unattractive people. Physically attractive people are given more help, receive more awards, and are perceived as more credible (and are therefore more persuasive) than their physically unimposing counterparts.[2]

On the other hand, attractiveness may not always be an asset. Recent research reveals that a businesswoman perceived as attractive may suffer unpleasant—and unfair—consequences from the perception. Because of her appearance, others may consider her unintelligent, self-centered, and fickle. Others may assume that she gained her power because of her looks rather than her ability. Being perceived as attractive may also make a businesswoman the target of co-workers' jealousy, gossip, and sexual harassment.[3]

Clothing and Other Artifacts

Most of us assume that people wear clothes for protection and modesty, but that isn't always the case. Darwin found that the natives of Tierra del Fuego never wore clothes, in spite of severe weather conditions; and modesty in some cultures—particularly those that are not westernized—is not related to wearing, or not wearing, clothes.

If protection and modesty are not the primary reasons for wearing clothes, there must be other important reasons why people wrap themselves in cloth, leaves, bark, or skins. These reasons include communication. Others take note of what you wear—just as you take note of what they wear—to assess your current economic and education levels; your social, economic, and educational background; your level of success, social position, and sophistication; and your trustworthiness and moral character.

Although it may not be fair—or wise—to judge people by their clothes, these judgments are a fact of life. Of course, what you wear matters more in some situations than in others and matters more to some people than to others. Your friends probably allow you more latitude in style and color than does your employer, and your choice of clothing for an informal party may be less consequential than your choice of clothing for a business luncheon.

What you wear in a business setting is important; what you wear to a job interview is crucial. An interviewer's first impression of you comes from what you wear; if that initial impression is unfavorable, your opportunities may be closed off immediately. Dressing too differently from your interviewer may result in a poor evaluation, as may dressing in anything but conservative garb. Men should wear dark suits (blue or gray—black is too solemn) and solid white shirts with solid ties, although discreet diagonal stripes are not too out of line. Women do best in skirted suits (which may be dark, but medium gray or blue is preferable) and white blouses, although gray and pink are acceptable. Whether or not you are comfortable with your appearance, you can control—at least to some extent—how the interviewer perceives you by choosing your clothes carefully.

Hairstyle, cosmetics, and jewelry also affect your appearance. For example, long hair on a man is associated with an artistic, casual, possibly romantic person, and short hair is associated with an athletic, energetic one. Moderate-length hair connotes seriousness, a business-like attitude, and decisiveness.

Although trends in makeup change rapidly, the one constant seems to be that "less is more." Women, especially those under 35, who wear subtle makeup, are perceived more positively than women whose makeup is obvious. However, "less is more" does not mean "none is best." A woman who wears no makeup at all may be perceived as too conservative and lacking in individuality.

Unlike clothes and makeup, which merely suggest characteristics, certain accessories communicate specific messages. Wedding bands, college rings, and religious symbols all convey particular and relatively unambiguous messages. Jewelry may also be used to communicate social status and economic level, but as with makeup, less is more in a business setting.

You react to what you wear just as others do: You may find that putting on your jogging outfit gets you ready, both physically and mentally, to run; putting on your favorite dress-up outfit helps get you in the mood for a sophisticated party. Your mood affects what you choose to wear, and what you choose to wear in turn affects your mood. Dress how you *want* to feel and, sure enough, you just might feel that way!

Find out your own style of dressing by taking Knowledge Checkup 3.3. Are you communicating what you want to with what you wear?

KNOWLEDGE CHECKUP 3.3

You Are What You Wear

Assess your clothing habits by responding to the following seven questions.

1. Do your clothes tend to be bright or muted in color, solids or prints, loose or tight fitting?

2. How would you describe the style of clothes you select? Is the style current or old-fashioned?

3. Do you dress to suit the occasion? How do you know?

4. How do you dress when you feel "up"? How do you dress when you feel "down"?

5. How do you dress when you feel fatter or thinner than usual?

6. Do you wear jewelry? If so, how much and how often? Do you wear jewelry only on particular occasions?

7. Select one scenario (for example, at work) and describe what you would typically wear. Now describe what you want to communicate with what you wear; contrast your answer with what you think you *do* communicate. What should you wear in that situation to make it more likely that you will communicate the desired message?

FACE AND EYES

You communicate more about your emotions with your face—especially your eyes—than with any other part of your body. You also depend more on other people's facial cues than on any other nonverbal behavior to ensure successful interactions. Facial cues may communicate five dimensions of meaning:

1. The extent to which communication is experienced as pleasant or unpleasant, good or bad (Does this person find interacting with you a pleasant experience?)

2. The level of interest in the communication (Is this person interested in you or what you're saying?)

3. The intensity of involvement in the communication (Is this person involved in your interaction?)

4. The spontaneity of the response (Is this person controlling his or her facial expressions or behaving naturally?)

5. The extent to which communication is understood (Does this person understand what you're saying?)

Looking at others' faces has early roots. Early in life you learned to search out the faces that meant warmth and security; soon after your birth, you recognized and were attracted to the faces of those who cared for you. Later you learned that this part of the body communicated even more useful information. Now you spend a lot of time looking at faces because faces identify people more than any other aspect of the body. Even young children, when they're asked to draw themselves, typically produce a large head with eyes, nose, mouth, and ears attached to a small body with little more than stick arms and legs. The head is what is important: it is what you speak to and what speaks back to you.

Because the face can be so revealing, you have probably learned a number of adaptive techniques, or ways of manipulating your facial expressions, to communicate a desired message. You can **qualify** your expressions by adding a second facial expression to change the impact of the first one. For example, after looking angry and yelling "I can't stand it any longer!" you might look sad or confused in order to communicate, "I'm hurt and sad, as well as angry, and I want to talk about this."

You can **modulate** your facial expressions to communicate feelings stronger or weaker than the ones you're actually experiencing. For instance, to make the statement "I'm really upset with you" more intense, you could squint your eyes to show that you really mean what you're saying.

You can **falsify** your facial expression by showing an emotion when none is felt (you may have no particular feeling about your friend's new coat, but to maintain your friendship you look excited); evincing little or no facial expression when you experience a particular feeling (you may feel angry about your friend's lateness, but keep your expression neutral to avoid an argument); or covering a true emotion by displaying a false one (you may express pleasant surprise when your parents unexpectedly show up to cover your real feeling of dismay).

Although overall facial expressions are interesting, the eyes hold perhaps the greatest fascination. Everyday expressions confirm the emphasis on sense of sight: You don't say "I feel/smell/hear/taste what you mean," or "I'll feel/smell/hear/taste you later," but "I *see* what you mean" and "I'll *see* you later." Old friends, of course, are a "sight for sore *eyes*." The evil eye, a glance that can inflict harm, must, of course, always be guarded against! Looks can kill—at least figuratively!

Eyes receive a lot of attention for several reasons, mostly because the eyes, many people believe, reveal whether a person is being honest or deceptive. Eyeshifting, excessive blinking, and frequent glances downward are often interpreted as signs of lying, while maintaining eye contact (without staring) is considered a sign of honesty. Eye behavior, like other aspects of nonverbal communication, is culture-bound. For example, Chinese are taught that "nice" girls must look down, and some Native American groups teach that looking down or away shows respect.

You use your eyes to initiate interaction and, by maintaining eye contact during a conversation, signal your level of interest and involvement in another person. However, assessing others' interest by the amount of eye contact they make can be difficult: Some people look at a partner in conversation only 25 percent of the time, while others look as much as 70 percent, depending on their culture's conventions and their personal preferences.[4] On the other hand, each person is relatively consistent in her or his use of eye contact, so once you know someone's typical pattern, you should be able to spot and interpret variations.

Eye contact can also show relative power and status. Although increased eye contact can communicate interest and involvement, too much eye contact can indicate a subservient position, or low power. People with low power pay more attention to those with high power—low power people look more at those with high power. However, just as too much eye contact is associated with low power, so is too little. Low-power people are more likely than high-power people to avert their eyes or look downward.

Perhaps the most reliable measure of interest is pupil size. Your pupils enlarge when you're interested in a subject and contract when you're uninterested. By noticing others' pupil size—certainly not something they can easily control—you can gauge their level of interest.

You also use your eyes to regulate the flow of conversation. Typically, a speaker looks away from the other person, glances back now and then to check for feedback, and then establishes full eye contact to indicate when it's the other person's turn to talk.

Facial cues can communicate the emotion you're experiencing, but your eyes indicate its intensity. For example, your face may communicate interest and happiness, but the most intense expression of both, love, comes only from your eyes.

Paying attention to the facial expressions and eye behavior of others will increase your sensitivity to the communicative function of the face. The following activity should help you increase your skill.

SKILL CHECKUP 3.1

Increasing Your Skill at Interpreting Facial Expressions

1. What emotions are being communicated by facial expressions in each picture?

2. What levels of interest and involvement are communicated facially by each person in each picture?

3. In each picture, what intensity of emotion is revealed by facial expressions?

4. Do the two persons seem to understand each other?

5. Do their facial expressions reveal their relative status?

6. What nonverbal information did you use to answer questions 1 through 5?

7. Did anything besides facial expressions help you answer the questions?

CONTEXTS OF INTERACTION

Because meaning is contextual, nonverbal behaviors have little meaning outside the situation in which they occur. For example, nonverbal behaviors that communicate sorrow—slumped body, hand pressed against forehead, downward glance, and sighs—can also communicate overwhelming happiness. You are more likely to interpret the behavior as sorrow if the physical context is a hospital and more likely to interpret it as happiness if the context is a game show and the person's score indicates she just won $10,000. Some context is needed to interpret the behavior correctly.

Two contexts are important: physical and psychological. The **physical context** is composed of objects and their arrangement in the environment. It may include architecture, furniture, room color, and temperature. The **psychological context** includes a person's thoughts and feelings toward aspects of the physical context. For example, a student may feel that the seat she occupies in a classroom is "her space."

Physical Context

A physical context may be analyzed along a number of dimensions. For example, a physical context may be assessed according to its degree of *formality* (most business offices are supposed to be formal), *comfort* (family rooms are supposed to be warm and comfortable), *privacy* (bathrooms are supposed to be private), *familiarity*—how usual or unusual it is (modern office buildings are supposed to be strikingly unusual), and *closeness*—how close it encourages you to be with others (living rooms are supposed to be arranged so that people can feel close).

To create a desired effect (formal or informal, comfortable or uncomfortable, private or public, familiar or unfamiliar, close or distant), you may adjust a room's color, temperature, and furnishings. For example, red is perceived as hot and full of vitality, whereas pale blue and green are cool and calm. Brown is unhappy, purple can be depressed or dignified, and white is neutral, which may account for its widespread use in a variety of shades.[5]

Color and temperature interact. For example, a white room seems cooler than a red room when the temperature is identical. If your goal is comfort for your guests, keep in mind that perceptions of attractiveness decrease as temperature and humidity increase. Cool temperatures are better for working and warm ones for relaxing, although *cooler* and *warmer* are relative terms.

Next to raising or lowering the thermostat, the easiest way to change the environment is with furnishings and lighting. Rooms with indirect lighting, comfortable furniture, and carpeting and drapes are perceived as attractive, and increase feelings of happiness and energy; rooms with direct lighting, few sound-absorbing furnishings, and uncomfortable furniture cause occupants to feel tired and bored.[6] Chairs, for example, can greatly influence others' responses to a room: High-backed chairs covered with expensive cloth are more formal than low-backed ones in corduroy; soft, cushioned chairs are generally more comfortable than ones without cushions; several chairs indicate that a room is not private, that it is open to more than one person at a time; and grouping chairs close together, facing each other, encourages interaction.

Knowledge Checkup 3.4 will help you analyze the environment you're in at this moment. Specifically, you will describe those aspects of the setting on which you base your perceptions of formality, comfort, and so on.

KNOWLEDGE CHECKUP 3.4

Analysis of Your Environment

Analyze the environment you are in right now in terms of formality, comfort, privacy, familiarity, and closeness. Indicate which part of the environment—color, temperature, furnishings, or lighting—you used as the basis for your assessment. For example, if you describe the room as uncomfortable, specify why. Is it the uncushioned chair, the bright lighting, the lack of seating?

1. Formality:

2. Comfort:

3. Privacy:

4. Familiarity:

5. Closeness:

Suppose you wanted to change the environment—for example, make it more formal or more private. What adjustments would you make and why?

Psychological Context

Psychological context may be divided into territoriality and personal space.

Territoriality is a feeling of ownership toward some fixed area. It may not be strictly logical to lay claim to certain areas of your environment, but you do it anyway. You *feel* that the room you sleep in is *your* room and the roses you tend are *your* roses. Because you feel that pieces of your environment belong to you, you feel protective toward them, personally insulted if someone makes an unkind remark about them, and sad if something happens to them.

To lay claim to a piece of territory requires that you mark it with your ownership. You may leave an "occupied" sign on an airplane seat, drape your coat over the back of a chair in a restaurant, or spread your books on a desk in the library to indicate that the place is yours and that you will be returning to claim it—*so others keep off!* You may also formally mark your territory with your name or some representative symbol, such as a club's emblem or your initials. "This room belongs to _____" is a popular sign for those who want to emphasize that trespassing will not be tolerated.

You may also mark the boundaries of your territory. For example, a fence may separate your property from your neighbor's; painted lines separate your parking space from the next ones; and a door clearly separates your room from the rest of the residence.

In a business setting, territory shows status. For example, the boss usually has a private office and the privilege of entering subordinates' work areas without knocking first. Similarly, the people with the most power and prestige most often get the largest and best-located offices.

Knowing your own and others' feelings about fixed areas of the environment—who lays claim to what—can help ensure smooth interactions. You shouldn't invade others' territory unless you're ready for a fight. Mark your own territory clearly if you want others to know that it's yours. Knowledge Checkup 3.5 will help you recognize those public and private environments to which you lay claim.

KNOWLEDGE CHECKUP 3.5

Analysis of Territory

What territory do you claim in each of these environments and how do you defend your territory from "attack"?

1. In public environments (choose your school, classroom, or workplace)

2. In private environments (choose your home, garden, or car)

Personal space is an invisible bubble of space around you—a body buffer zone. It is larger in front than in the back, and varies in overall size depending on where you are and with whom you're interacting. Your personal space

Photo A   Intimate Distance

Photo B   Personal Distance

probably contracts when you're with friends—you let friends get closer to you than strangers before you begin to feel uncomfortable. Unlike territory, which remains fixed, your personal space goes where you go.

In your next conversation with an acquaintance, try an experiment. As you talk, slowly, subtly, move closer to the other person and watch what happens. Most likely, the person will back away, countering each of your movements forward with a movement backward without consciously being aware of what is happening.

As the experiment demonstrates, you hardly notice your personal space until someone violates it. Crowded elevators and theaters are uncomfortable partly because your space requirements are not met. When doctors and nurses touch you, they breach the bubble and may leave you feeling exposed and vulnerable. Such violations may trigger a variety of nonverbal defensive reactions: You may shift your body away from the intruder, cut off eye contact to gain distance (a popular technique in elevators), or show nervous reactions, such as tightening your jaw, stroking your face, or tapping your fingers.

You protect your personal space because it serves several important purposes. Most importantly, it buffers you from other people who might pose a threat. It also gives you room to breathe, move about, and act as you choose, free from crowding. It satisfies your psychological need to be separate from other people.

Personal space requirements vary with age, gender, and personality, among other things. For example, as people get older their space requirements increase; interacting females require less space than interacting males; and introverts and people with low self-esteem require more than usual space between themselves and others. Culture also plays a significant role in personal

Photo C   Social Distance   *Photo D   Public Distance*

space requirements. For example, Mexican-Americans often feel a need for less personal space than Anglos do.

Perhaps the most important overall determinant of spatial distancing is the relationship between the participants, including both the activity in which they are engaged (for instance, some sports require close contact) and their feelings for each other.

Personal space can be broken down into four zones:

1. Intimate distance, from touching to eighteen inches, is reserved for intimate activities, including passing secrets and having confidential conversations.

2. Personal distance, from eighteen inches to four feet, is used for discussing personal subjects.

3. Social distance, from four to twelve feet, requires a louder voice than intimate or personal distance and is thus used for more impersonal conversations, such as business transactions.

4. Public distance, twelve feet and beyond, is usually used for small group meetings and for hailing people. Distances farther than twenty-five feet limit communication to shouts and broad nonverbal gestures.[7]

Increasing your sensitivity to your own and others' personal space requirements, as well as knowing the norms and expectations for using the space in your environment, increases your ability to communicate skillfully. Recognizing how people use space and react to violations of space should help you to respond quickly and appropriately when problems of perceived inappropriate behavior arise. Knowledge Checkup 3.6 provides you with the opportunity to apply the information on personal space in an analysis of a common setting.

KNOWLEDGE CHECKUP 3.6

Personal Space Analysis

1. Select one setting, such as a department store, and observe the interaction distances that seem usual between various individuals. For example, how much distance do you notice between store clerks and customers, store clerks and other store clerks, and managers and employees?

2. Based on the average distances between the people you observed, note reactions when one person comes too close to another or when one person touches another. How do people react to these violations of their space? How could they avoid violating each other's personal space?

TOUCH

Touch is the most relevant sense at the beginning of your life—it is how you first orient yourself to the world. By the time you learn to speak, however, sight and sound predominate and touch becomes less important. Nonetheless, the need for touch remains, although opportunities for touching and being touched decrease. The elderly may be the most touch-deprived members of western society and, therefore, the loneliest.

Your skin is a sensitive receiver of communication: Pats, pinches, strokes, slaps, punches, shakes, and kisses all convey meaning. Touches may signal a particular relationship. Some touches are professional, functional ones, as when a doctor performs a physical examination. Social touches, such as handshakes, fulfill norms associated with greeting, acknowledgment, and parting. Friendship touches, such as shoulder-patting and hugging, convey the message that "We're friends," "I like you," or "I appreciate you." Intimate touches, such as kisses, can communicate love, while sexually arousing touches can increase the physical and emotional pleasures of lovemaking.

The messages that touch communicates depend on how, where, and by whom you're touched. Slight variations in touch can communicate great differences of emotion. Your father may touch your shoulder lightly to say "Listen to me," apply slight pressure to say "Seriously consider what I say," or squeeze forcefully to communicate "You'd better do as I tell you!"

The same type of touch on different parts of your body communicates different messages. A slap across your face may evoke fear or anger, while a slap across your back may cause happiness. Similarly, stroking your hand may communicate concern, while the same touch on your head may communicate affection.

In addition to receiving messages, your skin also sends them. Polygraphs, for example, operate on the assumption that changes in your internal state are reflected in changes in your skin, and that these changes can be measured to determine whether you're lying.

The importance of touch for children has been well documented.[8] In general, the more touching an infant receives, the higher the probability that he or she will become a well-adjusted child, adolescent, and adult. Lack of touching during infancy has been implicated in health problems (such as allergies and eczema), academic problems (such as learning disabilities and low scores on intelligence tests), and decreased capacity for mature, sensitive tactile communication in adulthood (such as problems with showing affection by hugging). Feelings of trust and liking for others, on the other hand, have been linked to positive early tactile experiences. Parents who avoid touching their children, or touch them only on certain "neutral" body parts, often communicate that some parts are "better" than others, some are "more important" than others, and some parts are "bad." The result may be an adult alienated from her or his body.

Most people, except those who have been abused, raped, or brought up in low or no-touch families, associate touching with positive messages. Handshakes, probably the most common type of touch, connect people and help begin interactions on a note of shared status. Many cultures worldwide use touch to express affectionate greetings: Americans kiss, Eskimos rub noses, and Burmese press their mouths and noses to another's cheek and inhale deeply.

Avoiding touching is often associated with a negative attitude. We communicate dislike, disrespect, and refusal by *not* touching. Because we normally close a deal with a handshake, refusing to shake hands equates with refusing to complete a deal.

Uses of Touch

Touch is most useful for communicating intimacy, involvement, warmth, reassurance, and comfort. Touch has proven therapeutic power that nurses and other health-care professionals employ to help their patients emotionally as well as physically. The therapeutic benefits of touch may derive in part from the effect that touch has on a recipient's willingness to talk. Because touch implies reassurance and caring, it encourages self-disclosure.

Touch helps to persuade people. For example, a request for the return of a quarter left in a phone booth meets with greater success when the new booth occupant is touched on the arm than when not touched. Similarly, requests to sign a petition receive almost twice as many positive reactions when touch is involved.[9]

Touch is also useful for communicating power relationships. Generally, the person who initiates the touch is perceived as more powerful, more dominant, and of higher status than the one who is touched. In interviews, for example, while an initial greeting handshake is mutual and customary, the handshake that ends the interview is the prerogative of the interviewer, the person with more power in the situation. The interviewer may or may not offer to shake hands, but the lower status interviewee should not make the offer.

Expectations for Touch

Cultural background largely determines expectations about touch. For example, the least touchable cultures include Canadians of Anglo descent, Germans, Chinese, and English—generally the upper class. The most touch-oriented cultures include Latin Americans, Russians, and Netsilik Eskimos. American culture falls between the extremes; although American culture may be classified as nontouch, it is less extremely so than the Chinese or German cultures.[10]

Regardless of cultural background, touch is expected in some situations and not in others. For example, you are more likely to touch another person when giving him or her information or advice, asking a favor, expressing worry, or sharing an intimate conversation. You are also prone to touch a communication partner who is excited. You are less likely to touch another person when you are asking for information or advice, giving an order, agreeing to do something, participating in a casual conversation, or feeling excited. Casual, friendly settings, such as parties, are apt to encourage more touch than are formal work settings.

Whether your expectations about touch are violated depends on several considerations: Where is the touch? How long does it last? How much pressure or intensity is used? What is your relationship with the person touching you? What are the circumstances—for example, are other people watching?

Reactions to being touched in the wrong place or by someone you don't like can range from politely ignoring the gesture to starting a fight. If someone offers a limp handshake, you probably won't respond visibly, although you may form a particular impression of the person; if someone punches you in the arm, however, you are likely to respond with a punch of your own, a verbal attack, or a scream.

Being sensitive to responses to touch can help improve your relationships. You can use touch to increase your persuasiveness, appear powerful, and communicate warmth, intimacy, and comfort—but only if your touch doesn't violate the other person's expectations.

Knowledge Checkup 3.7 calls for an analysis of your responses to being touched by acquaintances, friends, and close friends, as well as the touch you engage in with family and friends.

KNOWLEDGE CHECKUP 3.7

Analyzing Responses to Touch

1. How comfortable are you with being touched? Circle the words that indicate how you feel when touched by the person indicated in each question.
   a. How comfortable do you feel when touched by an acquaintance?

   comfortable   somewhat comfortable   somewhat uncomfortable   uncomfortable

   b. How comfortable do you feel when touched by a friend?

   comfortable   somewhat comfortable   somewhat uncomfortable   uncomfortable

   c. How comfortable do you feel when touched by a very close friend?

   comfortable   somewhat comfortable   somewhat uncomfortable   uncomfortable

2. How often do people in your immediate family touch each other?

   very frequently   frequently   seldom   never

3. Pick two people with whom you interact regularly, a close friend and an acquaintance from work or school.
   a. How often do you and your close friend touch each other?

   very frequently   frequently   seldom   never

   b. How often do you and the acquaintance you picked touch each other?

   very frequently   frequently   seldom   never

   c. Where do you touch each person (if at all)?

   d. Describe the types of touches you give each person.

4. How do your feelings of comfort concerning being touched relate to how often people in your family touch and how often you touch others?

5. How do you respond to touches that are unexpected and uninvited?

6. Would you like to increase the touching you receive and the touching you give?

VOICE

Independent of the words you speak, your voice communicates a great deal about you. All by itself, your voice offers strong clues to your age, emotional state, education, home region, and status. Variations in loudness (loud or soft), pitch (low or high), rate (fast or slow), quality (the particular resonance of your voice—for example, flat, breathy, nasal, throaty, or tense), articulation (slurred or clipped), and pronunciation (what syllables are stressed) give your vocal cues their unique character.

For example, when we express anger, we speak loudly, quickly, and with wide variations in pitch (although mostly high). When we communicate affection, we speak softly, slowly, in a low pitch, and with vibrancy. The vocal expression of joy is similar to the one for anger except that the voice is not quite so blaring. Sadness is expressed much as affection is except that pauses in sadness' expression are irregular.

People's stereotyped reactions to different voice qualities indicate the importance of controlling your vocal behavior. For example, breathiness in males is associated with youth and an artistic temperament, and in females with prettiness, petiteness, and shallowness. Wide variations in pitch for both males and females is associated with being dynamic and extroverted, and an increased rate for both connotes animation and extroversion.[11] Of course, stereotyping by voice has its pitfalls: basing your mental picture of a blind date on a telephone conversation may lead to surprises when the two of you meet face to face.

Two other aspects of vocal behavior that affect perceptions are nonfluencies and silence. **Nonfluencies**—vocal behaviors that interrupt or disturb the flow of messages, such as "ah," "you know," and "stuff like that," unnecessary repetition of words, stuttering, incomplete sentences, and corrections—are usually associated with low credibility and lack of confidence. Keep nonfluencies to a minimum, or even eliminate them, to appear more competent.

Silence—not speaking or making nonverbal vocal sounds, such as "um," when you are interacting with another person—is more varied in meaning. Silence may communicate anger, attentive listening, grief, depression, respect, awe, or the message "leave me alone." Silence often strains a relationship. For example, you may be uncomfortable with long silences and strive to keep them short. But take care—if you perceive silence as invariably negative, you may find yourself talking first and thinking later!

Skill Checkup 3.2 will help you practice using your voice to express emotions effectively.

SKILL CHECKUP 3.2

Expressing Emotions Effectively

Read the following sentence in different ways to communicate five emotions: anger, bewilderment, fear, happiness, and sadness. If a tape recorder is available, record your attempts.

There is no other answer. You've asked me that question a thousand times, and my answer is always yes.

1. Were you able to create five different meanings as you read the sentences?

2. What variations in loudness, pitch, rate, quality, articulation, pronunciation, silence, and intonation did you make in each case to create the desired effect?

3. How were you able to distinguish that you were expressing anger rather than bewilderment, bewilderment rather than fear, fear rather than happiness, and happiness rather than sadness?

Vocal cues play a significant role in communication aside from conveying emotions: they regulate and structure interactions, much as eye contact does. For example, if someone tries to interrupt when you are speaking, you can maintain your role as speaker in two ways. You can either fill your pauses with meaningless vocalizations such as "uh, well" or "but, uh," or you can alter your pitch and volume to signal "Don't interrupt me now!" The other person will rarely take over the speaking role if you use either of these techniques.

If, on the other hand, you want to stop speaking and let the other person begin, you can employ several techniques. You can use ascending pitch and volume, as if you were asking a question, and pause afterward. Alternatively, you can use falling pitch and volume and stretch out your final words. Of course, just keeping quiet is a sure signal that you're through, but your signal may go unnoticed for an embarrassingly long time if the other person is only half-listening. Listeners give priority to cues other than silence because silence can be ambiguous: it can mean either "I'm through" or "I'm thinking."

Sometimes when you are listening you want to say something, but the speaker is unwilling to relinquish control. After trying the usual nonverbal methods for communicating your desire to speak—raising your hand, moving forward and gesturing, raising your eyebrows, opening your mouth—you may be forced to use a vocal stutter-start. A stutter-start is the pronunciation of a word with a repetition of the first sound, such as "m-m-m-m-maybe," or the use of an elongated nonfluency, such as "uhhhhhh." You may, of course, interrupt directly and begin speaking, but then the other person is likely to interrupt you and to maintain the speaking role.

Another way to regulate a conversation is to encourage the other person to *continue* speaking. In addition to the nonvocal behaviors that communicate "I'm listening, please go on," such as head nods, sustained eye contact, and appropriate facial expressions, you may use encouraging vocalizations such as "uh-huh," "hmmmmm," "ahhhhh," and "ohhhhh."

KNOWLEDGE CHECKUP 3.8

Using Vocal Cues to Regulate Conversations

Read the dialogue that follows and note the vocal cues used to regulate the conversation in the following ways: (1) to maintain the role as speaker, (2) to get the other person to speak, (3) to take over as speaker, and (4) to get the other person to continue speaking. The conversation, between a student in a communication class and the instructor, takes place after class in the instructor's office.

Student: I . . . well . . . had a little trouble understanding today's lecture on the voice. I . . .

Instructor: What specifically did you have trouble with?

Student: *(Leans forward and points at the instructor as if to speak.)*

Instructor: *(Raising the pitch of his voice and speaking quickly.)* If you would ask questions in class, maybe you wouldn't have this problem.

Student: B-b-b-but, I have trouble asking questions in front of the other students.

Instructor: I used to have the same problem when I was a student. *(Leans back in chair, looks at student for several moments.)*

Student: Gee, I would never have guessed that.

Instructor: *(Lowering his pitch and speaking slowly.)* As I was saying, I used to have that problem until I realized that if I didn't understand something, and didn't ask, I would never get the information I needed.

Student: I think I see what you mean.

Instructor: Hmmmmmm.

Student: But sometimes it's just hard for me.

Instructor: *(Pitch rising as he speaks.)* But, you have to do it. *(Pause.)*

Student: I guess you're right.

Instructor: Uh-huh.

Student: *(Pitch lowering, rate decreasing, and final two words stretched.)* I'm just going to have to do it.

Instructor: If you give it a try, I'll work with you on it.

Your analysis of the dialogue may have revealed:

Student: I . . . well . . . (**vocalized pause used to maintain his role as speaker**) had a little trouble understanding today's lecture on the voice. I . . .

Instructor: (**interrupts to take over as speaker**) What specifically did you have trouble with?

Student: *(Leans forward and points at the instructor as if to speak in an attempt to take over as speaker.)*

Instructor: *(Raising the pitch of his voice and speaking quickly.)* (**rising intonation to maintain his role as speaker**) If you would ask questions in class, maybe you wouldn't have this problem.

Student: B-b-b-but (**stutter-start to take over as speaker**), I have trouble asking questions in front of the other students.

Instructor: I used to have the same problem when I was a student. *(Leans back in chair, looks at student for several moments.)* (**uses silence to get other person to speak**)

Student: Gee, I would never have guessed that.

Instructor: *(Lowering his pitch as he speaks slowly.)* (**falling intonation to maintain his role as speaker**) As I was saying, I used to have that problem until I realized that if I didn't understand something, and didn't ask, I would never get the information I needed.

Student: I think I see what you mean.

Instructor: Hmmmmmm. (**vocal encourager to get other person to continue speaking**)

Student: But sometimes it's just hard for me.

Instructor: *(Pitch rising as he speaks.)* (**rising intonation to maintain his role as speaker**) But, you have to do it. *(Pause.)* (**silence to get the other person to speak**)

Student: I guess you're right.

Instructor: Uh-huh. (**vocal encourager to get other person to continue speaking**)

Student: (*Pitch lowering, rate decreasing, and final two words stretched.*) (**falling intonation and stretching final words to get the other person to speak**) I'm just going to have to do it.

Instructor: If you give it a try, I'll work with you on it.

BODY MOVEMENTS

Body movements are motions such as gestures; head, arm, finger, leg, and toe movements; and changes in posture or trunk position. Some self-help books on nonverbal behavior suggest easy and clear interpretations of body movements. Merely by focusing on body movement, the writers contend, you can successfully understand and manipulate other people. Wrong! Although body movements provide a wealth of information, interpreting that information is not that simple. For example, according to some authors of popular books, crossing your arms on your chest, crossing your legs, and pointing your index finger are all supposed to signal defensiveness. Rubbing your eyes, touching your nose, and glancing sideways are all supposed to communicate suspicion. Rubbing your hand through your hair or taking short breaths is supposed to indicate frustration.

Although any of these examples *may* be true at particular times and in particular circumstances, they are overgeneralizations. It's hard to interpret body movements without paying careful attention to the specific situation, including your relationship with the other person and the cultural context in which you're interacting. The same gesture may mean different things in different cultures. For example, what Americans recognize as the "A-OK" gesture, meaning "everything is fine," is a vulgar sexual invitation in Greece.

Types of Body Movements

Body movements fall into five categories: emblems, illustrators, regulators, affect displays, and adaptors, shown in the photos on the following pages.

Emblems have direct verbal translations, such as the "A-OK" gesture, the "come here" signal, and the waves that mean hello and good-bye.

Illustrators, like emblems, are used intentionally, but they add to or support what is said, as when you hold your hands different distances from the ground to indicate the relative heights of two friends, or point to your car when talking about it.

Photo A   Emblem

Photo B   Illustrator

Regulators, also used intentionally, influence who talks, when, and for how long. For example, waving to greet another person may initiate a conversation; moving backwards toward a door may signal the end of an interaction.

Less awareness and intentionality characterize affect displays and adaptors. **Affect displays**, body movements that express emotions, are most commonly associated with the face—in fact, fear, anger, surprise, disgust, sadness, and happiness are six facial expressions that can be identified across all cultures. Other body movements may also express emotions. Foot-tapping, fidgeting, covering your mouth while speaking, and shifting your weight from foot to foot may indicate nervousness or boredom, depending on the context.

Photo C   Regulator

Photo D   Affect Display

Adaptors, which are seldom intentional, are body movements performed by habit. Your first use of adaptors was to satisfy some physical need: You had an itch, so you scratched it; your hair needed grooming, so you patted it; or you had something caught between two teeth, so you used a fingernail to dislodge it. Interestingly, these adaptive behaviors satisfied not only your physical needs, but also your psychological needs. For example, patting your hair calmed you down, perhaps by distracting you from a stressful situation. Therefore, adaptors may indicate psychological states. Scratching when there is no itch may indicate nervousness, and stroking your hair may be your way of calming yourself.

Uses of Body Movements

Body movements may also be categorized according to their uses. One use of body movements is to communicate degree of pleasure or displeasure, liking or disliking. For example, you may lean forward, face the other person directly, and assume a position that mirrors the other person's position to communicate liking. You may communicate dislike by reversing these behaviors, as well as by crossing your arms in front of you and tensing your body. In general, movement toward something with an open body position (such as open arms) indicates liking, and movement away from something with a closed body position (such as crossed arms) indicates disliking.

Body movements may also communicate level of interest or arousal. Closing your eyes momentarily may mean simply that you're tired, but try persuading the other person of that! Looking tired and closing your eyes are usually interpreted as lack of interest.

Photo E   Adaptor

Photo F   Open and Closed Positions

Finally, body movements may be used to communicate feelings of dominance or submissiveness, power or powerlessness. Dynamic gestures and erect posture indicate feelings of power or dominance, whereas slow, hesitant gestures and a slumped posture indicate feelings of powerlessness or submission.

Gestures are movements made by a particular part of your body, such as your hands. Your hands provide some of your most expressive gestures: You wave hello and good-bye, suggest that someone is crazy by moving your index finger in a circle while pointing to the side of your head, and suggest that you're thinking by rubbing your chin. Gestures can also communicate emotions. For instance, you drum your fingers to indicate impatience or boredom, or hit a table to emphasize that you really are angry.

Consider the gestures that accompany these sentences:

Me? What did I do?
Take it! I give up!
You can trust me on this one.
Whew! That was a tough job!

Clearly, gestures can communicate very specific pieces of information.

Postures, movements that involve your whole body, are more useful for communicating general attitudes. For example, the angle at which you turn your body toward another person may reveal your desire to include or exclude her or him. Turning your back on someone is typically interpreted as rejection, whereas standing face to face is seen as acceptance. Whether or not you mirror another's movements may indicate your liking or perceptions of similarity. Films of group therapy sessions, when slowed down and viewed carefully, often reveal an intricate dance: people mirror the behaviors of individuals they like or want to encourage to like them and exhibit opposite body movements to individuals they dislike or reject. The changes in posture are subtle and rarely consciously performed. You may notice similar behavior in the way a seated group of people cross their legs. One change can set off a chain reaction—those who have positive feelings for the person who moved shift to a similar position, while the others quickly move to an opposite position.

Skill Checkup 3.3 provides you with the opportunity to compare what happens when you mirror and don't mirror another person's body movements.

SKILL CHECKUP 3.3

Increasing Perceptions of Similarity

If you want to examine perceptual differences based on body movements, interact with a person who does not know you well (and thus does not know your usual body movements) and mirror that person's movements. Use similar gestures, posture, eye contact, facial expressions, touch patterns, and vocal characteristics. Note any reactions. Does it seem that this person likes you and feels comfortable with you?

Repeat the activity with another person, only this time use dissimilar gestures, posture, and so on. Note the reactions.

How do the reactions differ in the two situations? What does this imply about how mirroring behavior can be used as a persuasive device?

NONVERBAL CLUES TO DECEPTION

Commonplace lies, like explaining why you missed class, normally do not make you feel anxious. The consequences of being found out are not serious, and the length of time you must maintain the deception is relatively short. By the same token, you will find it more difficult to catch someone else in a minor deception than in a complex fabrication.

Many nonverbal clues may suggest that someone is telling a white lie. But because the clues are deviations from the liar's normal behavior, you need to know the normal behavior in order to assess the situation.

Some of the more reliable clues to deception are vocal: liars tend to hesitate and pause more, speak rapidly, and sound nervous. Several gestures, including a lot of self-touching and hand movement, may also tip you off. Also, liars tend to look away from you much of the time and avoid your gaze after brief eye contact. In contrast, facial gestures are too easily controlled to offer many useful clues to lying.

If everyday lies are distinguished by low anxiety, uncommon lies are distinguished by the opposite. When stakes are high and lying must continue for a long time, liars often become extremely nervous. They tend to make very little eye contact, shift their eyes, move their feet a lot, fidget, shift their weight, twitch, and make nervous facial gestures, such as licking their lips. Careful observation will reveal that the pupils of their eyes dilate at the moment they tell their lie.

You cannot, however, identify a liar on the basis of a single behavior; only when telltale behaviors appear in groups should you begin to suspect that a speaker is not telling the truth. Because most of the behaviors that indicate lying can also indicate nervousness, be careful not to assume that nervousness *equals* lying. (How calm would you be if you were falsely accused of cheating on a final exam? As you explained your side of the story, would you behave as if you were nervous?)

FEELING = BEHAVIOR = FEELING

This chapter has emphasized how nonverbal behavior can reveal your emotions. That is, how you feel determines how you behave. The opposite is also true: How you behave often determines how you feel. *Acting* as if you're happy is a good way to become happy, just as *acting* as if you're tired is a sure path to feeling that way. You may have already learned that you can stop feeling tired and reenergize yourself when you're studying by sitting up straight, taking a deep breath, putting your shoulders back, and looking intently at the work you're doing. You *act* alert, so you *feel* alert!

SKILL CHECKUP 3.4

From Behaving to Feeling

Think of something that you believe very, very strongly. Picture yourself describing your belief (or watch yourself in a mirror, or ask another person to observe you).

Note how you behave: how you stand, how your face looks, how you gesture, what your voice sounds like, and what touch behaviors you exhibit.

Then select a topic about which you are neutral and, using all the behaviors you observed when you were intensely interested, talk about the neutral topic. After a few moments, note how you feel. Does the neutral topic now excite you?

Select any emotion and *act* as if you're experiencing it. Note your behavior and, whenever you want to feel that way, just *behave* the way you want to feel!

Nonverbal communication—which helps you transmit feelings and emotions, regulates your interaction with others, and works together with verbal communication to create messages—has many aspects. Physical appearance, facial gestures, eye behavior, touch, vocal characteristics, body movement, and the physical and psychological contexts within which each of these takes place all contribute to nonverbal communication. Understanding the role of nonverbal communication and developing skills in this area of human interaction are crucial to your development as a competent communicator.

COMMUNICATION COMPETENCY CHECKUP

BIG GEORGE   By Virgil Partch

"I think you'd better cool it, Randy. Your father is giving you one of his meaningful glances."

Randy's father wants to watch the movie on television and Randy wants to play his drums. The situation appears explosive and Randy is given some good advice.

1. Based on the nonverbal information in the cartoon, what do you know about each of the three characters—for example, their age, gender, emotional state, and how they're interacting?

2. The father is giving one of his "meaningful glances." Describe how his facial expressions and eye behavior convey his emotion and attempt to regulate the interaction.

3. Describe the situation with respect to invasion of territory and personal space.

4. How might the father use touch to communicate the same information he conveys with his meaningful glance?

5. Read the cartoon caption as if you were calm. Pretend you are the person speaking to Randy. Read it as if you were worried about what might happen if the drumming continued. Read it as if you were mocking Randy's father. Read it as if this were the third time you needed to repeat the statement to Randy, and you were angry. How do the readings differ in loudness, pitch, rate, voice quality, articulation, and pronunciation?

6. Randy's response to the caption is, "I'm not doing anything!" What nonverbal behaviors might indicate that he is lying?

NOTES

1. This material was adapted from an instrument developed by Cortes and Gatti. For the full instrument, see: J. B. Cortes and F. M. Gatti, "Physique and Propensity," *Psychology Today* 4 (May 1970): 42–44, 82–84.

2. For summaries of the research on the role of physical attractiveness in human interaction, see: Dale Leathers, *Successful Nonverbal Communication: Principles and Applications* (New York: Macmillan, 1986); Loretta A. Malandro and Larry L. Barker, *Nonverbal Communication* (Reading, MA: Addison-Wesley, 1983); and Virginia P. Richmond, James C. McCroskey, and Steven K. Payne, *Nonverbal Behavior in Interpersonal Relations* (Englewood Cliffs, NJ: Prentice-Hall, 1987).

3. Nancy Baker, *The Beauty Trap* (New York: F. Watts, 1984). For a summary of research, see: "When Beauty Can Be Beastly," *Chicago Tribune*, 21 October 1985, sec. 4, p. 22.

4. A. Kendon, "Some Functions of Gaze Direction in Social Interaction," *Acta Psychologica* 26 (1967): 34–35.

5. Judee K. Burgoon and Thomas J. Saine, *The Unspoken Dialogue: An Introduction to Nonverbal Communication* (Boston: Houghton Mifflin, 1978), p. 110.

6. Maslow and Mintz compared reactions to photographs of faces made in a "beautiful" room (one with windows, attractive draperies, and indirect lighting), an "average" room (a professor's office), and an "ugly" room (a storage area with a single overhead lightbulb). See: A. H. Maslow and N. L. Mintz, "Effects of Aesthetic Surroundings: I. Initial Effects of Three Aesthetic Conditions Upon Perceiving 'Energy,' and 'Well-Being' in Faces," *Journal of Psychology* 41 (1956): 247–54; and N. L. Mintz, "Effects of Aesthetic Surroundings: II. Prolonged and Repeated Experience in a 'Beautiful' and 'Ugly' Room," *Journal of Psychology* 41 (1956): 459–66.

7. Edward T. Hall, *The Hidden Dimension* (Garden City, NY: Doubleday, 1966).

8. R. Heslin and T. Alper, "Touch: The Bonding Gesture," in *Nonverbal Interaction*, ed. John M. Wiemann and Randall P. Harrison (Beverly Hills, CA: Sage, 1983), pp. 47–75; Ashley Montagu, *Touching: The Human Significance of the Skin* (New York: Harper and Row, 1971).

9. Chris R. Kleinke, "Compliance to Requests Made by Gazing and Touching Experimenters in Field Settings," *Journal of Experimental Social Psychology* 13 (1977): 218–23; Frank N. Willis and Helen K. Hamm, "The Use of Interpersonal Touch in Securing Compliance," *Journal of Nonverbal Behavior* 5 (1980): 49–55.

10. For a summary of studies on cross-cultural touch behavior, see: Robert G. Harper, Arthur N. Wiens, and Joseph D. Matarazzo, *Nonverbal Communication: The State of the Art* (New York: John Wiley and Sons, 1978), pp. 260–63, 295–97.

11. David W. Addington, "The Relationship of Selected Vocal Characteristics to Personality Perception," *Speech Monographs* 35 (1968): 492–503; and David W. Addington, "The Effect of Vocal Variations on Ratings of Source Credibility," *Speech Monographs* 38 (1971): 242–47.

FOR FURTHER INVESTIGATION

Burgoon, Judee K., David B. Buller, Jerold L. Hale, and Mark A. DeTurck. "Relational Messages Associated with Nonverbal Behaviors." *Human Communication Research* 10 (1984): 351–78.

Druckman, D., R. M. Rozelle, and J. C. Baxter. *Nonverbal Communication:. Survey, Theory and Research*. Beverly Hills, CA: Sage, 1982.

Edinger, J. A., and M. L. Patterson. "Nonverbal Involvement and Social Control." *Psychological Bulletin* 93 (1983): 30–56.

Ekman, Paul, and Wallace V. Friesen. *Unmasking the Face: A Guide to Recognizing Emotion From Facial Clues*. Englewood Cliffs, NJ: Prentice-Hall, 1975.

Ekman, Paul, Wallace V. Friesen, and J. Baer. "The International Language of Gestures." *Psychology Today* 18 (May 1984): 64–69.

Goffman, Erving. *Relations in Public*. New York: Basic Books, 1971.

Henley, N. M. *Body Politics: Power, Sex, and Nonverbal Communication*. Englewood Cliffs, NJ: Prentice-Hall, 1977.

Hickson, Mark, III, and Don W. Stacks. *NVC: Nonverbal Communication—Studies and Applications*, 2d ed. Dubuque, IA: Wm. C. Brown, 1989.

Jones, Stanley E., and Elaine Yarbrough. "A Naturalistic Study of the Meanings of Touch." *Communication Monographs* 52 (1985): 19–56.

Knapp, Mark L. *Nonverbal Communication in Human Interaction*, 2d ed. New York: Holt, Rinehart and Winston, 1978.

LaFrance, Marianne, and Clara Mayo. *Moving Bodies: Nonverbal Communication in Social Relationships*. Monterey, CA: Brooks/Cole, 1978.

Leathers, Dale G. *Successful Nonverbal Communication: Principles and Applications*. New York: Macmillan, 1986.

Malandro, Loretta A., and Larry L. Barker. *Nonverbal Communication*. Reading, MA: Addison-Wesley, 1983.

Mehrabian, Albert. *Silent Messages: Implicit Communication of Emotions and Attitudes*, 2d ed. Belmont, CA: Wadsworth, 1981.

Molloy, John T. *The Men's and Women's Dress for Success Book*. Englewood Cliffs, NJ: Prentice-Hall, 1976.

Mulac, Anthony, Lisa B. Studley, John W. Wiemann, and James J. Bradac. "Male/Female Gaze in Same-Sex and Mixed-Sex Dyads: Gender-Linked Differences and Mutual Influence." *Human Communication Research* 13 (1987): 323–44.

Richmond, Virginia P., James C. McCroskey, and Steven K. Payne. *Nonverbal Behavior in Interpersonal Relations*. Englewood Cliffs, NJ: Prentice-Hall, 1987.

Rosenfeld, Lawrence B., and Jean M. Civikly. *With Words Unspoken: The Nonverbal Experience*. New York: Holt, Rinehart and Winston, 1976.

Rosenfeld, Lawrence B., Sallie Kartus, and Chett Ray. "Body Accessibility Revisited." *Journal of Communication* 26 (1976): 27–30.

Rosenthal, Robert, and Bella M. DePaulo. "Expectancies, Discrepancies, and Courtesies in Nonverbal Communication." *Western Journal of Speech Communication* 43 (1979): 76–95.

Schlenker, B. R. *Impression Management.* Monterey, CA: Brooks/Cole, 1982.

Thayer, Stephen. "Close Encounters." *Psychology Today* 22 (March 1988): 31–36.

Thourlby, W. *You Are What You Wear.* New York: New American Library, 1978.

Weimann, John M., and Randall P. Harrison, eds. *Nonverbal Interaction.* Beverly Hills, CA: Sage, 1983.

CHAPTER 4

▶ ## *Conceiving the Self*

*This chapter on self-concept will help you to practice and develop communication competencies that fall into three broad categories: (1) **communication codes,** which include listening effectively and using words that are appropriate to a particular situation; (2) **basic speech communication skills,** which include expressing ideas clearly and asking and answering questions effectively; and (3) **human relations,** which include expressing feelings to others. Specifically, the competencies you will gain will enable you to do the following:*

▶ *Identify the important elements that make up your self-concept, including your social identity, personality characteristics, values, physical characteristics, and ego-extensions.*

▶ *Describe two principles of self-concept development—reflected appraisal and social comparison.*

▶ *Distinguish among the person you are, the person you **wish you were** or think you **should be,** and the person you present to others.*

▶ *Assess how you feel abut yourself—your self-esteem.*

▶ *Recognize the effects that high and low self-esteem have on communication.*

▶ *Use several techniques for increasing your self-esteem.*

*D*ump the contents of your purse or wallet on the table in front of you. Spread the items out so you can look at each one separately. Now, pretend you found the purse or wallet—that it is not yours—and you're trying to figure out what kind of person owns it.

Look at the driver's license. How does the picture look? Would you want to have this person for a friend? Is this an attractive person?

Are there any family pictures? If so, what do they tell you about this person? If there are none, what might this suggest?

Are there any membership cards from social or work groups? Can you guess the person's leisure activities and job? Is there a college identification card?

How much money is there? How many credit cards? What can you conclude about this person's financial state?

Take your time and consider each item. See how much you can find out about this person. Then ask yourself: *Am I the person these items suggest I am?*

WHO YOU ARE: YOUR SELF-CONCEPT

Who you are is the foundation for all your communication. The individual needs, interests, and strengths that distinguish you from others are revealed in your communication. Although English is your common language, you and the people around you often use different words to express similar experiences. These differences reveal something about how each of you sees the world. For instance, you may see a sunset and comment that it is getting late, whereas a photographer may see it and remark on the stunning contrast in light and dark.

The meanings you attribute to the words you hear are also slightly different from others' interpretations—again reflecting your uniqueness. You may even use a special vocabulary to express who you are and what you do. For example, if you're a computer enthusiast, you may use the words *input* and *output* to explain things unrelated to computers.

Who you are includes how you feel about yourself, and, in turn, how you feel about yourself is reflected in how you communicate. If you think of yourself as shy, you may avoid asking for a date; if you think of yourself as a good listener, you may encourage others to talk to you.

Who you are (the I-am me), what you would like to be (the I-wish-I-were me), and the person you present to others (the here-I-am me) form the foundation for how you communicate. Thus, improving your communication competency begins with an examination of who you are, how you came to be that person, and how your self-perception affects how you communicate.

The Person You Are

Your self-exploration began with an examination of the contents of your purse or wallet. Now, continue the process by answering the question "Who am I?" in Knowledge Checkup 4.1.

KNOWLEDGE CHECKUP 4.1

Who Am I?

Complete each sentence:

1. I am

2. I am

3. I am

4. I am

5. I am

The varied responses you give to the question "Who am I?" provide information about your **self-concept**—the totality of your thoughts and feelings about yourself. Your responses most likely describe the *content* of your self-concept—your social identity, personality characteristics and values, physical characteristics, and ego-extensions.[1]

Social Identity

Your **social identity**, the groups or categories to which you are socially recognized as belonging, begins with your birth. You are classified by gender, race, religion, and family role (brother, sister, only child, youngest, firstborn), and given a name. Your birth certificate discloses several of the categories into which you were placed—the categories that provided you with an immediate social identity.

As you grow up, you add new classifications for yourself. You become a student, a member of a political party, a member of various groups and clubs. The groups to which you belong reflect your cultural identity (based on shared language, history, values, or territory), your religious beliefs, your political ideology, your interests, your work, and other aspects of how you view yourself.

What you are also includes what you *were* but are not now, such as an athlete, a biology major, a soldier, a president of your sorority or fraternity. Some former social identities you may want to conceal; others you may want to use to gain status. For example, you may not want your current friends to know that you were once a biology major, or you may seek recognition by referring to your past activities as president of a campus club.

Personality Characteristics

The content of your self-concept is more than your social identity. The many personality characteristics you use to describe yourself also contribute to your self-concept. **Personality characteristics** are the qualities that constitute a person's character and that make him or her distinctive. For example, you may consider a friend "happy and easygoing" and a teacher "stern." Before discussing some of the more than 20,000 personality characteristics, complete Knowledge Checkup 4.2.

KNOWLEDGE CHECKUP 4.2

Bem Sex-Role Inventory[2]

Indicate the degree to which each statement is true of you.

Write 1 if the statement is never or almost never true of you.
Write 2 if it is usually not true of you.
Write 3 if it is sometimes but infrequently true of you.
Write 4 if it is occasionally true of you.
Write 5 if it is usually true of you.
Write 6 if it is always or almost always true of you.

_____ **1.** I am self-reliant.
_____ **2.** I am cheerful.
_____ **3.** I am independent.
_____ **4.** I am affectionate.
_____ **5.** I have a strong personality.
_____ **6.** I am sympathetic.
_____ **7.** I act as a leader.
_____ **8.** I am eager to soothe hurt feelings.
_____ **9.** I am analytical.
_____ **10.** I am warm.

The ten personality characteristics you just considered describe two types of personalities. The odd-numbered represent a stereotypical "masculine" personality and the even-numbered items represent a stereotypical "feminine" personality. Add your responses to the odd items to obtain your "masculine" score. Then add your responses to the even items to obtain your "feminine" score. Total scores above twenty in either category are considered high and scores below twenty are considered low.

If you scored high on masculine and low on feminine, you are classified as "masculine." If you scored low on masculine and high on feminine, you are classified as "feminine." High scores on both lead to your classification as "androgynous," and low scores on both lead to your classification as "undifferentiated." These classifications exist apart from gender or biological-sex categorization. Both males and females may fall into all four personality categories.

A person who describes herself or himself as androgynous—both highly masculine and highly feminine—has the largest repertoire of communication behaviors to call upon. For example, this person may behave both empathically and objectively, and both assertively and cooperatively, which increases the person's adaptability—one of the qualities of the competent communicator. Sex-typed individuals—masculine or feminine—exhibit a smaller range of communication behaviors and, therefore, are less adaptable than androgynous individuals.

Masculinity and femininity are only two of the many different personality characteristics that affect communication. For example, five others that have been studied are the following:[3]

Self-monitoring—sensitivity to one's communication out of concern for being appropriate. For example, high self-monitors are more likely than others to initiate conversations (the appropriate response to awkward silences) and reciprocate intimacy (the appropriate response to another's intimate behaviors).

Extroversion-introversion—outgoing and focused on the world outside the self versus focused on the inner world of the self. Extroverts speak more than introverts and spend less time pausing. Also, extroverts tend to display more nonverbal actions, such as gestures, than do introverts.

Dominance-submissiveness—controlling and authoritarian versus yielding and obedient. People with a dominant personality communicate more assertively and confidently than those with a submissive personality. They also participate more in groups and interrupt more.

Need for affiliation—concern with being included in others' activities. People with a high need for affiliation prefer to interact at closer distances and maintain more eye contact than those with a low need for affiliation.

Need for approval—concern with receiving praise and other positive feedback. People with a high need for approval watch others' nonverbal vocal characteristics, such as pauses, more than those with a low need for approval do.

Other examples of personality characteristics include sociability, tolerance, and concern with making a good impression (from the *California Psychological Inventory*); exhibitionism, autonomy, and nurturance (from the *Edwards Personal Preference Schedule*); and relaxed versus tense, conservative versus experimenting, and trusting versus suspicious (from the *Sixteen Personality Factor Questionnaire*).[4]

Values

Values reflect the importance you attach to both different ways of behaving, such as being honest, and the goals to which you aspire, such as a peaceful world. Values motivate you to behave one way or another. Knowledge Checkup 4.3 is designed to help you clarify several values.

KNOWLEDGE CHECKUP 4.3

Clarifying Important Values[5]

Rank the items within each set of values from most important to you (1) to least important to you (9).

It is important to be

_____ Ambitious (hard-working, aspiring)
_____ Broadminded (open-minded)
_____ Capable (competent, effective)
_____ Courageous (standing up for your beliefs)
_____ Forgiving (willing to pardon others)
_____ Helpful (working for the welfare of others)
_____ Honest (sincere, truthful)
_____ Loving (affectionate, tender)
_____ Responsible (dependable, reliable)

It is important to have

_____ A comfortable life (a prosperous life)
_____ A world at peace (free of war and conflict)
_____ A sense of accomplishment (lasting contribution)

	Family security (taking care of loved ones)
	Freedom (independence, free choice)
	Happiness (contentment)
	Salvation (being saved, eternal life)
	Self-respect (self-esteem)
	Wisdom (a mature understanding of life)

In a national survey, people across the United States were asked to rate these values. For the "important to *be*" values, *honest* was ranked first, *responsible* second, *ambitious* third, *forgiving* fourth, *broadminded* fifth, *courageous* sixth, *helpful* seventh, *loving* eighth, and *capable* ninth. For the "important to *have*" values, *family security* was ranked first, *a world at peace* second, *freedom* third, *self-respect* fourth, *happiness* fifth, *wisdom* sixth, *a sense of accomplishment* seventh, *a comfortable life* eighth, and *salvation* ninth. A few differences between males and females were found. Males ranked *capable* and *a comfortable life* higher than females did, and females ranked *salvation* higher than males did.

These results are averages; each value received every possible ranking. How you compare with the national results isn't important. What's important is for you to realize what values are important for you and understand how they help define who you are.

What is the relationship between your ranking of particular values and your behavior? For example, if you ranked *honesty* first, ask yourself if you have ever cheated on your income taxes or if you have ever kept extra change you received by mistake from a salesperson. Your behavior should be consistent with the values you respect most.

If you value honesty highly, you are more likely to communicate directly and openly, especially if you also value being courageous. Of course, if you value being ambitious more highly than being honest, you might stretch the truth during a job interview to increase your chances of getting hired. The issue gets more complicated if you consider how much you value self-respect. Will you respect yourself if you stretch the truth during the job interview?

Completing questionnaires like Knowledge Checkup 4.3 and observing your communication behavior should help you determine what your values are and which are most important. Knowing your values is the first step toward analyzing them and their relationship to how you behave. You will then be better equipped to change your values or your behavior as you see fit.

Your social identity is relatively unambiguous—you know the groups to which you belong; personality characteristics and values, however, are less demonstrable. You may be certain you're a student, but unsure about your warmth, true intelligence, or honesty. Your social identity is more easily verified than your psychological one. You may have a driver's license that clearly identifies you as a driver, but where in your wallet or purse is a document to prove that you're gentle, humorous, or forgiving?

Physical Characteristics

Your **physical characteristics**, your body's traits, make up a third category of elements that contribute to your self-concept. While the characteristics may be clear—indeed, you are a certain height and weight and have eyes a particular color—how you feel about individual body parts and your body in general may be less certain. Born without a notion of self, your first identity was a physical one. Lying in your crib, you noticed hands that came and went from view. One day, you realized that the hands were *you*—and, still without being aware of it, your physical self-concept began to form. Your physical self remains important even now, which may be why you diet, lift weights, run, or apply makeup.

Ego-Extensions

Your self-concept extends beyond social, psychological, and physical characteristics to elements in your environment. You experience environmental elements, **ego-extensions**, as part of yourself. Something is an ego-extension if you refer to it as *my* or *mine*, feel pride or shame for it, and accept praise or blame for it as your own. For example, if you refer to the school you graduated from as "my school," if you are proud of its history and traditions, and if you consider criticism of it a personal attack, your school qualifies as an ego-extension.

Your ego-extensions may take many forms, including your car, family members (attacks on family members, especially mothers and fathers, are perceived as personal attacks by over 90 percent of us), country, state, city, neighborhood, and work. For example, if a teacher gives you a failing grade and says, "This is terrible, but don't take it personally—I'm criticizing your work, not you," you may not be able to remain objective.

Your self-concept is complex, containing your social identity, personality and physical characteristics, values, and ego-extensions. How is it that your particular self-concept came to be what it is?

The Sources of Self-Concept

Two primary theories explain how particular elements come to form your self-concept. The first, reflected appraisal, suggests that you are influenced by the communication you receive from others, especially when it focuses on you. The second, social comparison, contends that you learn about yourself by comparing yourself to others.

Reflected Appraisal Reflected appraisal holds that your view of yourself is consistent with the view others hold of you, and that you have come to view yourself as you do *because* of the views of others. Some consistency between your self-perceptions and others' perceptions of you is essential for getting along in society. Think of the problems you would encounter if, because you thought of yourself as intelligent, outgoing, and an effective communicator, you wanted to lead a team project, but your classmates saw you as below average in intelligence, withdrawn, and a poor communicator.

At the root of reflected appraisals are the messages others send you about yourself. Not all messages carry the same weight, however. An appraisal from your best friend matters more to you than an appraisal from a relative stranger.

To take someone's opinion seriously, you must perceive the person as a **significant other**, that is, someone whose opinion of you matters or whose judgment you trust. Friends exert more influence than strangers, and members of your family usually exert more influence than outsiders, because you consider friends and kin qualified appraisers of you who have your best interests at heart.

For an appraisal to be accepted as true, it must first be personal. The other person must know a great deal about you and adapt an appraisal specifically to you. Second, an appraisal must be consistent with past appraisals so that you do not dismiss it as a mistake or an anomaly.

Part of reflected appraisal is the notion of projecting another's appraisal. Without the other person present, you can *imagine* what her or his evaluation will be. The "little voice" that warns what your mother will say if you fail a test, or what your religious leader will think if you act improperly, exists because you can assume another's point of view, see yourself as that person sees you, and imagine and use a reflected appraisal.

Who are your significant others? Skill Checkup 4.1 will help you identify them.

SKILL CHECKUP 4.1

Identifying Your Significant Others

You can recognize your significant others—the people whose appraisals affect how you view yourself—by answering four questions:

1. Which people know me best and have my best interests at heart?

2. Which people, in my opinion, are competent to judge me?

3. Whose comments seem to have the greatest influence on how I think about myself and how I behave?

4. If each person identified in my answers to questions 1, 2, and 3 described me to someone, what would she or he say?

Your answers to question 4 are the reflected appraisals that helped form your self-concept.

Finally, reflected appraisal includes what you think others in general—or **generalized others**—consider correct or proper. It is your interpretation of the attitudes of society in general. From years of watching television, for example, you may have formed the belief that conflicts are unhealthy unless they can be resolved in thirty or sixty minutes. Consequently, when you are involved in a real conflict—one that takes more than thirty or sixty minutes to resolve—your self-appraisal may be: "I am a bad person for engaging in unhealthy conflict. I had better run away or give in, or shout so loudly that I get my way, and end this problem immediately." How you communicate will be based on an appraisal from generalized others.

Social Comparison According to the principle of **social comparison**, you compare yourself to others to learn about yourself, and you evaluate how you measure up by the standards set by those others. For example, suppose you compare your height to that of your friends. If you are taller, and if being tall is valued by your friends, you can make two appraisals: You are taller than some others, and that is good.

Comparisons take at least two forms: *better or worse* and *same or different*. Assessments of such traits as intelligence, strength, and creativity define whether you are better or worse, while comparisons of religious background, social class, and home region tell whether you are the same or different.

Comparisons let you see yourself as smart or stupid, or attractive or ugly, depending on whom you compare yourself with. To compare better, change your source of comparison—you don't have to change yourself!

SKILL CHECKUP 4.2

Identifying Your Social Comparison Groups

You can recognize your social comparison groups by answering four questions.

1. In what area is a comparison made? (For example, is the comparison based on wealth, intelligence, or social skill?)

2. In the selected area, which people am I better or worse than?

3. In the selected area, which people am I the same as or different from?

4. What do my comparisons tell me about who I am? (For example, do I put myself down or inflate my ego by selecting unrealistic people with whom to compare myself?)

The information you gather through reflected appraisals and social comparisons becomes the content of your self-concept. Because you are a complex, multifaceted, multidimensional being, the elements of your self-concept are voluminous. Once you have amassed your self-perceptions, you need to organize them.

Organizing the Elements of Your Self-Concept

The elements of your self-concept are not random and disorganized. Rather, they are ordered in a way that makes it possible for you to behave relatively consistently. The order can be pictured as a circle with elements that are most important to you at the center and ones that are less important to you toward the outside. For example, thinking of yourself as a devoted son or daughter may be more central to your self-perception than thinking of yourself as a conscientious student.

Consider the following situations:

▶ You have to stay on campus over spring break to research a term paper. Your parents call to remind you that a family gathering is taking place and that you're expected to be there. Your mother asks whether you will be coming home. Going home means not getting your research done. What would you tell her?

▶ You want to get an A in a course that is part of your major concentration, but your work so far has been at the B level. Your friend offers to write a term paper for you that is more likely to get an A than the one you are writing; with an A paper, you probably could earn an A in the course. If there were absolutely no possibility of getting caught, what would you tell your friend?

You can determine the relative importance of the elements in your self-concept by examining your responses to hypothetical situations such as these, *as well as by observing your behavior in real-life situations.* If, in the first scenario, you tell your mother you're coming home, you may value family security more than individual accomplishment. If, in the second scenario, you tell your friend

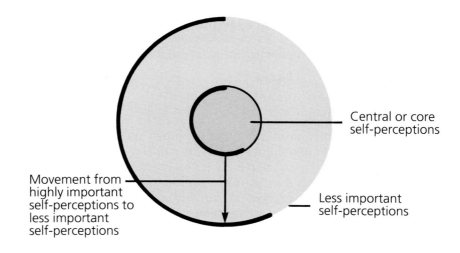

Central or core
self-perceptions

Movement from
highly important
self-perceptions to
less important
self-perceptions

Less important
self-perceptions

▶ **FIGURE 4.1**   Circle of Self-Perceptions

that you'll write the paper yourself, you may value honesty or responsibility above ambition.

Communication problems may arise when two people who have the same elements in their self-concepts rank the elements differently. For example, you and a friend may hold honesty as an important value, but you may believe in honesty at all costs while your friend believes he should be honest as long as honesty doesn't hurt anyone. Right versus wrong is not the issue as you communicate. Rather, difficulties arise because you have honesty at different places in your circle of self-perceptions—such as when you want to share your real feelings with a third person about her behavior and your friend suggests you withhold the truth because it could hurt her.

The Person You Wish You Were

The extent to which you think of yourself as a failure or a success, a good person or a bad one, depends largely on your notion of whom you would like to be. At least three images form your desired self-concept: the *idealized self*, the *serious self*, and the *should self*.

The Idealized Self

Your **idealized self** is what you would be if you were perfect. Elements of this image emerge when you say, "If I were . . . , then everything would be OK." When you feel overwhelmed by problems, you may temporarily invoke your idealized self. If you feel the need to be successful, you may dream that you can do anything and accomplish anything. And if you feel the need to be loved, you may dream of being attractive and desirable.

The Serious Self

Your **serious self** is a more realistic image than your idealized self, which conforms more to your capabilities and the restrictions of your environment. Even young children know the difference between an idealized image and a serious one. They clearly recognize the self-picture that is possible and, therefore, worth striving for. Thinking about an idealized image, such as being a basketball star, may be fun, but most children's real effort is spent pursuing a serious image, such as being a teacher. A child who is asked "If you could be anything, what would you want to be?" may answer "Superman," but that same child would probably admit that being Superman isn't *really* possible because he understands that the idealized self is simply a pleasant dream.

Comparing yourself to your idealized image is bound to leave you feeling inadequate. Comparing yourself to your serious image, however, is more fruitful because the serious self can be achieved.

The Should Self

The third component of the desired self-concept is the **should self**, which contains all the "oughts" and "shoulds" that serve as your moral guideposts. These standards, against which you constantly measure yourself, come from your family, school, friends, and the mass media. Your "shoulds" represent the moral standards of society; transgressing them usually results in guilt or anger with yourself.

"Shoulds" result not merely from your socialization, but also from the unique demands you place on yourself. Getting A's may not be a society-wide "should," but *you* may think that there is no alternative, that anything less than an A represents failure. You may be convinced that eating more than one scoop of ice cream is disgustingly self-indulgent, or that sleeping for more than eight hours is inexcusably lazy, or that watching television is a waste of time. In addition to all the "shoulds" that you adopt, you may generate hundreds more on your own. And every "should" increases the likelihood that you will view yourself as a bad person.

The Person You Present to Others

Regardless of the person you are and the person you would like to be, the only person others know is the one you present to them. Most of us distinguish actors from the characters they play; however, others do not distinguish you from the person you portray. As Kurt Vonnegut wrote in *Mother Night*, "We are what we pretend to be, so we must be careful about what we pretend to be."[6]

The person you think you are and the person you would like to be, together with your "shoulds," form the foundation for all your behavior. Acting in ways that do not fit your conception of yourself is difficult and often uncomfortable. If you must behave in ways that contradict how you see yourself, you are likely to distance yourself from the image you are presenting. For example, if you consider yourself shy, you might offer a toast at a dinner party something like this: "Well, gee, . . . this isn't something I do a lot. In fact, this is the first time. I feel really awkward about standing up here. . . ." You would thus try to show the other guests that being the center of attention is not part of how you see yourself.

Three additional factors influence the person you present to others: the perceived requirements of the situation, others' expectations, and your objectives for communicating.

The Requirements of a Situation

Your perceived requirements of a situation stem from the situation's immediate demands, the demands of similar past situations, and the implications of your behavior for similar situations in the future. For example, one rule-of-thumb for child rearing is "Be consistent in what you tell your child—don't change from situation to situation." Consider the following dialogue:

> **Child:** I want some ice cream.
> **Mother:** No. That's a rule we have in this house: No junk food before dinner.
> **Child:** I want ice cream. I want ice cream! I want ice cream!!

The immediate demand for the parent is to respond to the child's request for ice cream: Should an exception to the rule be allowed, or should a firm no be repeated? Situations that parallel the current one include the many times the child asked for cookies, cake, or candy and was refused. If the mother refuses the child's request for ice cream, her behavior would be consistent with past situations and the child might eventually learn to accept the house rule. But if she allows the child to have some ice cream, she probably opens the door to a flood of future requests for snack-time goodies.

The parent's message to the child reflects her definition of a good parent: "A good parent should not allow a child to eat junk food before dinner." In addition, her message reflects her analysis of the implications of her response for future interactions. The result may not please the child, but it is appropriate from the parent's perspective.

Others' Expectations

What you think people expect of you also affects how you behave. "People" includes both those with whom you are interacting and significant others who are now absent but helped form your self-image. Your goal is to be consistent with what both groups expect of you. Those expectations may be unclear, especially for a new situation, and the expectations of one group may differ from the expectations of the other group. For example, ambiguity and conflict commonly mark dating situations, especially when dating first begins. Consider these inner thoughts of two young teenagers on a first date:

He: *She wants me to put my arm around her shoulder—she expects that.*

She: *My mother knows his mother and she told me that he's a nice guy. I'm sure he won't try anything.*

He: *Should I put my arm around her?*

She: *I get the feeling he wants to put his arm around my shoulder. That's OK with me!*

He: *If I put my arm around her and she screams, what will I do? But if she expects me to put my arm around her and I don't, what will she think? And if I do and she screams, what will happen? And if I don't and she thinks I'm an idiot, will that mean I'll never see her again? And what will my mother think if it gets back to her that I put my arm around her friend's daughter and she screamed? And what if it gets back that I didn't, and should have, and my mother's only son is an idiot?*

She: *I think he thinks that I think that he shouldn't put his arm around me. Then he must think I'm stuck up.*

And so the evening goes. No one is sure what to do. No one knows what image to live up to, what expectations to fulfill, or even what the expectations are.

The Goals for Communicating

The self you present to others stems from several objectives, which further complicates the issue of how to behave. First are the goals you have for interacting: You may want to get hired for a particular job, impress a professor with your intelligence, persuade your parents that you're a dutiful child, or have your love reciprocated. There are as many goals as there are people and interactions. How you communicate reflects what you want, either directly or indirectly.

Second is your objective to remain consistent with your image of yourself and avoid doing anything that might lower your self-evaluation: if the teenaged boy puts his arm around the teenaged girl and she screams, his view of himself as a nice guy will be challenged and he may well lose some respect for himself. On the other hand, if he doesn't try to put his arm around her and later finds out that she wouldn't have screamed, he will probably feel just as downcast.

Third may be your objective of "trying on" a social identity. All of us test new behaviors and experiment with new elements of our self-concept, although adolescence is the heyday for such testing. Is the teenaged male a playboy? The only way he can find out is to try on the behavior and see how it feels. If it's comfortable and others seem to approve, he may decide to keep it as an element of his self-concept. Is the teenaged girl assertive? The only way she can find out is to tell her date that she wants him to put his arm around her, and see how it feels to have communicated assertively.

HOW YOU FEEL ABOUT YOURSELF: YOUR SELF-ESTEEM

To get a quick idea of how you feel about yourself—**self-esteem**—answer the questions in Knowledge Checkup 4.4.

KNOWLEDGE CHECKUP 4.4

Analyzing Self-Esteem[7]

Indicate the extent to which you agree or disagree with each statement.

Write 1 if you strongly disagree with the statement.
Write 2 if you disagree.
Write 3 if you neither agree nor disagree.
Write 4 if you agree.
Write 5 if you strongly agree.

_____ **1.** I am generally satisfied with myself.
_____ **2.** I feel that I have a number of worthy qualities.
_____ **3.** I am able to do things as adequately as most people.
_____ **4.** I think of myself in mostly positive ways.
_____ **5.** I have few regrets about my life.
_____ **6.** I wouldn't change much if I had the chance to live my life over again.
_____ **7.** I feel like a useful person.

Add up your responses to the seven items. The higher your score, the higher your self-esteem. Scores of twenty-one and higher suggest positive self-esteem, while scores below twenty-one suggest low self-esteem.

Although the test is short, it should give you a general idea of how you feel about yourself. You may disagree with the results and say something like, "Sure, I have a high score, but so what? I still hate the way my nose hooks and I don't do well in foreign language courses," or "My low score doesn't take into account that I'm a great pianist and play guard on the varsity basketball team."

Such statements reflect the relationship between your general attitude toward yourself, as measured by the test, and your attitude toward parts of yourself. You may like some elements of your self-concept and not others. Thus you may take pride in your social abilities yet be embarrassed by your math deficiencies.

Whether you should focus on the overall evaluation or the individual assessments depends on what you want to know about yourself. Regardless of where you focus, keep in mind that generalizing from smaller parts to the whole or from the whole to smaller parts can lead you astray: If you feel good about your work in school, avoid the generalization that you feel good about yourself. If you are upset with yourself in general, avoid concluding that you do not think highly of your singing ability. Instead, consider the whole and its parts together to gauge your self-esteem accurately.

Your level of self-esteem tends to be reflected in your communication. As you might suspect, communicators with high self-esteem are at a distinct advantage. Individuals who like and accept themselves tend to remain open-minded when they encounter new ideas, opinions, and beliefs. They can also change their minds more easily than people with low self-esteem because they are confident and unthreatened by others' ideas. As a result, their interactions are supportive and friendly, which leads to greater involvement with other people and the possibility of more intimate relationships. Consider the following dialogue between Barry, who has low self-esteem, and his boss.

Boss: I'd like you to tackle the Swegard account.
Barry: I already worked on it.
Boss: I'd like you to try out some new ideas. I have some suggestions that you might consider.
Barry: What's wrong? Didn't you like what I did?
Boss: It's not that. I just think a new approach . . . .
Barry: Well, I just don't see how to go about it any other way. I'm sorry you have a problem with me.

Barry's reactions indicate his inability to accept change and his unwillingness to consider alternatives. He perceived the request for change as an attack on him, and rather than talk with his boss to discover what was desired, he responded defensively and created a poor impression.

People with high self-esteem also tend to show sensitivity toward others and empathy, the ability to see things from another's perspective. Both of these characteristics hone the accuracy of a person's perceptions and contribute to effective conflict resolution. The ability to see a conflict from the other person's perspective strongly influences whether a mutually agreed-upon solution will be found.

Finally, self-esteem directly affects language. People with high self-esteem tend to have rich vocabularies and confident-sounding voices, whereas people with low self-esteem tend to use language filled with clichés and jargon. When things go wrong, the person with low self-esteem may say, "It never rains but it pours," or "Why does it always happen to me?" whereas the person with high self-esteem will probably give a clear description of the situation and its consequences. Language reflects feelings about the world, whether it is a place to trust others, act spontaneously, and be happy, or a place to withdraw, act defensively, and feel unhappy.

Improving Your Self-Esteem

Your communication reflects how you feel about yourself. The discussion so far reveals that one sure way to improve your communication is to increase your self-esteem. Among the methods of raising your self-esteem are confronting your "should" messages, focusing on the positive, and eliminating your self-put-downs.

Confronting Your "Should" Messages

A prime source of low self-esteem is the "should" image you hold. If your self-esteem is low, you can boost it by discovering your "should" messages, assessing their reasonableness, and then refuting unreasonable ones. For example, to confront the message "I should get A's in all my classes," you might say: "Earning A's in all my classes is desirable, but expecting to may be unreasonable. I am better at some things than others. I can reasonably expect to get A's in some courses and not others. I can't reasonably expect to earn all A's, although I will strive for them." Analyzing and refuting unreasonable "should" messages provides information that clarifies your strengths and weaknesses and the demands you place on yourself. It also lays the foundation for improving your self-esteem because you begin to set realistic goals.

●SKILL CHECKUP 4.3

Confronting "Should" Messages

1. Complete each of the following sentences:

   a. To be a good family member, I should

   b. To be a good friend, I should

   c. To be a good student, I should

2. What unreasonable and reasonable demands does each "should" statement in question 1 make?

3. How do the unreasonable demands prevent you from feeling better about yourself?

4. Refute each "should" statement in question 1 and substitute a more realistic goal.

Focusing on the Positive

All communication is open to interpretation, and your interpretation of a specific event can either increase or decrease your self-esteem. Assume that you are asked to lunch by a co-worker, Leslie. You could say to yourself, "I guess Leslie likes my company and would enjoy having lunch with me—perhaps to discuss something important." You could also say, "Leslie probably needs a favor and thinks I'm the sucker who will do it. That little schemer probably doesn't care about me at all and is using lunch to set me up." The first interpretation enhances your self-esteem; the second decreases it.

The next time you find yourself in an ambiguous situation, try to analyze how much your interpretation reflects or affects your self-esteem. Do you interpret situations positively or negatively? If you tend to interpret situations negatively or make negative statements, your self-esteem is likely low. If your interpretations or statements are predominantly positive, your self-esteem is likely high.

If you want to change, you must first recognize your problem. Skill Checkup 4.4 is designed to help you analyze and correct unfounded negative interpretations.

SKILL CHECKUP 4.4

Analyzing Negative Interpretations

To determine whether you are interpreting a situation negatively, ask the following questions:

1. Is what I am saying really true?
2. Am I being unfair?
3. Is there something bothering me that has nothing to do with this issue?
4. Am I responding to the other person or using her or him as a scapegoat?

If your analysis indicates that you view matters negatively, consider focusing on the positive. Make the *choice* to change your interpretation.

Eliminating Your Self-Put-Downs

A third method for improving your self-esteem is to attack your self-put-downs. We are all experts at putting ourselves down; in fact, no one can do a better job than we can. We know all our weaknesses, including the ones most vulnerable to attack. The book *Vulture: A Modern Allegory on the Art of Putting Oneself Down* describes self-put-downs in terms of vultures.[8] Consider, for a moment, the real vulture, an unattractive bird with sharp claws and a pointy beak whose favorite activity is picking on the weak, the helpless, and, preferably, the dead. It dives into the flesh and picks away at it.

The imaginary, psychological vulture is similar to that bird: it is ugly and hungry, eager to pounce on its psychological food, your self-concept. Every self-put-down is a call to the bird to attack. It screams to the bird that you are weak, helpless, and have an ailing self-concept. What do you call yourself when you lock your keys in the car? What do you call yourself when you trip over the edge of the carpet? Every self-put-down—"Idiot!" "Klutz!"—summons the vultures!

Put-downs may be either obvious or subtle. The obvious ones have a clear physical referent, like the keys dangling in the ignition of the locked car or the frayed edge of the carpet on which you tripped. The subtle put-downs impose limitations on you that, though not obvious, are destructive. Some typical ones are the following:

> "I could never jog five miles a day."
> "I could never write a paper longer than ten pages."
> "I could never stick to a diet for more than a week."
> "I just can't stop smoking."

Vultures tend to congregate in six areas. There are *intelligence* vultures ("I'm dumb," "I'm no good in math," "I'm no good at foreign languages"); *creativity* vultures ("I'm not imaginative," "I can't draw as well as Mary," "I can't sing like George"); *family* vultures ("I'm the black sheep in the family," "I should call home more often," "My brother is the favorite child"); *relationship* vultures ("I'm no good at meeting people," "I'm boring"); *physical* vultures ("I'm too short/tall/fat/thin," "My ankles are fat," "My teeth are crooked"); and *sexual* vultures ("I'm not sexy," "I'm boring in bed").

The results of self-put-downs are obvious: You avoid the areas where the vultures lurk, including math classes, drawing, your parents, and dates, and you wear clothes that hide this or that part of your body. You act and communicate how you feel. The goal of Skill Checkup 4.5 is to help you kill off your vultures!

SKILL CHECKUP 4.5

Killing off Your Vultures[9]

To kill off your vultures, follow this five-step process:

1. Pat yourself on the back by saying something good and true about yourself. You can surely think of something for which to compliment yourself.

2. Pat someone else on the back by saying something good and true about another person. Not only will you feel good about yourself for complimenting another person, but you'll also find that compliments beget compliments.

3. Recognize your self-put-downs. This is hard because you probably utter so many put-downs every day. To make sure you catch them all, you may want to ask a friend for help. Be sure to identify both the obvious and the subtle ones (and don't argue when your friend points them out). This step is crucial: You can't cure what you don't recognize!

4. Block each put-down. As you hear it coming out, put your hand over your mouth (literally, if you have to). Soon you'll feel a negative statement coming and you'll be able to head it off before you say it.

5. Turn the put-down around: Put it in the past tense and eliminate its evaluative component. For example, when you trip over the edge of the carpet, say, "I *used* to be *clumsy*, but I'm not anymore. I *tripped*, that's all, and that's human."

As you work on raising your self-esteem, remember to be realistic: Don't expect too much too soon! Plan on some hard work. You view yourself as you do because you get some payoff (you get to sulk, or you get to feel sorry for yourself because people ignore you, or you get an excuse for being a poor student). Changing your self-concept and self-esteem means giving up the old rewards for new and better ones.

Imagine that the person standing off to one side, who seems to be avoiding interaction with the other party-goers, complains to you that he doesn't like himself and thus avoids people.

1. What can you do to help him identify the elements of his self-concept that may be responsible for his problem?

2. With an understanding of the thoughts and feelings he has about himself, how would you identify his idealized self, his "should" self, and the self he presents to others? How would an understanding of these different aspects of self help him understand the present situation and his problem?

3. Develop three strategies for helping him improve his self-esteem: one for helping him confront his "should" messages and replace them with more realistic goals; one for helping him recognize the unreasonableness of his negative interpretations and focus instead on the positive aspects of the situations in which he finds himself; and one for eliminating his self-put-downs by substituting statements that recognize that being human means accepting imperfection.

NOTES

1. For detailed descriptions of the various ways the content of self-concept has been described, see: William H. Fitts, *The Self Concept and Self-Actualization* (Nashville, TN: Counselor Recordings and Tests, 1971), chapters 1 and 2; Morris Rosenberg, *Conceiving the Self* (New York: Basic Books, 1979), chapter 1; and L. Edward Wells and Gerald Marwell, *Self-Esteem: Its Conceptualization and Measurement* (Beverly Hills, CA: Sage, 1976), especially chapter 3.

2. Adapted from: Sandra L. Bem, "The Measurement of Psychological Androgyny," *Journal of Consulting and Clinical Psychology* 42 (1974): 155–62. The original inventory developed by Bem contains sixty items: twenty masculine, twenty feminine, and twenty neutral (neither masculine nor feminine exclusively).

3. For a summary of research conducted on communicator characteristics, see: Howard Giles and Richard L. Street, Jr., "Communicator Characteristics and Behavior," in *Handbook of Interpersonal Communication,* ed. Mark L. Knapp and Gerald R. Miller (Beverly Hills, CA: Sage, 1985), pp. 205–62.

4. Harrison G. Gough, *Manual for the California Psychological Inventory* (Palo Alto, CA: Consulting Psychologists Press, 1956); Allen L. Edwards, *Manual for the Edwards Personal Preference Schedule* (New York: The Psychological Corporation, 1959); Raymond B. Cattell, *16PF* (Champaign, IL: The Institute for Personality and Ability Testing, 1969).

5. Adapted from an instrument developed by Milton Rokeach, in Rokeach, *Understanding Human Values* (New York: Free Press, 1979). The original questionnaire contains eighteen "to be" and eighteen "to have" values. The values here were those ranked one through nine by the national sample as reported in Milton Rokeach and Sandra Ball-Rokeach, "Stability and Change in American Value Priorities, 1968–1981," *American Psychologist* 44 (1989): 775–84.

6. Kurt Vonnegut, Jr., *Mother Night* (New York: Dell Books, 1966), p. v.

7. Adapted from the *Rosenberg Self-Esteem Scale*. Morris Rosenberg, *Conceiving the Self* (New York: Basic Books, 1979), p. 291.

8. Sidney B. Simon, *Vulture: A Modern Allegory on the Art of Putting Oneself Down* (Niles, IL: Argus Communications, 1977).

9. The steps to killing off vultures are adapted from those presented by Sidney Simon on pages 34–44.

FOR FURTHER INVESTIGATION

Austin-Leff, Genelle, and Jan Sprague. *Talk to Yourself.* Boston: Houghton-Mifflin, 1976.

Bem, Sandra L. "Sex Role Adaptability: One Consequence of Psychological Androgyny." *Journal of Personality and Social Psychology* 31 (1975): 634–43.

Centi, Paul J. *Up With the Positive, Out With the Negative: How to Like the Person You Are.* Englewood Cliffs, NJ: Prentice-Hall, 1981.

Cole-Whittaker, Terry. *What You Think of Me is None of My Business.* LaJolla, CA: Oak Tree Publications, 1979.

Dyer, Wayne W. *Your Erroneous Zones.* New York: Avon Books, 1976.

Gergen, Kenneth J. *The Concept of Self.* New York: Holt, Rinehart and Winston, 1971.

Gergen, Kenneth J. "The Happy, Healthy, Human Being Wears Many Masks." *Psychology Today* 5 (May 1972): 31–35, 64–66.

Goffman, Erving. *The Presentation of Self in Everyday Life.* Garden City, NY: Doubleday, 1959.

Hamachek, Don E. *Encounters with the Self,* 2d ed. New York: Holt, Rinehart and Winston, 1978.

Hamachek, Don E. *Encounters With Others: Interpersonal Relationships and You.* New York: Holt, Rinehart and Winston, 1982.

Rokeach, Milton. *Understanding Human Values.* New York: Free Press, 1979.

Rokeach, Milton, and Sandra Ball-Rokeach. "Stability and Change in American Value Priorities, 1968–1981." *American Psychologist* 44 (1989): 775–84.

Rosenberg, Morris. *Conceiving the Self.* New York: Basic Books, 1979.

Samuels, Shirley C. *Enhancing Self-Concept in Early Childhood: Theory and Practice.* New York: Human Sciences Press, 1977.

Simon, Sidney B. *Vulture: A Modern Allegory on the Art of Putting Oneself Down.* Niles, IL: Argus Communications, 1977.

Weinberg, George. *Self Creation.* New York: Avon Books, 1978.

CHAPTER 5

▶ # *The Self and Others*

*This chapter on the self and others will help you to practice and develop communication competencies that fall into three broad categories: (1) **communication codes**, which include listening effectively and using words and nonverbal cues that are appropriate to a particular situation; (2) **basic speech communication skills**, which include expressing ideas clearly and asking questions to obtain information; and (3) **human relations**, which build and maintain personal relationships and include describing another's viewpoint, expressing feelings to others, and indicating differences of opinion. Specifically, the competencies you will gain will enable you to do the following:*

▶ *Describe how you perceive objects and people.*

▶ *Explain the role of self-fulfilling prophecies in your interactions with others.*

▶ *Apply several techniques for increasing your perceptual accuracy.*

▶ *Recognize verbal and nonverbal behaviors that indicate stress.*

▶ *Identify the presence or absence of personal communication anxiety.*

▶ *Define communication anxiety and specify its causes and effects.*

*R*ead the following story *once*:

> The students at Lower Valley State College wanted to build a new gymnasium. Although the university raised $2.7 million from student fees, alumni contributions, and fund-raising events, the students needed to raise another half-million dollars to purchase some special equipment. After speaking with the leader of the university's fund-raising drive —an efficient, well-organized, cold person—they came up with several schemes: a bake sale on the university's plush green lawn, selling cake for two dollars a slice; a carnival on the university's soccer field, with a five-dollar admission; and the sale of certificates that allowed the bearer to "buy a higher grade" in a course. In the end, the money was raised and the special equipment bought.

Without looking back at the story, write down as much of it as you remember. When you've finished, check your version against the original. How many pieces of information did you omit? If you omitted information, what was it? Did you add any details not in the original story? If you added details, how did they change the story? For example, did your additions make the story more interesting? Did you modify any pieces of information? If you did, what effect did your modifications have on the story? Was your version of the story shorter or longer than the original? What do the details you chose to see and remember, and the changes you made, tell about how you perceive things?

PERCEPTION

Perception is the process of becoming aware of objects and events, including yourself. How you perceive yourself forms the basis for your perception of the world, and how you perceive the world affects and reflects how you communicate.

Perception is an *active* process; the world may offer an infinite variety of details, but it does so passively. You need to make sense of the random pieces of information that are presented: You need to determine what you will perceive, how you will organize it, and how you will interpret it. *You* are the *cause* of what you perceive; you are the one in control, the one who determines what you perceive.

Selective Perception

The data available to your senses are too many to be grasped in their totality. You therefore need to engage in **selective perception**; that is, you need to choose what to focus your attention on. What you choose to perceive determines the subject matter of your communication.

Objects that are brighter or larger or easily distinguishable from their surroundings in some other way are more likely to attract your attention than are objects that seem to fade into the background. You focus on the Hawaiian shirt at a graduation ceremony, the tallest building on a street, or the loudest person in a room, because these things stand out. Of course, the choice to pay attention is yours: You can choose to concentrate on the sea of black robes instead of the colorful shirt, the entire skyline instead of the skyscraper, or the hum of voices instead of the outstanding one.

An object's distinctiveness is one determinant of selection; another is your purpose for selection. If you're hungry, restaurant signs attract your attention; if you're looking for a fight, possible insults receive your focus; and if you want company, people passing by may draw your notice.

The selection process is essentially the same whether you choose to focus on people or objects. What the person or object looks like in comparison to its context, together with your own needs, wants, and desires, determines where you focus your attention and what you select to perceive.

If the focus of your attention is not a person, the perception process moves quickly to selective organization, which will be discussed further. But if the focus of your attention is a person or a personal characteristic, something else happens: you make a snap judgment. When the Hawaiian shirt grabs your attention at graduation, you may immediately decide that its wearer is a jerk, a nerd, or someone you want to know better.

Snap judgments, which usually relate to liking, are based on your past experiences with similar people or characteristics or on cultural stereotypes. Snap judgments help you decide whether to continue focusing your attention on the person. If your initial judgment is positive, you'll choose to take more and more cues about the person; if your judgment is negative, you'll dismiss the person from your attention and move on to other aspects of your environment.

Selective Organization

Once you've chosen what to attend to, your next task is to organize the information in a way that makes it possible to interpret. To understand the information you amass, you must be able to see how parts relate to each other and how they interrelate to form the whole. **Selective organization** is the process of fitting together the information you selectively perceive to form a whole. Just as what to perceive is your choice, so is how to organize it.

General tendencies guide how you organize what you perceive. You tend to accentuate details that you consider essential and minimize those that seem less important to you; to fill in gaps so that details relate easily and logically to each other and to eliminate details that don't fit or make sense; and to put all the information you gather into a context that facilitates a recognizable pattern.

You would organize the material from a speech on affirmative action quotas in one way if you were a lawyer specializing in affirmative action cases, in another way if you were a person discriminated against, and yet in a different way if you were a student writing a term paper on affirmative action. If you were a lawyer, you would selectively perceive data related to legal issues and

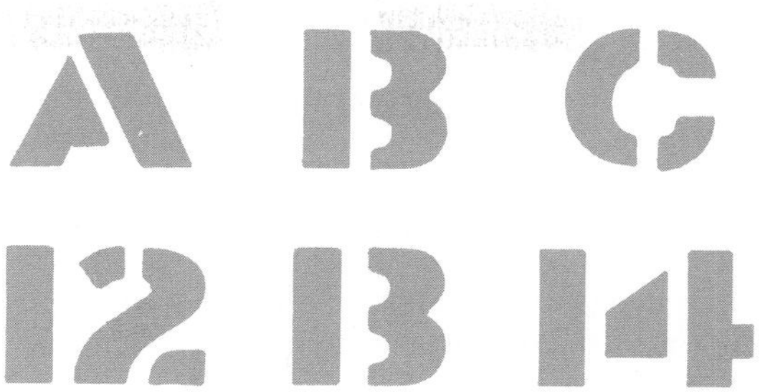

A B C
12 13 14

▶ **FIGURE 5.1**   What Do You See?

organize them into a coherent speech, filling in gaps left when the speaker handled other topics. You would probably place the information into a recognizable pattern such as "arguments in favor of *X*," or "arguments against *Y*." If you were a victim of discrimination, you would focus on information related to your particular problem and, like the lawyer, fill in gaps and eliminate anything that seemed irrelevant; you might also create a pattern out of the pieces you accumulate, such as "useful versus useless information." If you were a student new to the topic, you might take notes quickly, not sure what to focus on, but hoping that the speaker's tone of voice and method of organization would offer clues about what to report on later. Regardless of your purpose, you must organize the speaker's words—often without consciously thinking about it—so that meaning can be attributed to them. If a speaker does not organize a speech in a way that is meaningful to you, all you reap is a collection of unrelated, irrelevant facts.

The goal of filling in details (or eliminating them) is to create a unified whole of the information you receive. Look at the top line in figure 5.1 as you hold your hand over the bottom line. What do you see? Now repeat the same process for the bottom line.

Although the letters are fully formed, you probably have no trouble organizing the top line into *A*, *B*, and *C*, and the bottom line into *12, 13,* and *14*. If you take another look at the middle figures in the two sequences, however, you may notice that both figures are essentially the same. Because you created a context out of the surrounding figures, you determined that the middle figure is a *B* in the first line and a *13* in the second line. The other possible sequences—*A, 13, C,* and *12, B, 14*—seem illogical because you have been raised in a culture where A's, B's, and C's, like 12's, 13's, and 14's, come in packages.

The selective organization process is essentially the same for a person as it is for objects, letters, or numbers. For example, you commonly add details to people who are the focus of attention. Research shows that if you perceive someone as attractive, you add positive traits such as "kind," "friendly," "smart," and "happy." And you tend to add negative traits to complete the picture of someone who is less attractive.[1]

Ways of Organizing Perceptions of Others

There are two primary approaches to organizing impressions of other people. The first assumes that *traits interact with each other* to form the total picture of a person.[2] Traits are not independent of each other; rather, they combine and assume relative importance to form the overall impression. Consider the following list of characteristics you might perceive in someone.

> intelligent
> skillful
> industrious
> cold
> determined
> practical
> cautious

What would be your overall impression of a person who possesses these traits? How do the traits interact to form your impression? One way to determine the answer is by simple substitution. For example, if you substitute *warm* for *cold*, does your impression change dramatically? Some traits are central to an overall impression, so changing any or all of them changes the impression. Your first response to the list might have been that this is an unhappy, stingy person who is unpopular. But after substituting *warm* for *cold*, you might think that this is a generous, happy, good-natured person.

Although the warm-cold trait is central when you evaluate a person's sociability, it becomes less important when you evaluate honesty. In such cases, the blunt-polite trait appears to be more central. Which traits are central depends on the nature of the evaluation.

The second approach to organizing your impressions is based on *your ideas about the behaviors that characterize particular types of people or how people should behave in certain situations.* You have ideas about how certain types of people, such as extroverts, shy people, students, teachers, and parents, should behave. You also have ideas about what certain events, such as lectures, wedding ceremonies, and football games, should be like. You use these ideas to organize what you see and to make predictions about what else you should or should not see. You therefore evaluate what you see according to how well it fits your idea of what the person or event should be like.

Perceiving people is different from perceiving objects, if for no other reason than that you have many more things in common with another person than you do with an object. When the focus of perception is a person, you attribute qualities to the person that, for you, seem to go together. For example, *happy* and *independent* may be related in your mind, so that someone you perceive as happy you also perceive as independent. As with everything else, who you are determines what you attribute to another person. In someone you like, you see characteristics that you value for yourself; in someone you dislike, you see characteristics that you find objectionable for yourself. If you are proud of your ability to run long distances, you'll admire this trait in others. If you dislike your tendency to shout when you're angry, you'll dislike this trait in others.

Selective Interpretation

Interpretation is just as much your choice as what you perceive and how you organize it. In **selective interpretation**, you choose how to explain the information you selectively perceive and selectively organize. How you interpret what you perceive depends on who you think you are, who you would like to be, and who you think you should be. It also depends on your knowledge and expectations of the people and objects in your environment as well as how you feel at the moment. Many variables enter into your interpretation of what you perceive, which is why two individuals' perceptions are never the same. Just as no two people are identical, no two interpretations are identical.

How would you interpret your date, Dale, telling you: "I had a great time tonight. Let's get together again"? If you see yourself as desirable, you might think: "Sure, why not? I'm a *good* person!" If you see yourself as desirable, yet also assume that your date will say something nice because doing so is only good etiquette, you might think: "Well, it sounds good, but maybe Dale thinks it's *necessary* to tell me this!" If you see yourself as desirable, assume that your date will say something nice, *and* you have a bad stomachache, you might think: "Shut up! I have to get home before I get sick on your front porch! Are you trying to *kill* me?"

After you selectively perceive and organize cues from another person—whether they are nonverbal, such as clothing and posture, or verbal, such as spoken words—you attribute a motive to the person, make a general judgment, and finish by making a prediction. Consider the following:

"Dale wants to see me again because Dale thinks I'm a nice person. I can expect Dale to like me more and more as we continue to date."

"Dale acted politely because Dale is a polite person who can be expected to behave politely in the future."

"Dale kept talking because Dale could see I was in pain and wanted to inflict further pain on me. Dale is a cruel person who can be expected to try to hurt me whenever the opportunity arises!"

Knowledge Checkup 5.1 will help you understand your own perception process—what you select to perceive, how you organize the information, and how you interpret it—and what it reveals about you.

KNOWLEDGE CHECKUP 5.1

Analyzing Your Perception Process

Describe what you see in this picture.

1. What details of the picture do you select to perceive?

2. How do you organize the details you select to perceive?

3. How do you interpret the details that you select to perceive and organize?

4. The picture is ambiguous. Because it presents a great deal of information that is unorganized and uninterpreted, there is no right or wrong way to perceive it. What does your description of the picture—what you selectively perceive, selectively organize, and selectively interpret—tell you about yourself and your perception process?

What you chose to see in the picture, how you chose to put the details together, and how you made sense of the details reflect what is important to you. Were you more concerned with the man and woman than where they were? Did you describe characteristics you perceived in them? Did you go into detail about their relationship, and, if you did, how did you describe the relationship? Did you perceive the scene as calm or tense? Were the man and woman looking at something or just staring off into the distance? What does your perception of this picture tell you about who you are?

The Self-Fulfilling Prophecy

What you believe about yourself and others has a tendency to come true. This notion is called the **self-fulfilling prophecy**. Consider, for example, the likely outcomes of the earlier interactions with Dale. If you believe that you are a good person and that Dale recognizes this (as in the first situation), you are likely to behave nicely the next time you two are together, which should increase the probability that Dale will, indeed, treat you nicely. If you believe that Dale was simply polite and didn't care about you as a person (the second scenario), you might treat Dale distantly and politely the next time you are together, which should increase the probability that you will be treated likewise. If you believe that Dale intends to harm you (the third situation), you might be suspicious of Dale's every move, convinced that danger lurks in every behavior; if you continue behaving accordingly, Dale just might treat you unkindly.

People behave in ways that increase the probability that their beliefs about themselves and others will come true. Consider how the self-fulfilling prophecy applies to the man in the following conversation. His basic belief was that he couldn't get any love. He was asked, "From whom can you get love? Anyone?" His responses, and the prompting questions, went like this:

"No, not *anyone*. The person needs to be a woman."
"Any woman?"
"No, she needs to be between eighteen and forty years of age."
"Any woman between eighteen and forty?"
"No, she needs to have long red hair."
"Any woman between eighteen and forty with long red hair?"
"No, she also needs to have blue eyes."
"Any woman between eighteen and forty, with long red hair and blue eyes?"
"No, she also needs to be between 5'3" and 5'7"."
"Any woman between eighteen and forty, with long red hair and blue eyes, between 5'3" and 5'7"?"
"No, she also needs a college degree."

"Any woman between eighteen and forty, with long red hair and blue eyes,
between 5′3″ and 5′7″, with a college degree?"

"No, she needs to have a degree in the helping professions, such as
teaching or social work."

"Any woman between eighteen and forty, with long red hair and blue eyes,
between 5′3″ and 5′7″, with a college degree in the helping professions
such as teaching or social work?"

"No, there's one more requirement. She has to love me *first*."

"And what's the problem?"

"I'm unlovable."

This man created his own experience of "getting no love" by making his
requirements so strict that few women could possibly meet them. But if even
one person matched his description, the final obstacle *guaranteed* that his prophecy
would come true: he was unlovable. He could never perceive being loved
because he *saw himself as unlovable.* So before his experiences could change, his
self-perception needed to change. He was the cause of his experience.

Similarly, *you* are the cause of *your* experience.

INCREASING PERCEPTUAL ACCURACY

Many issues need to be addressed before you can increase the accuracy of your
perceptions. Given that *who you are determines what you perceive,* you may need
to change even who you are in order to perceive things more accurately.

What you perceive is limited by what you believe. Picture yourself as a
tube. At one end is a mesh screen through which you perceive your environment. If each thin wire in the screen were a belief, accumulating enough beliefs
would mean that eventually nothing could get through. From the inside, all you
could see would be your own screen. You would be trapped in your beliefs and
they would cloud your view of reality. From inside the tube, everything would
seem orderly, stable, and logical, resulting in the most dangerous of all beliefs:
What I see is what there is, and that is all there is.

Stretch Yourself

Increasing your imagination expands what you are capable of perceiving. The
more you can imagine, the more you can perceive.

Begin with your senses, because it is through your senses that you perceive
things. Try to complete Skill Checkup 5.1 with a friend. If a friend can't help you
or if you don't have time to do all the steps, then *imagine* how you would feel at
each key point in the activity.

SKILL CHECKUP 5.1

Increasing Sense Awareness and Sense Imagination

Increasing Sense Awareness

1. Cover your eyes, put cotton or earplugs in your ears, put on thick gloves and heavy shoes or boots, and plug up your nose.
2. With a friend along to make sure you're safe, take a walk.
3. After ten minutes, remove your gloves.
4. After another ten minutes, remove your nose plug.
5. After another ten minutes, remove your shoes or boots.
6. After another ten minutes, remove the cotton or plugs from your ears.
7. After another ten minutes, remove your blindfold.
8. Answer the following questions: What did you notice as the activity progressed? How did you perceive things as each obstacle to your senses was removed? Did you encounter a new environment every ten minutes?

Increasing Sense Imagination

1. What does winter *taste* like?
2. What is the *color* of worry?
3. What does time *feel* like?
4. What does a rainbow *sound* like?
5. What is the *smell* of silence?

To increase the accuracy of your perceptions, you need to break the habit of using your senses in usual ways and stop making common, automatic associations. Expand your imagination!

Many of the associations people make stem from fixed ways of looking at things that they learned as children and never bothered to change. For example, consider your automatic responses to the following word combinations:

bread and _____

ham and _____

hot and _____

short and _____

If you said "butter," "eggs" or "cheese," "cold," and "tall," you made habitual responses. These associations are made almost by reflex. Skill Checkup 5.2 provides you with the opportunity to break old habits and form new associations.

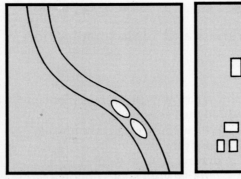 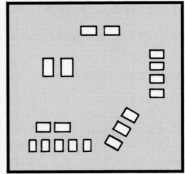

▶ **FIGURE 5.2**   Droodles

SKILL CHECKUP 5.2

Forming New Associations[3]

Part I

Look at the droodles in figure 5.2 and see how many titles you can create for each. (A *droodle* is a drawing that doesn't make sense until it has a title.) Just to get you started, a possible title for the first droodle is "two corpuscles who loved in vein." Let your imagination run wild!

Part II

Pick two words at random from the following list. Combine them to invent a new product or something that improves on either of the two original items. (For example, an "apple suitcase" can be a suitcase in the shape of an apple, a suitcase made especially to transport apples, or maybe a suitcase made of apple skins.) Do this for two pairs of words.

apple	suitcase	glass	basket
bottle	hook	shoe	pen
hand	star	phone	wax
chair	magazine	band	comb
tar	disk	clip	typewriter

Association 1

Association 2

Part III

Write two rhyming words that apply to each of the following definitions. For example, "boob tube" is a pair of rhyming words that together define "television."

1. A corpulent feline

2. A musical stringed instrument known for its soft, rich sounds

3. A man whose health is delicate

4. An angry young male

5. A person who murders for the fun of it

Activities such as these help you develop skills that expand how you perceive things. If you have the opportunity, share your responses with your classmates. Sharing perceptions expands your perceptual frame and enriches your way of looking at things. In what other ways did people see the droodles? What word combinations struck you as unique and imaginative? How did your rhymes compare with those created by others? Did you all agree that a corpulent feline is a *fat cat*, the stringed instrument is a *mellow cello*, a man with delicate health is a *frail male*, an angry young male is a *mad lad*, and a person who murders for the fun of it is a *thriller killer*?

Remain Open-Minded

To ensure accurate perceptions, you must be receptive to new information, assumptions, beliefs, and opinions, even when they seem to contradict your own positions. Increasing your perceptual accuracy requires, above all else, open-mindedness.

Being open-minded means recognizing that there may be more to see than you see, more to touch than you touch, more to hear than you hear, more to smell than you smell, more to taste than you taste—more to know about one subject, one person, or one world than you, alone, could ever know.

Being open-minded also means recognizing that you may perceive things that aren't there, eliminate inconvenient pieces of information, and otherwise push, pull, stretch, and bang the world to fit your preconceived notions.

Finally, being open-minded means recognizing that you may draw conclusions too quickly, state them too assuredly, and assume that if an answer works for you, it must work for everyone.

You can increase your open-mindedness by making yourself available to new and varied experiences. Your object is to gain additional information about your world.

SKILL CHECKUP 5.3

Increasing Your Open-Mindedness

1. *Talk to people.* The more you interact with others, the more you will learn and the greater your personal storehouse of varying perceptions will grow.
2. *Share your perceptions and listen to the feedback you receive.* Avoid being defensive when you check your perceptions. Keep in mind that your view is a personal interpretation.
3. *Deal with contradictions—don't ignore them.* Contradictions are often predictable once you recognize their origin—so gather them, look at them, reconcile them when you can, and understand why you can't when you can't.
4. *Continue gathering information on a subject, even after you have reached a decision.* Recognize that what you know is only a fraction of what there is to know. Stay open to new information.

To be open-minded, you must accept change and be willing to adjust your thoughts and beliefs. There is no point in gathering new information if you don't intend to evaluate it and act on it.

Increase Empathy

To improve your perception of other people, you must strive to increase your empathy, your ability to experience the world as others do. Of course, you can never see things exactly as someone else would, but trying is important. When you empathize with another person, her or his experience becomes your own, you understand her or his reasons for behaving and feeling in particular ways, and you understand these things *as the other person understands them.* The goal is something like the Vulcan mind-meld that Mr. Spock performs occasionally on *Star Trek.* Placing his fingertips on another's head, he and the other become one, and Spock comes to know the other person (or, in some cases, the other thing) as the other person knows *himself or herself.*

Although earth-bound creatures will never perform a Vulcan mind-meld, empathy may be achieved in other ways. For example, groups of handicapped students have invited those who can walk to "spend the day paralyzed from the waist down," or those who can see to "spend the day blind," or those who can hear to "spend the day deaf." With the help of wheelchairs, blindfolds, and earplugs, you can enlarge your own perception of the world.

Incorrect assumptions about another person may also be revealed by engaging in role reversal. Switch positions with someone with whom you have an ongoing argument, regardless of what the argument is about, and try to see the situation from the other's perspective. What does this person think, feel, and want? How does this person see you in the situation and interpret your behaviors? Empathy for the other person's position should provide insights that allow you to resolve your differences.

Unless you are a member of a helping profession—a psychologist, social worker, or nurse, for instance—your ability to empathize probably does not extend too far beyond the people with whom you share your most personal relationships. Empathy requires a great deal of information about the other person, information gathered open-mindedly over long periods of time. The questions posed in Skill Checkup 5.4 should help you gather the information necessary to assess the empathy in one of your friendships.

SKILL CHECKUP 5.4

Assessing Empathy in Friendship

The following questions can help you determine the degree to which empathy is part of a friendship.

1. Does your friend understand most of what you say?

2. Does your friend understand how you feel?

3. Does your friend appreciate what your experiences feel like to you?

4. Does your friend try to see things through your eyes?

5. Does your friend ask you questions about what your experiences mean to you?

6. Does your friend ask you questions about what you're thinking?

7. Does your friend ask you questions about how you're feeling?

Have your friend answer the same questions. Compare your answers. The results might well contribute to greater empathy in your relationship.

STRESS AND COMMUNICATION

What you select to perceive, together with how you organize and interpret it, is up to you. Events in the world are neither good nor bad, *but your perception makes them one or the other*. Nothing inherent in any event makes it *anything*: what matters is your perception of the event. *You* determine what an event means for you and, in turn, what it means for you determines your reaction.

How would you perceive the following series of events?

It's 7:00 *A.M.* and the alarm jars you out of a restless sleep. You remind yourself that it is Tuesday, which means you must attend three classes and work for four hours after school. Today you must also take a test and find out about the raise you were promised. And, to top it off, you need to resolve an argument you had yesterday with your friend. You stare at your face in the mirror and don't know whether to laugh or cry.

Would you define this situation with words such as *unbearable* or *overwhelming* and choose to cry? Would you call it *challenging* or *exciting* and begin to prepare yourself mentally? Or would you shrug your shoulders, see your situation as *bizarre* or *weird*, and choose to laugh?

Perhaps the word you would choose is *stressful*, an increasingly common word these days. **Stress** is the feeling of strain or pressure that arises from any event you perceive as interfering with what you consider normal.

The creation of stress is rather straightforward: (1) an event occurs, (2) you perceive it to have a particular effect on you, (3) the event is related to something you need or want, and (4) you feel strained or pressured. Consider, for example, that awful Tuesday morning. The test is a stress-triggering event. The test makes you nervous: you want a high grade on the exam so you can get a high grade in the course and feel more confident about applying to medical school. As a result, even though you studied hard, feel you have a good grasp of the material, and did fairly well on previous tests, you feel anxious and use the word *stressed* to describe yourself.

The perception of an event as stressful is important because of its consequences for you. Your reactions to stress may be relatively mild, such as gritting your teeth, biting your fingernails, or chewing pencils. They may be somewhat severe, such as insomnia, argumentativeness, over- or undereating, or using drugs to mask your feelings. They can be extremely severe, too, including withdrawal, depression, or even suicide. Although your reactions to stress may vary from another person's, stress always affects how you communicate.

Communication Indicators of Stress

Both positive and negative events may be sources of stress. For example, a test for which you feel prepared and confident and a test for which you feel unprepared and insecure may both trigger feelings of stress. In either case, you will communicate your stressful feelings through both verbal and nonverbal behavior. Knowledge Checkup 5.2 will help you identify your verbal and nonverbal indicators of stress.

KNOWLEDGE CHECKUP 5.2

Communication Indicators of Stress

Check each behavior you display when you feel pressured.

1. Talking a great deal about what you feel is pressuring you
2. Talking less than usual
3. Encouraging others to talk faster
4. Attacking people verbally
5. Using swear words
6. Making errors in grammar or pronunciation
7. Lacking quick recall or repeating yourself
8. Using vocalized pauses such as *uh, um,* and *er*
9. Using a sarcastic or nasty tone of voice
10. Emphasizing words when unnecessary
11. Speeding up at the ends of sentences
12. Using a higher pitch than usual
13. Speaking quickly
14. Drumming your fingers
15. Clenching your fists
16. Clenching your jaw
17. Scratching repeatedly
18. Biting your nails
19. Blinking your eyes rapidly
20. Squinting
21. Avoiding eye contact
22. Eating too much or not at all
23. Drinking or smoking more than usual
24. Perspiring or trembling hands
25. Pacing
26. Shifting your weight from foot to foot
27. Wiggling
28. Withdrawing

The first eight behaviors listed in Knowledge Checkup 5.2 are particularly common in people who feel stressed. For example, in a situation that is free of conflict, stressed people often appear self-engrossed because they tend to push conversation toward their own areas of expertise or interest (such as the source of their stress). If their attempts to dominate a discussion fail, they may remain quiet, or they may grow impatient and use a variety of interjections, such as "yes, yes, uh-huh, yes," to encourage the other person to hurry up. When you have a test, that topic tends to consume all your thoughts. Because you are anxious, talking with your roommate seems to be an either-or proposition: either you talk about the test—and you use impatient interjections to get your roommate to hurry up and change to your topic—or you don't talk at all.

In a situation that involves conflict, people who feel stressed tend to attack the other person rather than discuss the underlying issues. Also, when asked for clarification or further explanation, they often repeat exactly what they said the first time. Finally, stressed people have a tendency to swear for emphasis. Consider the following conversation in which Robert is stressed:

Jon: Where were you last night?
Robert: I told you I went to the library.
Jon: I went to look for you.
Robert: I already told you! I went to the library!
Jon: Okay, I was just asking.
Robert: I went to the *%&! library to study for that %&*! test!

Items 9 through 13 in the knowledge checkup are nonverbal reactions that affect verbal presentations. For example, a sarcastic tone narrows the possible interpretations of your message, and emphasizing the wrong words is likely to confuse your listener.

The remaining behaviors on the list are nonverbal reactions to stress that may or may not accompany verbal behavior. Many more nonverbal than verbal behaviors indicate feelings of stress, which is why hiding your perception that an event is stressful is often difficult.

Adding to our feelings of stress are the many evaluative messages we constantly send ourselves: "There's no time to relax," "I shouldn't put this off until later," "I should be busy all the time," or "I must be losing my mind because I can't remember anything."

COMMUNICATION ANXIETY

A form of stress specifically related to communication is called **communication anxiety**—the fear of engaging in communication interactions. This fear is based on both self-perceptions (Do I have the skills to communicate effectively?) and perceptions of the situation (Will the advantages from interacting outweigh the possible negative outcomes?).

KNOWLEDGE CHECKUP 5.3

Communication Anxiety[4]

Indicate the degree to which each of the following five statements applies to you.

Mark 1 if you strongly agree.
Mark 2 if you agree.
Mark 3 if you are undecided.
Mark 4 if you disagree.
Mark 5 if you strongly disagree.

There are no right or wrong answers. Work quickly so that you record only your first impressions.

1.	When communicating, I am usually calm and relaxed.	1	2	3	4	5
2.	I find the prospect of speaking mildly pleasant.	1	2	3	4	5
3.	In general, communication makes me uncomfortable.	1	2	3	4	5
4.	I don't like to use my body and voice expressively.	1	2	3	4	5
5.	When communicating, I am usually tense and nervous.	1	2	3	4	5

Add your scores for items 3, 4, and 5. This is Score A.
Add your scores for items 1 and 2. This is Score B.
(18 – Score A) + Score B = _____ Total Score

According to a national survey, a score of 14 or above indicates that you perceive yourself as more anxious about communicating than the average person.

If you suffer from communication anxiety, you tell yourself "I lack the ability and/or confidence to share my true self with someone else," "I can't interact when I'd like to," and "There's more to be lost than there is to be gained by communicating." When communication anxiety is emotionally based it is sometimes labeled **communication apprehension,** and when it is caused by a perceived lack of skills it is sometimes called **reticence.** The general term **shyness** may also be applied to those who are fearful and believe they lack communication skills.

No matter which term is selected, once you believe yourself to be communicatively anxious, you act accordingly. You may not think others take you seriously so you are afraid to seek help; you therefore become increasingly isolated, nonassertive, and withdrawn. Severe sufferers feel stressed even when just *thinking* about speaking. Communication anxiety is not an isolated phenomenon. Between 80 and 93 percent of all people feel some communication anxiety, and 15 to 20 percent of all college students have high levels of communication anxiety.[5]

Communication Anxiety and You

So far our discussion of communication anxiety has centered on people in general, with only a bit of attention to you in Knowledge Checkup 5.3. To give you even more personal insight, let's further test your anxiety quotient. Complete Knowledge Checkup 5.4.

KNOWLEDGE CHECKUP 5.4

How I See Myself

Check the one statement that best describes you.

_____ **1.** I am shy, and people usually see me as shy.
_____ **2.** I am shy, but people usually don't see me as shy.
_____ **3.** I am not shy, but people usually see me as shy.
_____ **4.** I am not shy, and people usually don't see me as shy.

If you checked the first statement, you probably perceive yourself as publicly shy. The second statement is often selected by people who are privately shy. If you selected the third option, you probably perceive yourself as generally quiet, but not actually shy. If you selected the fourth, you probably don't experience much, if any, anxiety in communication situations.

Public and Private Shyness

Some people are publicly shy; others are privately shy. Publicly anxious people display their shyness by avoiding eye contact, blushing, perspiring, or speaking in a quavering voice. Privately shy people mentally resist active communication, but seldom show outward signs of stress such as fingernail biting or sweaty palms. Famous people who admit to being privately shy include Carol Burnett;

Johnny Carson; Diana, Princess of Wales; and Barbara Walters. Each has gained success by learning to cope with anxiety.

Situational Shyness

Communication anxiety can be situational or general. Some people show anxiety in only one or a few communication contexts. For example, you may fear giving public speeches, but be totally at ease speaking with one other person, whether a friend or a stranger, or interacting in a small group. Or you may fear speaking with one person at a time, but have little anxiety about giving a public address.

Causes of Communication Anxiety

Communication apprehension seems to stem from authoritarianism—being raised in an authoritarian home, having attended authoritarian schools, and being exposed to an authoritarian religion.[6] These influential sources may have taught you to control what you say or emphasized the importance of being "seen but not heard." In addition, if your parents were shy, there is a 70 percent chance that you are shy.

Reticence often results when schools fail to teach students how to organize ideas or develop effective speaking and listening skills. Or it may come from parents who restrict their children's exposure to the question and answer process and thus stymie their children's normal language play and development of basic communication skills.

Communicatively anxious people tend to fear rejection, criticism, and imperfection. The primary fear of college students who experience communication anxiety is not being loved. Adult sufferers say that their greatest negative feelings arise from operating in a world they perceive as unfair.

Gender is not significant in communication anxiety. Although males tend to be shyer and females tend to have more public speaking anxiety, there seem to be few consistent differences between the sexes.

The Effects of Communication Anxiety

Most people with communication anxiety believe that they suffer negative consequences. Many feel that they have given up control of themselves to someone else or to some unknown force—that they are puppets whose strings are being pulled by their master, *fear*.

There are some demonstrated effects of communication anxiety. In classroom situations, communicatively anxious students volunteer rarely, if at all. They often drop classes that require oral communication or miss class when oral participation is necessary. These patterns can affect learning and grades.

Some anxious students even fail to graduate with only one requirement to complete—passing a speech communication course.

People with communication anxiety often choose college majors that require few, if any, oral presentations, such as research or technical fields. In the work place, if advancement depends on participating orally—whether one-on-one, in a group, or in a public setting—they may miss promotions and pay increases because they are handicapped by fear.

Dealing with Communication Anxiety

Communication anxiety is curable because it hinges on perceptions, which can be altered. If you believe that you lack communication skills, you can change that perception permanently by acquiring the necessary skills and practicing their use. Taking classes or workshops in assertiveness, public speaking, decision making, group action, and communicating with friends and strangers should help you to begin eliminating your anxiety. The more you learn, prepare, practice, and gain comfort with new and better skills, the less anxiety you will feel.

The belief that communication situations offer more disadvantages than advantages will also change as you develop new skills and change your focus from the negative to the positive. Because what you select to perceive is your choice, you can consciously decide to open yourself up to the positive consequences of your communication.

"This is nothing. When I was your age the snow was so deep it came up to my chin!"
©1979 Redbook Magazine and Jerry Marcus

Whether you find this cartoon funny or not tells as much about you as the cartoon.

1. Analyze the cartoon from the perspective of someone who finds it funny by applying the notions of selective perception, selective organization, and selective interpretation. Then do the same analysis for someone who does not find the cartoon funny. How could the same cartoon get two different reactions?

2. What could the taller of the two cartoon characters do to increase his perceptual accuracy?

3. What elements of this cartoon did you selectively perceive, organize, and interpret? For example, did you selectively interpret the relationship between the two characters as that of father and child? Did you perceive the two characters as having particular traits (for example, did you see the taller one as "stupid" and the shorter one as "amazed")?

4. How do your perceptions of the cartoon reflect who you are?

5. Assume that the shorter character perceives the situation as stressful. What communication behaviors might this person exhibit?

6. Assume that the shorter character tells you, "I think I'm lacking in communication skills." What behaviors might this person exhibit? What behavior might this person not exhibit? What are the possible consequences of this person's communication anxiety? How could the anxiety be overcome?

NOTES

1. For a discussion of implicit personality theory, see: Seymour Rosenberg and Andrea Sedlak, "Structural Representations of Implicit Personality Theory," in *Advances in Experimental Social Psychology*, vol. 6, ed. Leonard Berkowitz (New York: Academic Press, 1972), pp. 235–97.

2. The original research that considered how traits interact to form total impressions and the importance of central traits in the process was conducted by Solomon Asch, in Asch, "Forming Impressions of Personality," *Journal of Abnormal and Social Psychology* 41 (1946): 258–90.

3. These exercises are adapted from ones developed by Noller, Parnes, and Biondi. For more information and other exercises designed to develop creativity, see: Ruth B. Noller, Sidney J. Parnes, and Angelo M. Biondi, *Creative Actionbook* (New York: Charles Scribner's Sons, 1976).

4. The five items presented here are adapted from the "general" category of the *Communication Apprehension in Generalized Contexts Scale*. Virginia P. Richmond and James C. McCroskey, *Communication: Apprehension, Avoidance, and Effectiveness* (Scottsdale, AZ: Gorsuch, 1985).

5. Philip Zimbardo, *Shyness: What It Is; What to Do About It* (Reading, MA: Addison-Wesley, 1977), pp. 13–14.

6. For a discussion of the research supporting these and other causes of communication apprehension, see: Gerald M. Phillips, *Help for Shy People* (Englewood Cliffs, NJ: Prentice Hall, 1981), especially chapters 3 and 4.

FOR FURTHER INVESTIGATION

Albrecht, K. *Stress and the Manager.* Englewood Cliffs, NJ: Prentice Hall, 1979.

Asch, Solomon E. "Forming Impressions of Personality." *Journal of Abnormal and Social Psychology* 41 (1946): 258–90.

Communication Education 31 (1982): entire issue.

Delia, Jesse G. "Change of Meaning Processes in Impression Formation." *Communication Monographs* 43 (1976): 142–57.

International Communication Apprehension Newsletter (available from Dr. Arden Watson, The Pennsylvania State University, Delaware County Campus, 25 Yersley Mill Road, Media, PA 19063).

Journal of Human Stress.

Kelley, Harold H. "The Process of Causal Attribution." *American Psychologist* 28 (1973): 107–28.

Phillips, Gerald M. *Help for Shy People.* Englewood Cliffs, NJ: Prentice Hall, 1981.

Pines, Ayala M., Eliot Aronson, and Ditsa Kafry. *Burnout.* New York: Free Press, 1981.

Richmond, Virginia P., and James C. McCroskey. *Communication: Apprehension, Avoidance, and Effectiveness.* Scottsdale, AZ: Gorsuch, 1985.

Schneider, David L., Albert H. Hastorf, and Phoebe C. Ellsworth. *Person Perception,* 2d ed. Reading, MA: Addison-Wesley, 1979.

Sillars, Alan J. "Attributions and Communication in Roommate Conflicts." *Communication Monographs* 47 (1980): 180–200.

Snyder, Mark E. "Self-Fulfilling Social Stereotypes." *Psychology Today* 16 (July 1982): 60–68.

Sylvester, Sandra. *Living with Stress.* Kansas City, MO: National Catholic Reporter Publishing, 1985.

Zimbardo, Phillip. *Shyness: What It Is; What To Do About It.* Reading, MA: Addison-Wesley, 1977.

Zimbardo, Phillip, and Shirley Radl. *The Shyness Workbook.* New York: A and W Visual Library, 1979.

CHAPTER 6

▶ # *Effective Listening*

*This chapter on effective listening will help you to practice and develop communication competencies that fall into three broad areas: (1) **communication codes,** which include listening effectively to spoken English; (2) **oral message evaluation,** such as identifying main ideas and recognizing when someone does not understand your message; and (3) **basic speech communication skills,** such as asking questions, obtaining information, and summarizing messages. Specifically, the competencies you will gain will enable you to do the following:*

▶ *Identify your own listening patterns.*
▶ *Define listening and summarize the four stages of the listening process.*
▶ *Describe the three levels of listening.*
▶ *Explain the importance of listening as part of the communication process.*
▶ *List some of the barriers to good listening.*
▶ *Apply several techniques for improving your listening skills, including methods for focusing your attention, organizing material, and providing feedback.*
▶ *Use empathic listening skills.*

Close you eyes for a few minutes and listen to the sounds around you. What did you hear? Did you hear sounds that you didn't hear before you closed your eyes and concentrated?

What sounds can you identify? Did you hear any meaningless sounds? Did you hear sounds you didn't expect to hear?

Was it easy to listen with your eyes closed, or did thoughts distract you? What were you thinking? Were questions running through your head, such as "Why am I doing this?" Were you distracted by feelings, such as hunger or thirst? What barriers to effective listening did you encounter?

Close your eyes again for a few minutes and listen once more to the sounds around you. Mull over the questions you were just asked. Evaluate your experience: How well did you listen? That is, how well did you take information gathered through your sense of hearing and give it meaning? What evidence do you have to support your conclusion?

INVESTIGATING YOUR LISTENING PATTERNS

Each of us follows a general pattern while listening. Use Knowledge Checkup 6.1 to investigate your personal listening patterns.

KNOWLEDGE CHECKUP 6.1

Listening Self-Evaluation[1]

How often do you find yourself engaging in the following listening habits?

Write 1 if you almost always (91–100 percent of the time) engage in the habit.
Write 2 if you usually (71–90 percent of the time) engage in the habit.
Write 3 if you sometimes (31–70 percent of the time) engage in the habit.
Write 4 if you seldom (11–30 percent of the time) engage in the habit.
Write 5 if you almost never (0–10 percent of the time) engage in the habit.

_____ 1. I pay attention primarily to what the speaker is saying and give little attention to what the speaker is doing.
_____ 2. I let the speaker's lack of organization get in the way of my listening.
_____ 3. I interrupt if I have something I want to say.
_____ 4. I stop listening when I think I understand the idea, whether or not the speaker has finished.

_____ **5.** I fail to repeat what has been said before I react.
_____ **6.** I give little verbal or nonverbal feedback to the speaker.
_____ **7.** I pay attention only to the words and ignore the tone and pitch being used.
_____ **8.** I let emotionally charged words make me angry.
_____ **9.** If I consider the subject boring, I stop paying attention.
_____ **10.** I criticize the speaker's delivery or mannerisms.
_____ **11.** I do not take notes during lectures and phone calls.
_____ **12.** I let distractions interfere with my concentration.
_____ **13.** I do not recognize when I am too upset or tired to listen.
_____ **14.** I slump in my chair when listening in class.
_____ **15.** I try to give advice when someone is telling me his or her problems.

This quiz is based on the skills you need to be a good listener. Add the numbers you assigned to the fifteen items. This is your total Listening Self-Evaluation score. The average score is 54. Is yours higher or lower? By itself, your total score is less important than your responses to the individual items. Items on which you rated yourself 1, 2, or 3 indicate areas in which you need to improve.

Four basic principles should guide your study of listening:

1. _Poor listening cannot be remedied quickly._ Sharpening your listening skills requires patience and practice. Only you can put in the practice you need to become a skilled listener.

2. _There is no single "best" listening strategy._ Good listeners know how to decipher what various speakers mean in varying situations, and different situations require different listening strategies. Some speakers don't organize their ideas well; others do. Some realize that they must repeat their main ideas to ensure understanding; others ramble on without systematic repetition. Some people give you time to think about what they've said; others move rapidly ahead. Some speakers choose simple and clear words; others intentionally use language to confuse and confound. Regardless of the speaker's strengths and weaknesses, it is the listener's responsibility to adapt and to understand.

3. _Good listening depends on finding some personal benefit in the speaker's words._ Because listening is hard work, you need to find some reason for paying attention.

4. _When you listen, you must actively participate in the communication process._ You have a responsibility to interpret what's said, assess its value, decide how to use it, and respond accordingly.

What Is Listening?

Listening is the active process of receiving, attending to, and assigning meaning to sounds. It is *active* because it involves taking information from speakers, processing it, giving meaning to it, and, when appropriate, encouraging the continuation of communication by giving appropriate feedback.

Listening is the most important communication skill. There is no other skill that could make you as well informed and desirable as a companion. Listening is the key skill for becoming a good communicator, an effective counselor, and a skilled leader.

Despite its great value, listening is probably the most underrated of the sensory skills. Even though you spend at least 40 percent of your time listening, you probably received less than half a year of formal listening training in all of elementary and secondary school.[2] Compare that short time to the usual six to eight years devoted to formal reading instruction, twelve years to writing, and one year to speaking. Most people spend only about 9 percent of their time writing, 16 percent reading, and 35 percent speaking, so for your most used skill, you received the least training. Is it any wonder that the average American's listening skills are only about 25 percent as effective as they could be?[3]

So little emphasis is placed on listening training in the schools because most people assume that normal hearing equals good listening. In fact, hearing and listening are not the same. Hearing is merely the biological act of receiving sounds, while listening is a much more active process.

Listening is a learned skill. The effectiveness of your listening often depends on what is going on in your mind as well as on what is going on around you. You must learn to participate both mentally and physically in the communicative transaction. You must learn to listen in different ways at different times. And you must learn to listen to different people in different ways.

The Stages of Listening

The process of listening, of actively receiving sounds, usually proceeds through four stages: sensing, understanding, evaluating, and responding.

The Sensing Stage

First, you sense the message. Someone speaks, you hear the sounds, and, in some cases, you see actions that clarify or enhance the sounds.

The Understanding Stage

If the sounds are familiar, you interpret them and understanding takes place. If a person says "T-A-B-L-E" and if you understand standard American English, you combine the letters into the word *table* and picture an object with a flat surface and four legs. You comprehend the intent of the sounds as they combine. If someone points at a table and says the word, you have a further clue to the intended message.

The Evaluating Stage

After you understand the message, you may go through a stage in which you appraise it. If a speaker says, "Let's sit down at the table and talk," you may evaluate the message ("This is a good suggestion" or "This is a bad suggestion") and decide how you are going to respond ("I think I'll agree" or "I think I'll refuse").

The Responding Stage

In the responding stage, you do something with the message. For example, you may sit down at the table, indicating that you understand the message and choose to positively evaluate the invitation. Or you may say, "I don't want to sit down and talk right now," showing that you understand the message but do not want to accept the invitation. Even ignoring the message is a response, although an ambiguous one. It leaves the speaker wondering whether the message was received, whether it was understood, and whether the lack of response should be taken as an insult.

The Levels of Listening

There are three levels of listening, each representing a different degree of effectiveness. At the third level is inefficient listening, at the second level is minimal listening, and at the first level is good listening.

Level 3 Listening

Level 3 listening is characterized by listening now and then. You tune in and tune out, aware of the presence of others but mainly absorbed in your own thoughts.

You may be more interested in what you want to say than in what the other person is saying, listening only for pauses that will let you take control of the conversation. You may sit passively and offer little feedback to the speaker. You may think about unrelated matters and make little effort to perceive the message. In short, you are not paying attention to the speaker.

Level 3 listening can produce misunderstandings, hurt feelings, confused instructions, loss of important information, embarrassment, and frustration.

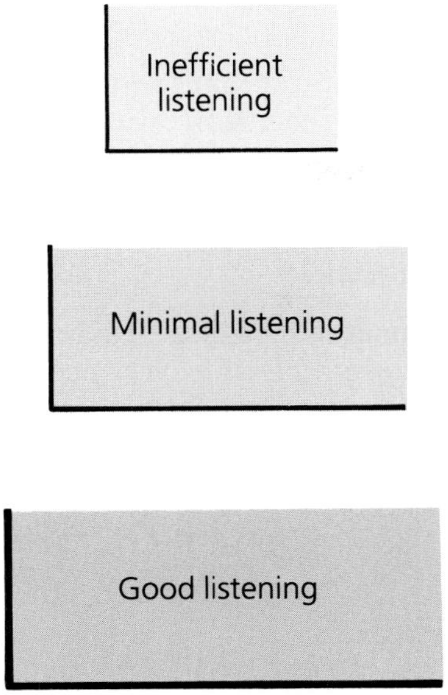

▶ **FIGURE 6.1**   The Three Levels of Listening

Level 2 Listening

In Level 2 listening, you hear words and sounds but do not actively try to grasp anything beyond surface meanings. Typical of this level is tuning out after you think you have enough information to guess the speaker's intent. As a result, you may grasp the basic meaning of the message, but miss the emotion and feeling and thus fail to comprehend the full content.

Level 2 listeners often seem emotionally detached from a conversation. Misunderstandings may occur because the listener often misses how the meaning of what is said is modified by the way in which it is said.

Level 1 Listening

Level 1 listening is active listening. You listen for main and supporting ideas, acknowledge and respond, give appropriate feedback, and pay attention to the speaker's total communication. In other words, a Level 1 listener is concerned about the content, the intent, and the feelings of the sender's message.

The Reasons for Listening

Listening is an important communication skill because it has so many uses. You listen for comprehension, appreciation, identification, evaluation, and to empathize and to gain self-understanding.

Comprehension

Comprehension involves grasping the meaning of the sounds you hear. Through comprehension you acquire information, ideas, and others' viewpoints. Comprehension is required in the classroom, at work, at home, and in social settings. By comprehending the messages you receive you gain new ideas, learn new skills, test ideas, and expand your perspective.

Appreciation

You listen appreciatively to music, to the sounds of nature, and to the actor's voice. Appreciative listening differs from comprehension because your purpose is not to gain information per se but to relax or to feel a particular way, such as peaceful, stimulated, or excited.

Identification

A doctor listens to the sound of a patient's heart to detect abnormality. A mechanic concentrates on the sounds of an engine to determine whether the car is running smoothly. You listen to the pitch of someone's voice to discern tension or relaxation. The sound of the wind, the roll of the thunder, and the crash of the waves all supply useful information about the probable severity of an oncoming storm.

Evaluation

You evaluate what is being said by carefully analyzing whether the ideas are acceptable to you, meet your expectations, and are logical. You evaluate the messages of commercials, salespeople, friends, and family members. In a work environment, whether you are an employer or an employee, you constantly evaluate and are evaluated.

Empathy

One of the most overlooked and underrated uses of listening is empathy—the ability to experience the world as others do. The easiest way to think of your role as an empathic listener is to picture yourself as a mirror. As someone explains her or his concerns, stressors, or conflicts, you reflect what you are hearing by restating the ideas in your own words. Usually, the person who seeks an empathic listener needs reflection, not advice. Empathic listening can reduce tensions, help solve problems, encourage cooperation, and promote good communication.

Self-Understanding

Listening to others' observations about you can lead to self-understanding and personal growth. Similarly, listening to yourself talk about who you are provides important data for self-analysis. Just by listening to yourself talk, you may discover that you feel more strongly about a topic than you had realized. You may become more intense than you would have predicted, or you may bring up arguments that you didn't realize were important to you.

BARRIERS TO EFFECTIVE LISTENING

To become a good listener, you must be aware of the barriers that may interfere with the accurate reception of messages. Knowledge Checkup 6.2 will help you answer the question "How can I tell if I'm not listening?"

KNOWLEDGE CHECKUP 6.2

Your Nonlistening Signals

Which of the following are your signals that you aren't listening to a speaker?

     1. I drum my fingers on my arm or on a solid surface.
     2. I slouch down in the chair if I am seated.
     3. I glance at my watch.
     4. I take off my glasses and play with them, or I play with some other object, such as a paper clip or pencil.
     5. I stare into space.
     6. I turn slightly away from the speaker.
     7. I yawn, sigh, or show other signs of boredom.
     8. I continually glance down at the floor or up at the ceiling.
     9. I cross my arms in front of my body.
    10. I engage in preening behaviors, such as smoothing my hair, cleaning my fingernails, or straightening my clothing.

Nonlistening Cues

You undoubtedly checked several items on the list. If you are aware of the behaviors that indicate you aren't listening, you can stop them and refocus your attention on the speaker. For example, if you observe yourself yawning and realize that you have quit listening because you're bored, stop yawning, focus on what the speaker is saying, and ask yourself, "Why is this material important for me?" Even if you don't find the material interesting, there may be important reasons for listening, such as to prepare for an upcoming test or to avoid appearing rude.

Overloading

One barrier to good listening is **overloading,** feeling as if you couldn't possibly listen anymore because you already have too much information to retain. You are capable of grasping and retaining only a limited number of ideas at any given moment. The human brain works like a computer in that it receives information, stores it, and then responds when the proper stimulus activates the retrieval process. Similar to a computer, the human brain can in effect overload and "blow a circuit." Receiving too much information at one time, becoming upset by certain messages, and feeling out of control because of the situation or the participants can cause poor listening. Sometimes you may need to tell the sender that you just can't listen any longer, or you may need to leave the receiving environment. Other times you may have no choice but to continue listening.

Feeling overloaded can be avoided in several ways. As explained later in this chapter, learning how to focus your attention and organize material, besides improving your listening skills in general, can be particularly useful for overcoming feelings of overload.

Arguing with the Speaker's Logic

If a speaker's ideas seem illogical or if the information doesn't seem valid, you may start to doubt the value of listening. For example, you may react negatively when you hear the word *always* but know there are exceptions, or when you realize that no evidence supports a conclusion, or when the speaker states that "everyone knows" but doesn't specify who "everyone" is. Nonetheless, to stop listening, or to listen without paying close attention, may not be the best response. Keeping an open mind and withholding final judgment will enable you to gather new information, some of which may be useful. There is always time to reject what a speaker has to say *after* you listen!

Responding to Emotionally Loaded Words

How do you feel when someone says to you:[4]

> "What you should have done was...."
> "You have to...."

"Only someone stupid like you would...."
"If you had done it my way...."
"See, I told you that would happen!"
"You do this all the time [sigh]."
"Your brother/sister always...."
"Are you going to be on time for a change?"

Such judgmental words and phrases—called **red flags**—can evoke strong emotions and interfere with your willingness and ability to listen. If, for example, you have strong feelings against abortion and your communication partner mentions that she is in favor of abortion, you may immediately turn off the rest of her message.

Red flags also include people who provoke strong negative reactions. For example, merely seeing someone with whom you're having an ongoing argument may be enough to trigger thoughts that interfere with your ability to listen. Your mind may concentrate on the last argument, how to approach the person, or how to escape with dignity.

Similarly, some topics may arouse negative emotions regardless of how they are discussed. For example, your feelings against the death penalty may be so strong that any mention of the topic—even by someone who agrees with you—interferes with your ability to listen.

In contrast, **green flag words** stir up positive feelings, although they too may interfere with listening. If you are an avid skier and the person you are conversing with says that he has recently been in Vail, Colorado, your mind might switch to a scene of yourself skiing down a beautiful, snow-covered mountain. Green light words for college students may include *spring break, party,* and *graduation.*

Green flags also include people who trigger strong positive emotions that interfere with your ability to listen. For example, meeting an old friend whom you haven't seen in years may cause such strong positive feelings that you fail to listen when she tells you she has only a few minutes to talk. Similarly, some topics may arouse positive emotions. For instance, your positive feelings toward parenthood may be so strong that you fail to listen to your acquaintance's reasons for deciding not to have children.

Both red and green flags lead you to stop actively participating in the listening act. Being aware of your red and green flags is the first step in combating their interference.

KNOWLEDGE CHECKUP 6.3

Your Emotional Triggers[5]

Identify your red and green flags by writing at least two items that cause you to react very positively or negatively.

Words and phrases	Positive	Negative
People		
Issues (topics)		

Once you are aware of some of your red and green flags, you can make a conscious effort to stop yourself from daydreaming or becoming irritated. You won't always be successful, but you can make progress.

Failing to Receive the Whole Message

Have you ever filled out an application form and found that on the line that said "Name" you wrote your first and last names in sequence before you saw that the directions said, "Print last name first"? This is an example of not allowing yourself to receive the whole message. You may also do this when you listen.

Read the following statement:

The cow jump over
over the noon.

Now go back. Did you read *jump* or *jumped*? Did you see both occurrences of the word *over*? Did you read *noon* or *moon*? Because you are probably familiar with the nursery rhyme "Hey Diddle, Diddle," you may not have needed more than the first two words to "know" what followed. If you knew the rhyme but caught all the deviations, you are probably alert to the importance of paying attention to an entire message. If not, you need to practice receiving entire messages before jumping to conclusions.

External Distractions

Listeners may have problems receiving a message if there are **external distractions**—people, objects, or events in the environment that divert attention. Have you ever had difficulty receiving a message when a lot of people were talking, when machinery such as a dishwasher was running, or when the television set was on? External distractors are not limited to environmental noise. You may be distracted by a speaker's clothing, dialect, pronunciation, or poor grammar, or by the general setting. One reason teachers avoid holding classes outdoors is that the many external distractors—people walking by, the weather, and so on—interfere with good listening.

External distractors are usually obvious and, once pointed out, easy to eliminate. A change of location may be enough to reduce noise or remove distractions, and recognizing that pronunciation and poor grammar are not good enough reasons to stop listening usually eliminates them as problems.

Internal Distractors

In comparison to external distractions, **internal distractors,** attention diverters that occur within you, are more difficult to recognize and often are more difficult to eliminate. Earlier you closed your eyes and listened to the sounds in your environment. Did any thoughts distract you? If so, they were internal distractors—they occurred within you and kept you from listening effectively. A study of what students think about during a lecture found that only 20 percent actually pay attention to the message, and only 12 percent concentrate fully. The others were thinking erotic thoughts, reminiscing, worrying, and so on.[6] Hunger, having the flu, and an itch on your left leg are all internal distractors.

Two products of internal distractors are egospeaking and daydreaming. **Egospeaking** is jumping into a communicative transaction because you have something you want to say, or because you feel that what you have to say is more important or more interesting than what the other person is saying. Egospeaking not only stops you from receiving the whole message, it irritates others because it is disrespectful. In addition, the moment you decide (consciously or unconsciously) to interrupt, you stop listening.

Once you realize what egospeaking is, you should be able to control it. Several physical clues will help you detect when you are about to egospeak. When most people start to interrupt, they literally jump into the conversation by raising their bodies, leaning forward, and moving their arms and hands upward, often pointing with a finger. If you catch yourself making such motions while someone else is talking, you are probably about to egospeak. Another way to detect that you are egospeaking is to listen to yourself. If you tend to enter conversations with such phrases as "That's interesting, but...," or "Uh-huh, but what happened to me was...," or if people ask, "What does that have to do with what we're talking about?" you are probably egospeaking. Egospeaking becomes a problem if it is a typical feature of your communication because if you egospeak often, you are probably not getting as much out of listening as you could.

Daydreaming, being lost in your own thoughts, is another common barrier to effective listening. When you daydream you may still be hearing sounds, but instead of focusing on what is being said you are floating in mental space—thinking of what you'll make for dinner, an upcoming test, your weekend plans, or anything else that, at that moment, strikes you as more interesting than the speaker's message.

To stop daydreaming you need to recognize that you are doing it, identify what set you off, and in the future try to avoid the action or situation that stimulated it. For example, were you slumping in your chair? Were you looking out the window? Did a green or a red flag send your thoughts flying? Keeping in mind that the speaker's message is important for you may help you avoid daydreaming.

MAKING LISTENING WORK FOR YOU

Several techniques can help you avoid or overcome barriers to effective listening. By learning to focus your attention, organize what you hear, receive the whole message, paraphrase the speaker's message, and provide the speaker with feedback, you can take an active role in the communication process and, as a result, become a more skilled listener.

Focusing Attention

To be a good listener, you must know how to focus attention on the speaker. This focusing skill helps in two ways: it allows you to pick up nonverbal cues and it shows the sender that you are paying attention.

People who wear glasses often say that they can't hear as well without their glasses. Although this may strike you as odd, it is probably true because without their glasses, some receivers may miss a speaker's facial expressions, gestures, and body positions. As a result, they may miss much of the total message.

By facing a speaker and watching carefully as she talks, you will catch both obvious and subtle cues about her intentions and emotions. Noting such factors as her breathing patterns, facial color, leg and arm positions, finger movements, and physical distance will help you to interpret her message.

Paraphrasing

Listening with the intent of **paraphrasing**, restating the speaker's message in your own words, will force you to focus on the message being presented. Indeed, one of the most effective ways of checking whether you have received a message is to repeat it back. Restating not only gives you a chance to check the ideas you have received but also informs the other person that you are listening. Given how rare good listening is, paraphrasing to demonstrate your attentiveness can be a great compliment. In addition, if you force yourself to paraphrase, you will find you must listen to the entire message without interrupting.

Paraphrasing is an excellent device to use in telephone conversations. Repeating the name and number of a caller who is leaving a message makes you focus on important details and note them accurately. Restating the details of an order, the directions for how to get someplace, or what a caller wants saves time in the long run by eliminating unnecessary mistakes.

Skilled paraphrasers repeat only the speaker's general idea—not the entire message. Paraphrasing starters include "It sounds as if you…," "You seem to be saying…," "It appears to me that you believe…," "What I perceive is…," "What I heard you say was…," and "So you believe that…." When paraphrasing is done well, it is the best way to prove that you are focusing on the speaker and listening thoughtfully.

Taking Notes

Some people find that taking notes improves their listening because it requires them to concentrate on what the speaker is saying. Since an average sender speaks 150 words per minute (about half the number of words on a typed, double-spaced page) and an average receiver can grasp meaning at rates as high as 300 words per minute, listeners should have time to jot down a speaker's ideas.[7]

To make your notes most useful, concentrate on the main ideas and supporting evidence. Write down only what is necessary to remember the most important information, use key words, and avoid writing complete sentences or every word the speaker says. By putting the ideas in your own words, you can check your understanding and immediately review the speaker's message.

Note-taking is a skill that must be practiced. It should be an automatic part of your listening routine in class, while talking on the phone, and when you feel you can't concentrate on or remember a spoken message without some reinforcement.

Repeating

Another way to focus your attention and increase your comprehension is by repeating. For example, when a person is introduced to you, focus your attention on the name and immediately repeat it by saying something like, "It's nice to meet you, Marcia." Call the person by name several times during your conversation. Then, when departing, repeat the name again. The more you repeat the name and look at the person, the stronger your memory is likely to be.

Physically Paying Attention

Most people don't realize how much their bodies reflect whether they're focusing on what is being said. For example, when you're interested in what another person is saying, you lean forward; when you're enthusiastic about an idea, your posture straightens; and when you're disturbed by what is being said, your body tightens.

Good listeners recognize that sometimes they must change body position in order to focus more intently. Think of your body as an auto engine. If you drive a gear-shift car, you know that at certain times you need to upshift or downshift. You need more engine power to get up a hill and less to cruise comfortably down a flat highway. Similarly, in listening, you must upshift or downshift your body when it needs a change in power. Level 3 listening doesn't take a lot of effort; much like easy driving, third gear will do. Level 2 listening takes more power, and Level 1 requires great concentration and physical involvement. Sitting or standing upright with your eyes on the speaker are your most powerful listening positions. They force you to focus all your attention on the speaker and the immediate situation.

Right now, while you are reading this book, sit up straight, center all your attention on the words you are reading, ignore any outside sounds, and underline the key words on this page. You will find that your power of concentration increases immediately because you have, in effect, shifted into first gear. Stay in this position as long as necessary to grasp the material you are reading. Once you have identified the general trend, shift out of first gear. (It helps to know that in writing and speaking, the writer or speaker usually makes a statement and then clarifies by defining terms and giving examples. You may need first gear for the statement, second gear for the definition, and, if you understand what is being said, third gear for the examples.) Shift back to first when a new idea is presented. When you are not in first gear you can relax your body, but you should still stay alert (Level 2 listening, second gear). Because active listening is hard work, it is tiring to maintain maximum alertness. Certain activities, such as appreciative listening, usually require only third gear. In contrast, listening for comprehension, as in class lectures, usually requires frequent shifting from gear to gear. Such shifts do not take place automatically. You must psychologically and physically shift gears for yourself during the act of listening.

Organizing Material

You can help yourself remember what is said by using three organizing techniques: chunking, ordering, and reordering.

Chunking

Chunking is the grouping of bits of information according to a mutual relationship. This allows you to condense information for easier recall. For example, while discussing a story in an American literature class, you could group the terms that describe each character so that later you remember each person's physical and emotional description rather than random details.

Ordering

Ordering is the arranging of bits of information into a systematic sequence. Thus, in chemistry class you can more easily remember a process by organizing it into a step-by-step progression. For example, first, get the equipment for the experiment; second, get the necessary chemicals; third, study the lab manual to determine the order in which the chemicals are mixed; and fourth, mix the chemicals.

Reordering

Reordering is the changing of an existing system of organizing information so that a new or different sequence is developed. Reordering is useful when you have difficulty remembering material in the sequence in which it is presented. For example, rather than remembering the causes of World War I by dates, you might remember them according to the causes in each country going from west to east (England, France, Germany, and Austria-Hungary).

SKILL CHECKUP 6.1

Chunking, Ordering, and Reordering

1. Chunk the following: apples, peas, carrots, pears, string beans, lemons, limes, radishes

2. Chunk these: Detroit, St. Louis, Mississippi, Pennsylvania, Denver, California, Miami, Memphis, Florida

3. Order these: World War I, Spanish American War, American Revolutionary War, Civil War, World War II, Vietnam Conflict

4. Order these: Virginia, Colorado, Arizona, Florida, Hawaii, Kansas, Louisiana, Delaware, Georgia, New York, Michigan

5. Reorder your answer for item 4

6. Reorder these alphabetically listed cities: Ann Arbor, Michigan; Cleveland, Ohio; Columbus, Ohio; Dayton, Ohio; Detroit, Michigan; Flint, Michigan; Toledo, Ohio; Traverse City, Michigan

Possible answers

1. Fruits (apples, pears, lemons, limes) and vegetables (peas, carrots, string beans, radishes)
2. Cities (Detroit, St. Louis, Denver, Miami, Memphis) and states (Mississippi, Pennsylvania, California, Florida)
3. American Revolutionary War, Civil War, Spanish American War, World War I, World War II, Vietnam Conflict
4. Arizona, Colorado, Delaware, Florida, Georgia, Hawaii, Kansas, Louisiana, Michigan, New York, Virginia (alphabetical order by first letter)

5. Other methods could be spatial—going from the west coast to the east or vice versa, or from the largest population total to the smallest or vice versa

6. Among the many possibilities would be to chunk the cities by state: Ohio—Cleveland, Columbus, Dayton, Toledo; Michigan—Ann Arbor, Detroit, Flint, Traverse City

Providing Feedback

As a listener, you can use feedback to stop speakers from using unfamiliar vocabulary, to discourage them from digressing and speaking in circles, to alert them to the need for examples, to make them focus on the issue, to signal the need for specifics, and to suggest that thoughts be organized more comprehensibly. The focus of Skill Checkup 6.2 is on the methods others use with you to provide feedback that indicates they're listening.

SKILL CHECKUP 6.2

Listening Feedback Cues

For each category, list several ways in which *others* let you know they are listening to you. Examples are included to help you get started.

1. Nonverbal cues: *(raised eyebrows, sustained eye contact)*

2. Verbal cues: *(uh-huh)*

3. Nonverbal and verbal cues combined: *(nodding and saying yes)*

Look at the feedback cues you just listed. Do you use them when you are listening? Obviously, if they are encouraging when others use them on you, they will be encouraging when you use them on others.

Good listeners also use questions as feedback. By listening to a speaker's message carefully, you can determine the best question to ask to ensure that you understand the true intent.

S K I L L   C H E C K U P   6 . 3

Feedback Questions

Here are some speakers' statements. Based on the problem, indicate two questions you would ask as feedback.

1. "All you have to do is connect that little thingie to the other jobbie and the engine will work." Problem: You don't understand what to do.

2. "I bought you a notebook, file cards, and some other stuff." Problem: You want to know specifically what else was purchased.

3. "I believe that the tax bill is bad for the economy!" Problem: You want to know why the speaker has this belief.

4. "There are four reasons for wearing seat belts. I think those are enough cause for passing the law." Problem: You don't know what the reasons are.

DEVELOPING EMPATHIC LISTENING SKILLS

Empathic listening, listening to understand another person's message from her or his point of view, requires attention to both the content and the feeling of the message. You must establish rapport, communicate acceptance, and encourage the speaker to continue talking.

If you already are or plan to become a helping professional, working in psychology, social services, teaching, speech therapy, law, or medicine, you must have good empathic listening skills. Empathic listening requires that you understand the basic helping process model:

INVOLVING　➤　EXPLORING　➤　RESOLVING　➤　CONCLUDING

Involving yourself in another person's life requires acting as a mirror to reflect his or her problems or needs. You then help the person to *explore* the situation. This is often accomplished by listening carefully and posing feedback questions that stimulate the other person to talk and think about his or her problem. The goal is to help the person to *resolve* the problem through either personal insight or a series of experiences that provide useful skills. In the *concluding* step, the listener summarizes the involving, exploring, and resolving steps and indicates possible future actions.

To be a good empathic listener, you should restate what is said and use verbal and nonverbal feedback to show that you understand. Only if the troubled person asks for advice or if you are trained to help people achieve behavioral change should you get involved beyond reflecting. People who try to play Dear Abby without the appropriate training, no matter how good their intentions, often do more harm than good.

In empathizing you must listen not only to the speaker's words but also to the feelings behind the words. You must see the world through the other's eyes, suspending judgment in order to understand the speaker's thoughts and feelings as the speaker experiences them.

To carry out the process, the empathic listener should keep these questions in mind: What is the real problem (why is the person asking for help)? What is the person feeling (about himself or herself, the problem, you, and the process of getting help)? How can you be helpful (what can you realistically do)?

Good empathic listeners act as mirrors who reflect the actual situation rather than create new pictures. One of the most difficult things you, as an empathic listener, must do is to stop yourself from interrupting the emotional flow of a speaker who needs to express his or her feelings. Interrupting, giving advice, or even asking questions at an inappropriate time may thwart the effectiveness of the interaction.

Paraphrasing is an especially productive way to probe a speaker for more information. In addition, your feedback should describe rather than evaluate, be specific rather than general, and take into account the other person's needs. Try to avoid trite statements ("That's too bad," "This too shall pass," and "We all go through that"), but invite the person to tell more ("Would you like to talk about that?" "Tell me about it," and "I'd be glad to listen").

Noting how you respond to others' statements and actions can help you determine whether you listen empathically. Knowledge Checkup 6.4 will help you assess your usual response to others—whether you listen empathically or with some other style.

KNOWLEDGE CHECKUP 6.4

Assessing Your Empathic Listening[8]

Circle the letter that best describes your first response to the person in each situation. The goal is to tell how you would *actually* respond, not what the right response would be or how you would *like* to respond. Each is a work-related example. Put yourself into the situation, whether or not you have actually had the experience.

1. "I don't know what I'm going to do. I'm making all kinds of mistakes, and I know my supervisor is unhappy with me. He's already yelled at me two times."
   a. "Why do you make mistakes?"

b. "Why don't you tell your supervisor how you feel?"

c. "It's scary to have someone yell at you when you make mistakes."

d. "Perhaps your supervisor has good reason to yell at you. You should do something about making so many mistakes."

2. "The policy is supposed to be to promote from within the company. And now I find that this new person is coming in to replace my boss. I had my eyes on that job; I've been working hard for it. I know I could prove myself if I had a chance. Well, if that's what they think of me, I know when I'm not wanted."

    a. "It can be disappointing when the company seems to have forgotten about you by hiring an outsider, especially when you put a lot of hard work into your job."

    b. "Maybe your qualifications don't compare with those of the new person."

    c. "You should make sure they know your views and let them know your interest in advancement."

    d. "Did they discuss it with you at all?"

3. "My supervisor often makes mistakes and then has me handle the situation for him. To add insult to injury, he constantly forgets who caused the problem, and says to me, 'It's your fault, you should watch for those mistakes.'"

    a. "I wouldn't let anybody treat me that way."

    b. "It sounds like you're caught in a double bind; you resent being treated this way and are wondering what you can do about it."

    c. "What kinds of mistakes does he ask you to cover up?"

    d. "You should quit that job and find one where you're treated fairly."

4. "It happens every time the manager appears in my department. She just takes over as if I weren't there. When she sees something she doesn't like, she tells the employee what to do and how to do it. The employees get confused, I get upset, and finally she leaves. I'm responsible to her, so what can I do?"

    a. "You should discuss your problems with your boss."

    b. "When did this start to happen?"

    c. "The boss must be the boss, I suppose, and we all have to learn to live with it."

    d. "It upsets you that your manager takes over and gives conflicting directions. You're not sure what would be the most appropriate way to confront her about your feelings about her behavior."

5. "It's happened again! I was describing an office problem to my boss and she started staring out the window. She doesn't seem to be really listening to me because she has to ask me to repeat things. I feel she's superficially giving me the time to state my problems, but she ends up sidestepping the issue."

    a. "You should stop talking when you feel she's not listening to you. That way she'll start paying attention to you."

b. "You can't expect her to listen to every problem you have; anyway, you should learn to solve your own problems."

c. "What kind of problems do you talk to her about?"

d. "It's frustrating to have your boss behave this way when you're talking about problems that are important for you to solve."

Listed below are the possible responses for each of the five situations. If you circled answer a in situation number 1, circle 1a below (in the "asking for information response" category), if you circled answer b, circle 1b below (in the "recommendation response" category). Do this for your five responses.

Empathic response: 1c, 2a, 3b, 4d, 5d
Recommendation response: 1b, 2c, 3d, 4a, 5a
Asking for information response: 1a, 2d, 3c, 4b, 5c
Critical response: 1d, 2b, 3a, 4c, 5b

Underline the category in which you have the most circled answers. This is your general listening response style.

Empathic Response Style

If your general response style is empathic, you are probably nonjudgmental as you listen. Empathic listeners tend to focus on the essential themes and feelings that are being expressed and at the same time try to build rapport and mutual understanding. Empathic listeners also demonstrate a good grasp of paraphrasing because their feedback reflects both the content and the feelings of the speaker.

Recommendation Response Style

If your general listening response style is to make recommendations, you are probably an advice offerer who tells the speaker what to do and what not to do. You attempt to solve the problem or to do the thinking for the talker.

Asking for Information Response Style

If your general listening response style is to ask for additional information, you probably want to clarify your understanding before you react. This approach is usually positive, but if you overuse it a speaker may feel grilled or that you aren't dealing specifically with the problem and how she or he feels. As a result, your delay may be perceived as disinterest or lack of involvement.

Critical Response Style

If your general response style is to criticize, you show a tendency to judge, approve, or disapprove of the messages you receive. Instead of focusing on content and emotion, you are probably listening for information that may be used to evaluate the speaker. Critical responses often cause conflicts because the speaker feels attacked and thus may lash out at you in frustration.

Hearing may be natural, but effective listening is not. It requires work: you need to evaluate your listening strengths and weaknesses; you need to recognize the barriers that interfere with your ability to be a good listener; and you need to develop the skills necessary to overcome those barriers. In addition, if you want to help others, you need to develop empathic listening skills. Given the large amount of time you spend listening, the work is well worth the effort.

COMMUNICATION COMPETENCY CHECKUP

M. Gordon

"I have a task and that is talking to you. You have a task of listening to me. I hope you do not finish before I do."

Speakers and listeners are engaged in a cooperative effort. The speaker in the cartoon hopes they're both up to the task.

1. Why is the speaker concerned that his audience members have good listening skills?

2. The speaker hopes that audience members won't finish listening before he finishes speaking. What barriers to effective listening could cause this problem?

3. What techniques could audience members use to improve their listening skills and thus maintain attention throughout the speech?

4. At a reception after the speech the speaker and several audience members discuss the talk. He tells them, "I was really afraid that the way I presented the material would confuse many listeners." What would a person with an empathic response style say to the speaker? What would a person with a recommending response style say to the speaker? What would a person with an asking-for-information response style say to the speaker? What would a person with a critical response style say to the speaker? How would the speaker probably react to each audience member's remarks?

NOTES

1. Adapted from: Lyman Steil, *Your Listening Profile* (New York: Sperry Corporation, 1980), p. 6.

2. For a discussion of several studies concerning how communicating time is divided (among listening, speaking, and writing, for example), see: Andrew D. Wolvin and Carolyn Gwynn Coakley, *Listening*, 2d ed. (Dubuque, IA: Wm. C. Brown, 1985), pp. 7–9.

3. Reported in Lyman Steil, "What Is Your Ear-Q," *Cereal Foods World* 20 (March 1975): 136–38.

4. Adapted from: Madelyn Burley-Allen, *Listening: The Forgotten Skill* (New York: John Wiley and Sons, 1982), p. 44.

5. Adapted from a handout by George Tuttle and John Murdock, "Approaches to Teaching Listening as a Communication Behavior in Businesses and Organizations," a workshop at the Speech Communication Association Convention, Anaheim, CA, November 11, 1981.

6. Cited in Ronald B. Adler, Lawrence B. Rosenfeld, and Neil Towne, *Interplay: The Process of Interpersonal Communication*, 4th ed. (New York: Holt, Rinehart and Winston, 1989), p. 182.

7. David B. Orr, "Time Compressed Speech—A Perspective," *Journal of Communication* 18 (1968): 288–92.

8. Madelyn Burley-Allen, *Listening: The Forgotten Skill* (New York: John Wiley and Sons, 1982), pp. 85–89.

FOR FURTHER INVESTIGATION

Arnold, William. *Crisis Communication.* Dubuque, IA: Gorsuch, Scarisbrick, 1980.

Burley-Allen, Madelyn. *Listening: The Forgotten Skill.* New York: John Wiley and Sons, 1982.

Drakeford, John W. "Tuning Out: The Most Debilitating Social Disease." *New Woman* (July 1983): 66–69.

Dyer, Wayne. *Your Erroneous Zones.* New York: Avon Books, 1976.

Goss, Blaine. "Listening as Information Processing." *Communication Quarterly* 30 (Fall 1982): 304–7.

Kinlaw, Dennis. *Listening and Communication Skills.* San Diego, CA: University Associates, 1981.

Raudsepp, Eugene. "The Art of Listening Well." *INC* (October 1981): 135.

Steil, Lyman. *Your Listening Profile.* New York: Sperry Corporation, 1980.

Steil, Lyman. "Secrets of Being a Better Listener." *U.S. News and World Report* (May 26, 1980): 65–66.

Wolff, Florence, Nadine Marsnik, William Tacey, and Ralph Nichols. *Perceptive Listening.* New York: Holt, Rinehart and Winston, 1983.

Wolvin, Andrew D., and Carolyn Gwynn Coakley. *Listening*, 3d ed. Dubuque, IA: Wm. C. Brown, 1988.

CHAPTER 7

▶ # *Interpersonal Processes*

*This chapter on interpersonal processes will help you to practice and develop communication competencies that fall into two broad categories: (1) **basic speech communication skills**, such as expressing yourself clearly and presenting your point of view, and (2) **human relations**, which include describing another's viewpoint, expressing your feelings to others, and performing social rituals. Specifically, the competencies you will gain will enable you to do the following:*

▶ *Define the framework for a relationship, including personal and relational goals, the structure of the relationship, and the rules of the relationship.*

▶ *Distinguish relationship structures according to dominant/submissive and loving/hostile behaviors.*

▶ *Specify the universal rules for relationships.*

▶ *Identify the components of relationship commitment and assess your commitment in an important relationship.*

▶ *List the components of intimacy and distinguish an intimate experience from an intimate relationship.*

▶ *Identify the resources offered in relationships.*

*H*ow many different types of relationships do you have? You may know people you consider work partners, colleagues, superiors, subordinates, acquaintances, relatives, parents, pals, friends, buddies, or lovers. How many different names do you have for your variety of relationships?

Select three different types of relationships that you have and list several words you might use to describe each one. For example, you might describe your friendship relationship with the words *caring* and *dependent*.

Do your descriptions relate to each relationship's goal, such as "to have fun," "to get a job done," or "to keep from being bored"? Do they refer to whether you are the superior person in the relationship—the "leader"—or the subordinate one—the "follower"? Do some characterizing words focus on the amount of love and affection or hate and hostility you have in the particular relationship? Did you concern yourself with some of the rules that make each relationship unique, such as "we date each other exclusively," or "we have a fifty-fifty partnership in the business"? Did you use such words as *commitment* or *intimacy*?

What do the variety of types of relationships you have and the myriad ways you describe and distinguish them reveal about yourself?

DIMENSIONS OF RELATIONSHIP PROCESSES

Relationships come in a variety of forms, from the work-on-a-class-project type to the live-together-forever type. Several sets of dimensions distinguish each relationship from others. One set of dimensions describes the framework for a relationship, such as the rules that guide your behavior. Another set helps you judge the quality of a relationship, such as its levels of intimacy and commitment. At the outset of this chapter, you should examine your own idea of what a relationship is, because your definition of a relationship predicts its content. Complete Knowledge Checkup 7.1.

KNOWLEDGE CHECKUP 7.1

Relationship Want Ads

Write three want ads for people to fill the following relationship vacancies in your life. Specify the characteristics you want in the other individual as well as the personal qualities you have to offer.

1. Advertise for a person with whom you wish to establish a *work relationship*.

2. Advertise for a person with whom you wish to establish a *casual friendship*.

3. Advertise for a person with whom you wish to establish a *loving and caring relationship*.

How do your three advertisements differ from each other?

The differences among the advertisements you wrote in the knowledge checkup reflect, first of all, the differences in your goals for each relationship. Although the general goal for each—a work relationship, a friend relationship, or a loving relationship—is prescribed, you meet your specific needs and desires by seeking particular characteristics in a partner in a relationship.

The characteristics you want in a partner reflect how you expect to interact with her or him. For some people, the patterns of interaction in all three relationships might be similar, even if the goals are different. For example, you might want to be the person who controls what happens, whether the goal is to complete a project with a work partner or to see a movie with a friend. For other people, the patterns of interaction may differ for each relationship. For example, you may picture yourself the boss with your work partner, the equal of your friend, and the subservient member of your loving relationship.

You may also believe that different rules of behavior apply to each relationship. For example, "Do your fair share" might guide a work relationship, and the rule "Stick up for the other person" might guide the friend relationship; in the first instance, you want someone who is hard-working; in the second, you seek someone loyal.

Finally, the advertisements you wrote identify what you see as the desirable resources of each relationship—that is, what you want each relationship to provide. Do you picture the work relationship as giving you the chance to get a good grade, earn a promotion, or impress someone? Do you see the friendship as releasing you from boredom? Do you imagine that the loving relationship will supply security, respect, and intimacy?

If you analyze your ads carefully, you'll find a lot of useful information about how you personally define your relationships. On a more formal note, the *Random House Dictionary of the English Language* defines **relationship** as "a connection, association, or involvement . . . an emotional or other connection between people." Synonyms include *dependence, affinity, concern, alliance, affiliation, association*, and *tie*. Each of these words reveals the complexity of human connectedness.

You consider yourself involved in a relationship if your actions, thoughts, and emotions follow specific patterns. You observe your communication behaviors and notice whether your interaction with the other person seems mutually influential and structured. For example, two people eating in a restaurant share a relationship if they are sitting together, taking each other into account as they talk, and influencing each other at least to the extent that what one says is in response to what the other says.

Relationships are complex. To understand them means breaking them down into their component parts and looking at each part separately, even though you rarely sit down and consciously analyze them—relationships often seem to just happen. For the sake of analysis, however, the components of a relationship are divided into two broad categories: those related to the framework for interaction and those related to the relationship's quality or outcomes.

THE FRAMEWORK FOR INTERACTION

Each of your relationships has goals, structure, and rules that form the context within which you and the other person interact. Your communication both reflects and determines each of the three dimensions for each of your relationships.

Goals

Relationships form because of some **goal,** or outcome, that each person wishes to achieve. The goal may be to learn something about yourself, to learn something about the environment, to overcome loneliness, to change another's attitude or behavior, to complete a project, to kill time, to release tension, to be entertained, to help someone, or to become intimate with someone. There may be as many goals as there are individuals and relationships.

Reread the three ads you wrote and consider what your goals were for each type of relationship. You may find that your love, friend, and work relationships have different goals and that these goals are reflected in the characteristics you included in each ad. Assume, for example, that you seek a person with whom to share a loving relationship who is kind and considerate, a friend who jogs and likes spicy food, and a work partner who is responsible and has good research skills. Each set of characteristics reveals different relationship goals: to share a long-term intimate relationship, to provide companionship, and to complete some task efficiently.

Comparing the characteristics you listed in each of your ads with those listed by your classmates should help to clarify your goals for these three types of relationships. An advertisement for a work partner that focuses exclusively on intelligence, experience, and a willingness to work hard reveals different goals from one seeking a partner who is easy-going and flexible. Someone advertising for a friend who is a good listener has a different goal from someone who seeks a person with whom to share weekends of mountain climbing. An advertisement for a partner in a loving relationship that lists quiet, warm, and considerate as desired characteristics displays different goals from an ad that seeks someone wild, exciting, and willing to take risks.

Researchers pay more attention to close, personal relationships—intimate ones—than to any other relationship because intimacy offers great rewards and exacts great costs. **Intimate relationships** provide stimulation (an escape from loneliness and boredom) and an opportunity to share experiences (whether a beautiful sunset or a horrible test grade). Relationships frequently present a nonthreatening arena in which to try out new ideas and behaviors and they often increase enjoyment of certain activities (a party with close friends is usually more fun than one with strangers). Intimate relationships also provide the opportunity for self-disclosure, the self-revealing communication that strips away the front you present to others and displays the person you think you *really* are. Accompanying the rewards, however, are potentially great costs, the greatest of which is rejection by the other person.

Regardless of the particular goals you have for an intimate relationship, you should bear two things in mind. First, people rarely set out to form an intimate relationship in a rational and intellectual way. Their conscious aim often is something other than to begin an intimate relationship. People seldom enter a classroom with a specific plan for leaving with an intimate relationship, although many individuals have met in class and eventually lived together or gotten married.

Second, most relationships are not formed with the primary goal of achieving intimacy. Usually, relationships form as accompaniments to everyday activities. For instance, you like to jog, so you meet people who share the same interest; you may not think about extending the relationship beyond your noon-time run. Or a class project may require you to work with another student; your only goal may be to fulfill the assignment.

Nonetheless, your specific goal may be to find someone with whom you can follow a path toward intimacy—a person with whom to share your innermost thoughts and feelings and, eventually, your love. If this is the case, your goal—to seek out and develop *an intimate relationship*—is predetermined and conscious, not a by-product of other relationships with different goals.

Structure

A relationship is like a dance—two people move together in a coordinated display. The partners may glide about smoothly, anticipating each other's movements and responding with grace, or they may appear awkward and out of step. Relationships are distinguished by the **structure** of their communication—how their talk is organized and coordinated—much as dancers are distinguished by their choreography.

Two dimensions characterize the structure of a relationship: dominance/submission and love/hostility. The dimension of dominance/submission describes how much control you and the other person have over each other, while the dimension of love/hostility reflects how much affection or love you give and receive. In figure 7.1, dominance and submission are the endpoints of the vertical line through the circle, and hostility and love are the endpoints

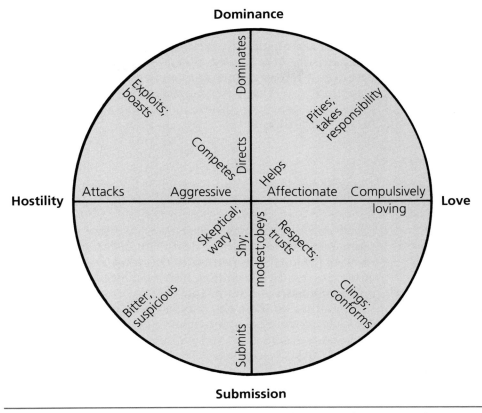

▶ **FIGURE 7.1**   Primary Components of Relationship Interaction

of the horizontal line. The two dimensions are independent of each other—that is, you can be both dominant and loving (stereotypical "parent" behavior), dominant and hostile (stereotypical "exploitive manager" behavior), submissive and loving (stereotypical "good little child" behavior), and submissive and hostile (stereotypical "downtrodden worker" behavior).

The behaviors indicated on the circle represent variations of the behaviors associated with dominance, submission, love, and hostility, and their combinations, such as loving *and* dominant, hostile *and* submissive. The terms that describe behaviors along the inside edge of the circle (*pities, clings, bitter,* and *exploits*) are extreme or exaggerated behaviors, and those toward the center (*helps, respects, skeptical,* and *competes*) are moderate or less exaggerated behaviors. For example, the exaggerated form of love is *compulsively loving,* whereas the moderate form is *affectionate.*

Your relationships take one of three possible structures: complementary, symmetrical, and parallel.

In a **complementary relationship,** one partner's behavior complements or completes the other's—the behaviors seem to go together. The relationship is based on differences (for example, one partner may be dominant while the other is submissive) which, when they come together, form a stable relationship. Each partner has particular duties and obligations, whether one "brings home the bacon" while the other "keeps the home fires burning," or one washes the dishes while the other dries. The partners work better in combination than alone.

The relationship between dominant and submissive behaviors is complementary. Dominance tends to provoke its opposite from the other person— subordinance—and submission tends to provoke its opposite—control.

A **symmetrical relationship,** unlike a complementary one, implies balance: the partners contribute equally to their relationship. Whereas the partners in a complementary relationship create a whole from their two separate parts, partners in a symmetrical relationship maintain their individual identities. In the ideal symmetrical relationship (for which there are few examples), power is equally distributed, independence is stressed, and both partners are either submissive or dominant.

Unlike dominant and submissive behaviors, which tend to provoke their opposites, loving behaviors tend to evoke love and hostile behaviors tend to provoke hostility. For example, when you tell someone "I love you," you probably expect a similar confession. An opposite or neutral response ("I don't love you!" or "Oh") is usually unexpected and unappreciated.

Combining a loving or hostile behavior with a dominant or submissive one tends to provoke the same feeling and the opposite behavior. Loving-dominant behaviors, such as "pities" and "takes responsibility" or "helps," tend to provoke loving-submissive behaviors, such as "clings" and "conforms" or "respects" and "trusts"; in other words, symmetrical feeling and complementary control behavior. For example, a parent's loving-dominant message, "You poor child—here, let me help you with your math homework," is likely to get a loving-submissive message from the child, such as, "Please help me. I'd really appreciate it."

Likewise, loving-submissive behaviors, such as "clings" and "conforms" or "respects" and "trusts," tend to provoke loving-dominant behaviors, such as "pities" and "takes responsibility" or "helps." For example, the loving-submissive message, "I think it's terrific that you know how to use the new computer in the office," is likely to evoke a loving-dominant message in return: "Let me show you how to use it. It's really not hard once you know what to do."

Hostile-dominant behaviors, such as "exploits" and "boasts" or "competes," tend to provoke hostile-submissive behaviors, such as "bitter" and "suspicious" or "skeptical" and "wary." For example, a manager's hostile-dominant message, "I've been on the job here twice the time you have, so do the job the way I say to do it," is likely to get an employee's hostile-submissive message in response: "Well, okay, but just because you've been here a long time doesn't make you a genius!"

In turn, hostile-submissive behaviors, such as "bitter" and "suspicious" or "skeptical" and "wary," tend to provoke hostile-dominant behaviors, such as "exploits" and "boasts" or "competes." For example, a child's hostile-submissive message, "Gee, I never get to do anything I want to do—how come?" is likely to get a parent's hostile-dominant message in return, such as: "I'm the parent and you'll do what I say!"

The third relational structure, **parallel,** is not represented in figure 7.1. It is a hybrid form in which complementary and symmetrical aspects are combined. One partner may be dominant and the other submissive at times; other times, the partners may reverse roles; and sometimes, both partners may be dominant or both may be submissive. Similarly, the expression of feelings depends on the situation. In general, the parallel structure is the most flexible, allowing contributions to the relationship to vary from time to time.

Knowledge Checkup 7.2 will help you analyze the structure of one of your relationships.

KNOWLEDGE CHECKUP 7.2

Relational Structure Analysis

Select an important relationship and, using figure 7.1 as a guide, indicate the extent to which you and your partner are dominant, submissive, loving, and hostile. Use the following ten-point scale to mark your responses.

1	2	3	4	5	6	7	8	9	10
almost never								almost always	

_____ **1.** I am dominant.
_____ **2.** My partner is dominant.
_____ **3.** I am submissive.
_____ **4.** My partner is submissive.
_____ **5.** I am loving.
_____ **6.** My partner is loving.
_____ **7.** I am hostile.
_____ **8.** My partner is hostile.

Using the terms *complementary, symmetrical,* and *parallel,* describe your relationship.

To determine whether you perceive your relationship as predominantly dominant-loving, dominant-hostile, submissive-loving, or submissive-hostile,

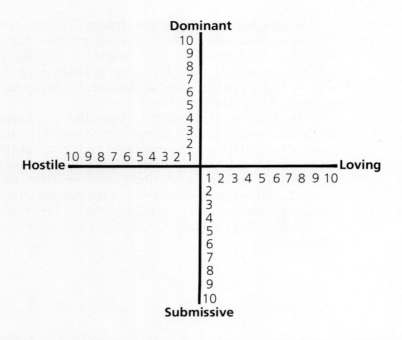

▶ **FIGURE 7.2**   Your Relational Structure Analysis

plot your responses on figure 7.2. For example, figure 7.3 shows plots for one person's responses to items 1, 3, 5, and 7 for himself, and to items 2, 4, 6, and 8 for his perceptions of his father. (The son's four scores for himself were plotted as follows: the response to item 1 was a 2, so a point was placed on the *dominant* line at number 2; the response to item 3 was a 7, so a point was placed on the *submissive* line at number 7; the response to item 5 was a 1, so a point was placed on the *loving* line at number 1; and the response to item 7 was a 6, so a point was placed on the *hostile* line at number 6. The four points were joined to form the four-sided figure.)

The son perceives himself as predominantly submissive and hostile (because the four-sided figure formed by his scores falls into the submissive-hostile quadrant) and his father as predominantly loving and dominant (because most of the four-sided figure formed by the scores for the father falls into the dominant-loving quadrant). Given the son's perception of their relationship as complementary for both control and affection, what predictions could you make for their relationship? (For example, do they fight with each other? If they fight, what do you think the underlying issue is?)

As you plot your responses to items, 1, 3, 5, and 7 (your perceptions of yourself) and to items 2, 4, 6, and 8 (your perceptions of your partner) on figure 7.2, consider the following questions:

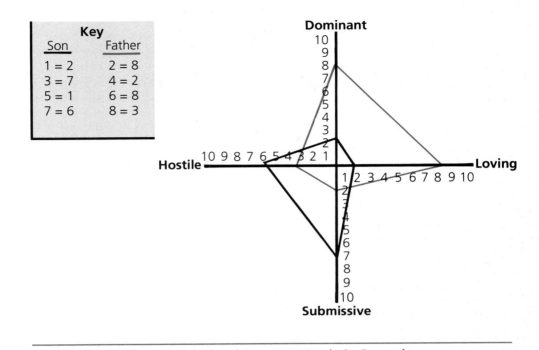

▶ FIGURE 7.3   Relational Structure Analysis: Example

1. Does your four-sided figure fall predominantly into any one of the four quadrants? What about your partner's?

2. How do the two figures compare? How do they describe the structure of your relationship?

3. What predictions could you make for your relationship?

Analyzing the structure of your relationships could help you discover why some are more satisfying than others. For example, the father-son relationship in figure 7.3 is likely to be unsatisfactory from the son's perspective: the two probably fight a lot, the son probably harbors a great deal of quiet resentment, and when they fight the underlying issue is probably *who's in control.*

Although most people prefer the parallel relationship structure, not every close relationship takes this form.[1] Do you insist on being dominant or submissive but have a partner who seeks equality? Do you wonder whether your expressions of love will receive loving responses? Questions such as these should help you further analyze the structure of your relationships.

Rules

Rules, the regulations that govern actions in a relationship, are necessary for you to make predictions about another person's behavior. If you don't know the rules governing your interaction, you can't predict whether the person to whom you nod and say hello will nod and say hello in return, ignore you, hit you, or start screaming! But because most people share the same rule for greeting behavior, you can predict a reciprocal response: a nod and hello will get you a nod and hello in return. Rules organize the world for you, add predictability, and reduce uncertainty.

Researchers who have conducted studies in various parts of the world uncovered a small number of universal rules that help structure all relationships.[2] Like all rules, some may be more important than others in particular relationships, and some may even be broken. There are five universal rules:

1. You should respect another's privacy.
2. You should look the other person in the eye during conversations.
3. You should not divulge something that is said in confidence.
4. You should not criticize the other person publicly.
5. You should seek to repay debts, favors, or compliments, no matter how small.

Several specific rules that help structure particular relationships, such as loving, friendship, and work relationships, also turned up.

1. You should stand up for the other person in her or his absence.
2. You should share news of success with her or him.
3. You should show emotional support.
4. You should trust and confide in each other.
5. You should volunteer your help in time of need.
6. You should strive to make the other person happy when you are with her or him.
7. You should not nag the other person.

If the friendship evolves into a love relationship, new rules arise, mostly concerned with self-disclosure and the expression of emotion. Should the love relationship culminate in marriage, the number of rules increases dramatically—the guidelines extend to virtually all forms of interaction, both with the marriage partner and with people outside the marriage. You may develop rules about whom you can dance with at a party (relatives may be OK, but not people you dated in the past), whom you can have lunch with, and even whom you can talk to on the phone. The multitude of rules arises from an attempt to keep the interaction orderly, but the very number of rules points to the high probability of conflict and friction between husbands and wives.

Unique rules, as well as universal rules, govern interaction in a work relationship. Less concern is placed on intimacy, but more is placed on task-maintenance rules, such as "Both people should accept a fair share of the workload" and "Workers should cooperate."

Rules also exist for topics that should and should not be discussed.[3] For example, in both platonic and romantic relationships, talking about the current or future state of the relationship is taboo because partners fear that such talk might destroy the relationship. Thus, you might want to talk about getting married, for example, but avoid the topic because you fear scaring your partner.

To further complicate matters, how rules apply to particular situations may be unclear. You may know that making eye contact with your date when you talk is important, but what are the rules for the first good-night kiss? When should it happen? Should it happen? How should you go about it? What should you say, if anything? How can you avoid looking like the village idiot or the most desperate person in town?

You may not consciously apply the universal rules, but you probably resort to them anyway because they create a structure that makes beginning interaction moderately predictable and not unpleasant. As a relationship grows, however, more rules need to be negotiated. Whether you and your partner sit down face to face and discuss existing rules or ones that need to be created, or whether you proceed in a less formal way, the task cannot be avoided. The more the relationship reflects your own and your partner's individual characteristics, the more specific the rules for your interaction must be.

Analyzing the rules of your relationships can help you make your interactions more satisfying. Knowledge Checkup 7.3 will help your analysis.

KNOWLEDGE CHECKUP 7.3

Analysis of Your Relationship Rules

Select an important relationship and answer each of the following questions.

1. What are three rules that you have for the other person?

2. What are three of the other person's rules for you?

3. What are three shared rules that give the relationship excitement?

4. What are three shared rules that give the relationship stability?

5. What are three shared rules that give the relationship personal and mutual benefits?

6. Write two positive and two negative statements about how you feel about the rules. (Are some hard to follow? Are they negotiable?)

7. How do you ensure that the other person follows the rules?

8. What does your partner do to make sure you follow the rules?

QUALITIES AND RESOURCES
OF RELATIONSHIPS

Once you understand the goals, structure, and rules that establish the framework for a relationship, you can begin to consider the relationship's quality and the resources it provides. You already have a sense of the characteristics that contribute to a relationship's quality—that is, its "goodness" or "badness." If asked, you could probably rank your relationships along a continuum from good to bad, from high quality to low. Similarly, you could probably also describe your relationships with respect to the resources, or benefits, they provide.

Whereas goals, structure, and rules are *either-or* propositions (your relationship has one goal or another, one type of structure or another, and one set of rules or another), qualities and resources exist in terms of *more or less* (your relationship is more or less intimate, more or less affectionate).

Two qualities that are important for understanding any relationship are commitment and intimacy, and four important resources are affection, esteem, information, and services.

Commitment

Nowadays *commitment* is a popular word to toss into magazine articles and sprinkle in conversation. It appears to imply a great deal about a relationship:

"He's afraid of committing himself to the relationship."
"She considers the expensive birthday present a commitment."
"If you're not committed to completing the project, why did you agree to do it in the first place?"

Before we take a closer look at the notion of commitment, complete the self-analysis in Knowledge Checkup 7.4.

KNOWLEDGE CHECKUP 7.4

Commitment Probe[4]

Do the following exercise twice. First think of a person with whom you have a friendship or intimate relationship—whether you are childhood pals, dating, living together, or married—and with that relationship in mind, mark each statement according to how *true* it is for you. Then think of a person with whom you have a work relationship and, with that relationship in mind, respond to the statements again.

Mark 1 if the statement is definitely false.
Mark 2 if it is mostly false.
Mark 3 if it is neither true nor false.
Mark 4 if it is mostly true.
Mark 5 if it is definitely true.

_____ **1.** It is likely that my partner and I will be together six months from now.
_____ **2.** I am not attracted to other potential partners.
_____ **3.** A potential partner would have to be truly outstanding for me to pursue a new relationship.
_____ **4.** It is likely that this relationship will be permanent.
_____ **5.** My partner is likely to continue this relationship.

Total your five responses. This is your commitment score.

A relationship identified as "casual dating" has an average commitment score of 13, one identified as "exclusively involved" has an average score of 17, and a marriage relationship has an average score of 21. Where does your friend or intimate relationship fit along this continuum?

Although the term *commitment* is often applied to relationships on a path toward intimacy—such as dating relationships—it is equally important in long-term work relationships, particularly partnerships. Scores below 16 indicate a weak or unstable work partnership, one likely to break up if an attractive offer comes along from outside the relationship. The higher the commitment score, the more stable the relationship and the higher the probability that it will continue.

Commitment, a pledge to the continuation of a relationship, has three aspects: your commitment, your perception of the other's commitment, and what it is you are committed to. In general, you link your commitment with the perceived commitment of the other person (consider your response to item 5 in the knowledge checkup). If you think your partner is less committed than you, you are likely to decrease your commitment; similarly, if you think the other person is more highly committed, you might increase your commitment. A relationship is unstable if the levels of commitment are unequal. For example, if you see your relationship as a long-term involvement to which you're highly committed, a problem may arise if your partner sees it as a casual pastime involving little commitment.

The phrase "commitment to a relationship" is vague, but you usually have a particular object in mind. For example, you may commit yourself to continuing the relationship even if you and your partner are separated by geographical distance, or you may commit yourself to increasing the intimacy of your relationship, or you may commit yourself to working together to increase business sales.

Intimacy

Intimacy is an umbrella term that includes, among other things, emotional closeness and intellectual sharing. Consider the following questions with respect to one of your relationships:

1. How much do you know about each other?
2. To what degree are you and your partner's lives intertwined and interdependent?
3. Do you trust each other?

Each of these questions relates to one aspect of intimacy and underscores the difficulty of defining precisely what intimacy is. Essentially, **intimacy** is a quality of a relationship based on detailed knowledge and deep understanding of the other person. Trying to enumerate specific behaviors ("This relationship is an intimate one because . . .") results in a long list that contains seemingly trivial items.

Intimacy is an expectation you have for a relationship, an anticipation that you and your partner will come to know each other more and more deeply, more and more personally—that you will continue to share intimate experiences.

Intimacy and intimate experiences are not identical. Although any relationship may include an **intimate experience**—a "one-night stand" or a moment of important personal sharing, for example—it is only in intimate relationships that continued intimate experiences can be expected.

The intimacy of a relationship may be determined by examining three factors, each related to the three questions you answered at the beginning of this section. First, what are the breadth and depth of the information you and your partner know about each other? Breadth refers to the number of topics you discuss and depth pertains to how important and personal the information is. As breadth and depth increase, so does intimacy.

Second, in what ways are your and your partner's lives interdependent? As you and your partner share and learn to depend on each other for services, support, and understanding, you become mutually dependent for the satisfaction of your needs, wants, and desires. Intimacy and interdependence, however, are not related in a simple way, such as when one increases the other increases. Rather, the most intimate relationships are characterized by an interdependence that allows each partner's maximum satisfaction but also has limits and flexibility—so that one person doesn't feel overwhelmed or smothered by the other.

Third, how much do you trust your partner to accept you as you are, to avoid purposely hurting you, to keep your best interests and the best interests of your relationship in mind, to share with you, and to continue the relationship? Your answers determine the degree to which you allow yourself to be vulnerable to your partner. Without trust, the information you share will be mostly superficial. You might fear being exploited, so you keep yourself separate from the other person, perhaps reaching out occasionally to have an intimate experience, but avoiding the belief that intimate experiences characterize your relationship.

Resources

Relationships, whether intimate or not, serve as sources for tangible benefits, such as money and gifts; intangible benefits, such as affection and emotional support; and service benefits, such as help with your gardening or getting you a book from the library. Important resources in a relationship include affection (expressing and receiving warmth, tenderness, and caring), esteem (obtaining confirmation of who you are in relation to others), services (having things done for you), and information (receiving needed information about yourself and the environment).

Affection and esteem are more important resources in love and friendship relationships than they are in work relationships. In contrast, service and information resources are more important in work relationships than they are in love and friendship relationships. Although some resources may be more important than others in a particular relationship, most relationships have many resources.

A relationship's framework—its goals, structure, and rules—and its qualitative aspects—including commitment, intimacy, and resources—may be joined together within a larger context, that of time. Because relationships are continuously evolving, you can expect that your goals will change; a relationship's structure will change, stabilize, and change even more; some rules will be clarified, others will be abandoned, and new rules will emerge; commitment will vary, as will what you and the other person commit yourselves to; intimacy will increase, stabilize, and continue to change; and new resources will be added, old resources may be discarded, and available resources will vary in importance.

How time affects a relationship depends on the relationship's unique characteristics. Changes are complex because alterations in one aspect of a relationship's framework, such as adding the rule "We date each other exclusively," or in one of its qualitative aspects, such as becoming more intimate, cause modifications in other dimensions of the relationship. For example, adding a rule about exclusivity will most likely cause changes in the relationship's goals (Is marriage now a goal?), structure (Should decision making be more evenly shared now?), and what resources are important (Are more services expected now?). Relationships are dynamic—continually adapting and developing—as they pass through time. A relationship is not a *thing*, but a *process*—an ever-changing process.

The teacher and student are involved in a conflict. An analysis of their relationship—goals, structure, rules, commitment, intimacy, and resources—will help clarify some possible sources of their trouble.

1. What are several goals the teacher might have for this teacher-student relationship? What are several of the student's possible goals?

2. Describe the probable structure of their relationship in terms of dominance/submission and love/hostility. Is the relationship complementary, symmetrical, or parallel?

3. List several rules that affect interaction between teachers and students. What new rules would you recommend for teacher-student relationships and what effects would they have on how teachers and students relate to each other?

4. How committed do the two people in the picture seem to their teacher-student relationship?

5. Does the relationship between teachers and students allow for the development of intimacy?

6. What common resources are available to teachers in their teacher-student relationships? What resources are available to students?

NOTES

1. Mark Randall Harrington, *The Relationship Between Psychological Sex-Type and Perceptions of Individuals in Complementary, Symmetrical, and Parallel Relationships* (Master's thesis, University of North Carolina at Chapel Hill, 1984).

2. A summary of the series of investigations, including comparisons of the rules for different types of relationships in different parts of the world, is available in: Michael Argyle and Monika Henderson, "The Rules of Relationships," in Steve Duck and Daniel Perlman, eds., *Understanding Personal Relationships* (Beverly Hills, CA: Sage, 1985), pp. 63–84.

3. A detailed analysis of taboo topics in relationships is available in: Leslie A. Baxter and William Wilmot, "Taboo Topics in Close Relationships," *Journal of Social and Personal Relationships* 2 (1985): 253–69.

4. Adapted from: Mary Lund, "The Development of Investment and Commitment Scales for Predicting Continuity of Personal Relationships," *Journal of Social and Personal Relationships* 2 (1985): 3–23.

FOR FURTHER INVESTIGATION

Altman, Irwin, and Dalmas Taylor. *Social Penetration: The Development of Interpersonal Relationships.* New York: Holt, Rinehart and Winston, 1973.

Argyle, Michael, and Monika Henderson, "The Roles of Relationships." In *Understanding Personal Relationships,* edited by Steve Duck and Daniel Perlman, pp. 63–64. Beverly Hills, CA: Sage, 1985.

Baxter, Leslie A., and William Wilmot, "Taboo Topics in Close Relationships." *Journal of Social and Personal Relationships* 2 (1985): 253–69.

Delia, Jesse G. "Some Tentative Thoughts Concerning the Study of Interpersonal Relationships and Their Development." *Western Journal of Speech Communication* 44 (1980): 97–103.

Derlega, Valerian J., ed. *Communication, Intimacy, and Close Relationships.* Orlando, FL: Academic Press, 1984.

Farrell, Warren. *The Liberated Man.* New York: Bantam Books, 1975.

Hendrick, Clyde, and Susan S. Hendrick. *Liking, Loving, and Relating.* Monterey, CA: Brooks/Cole, 1983.

Knapp, Mark L. *Interpersonal Communication and Human Relationships.* Boston: Allyn and Bacon, 1984.

Leary, Timothy. *Interpersonal Diagnosis of Personality.* New York: Ronald Press, 1957.

Lund, Mary. "The Development of Investment and Commitment Scales for Predicting Continuity of Personal Relationships." *Journal of Social and Personal Relationships* 2 (1985): 3–23.

Napier, Augustus, and Carl Whitaker. *The Family Crucible.* New York: Bantam Books, 1980.

Powell, John. *Why Am I Afraid to Tell You Who I Am?* Chicago: Argus Communications, 1969.

Wilmot, William W. *Dyadic Communication,* 3d ed. Reading, MA: Addison-Wesley, 1987.

CHAPTER 8

▶ *Interpersonal Relationships*

*This chapter on interpersonal relationships will help you practice and develop communication competencies that fall into three broad categories: (1) **communication codes,** which include listening effectively and using verbal and nonverbal cues that are appropriate to a particular situation; (2) **basic speech communication skills,** such as expressing yourself clearly, presenting your point of view, and asking questions to obtain feedback; and (3) **human relations,** which include describing another's viewpoint, expressing your feelings to others, and performing social rituals. Specifically, the competencies you will gain will enable you to do the following:*

▶ *Describe the role of attraction in new relationships.*
▶ *Recognize several important objectives to be accomplished during the beginning phase of a relationship.*
▶ *Apply the five steps of relationship formation to a new relationship.*
▶ *Recognize the role of information sharing in the maintenance of a relationship.*
▶ *Apply two techniques—developing a supportive and confirming communication climate and self-disclosing—for maintaining and enhancing your relationships.*
▶ *Apply several methods for increasing relationship satisfaction.*
▶ *Describe the characteristics that distinguish relationship termination processes.*
▶ *Recognize the most common communication strategies for relationship termination.*

*I*magine yourself at a party. You know a few of the people, but you're determined not to fall into the habit of talking exclusively with old friends. This time, you tell yourself, you're going to take the opportunity to make some new friends. What do you do? What determines whether you approach someone or not? After you do find someone you'd like to meet, what do you say? How do you get to know someone well enough in the space of a few minutes to kill the butterflies in your stomach, relax enough to get some moisture back in your throat, and take your mind off fears of looking like an idiot and sounding like a fool?

RELATIONAL DEVELOPMENT: BEGINNING, MAINTAINING, AND ENDING RELATIONSHIPS

Establishing a new relationship—one that goes beyond an hour or two of superficial cocktail chatter—is difficult for most of us. Getting close to another person seems to bring out our deepest insecurities and our best-hidden self-perceived flaws.

Although the romantic view of relationships is that they "just happen"— from the magical moment when two lovers swoon at first sight until the tragic end when circumstances pull them apart forever—relationships do not drop from the sky fully formed. Relational development, whether between lovers, friends, acquaintances, or co-workers, follows a predictable pattern. Relationships have a recognizable beginning, middle, and end, and what takes place during each phase is highly complex.

Beginning a Relationship

A relationship begins when you are attracted to someone and initiate interaction. Just because you are attracted to another person, however, does not automatically mean that you will initiate interaction. Interaction is usually initiated when you want to learn something about the other person—background, values, interests, and personality—and when you want to create a favorable impression. Regardless of where it may end, the relationship process begins with attraction.

On any given day, you encounter many people with whom you can choose to form a relationship. Not everyone, of course, has an equal probability of being chosen: you are attracted to some people and not to others, just as some are attracted to you and some are not. Each of us carries a mental list of criteria for attraction. Knowledge Checkup 8.1 will help you identify the reasons why you may be attracted to someone.

KNOWLEDGE CHECKUP 8.1

Characteristics Assessment

Rank the following characteristics in the order of their importance to you in describing a person with whom you would form a long-term relationship. Rank the most important characteristic 1 and the least important 13.

_____ adaptability
_____ college graduate
_____ creativity
_____ desire for children
_____ exciting personality
_____ good earning capacity
_____ good health
_____ good heredity
_____ good housekeeper
_____ intelligence
_____ kindness and understanding
_____ physical attractiveness
_____ religious orientation

Attraction

Think of people to whom you are attracted and the traits they share. Do they seem to have similar physical characteristics? Do they live nearby? Do they do things for you without asking for too much in return? Do they have qualities you lack but which seem to fit well with your own? Are they similar to you? Your answers to these questions correspond to the five bases of attraction: attractiveness, proximity, personal rewards, complementarity, and similarity.

Attractiveness **Attractiveness** is your impression of someone as good-looking or appealing. The first information you typically receive about a new acquaintance pertains to physical attractiveness. When you call someone attractive, you are usually referring to your perception of the person's physical attributes.

You may have a personal list of desired attributes, but no universal description of what people find attractive exists: such a description varies from person to person and from time to time. For example, at one time plumpness was considered attractive; now the preference is for thinness. Tall and slender, blue eyes, and a clear complexion might constitute attractiveness for many people, but not for all and certainly not for all time.

A paradox exists in evaluating attractiveness: although people may agree that person X is more attractive than person Y, they may strongly disagree on *why* person X is more attractive. However, even in the absence of consensus on a definition of physical attractiveness, attractiveness matters in forming initial impressions.

How high did you rank physical attractiveness in the knowledge checkup? A recent survey reveals that men rank the item third and women rank it sixth, which indicates that both groups give high importance to physical beauty.[1]

Often included as an aspect of attractiveness is "demeanor," how the other person behaves during an encounter. Someone who follows the rules for interacting, who, for example, maintains eye contact and doesn't criticize, is more likely to be found attractive than someone who is less socially adept. In this instance, "attractive" implies "comfortable." In general, attractive people are assumed to be warmer, more sensitive, kinder, more modest, and more sociable, and to make better husbands or wives than their unattractive peers.[2]

Proximity   Marrying the person next door doesn't happen just in 1950s musicals. To be attracted to someone takes some interaction, and you are most likely to interact with people whom you encounter frequently. Whether meeting at the mailbox when you both fetch your mail or sitting next to each other in a class, the effect is the same: you get the opportunity to communicate. **Proximity**, how near you are to someone, is an important determinant of attraction.

Familiarity, although it may breed contempt, more often breeds liking. As the other person becomes more predictable, interaction likely increases. Increased interaction, in turn, leads to other bases of attraction. You may go on to discover interests, physical attributes, and personality traits that enhance attraction.

The **mere exposure principle**, which states that increases in exposure increase liking, is the primary motive behind integrated housing and "forced" school busing. Prejudice appears to decline when interaction between different groups is increased.

Personal Rewards   According to an economic model of relationships, we are attracted to people with whom a relationship costs little yet provides many rewards. This calculation may seem self-serving, but it makes sense. Relationships have goals, and achieving goals entails costs. Costs may take many forms: You may have to do something for the other person in return for what he or she does for you; you may be expected to behave in a way that does not fit your self-image; or you may need to expend money, time, or emotional energy. Nevertheless, there is a reward: achieving your relationship's goal. The question is whether the rewards are sufficient to offset the costs.

The reward-cost balance is not simply assessed. The time and effort you invest in a relationship are not tangibly calculable, nor are the rewards you receive. Moreover, you may not even expect your rewards to correspond directly to your investment: depending on the relationship, you may be satisfied with less, or you may want more. Comparing costs and rewards of relationships is a psychological process, not an accounting procedure that leads to balanced books.

If you think your rewards adequately offset your costs, you will usually perceive a relationship as attractive. If you think your rewards are inadequate, you will probably find the relationship too costly and consider it unattractive. You can ultimately determine the attractiveness of a relationship, however, only after you assess the other relationships open to you. Can you form another relationship? Is the other relationship likely to provide more rewards than the current relationship?

If you are in a relationship that seems, on the whole, unsatisfactory, ask yourself what benefits make the relationship attractive. If you stay in an unattractive relationship, chances are that some reward makes the costs bearable. The reward may be hard to recognize at first, but it's there. Perhaps the reward is not being alone, or not having to change, or not having to seek out and develop another relationship.

Complementarity   **Complementarity** is the attraction of opposites. Although we often say that opposites attract, complementarity in fact is rather limited— not simply to particular people, but to particular people in particular situations. For example, a dominant older brother may enjoy his younger sister's submissive behavior, but he may be annoyed by such behavior in his friends.

Complementarity is at work when you find it enjoyable to talk to someone whose job is completely different from yours or who doesn't agree with you on certain issues.

But the excitement of exploring differences, although important in some relationships, is not as strong a source of attraction as its opposite, similarity.

Similarity   **Similarity** occurs when people have characteristics in common, whether looks, attitudes, opinions, values, beliefs, experiences, or ideas. This principle of attraction gets the most support from published research: birds of a feather *do* flock together. You are most attracted to those you perceive as similar to yourself. For example, husbands and wives tend to be of similar age (especially in first marriages), education, race, religion, and ethnic background. Partners also tend to hold similar attitudes, opinions, and socioeconomic status.

Review your ranking of the thirteen items in Knowledge Checkup 8.1 and study them in light of the similarity thesis. You may be surprised to find that you described someone whose characteristics are similar to your own and that you gave the highest rankings to those characteristics you find most important or attractive in yourself. If your ranking didn't follow this pattern, you do not consider similarity important in judging attractiveness. Knowledge Checkup 8.2 provides the opportunity for you to compare your ranking with that of the general population.

KNOWLEDGE CHECKUP 8.2

Comparing Your Preferences with General Preferences[3]

The following table shows how the thirteen characteristics in Knowledge Checkup 8.1 were ranked by the general population. The highest preference in a mate is ranked 1 and the lowest is ranked 13. For example, both males and females ranked "kindness and understanding" as the most important quality in a mate. Compare your rankings with those of the general population. Are there any significant differences? How might any differences affect your finding a mate? How important is it to know what the other person finds attractive? Are you willing to present a false image—lie—to find a mate?

Males	Females	
1	1	kindness and understanding
2	2	intelligence
3	6	physical attractiveness
4	3	exciting personality
5	4	good health
6	5	adaptability
7	7	creativity
8	10	desire for children
9	9	college graduate
10	11	good heredity
11	8	good earning capacity
12	12	good housekeeper
13	13	religious orientation

Objectives

Once you identify someone with whom you hope to form a relationship, you pursue two immediate goals: (1) to initiate contact and thus gather enough information to decide whether to continue the relationship, and (2) to leave the other person with a favorable impression of yourself.

Initiating Contact and Gathering Information Beginning a relationship is often anxiety-provoking. Regardless of your background and education, the odds are you received little or no training in forming relationships. Here are several steps you can take to improve your skills in this area.

Step One. *Look for Approachability Cues.* The first step in meeting new people is to look for **approachability cues**, indications that the other person is available for conversation. A person may be approachable when she or he smiles at you; is alone, relaxed, not busy, in a place where talking with strangers is OK (such as the student cafeteria), or talking with some of your friends; maintains eye contact with you for a moment beyond what is usual (three to ten seconds); has an open body position (arms and legs not crossed); evinces a good mood (pleasant facial expression); says or waves hello; or (if you're looking for a prospective mate) has an empty ring finger.

Step Two. *Initiate a Conversation.* Once you decide to approach someone, the second step is to initiate a conversation. One technique is to tell the person your reason for approaching. You may ask for information ("I'm new on campus. Can you tell me where the Student Union Building is located?"); introduce yourself ("I'm Bill. I wanted to meet you since we'll be sitting next to each other in this class."); talk about something you have in common ("Did you understand *one word* of the professor's lecture?"); or offer a sincere compliment ("That's a great picture of Bach on your shirt!").

Step Three. *Find Topics to Talk About.* The third step, finding topics to talk about, quickly follows the second one. Perceived similarities often provide topics of conversation. For example, you may attend the same school or classes; enjoy the same types of food, sports, or movies; or come from the same town. Although perceived differences may also suggest topics of conversation, such talk tends to separate you from the other person rather than bring you closer together.

Step Four. *Talk About a Variety of Topics.* The fourth step builds on the third. To gather enough information to decide whether to pursue a relationship, you need information on a variety of topics. Even very limited relationships, such as many between employers and employees, require a range of background knowledge.

You can make transitions to new topics by noting what the other person says and using the information to guide you. Rarely are casual conversations so structured that everything communicated is immediately pertinent. More often, extra or **free information**—elaborations—is provided as well. Use this free information to find new topics of conversation. For example, if you ask someone whether he likes Mexican food and he responds, "Yes. I also like Italian food, French food, and hamburgers and fries. In fact, I like just about every kind of food," you have more information than you requested. You can then use this free information to extend the conversation to talk about food in general, diets, and even travel to foreign places.

SKILL CHECKUP 8.1

Information Probe

1. Write a question someone could ask you about something you know. (Example: "What are your hobbies?")

2. List two follow-up questions the other person could ask you based on your answer. (Example: If your hobby is going to the theater, follow-up questions could be, "What plays have you seen lately?" and "Who's your favorite playwright?")

You can increase the probability of getting free information by asking questions that require detailed answers instead of ones that can be answered yes or no. A question-probe series, such as the one you developed for Skill Checkup 8.1, encourages the other person to offer additional pieces of information.

Other techniques for obtaining free information include giving compliments—direct ones, such as "That's a nice dog," or indirect ones, such as "How would you finish this report for the manager?" (which implies the other has knowledge you don't)—and telling something about yourself, which encourages the other person to speak about herself or himself.

Step Five. *Share Plans for Future Interaction.* The fifth step, sharing your plans for future interaction, completes the first phase of relationship development. If at the end of your first conversation you have enough information to conclude that another meeting is a good idea, communicate this to your partner. You may be indirect ("Are you planning to see that movie Professor Kolb recommended this weekend?") or direct ("I'd like you to come with me Saturday night to see the movie that Professor Kolb recommended.") Being direct is more threatening than being nondirect— for both of you, perhaps—but it is also more honest and likely to yield the information you need. Indirect statements or questions may be safer, but they are also less useful. Direct communications reveal what people are thinking, feeling, and wanting.

Creating a Favorable Impression You must convey three characteristics if you want to continue to interact: *cooperativeness, caring,* and *memorableness.* To be perceived as cooperative, you should follow conversational rules and behave according to the norms of the person with whom you're interacting. When you follow the rules, you make it easier for the other person to predict your behavior. You will also seem cooperative, which will further reduce the tension that often accompanies initial interactions.

To be perceived as caring, you should solicit information about the other person and listen attentively. Such attention tells the other person, "I care about what you have to say. You're important to me," which increases liking and creates a favorable impression.

To be perceived as memorable, you should communicate your most dynamic and interesting self-image. You may communicate information that shows you are unique, such as being from a family of ten children; adventurous, such as participating in a dangerous sport; or active, such as holding down several jobs.

Maintaining a Relationship

When you feel you have enough information to decide whether to continue a relationship, the initial phase of relationship development is complete. Deciding to pursue a relationship requires that you examine your goals and quickly assess the probability of attaining them. Will this person be helpful on the term project? Will this person be a good friend? Will this person be the type of spouse you seek? Whatever your needs, if the response is a tentative yes, you move into the second phase of relationship development: maintaining the relationship.

Objectives

Objectives during the maintenance phase of a relationship development include developing a framework for the relationship—goals, structure, and rules—and maximizing certain relational qualities—commitment, intimacy, and resources. Tentative explorations of who the other person is gives way to a more intense examination. Many decisions need to be made:

- What are your personal goals?
- What are your goals for the relationship?
- What is the best balance between dominance and submission and between love and hostility?
- What rules are important, and what new rules should be developed to meet the unique demands of your particular relationship?
- How committed should you be?
- How important is intimacy?
- What resources are crucial to goal attainment and relational satisfaction?
- How do the answers to all these questions change as the relationship develops?

You can't tackle all these questions in a totally rational way. You can't successfully make lists, check alternatives, assign weights to items, and develop equations. If people behaved this rationally, relationships wouldn't be so interesting or exciting! Rather, you usually answer these questions spontaneously and unconsciously.

Achieving Your Objectives

If you aim to answer many or all of the previous questions, you need information—and you will continue to need information throughout the life of your relationship. Information is the basis for relational decision making. Setting the stage for information sharing requires that you use your communication skills to create a confirming, supportive communication climate.

Supportiveness and Confirmation   You are willing to communicate openly and freely to the extent that you feel *valued*. **Supportive** and **confirming** behaviors communicate this message by indicating that you are acknowledged, understood, and accepted. **Attacking** and **disconfirming** behaviors communicate the opposite message and curtail effective communication. In an attacking and disconfirming environment, the aim is to protect yourself, not to share information.

Supportive language has several identifiable characteristics:[4]

1. Because it depends on "I" language, supportive language is descriptive and not evaluative. The emphasis switches from judging the other's behavior (attacking)—"You're too quiet"—to describing what you experience (supportive)—"When you don't talk I think you're angry."

2. Because it focuses on immediate thoughts and feelings, supportive language is spontaneous and not manipulative. The emphasis switches from following a calculated plan (attacking)—"I think it would be best if we considered dating other people"—to communicating honestly in the here-and-now (supportive)—"I want to date someone else."

3. Because it focuses on accepting the other person's feelings and putting yourself in the other person's place, supportive language is empathic and not indifferent. The emphasis switches from treating the other person in a neutral and detached way (attacking)—"I don't want to take sides in your fight with Sandy"—to communicating your understanding and caring for how the other person feels (supportive)—"I can feel how angry you are with Sandy."

4. Because it focuses on remaining open to new ideas, perspectives, and the possibility of change, supportive language is provisional and not certain. The emphasis switches from dogmatic declarations (attacking)—"We'll handle the problem this way"—to tentative conclusions (supportive)—"Let's try the idea and see if it works." People who communicate their certainty also communicate their superiority, their being *right* or *better*.

Just as supportive behavior is best understood by contrasting it with its opposite, attacking behavior, confirming behavior is best understood by contrasting it with its opposite, disconfirming behavior—the "what not to do."[5] How do you feel in each of the following situations?

- ▶ Someone fails to acknowledge what you say either verbally or nonverbally.
- ▶ Someone interrupts you in order to change the topic.
- ▶ Someone responds to your comment with an irrelevant or tangential remark.
- ▶ When you ask a simple question or make a simple statement, someone responds with an impersonal monologue, such as, "Why, when I was your age, I. . . ."

▶ Someone's comments are so ambiguous that you can't determine their true meaning.

▶ Someone's verbal and nonverbal behaviors contradict each other, such as when someone says, "I love you" with a giggle or a yawn.

Communicating that you value the other person entails more than simply avoiding these disconfirming behaviors—although that's an excellent start. You must also acknowledge the other person by communicating that you are physically and mentally available for the interaction. You can do so both nonverbally and verbally.

Nonverbal behaviors that communicate interest and attention include standing no more than a few feet from the other person, maintaining eye contact, making appropriate facial gestures, leaning toward and directly facing the other person, maintaining an open posture, and touching the other person. If you were actually to go out and employ these behaviors, you would probably find the other person speaking more, appearing more animated, and reciprocating your interest and attention.[6]

Verbal behaviors that acknowledge the other person communicate your understanding of what the other is both saying and feeling. Two useful techniques are paraphrasing—putting the other person's thoughts and feelings in your own words—and asking questions. Consider the following examples:

Statement: "I think it's time to change the work schedule—make some improvements. I'm not sure about who should take vacation time first, but I'm leaning toward John's going in early June and your going in late June."

Paraphrase: "You think the old schedule had some problems, right? You sound unsure about what specific changes might help things."

Question: "What are the advantages of changing the schedule?" or "What is the problem you're trying to solve?"

Reflecting thoughts and feelings demonstrates that you're listening and opens the way to continued communication. If your paraphrase is incorrect or your question misses the other person's point, further communication can clarify what was said. If your paraphrase or question is on target, the other person is encouraged to continue talking. Paraphrasing and asking questions compliment the other person, conveying "You are important to me, so I'm listening to what you say and taking note of how you feel."

SKILL CHECKUP 8.2

Giving Supportive and Confirming Responses

Each of the following three items presents a nonsupportive, defensive reaction. Give an appropriate supportive response that could substitute for the defensive one.

1. **Evaluative:** "You're a slob! Your clothes are all over the room!"
   Descriptive:
2. **Manipulative:** "Don't you agree that it's a good idea to do your homework right after school?"
   Spontaneous:
3. **Indifferent:** "There are always two sides to any argument."
   Empathic:

Provide a confirming answer for the following statement by reflecting both the content and the feelings expressed.

Statement: "I'm having a really hard time balancing classes and my work at the department store. I hope I don't mess up both!"
Confirming response:

Self-Disclosure **Self-disclosure**—intentionally letting the other person know who you are by honestly communicating self-revealing information—does much to maintain and develop a relationship. It enables shared knowledge and, therefore, makes it possible to develop joint views, joint goals, and joint decisions. It also helps the partners in a relationship to help each other; keep up with each others' lives; and learn what the other person is thinking, doing, and feeling.[7]

Self-disclosure varies according to the type of relationship. In intimate relationships, for example, there is much self-disclosure that shows a great deal of breadth and depth. In contrast, in nonintimate relationships, self-disclosure has little breadth and depth and accounts for only a small percentage of total communication. Many relationships are characterized by self-disclosure that has little breadth yet great depth. Business partners, for example, may discuss their thoughts and feelings about their work setting in great and personal detail, but avoid discussions of nonwork-related matters altogether.

No matter what its depth, breadth, and amount, self-disclosure fulfills several individual and relationship functions:[8]

1. catharsis, to help you "get something off your chest";
2. self-clarification, to help you learn about your own ideas by talking them out with another person;
3. reciprocity, to encourage the other person to disclose;
4. maintaining a relationship, to inform the other person of changes in your life;
5. enhancing a relationship, to open up new areas for discussion and increase the depth of messages; and
6. manipulation, to get the other person to do what you want.

Disclosure used for manipulation seems to deny the basic notion of honesty, but there are times when you can be both honest and manipulative. For example, you might tell another person "I love you" because you honestly feel that way and also because you know you can then ask for particular favors.

Disclosure involves both a willingness to talk *and* a willingness to listen to feedback. Before considering other aspects of disclosure, complete Knowledge Checkup 8.3. Select one person with whom you share an important relationship and keep that person in mind as you respond to the items.

KNOWLEDGE CHECKUP 8.3

Relational Disclosure and Feedback

This self-assessment is divided into two parts: willingness to disclose and willingness to listen to feedback. Before each item in the first part, place a number from 1 to 6 to indicate *how much you are willing to reveal*. A 1 indicates that you are willing to self-disclose nothing or almost nothing, and a 6 indicates that you are willing to reveal everything or almost everything. Use the values 2, 3, 4, and 5 to represent the points between these extremes.

Before each item in the second part, place a number from 1 to 6 to indicate *how willing you are to receive feedback about what you self-disclose*. A 1 indicates that you refuse or resist feedback, and a 6 indicates that you consistently encourage feedback. Use the values 2, 3, 4, and 5 to represent the points between these extremes.

Part 1: Extent to which I am willing to self-disclose my

_____ **1.** goals
_____ **2.** strengths
_____ **3.** weaknesses
_____ **4.** positive feelings
_____ **5.** negative feelings
_____ **6.** values
_____ **7.** ideas
_____ **8.** beliefs
_____ **9.** fears and insecurities
_____ **10.** mistakes
_____ **Total**

Part 2: Extent to which I am willing to receive feedback about my

_____ **1.** goals
_____ **2.** strengths
_____ **3.** weaknesses
_____ **4.** positive feelings

	5. negative feelings
_____	**6.** values
_____	**7.** ideas
_____	**8.** beliefs
_____	**9.** fears and insecurities
_____	**10.** mistakes
_____	**Total**

In general, total scores of forty and above are considered high, while those below forty are considered low. If you scored high on the first part and low on the second, you are probably more willing to disclose than you are to listen to feedback. If you scored low on the first part and high on the second, you are probably more willing to listen to what others have to say than you are to disclose things about yourself. If you scored low on both, you probably avoid self-disclosing and receiving feedback. And if you scored high on both, you are probably willing to disclose and receive feedback—a perfect candidate for a high-information-sharing relationship.

You can use your scores to create a **Johari Window**, a model that illustrates how your willingness to self-disclose and receive feedback operates in the relationship you had in mind when you completed the knowledge checkup.[9] Imagine a box that contains everything there is to know about you, including your goals, strengths, weaknesses, positive and negative feelings, and so on. The box is divided into four parts: (1) what you know about yourself, (2) what you don't know about yourself, (3) what others know about you, and (4) what others don't know about you. The result is the Johari Window shown in figure 8.1.

The upper-left pane of the window, which contains information about you that is known to yourself and others, is called the open area or **arena**. The lower-left area, which contains information about you that is known to yourself but not known to others, is called the **hidden area** because all your secrets are hidden there. The upper right-hand area, which contains information about you that is unknown to yourself but known to others, is called the **blind area** because you are blind to the information contained in it. Finally, the lower-right area, which contains information about you that is unknown to yourself and others, is called the **unknown area** because it contains things about yourself that remain to be discovered.

The window in figure 8.1 has four equal areas, but your own Johari Window would show different-sized areas, depending on the relationship. For example, your open area would likely be larger for a close friend than for a stranger. Figure 8.2 presents four different Johari Windows, each representing a different—and exaggerated—interaction style.

Known to self   Not known to self

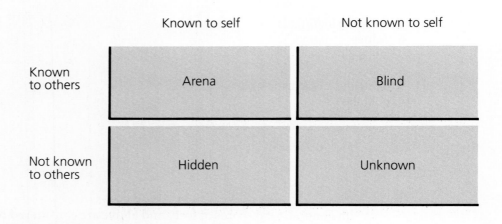

	Known to self	Not known to self
Known to others	Arena	Blind
Not known to others	Hidden	Unknown

▶ **F I G U R E   8 . 1**   Johari Window

Style I, with its small arena, depicts a person who is unwilling either to disclose or to receive feedback. This person takes few risks and often appears aloof and uncommunicative. The largest area is the unknown, indicating that this person has a great deal to learn about herself or himself.

Style II depicts a person who is willing to receive feedback but unwilling to disclose. This person may fear exposure, possibly because he or she perceives others as untrustworthy. Unlike the Style I person, this individual seems friendly and supportive at first—mainly because of a willingness to listen—but after a short time it becomes apparent that this person will not share anything personal, so the initial positive feelings turn to distrust. Style II people, because their largest area is the hidden one, are ultimately perceived as secretive and detached.

Style III depicts the opposite of Style II: this person is willing to disclose but unwilling to seek, encourage, or receive feedback. Unless interacting with a Style II person (who is willing to listen but not talk), a Style III person may be perceived as self-centered and egotistical. Style III people have large blind areas, indicating they have much to learn about themselves that others could provide. Unfortunately, Style III people won't listen.

Style IV people, with their large open areas, are willing to disclose information about themselves and to receive feedback. Although Style IV may seem to be the best of the four possibilities—given that a Style IV person has the highest probability of forming close and personal relationships—it is not without drawbacks. For example, a Style IV person may appear aggressive to a Style I person (insisting on interacting on more than a superficial level), demanding to a Style II person (trying to get the Style II person to talk), and egotistical to a Style III person (self-disclosing instead of silently listening to Style III's monologue). Style IV interaction can be intimidating to people who are unwilling to talk, unwilling to listen, or unwilling to do both. Used in

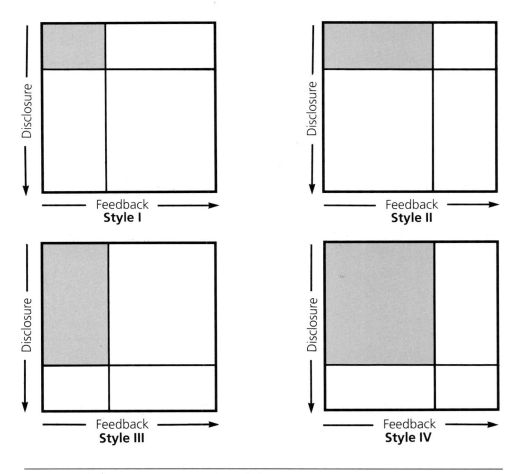

▶ **FIGURE 8.2** Interaction Styles

moderation, however, beginning with relatively low levels of self-disclosure and requests for feedback and building to higher levels, Style IV is the most successful interaction style for forming personal relationships.

Use figure 8.3 to draw your own Johari Window. Plot your "willingness to self-disclose" total score on the vertical axis and your "willingness to receive feedback" total score on the horizontal axis. With the points marked on each axis, draw lines down and across the window so that you have four areas. How does your Johari Window compare with the four styles in figure 8.2? Which area of your window is largest? What does your Johari Window indicate about your interaction with the person you had in mind as you completed the knowledge checkup?

If you scored low on Part 1 of Knowledge Checkup 8.3, consider developing skills to increase your self-disclosing communication. You may have trouble

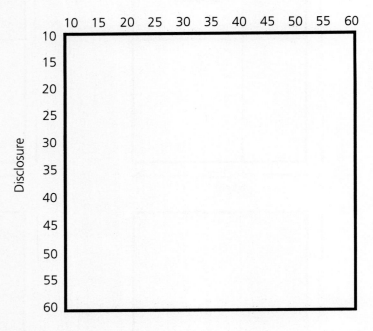

▶ **FIGURE 8.3** Your Johari Window

trusting people to respond to your disclosures in ways that are comfortable for you. The following skill checkup could help you develop some skill at self-disclosing while increasing your trust.

SKILL CHECKUP 8.3

Increasing Your Self-Disclosure

Examine your responses to Part 1 of Knowledge Checkup 8.3.

1. What aspects of yourself are you unwilling to share? Make a list of the information you keep to yourself in each of your weaker areas.

2. Select your least threatening secret and ask yourself what the most horrible consequences would be if you revealed it.

3. With your least threatening secret and its presumed consequences in mind, tell your secret to the person with whom you feel safest.

4. Observe what happens. You will probably learn that your secret is more threatening to you than it is to others and that the horrible consequences you imagine rarely come to pass.

5. Continue to think about each secret, its consequences, and telling it to someone. Remember that you do not have to reveal *every* secret or even *everything* about each secret.

As you gain experience in self-disclosing, you should become more skilled at knowing what to reveal and when. Also, your assessment of the potential risks should become more realistic.

If you scored low on Part 2 of Knowledge Checkup 8.3, consider developing skills to increase your receptiveness to feedback about yourself. You may doubt that others' comments will be relevant, or you may believe that others' comments can hurt you. Once you realize that feedback *may* be relevant (you can decide whether or not it is) and that *you choose* how to feel (you don't *have* to feel hurt by what someone says, although you can *choose* to—you can also choose to feel happy, sad, glad, or disappointed), you can begin to open yourself to feedback by not cutting off others' observations and by practicing requests for information. Phrases such as "Tell me what you think about what I just said" and "How do you feel about my. . . ?" encourage the other person to provide feedback. The resulting information will be only as useful as you decide to let it be.

What you choose to disclose depends on several considerations. Does the disclosure suit the relationship? For example, highly intimate disclosure in a nonintimate relationship is inappropriate. Is the disclosure relevant to the relationship? Disclosure about your family to your employer, for example, may not be pertinent to your relationship. Is the disclosure relevant to the immediate interaction? How likely is the other person to treat the disclosure with respect? How constructive is the disclosure likely to be for the relationship? Can you communicate your disclosures clearly and understandably?

Self-disclosure isn't an all-or-nothing proposition; it begins slowly with revealing positive aspects of yourself and progresses—if at all—to greater breadth, depth, and amount. Early disclosures test the situation: Is this person trustworthy? Will this person care about what I say? Each yes bolsters your willingness to self-disclose.

Despite its benefits, self-disclosure is risky. Telling your boss how you feel about the new organizational chart may lead to rebuke and early retirement, just as telling your friend how you *really* feel about his new shirt may result in hurt feelings. How will the other person feel about you after you disclose? What will happen to your relationship if you disclose your real feelings? You may well have to ask yourself whether you want to be polite or honest.

The primary fear associated with self-disclosing for both men and women is the fear of rejection.[10] Many men also fear that disclosing will make them look bad and cause them to lose control over other people: "If you know my weaknesses, I will no longer be powerful." Many women, on the other hand, fear the consequences of disclosure for the relationship: "If I disclose, you might use the information against me" or "Disclosing might hurt our relationship." For the majority of men, control is the primary objective; for the majority of women, the relationship itself is. These objectives affect how each gender discloses and the reasons each chooses to avoid disclosure. The fears associated with disclosing are great, but the rewards are great as well.

Ending a Relationship

Relationships end for a variety of reasons. Goals may be fulfilled and no new goals established. Goals may not be accomplished and there may be little chance of achieving them. The partners may continue to feel lonely despite their relationship. The patterns of interaction may be too fixed, too inflexible—or too boring. The initial attractiveness may fade and nothing new may replace it. New relationships may appear more attractive. Changes in either person may alter the possible rewards: the two may no longer agree on things that were once no problem and their interests may no longer be compatible. Sexual dysfunction, conflicts with work, financial difficulties, changes in commitment—and endless other possibilities—may plague highly intimate relationships. Relationships are fragile, and the possible threats to their well-being are numerous and powerful.

Several of the most common communication strategies for the disengagement process have been studied.[11] Six critical dimensions describe the variations in relationship disengagements. The first three dimensions are as follows:

▶ Was the onset of relational problems gradual or sudden? Most problems emerge gradually, making it difficult to determine their specific causes and the most clearly related consequences.

▶ Does only one partner want to end the relationship (unilateral desire) or do both agree (bilateral desire)?

▶ Is a direct or an indirect strategy used to end the relationship?

For example, if you want to end a relationship and the other person does not, you may confront the other person with your desire—a direct strategy. You may also say nothing but arrange to see the other person less—an indirect strategy. If both you and the other person wish to end your relationship, a direct strategy would be to talk it out and an indirect strategy would be to decrease the amount of time you spend together.

Strategies vary not only according to whether they're direct or indirect, but also according to whether they're self-oriented or other-oriented. Strategies that seem to have a self-orientation are *fait accompli* ("I've decided—this is over!"), *withdrawal* ("I'm going to be busy all next week"), *cost escalation* ("If you want me to go with you, you'll have to give up going out on Fridays with your other friends"), and *attributional conflict* ("It's your fault, *jerk!*"). Fait accompli takes control away from the other person, inflicting a blow to the other's self-esteem. Withdrawal also limits the other's control. Cost escalation raises the

STRATEGIES	DESIRE TO EXIT: UNILATERAL	DESIRE TO EXIT: BILATERAL
Direct	1. fait accompli: declaration that the relationship is over 2. state-of-the-relationship talk: discussion of dissatisfaction, relationship problems, and desire to exit	1. attibutional conflict: hostile argument focused on why termination is necessary 2. negotiated farewell: conflict-free discussion to formally end the relationship
Indirect	1. withdrawal: decrease of intimacy and/or contact 2. pseudo-deescalation: false declaration of a desire to reduce closeness when the goal is termination 3. cost escalation: increase in costs to the other person to maintain the relationship, (for example, treat the other disrespectfully)	1. fading away: decrease of contact without any discussion of the relationship 2. pseudo-deescalation: mutual false declaration of a desire to reduce closeness when the goal is termination

▶ **TABLE 8.1** Strategies for Relationship Disengagement

relationship's costs for the other person, and attributional conflict results in hostile communication of disparaging remarks.

In contrast, *state-of-the-relationship talk* ("Where is this relationship going?"), *pseudo-deescalation* ("I think we should see less of each other for awhile"—when the real goal is termination), *negotiated farewell* ("Let's rationally discuss how to end this without fighting"), and *fading away* (seeing the other person less and disclosing less) are more other-oriented. They allow some face-saving for both relationship partners.

Table 8.1 summarizes various methods of ending relationships in four possible situations: unilateral and bilateral desires to exit using a direct strategy, and unilateral and bilateral desires to exit using an indirect strategy. Except for the bilateral-indirect situation, each describes a self-oriented and an other-oriented strategy. The two indirect strategies for terminating a relationship when both people want it to end are other-oriented.

The final three dimensions on which disengagement processes may be distinguished are as follows:

▶ Does it take a long time or a short time to break away? Using an indirect strategy is likely to result in a drawn-out disengagement with several rounds of negotiations. Overreliance on indirectness is also likely to lead both partners to regret that they didn't use a more direct strategy to make the break quicker and less complex.

▶ Are there any attempts to repair the relationship? Partners are more likely to try to repair their relationship if they use an indirect disengagement strategy.

▶ Is the final outcome termination or a restructured relationship? Restructuring may result in a relationship that is successfully repaired and restored to approximately the same state it was in before problems arose, or it may lead to a different relationship with new goals, structure, or rules, or modified commitment, intimacy, or resources. The infrequency with which relationships are successfully restructured demonstrates the difficulty of accomplishing this task to both partners' satisfaction.

The most frequently used disengagement process involves a unilateral desire to exit (one person wants out) coupled with an indirect strategy (the person decreases contact, claims a desire to reduce contact when no contact is really the goal, or makes contact very costly for the other person), with no attempts at repair, which leads to termination without trying to structure a new relationship (the pair say good-bye with no expectation for future contact). For example, Leslie wants to break off with Dale. Leslie stops calling Dale. Dale calls Leslie and asks, "What's wrong?" Leslie tells Dale, "Nothing. I don't want to talk about it. Good-bye." Leslie hangs up.

INCREASING RELATIONAL SATISFACTION

Your relationships are what you make them. This is good news because it underscores your active role. You can begin relationships to meet your goals. You can improve relationships that need improvement. And you can end relationships that are best ended.

Here are some thoughts that might help you achieve more effective, satisfying relationships:

1. Be aware that *relationships have goals.* Understanding your goals, the other person's goals, and your mutual goals should provide a firm foundation for obtaining those goals. At the least, understanding all the goals should help you assess the relationship's possibilities.

2. Be aware that *relationships have structure* and that that structure can be changed to meet changing needs. Changing patterns of behavior is difficult, but recognizing the patterns that exist and determining which patterns might be better can help the relationship grow in responsible and beneficial ways.

3. Be aware that *relationships have rules*. The rules coordinate interaction and make it more predictable. You have to know the rules to follow them, so talking about rules and reaching mutual understanding can benefit you and your partner. And if you want to change a rule, recognize that doing so is a slow process, one that requires understanding the reasons for the rule in the first place.

4. Be aware that *relationships are always in process*. Like everything else, relationships change with time. Attempting to freeze a relationship at one moment in time is bound to fail. Relationships change as you and the other person change, and as the context for the relationship changes. Although this progression may seem obvious, few people behave as if change is inevitable. The comfort of old habits, old patterns, and old viewpoints can be more powerful than the reality of change. The moment comes when the relationship *as it is* no longer matches what either of the partners *thinks* it is, and the result of their shortsightedness is conflict.

5. Be aware that *relationships require attention*. Creating a supportive, confirming communication climate and appropriately self-disclosing are important ways of attending to your relationship. They ensure the exchange of information necessary for meeting your and your partner's needs as well as the needs of the relationship. Talk about your relationship with your partner and deal directly with relational issues.

COMMUNICATION COMPETENCY CHECKUP

1. For the man and woman looking at the right, what are the most plausible reasons for these two individuals' attraction to each other?

2. Based on the five steps for forming a new relationship, what specific recommendations would you make to each person?

3. Assume that your recommendations are good ones and that the two persons begin a relationship. Problems arise, however, because he avoids self-disclosing and she complains that he's too quiet and doesn't seem to care about her. What could each do to help maintain their relationship?

4. The relationship is crumbling. Because you are their friend, they come to you for help. What questions would you ask to gain understanding of their disengagement?

5. They are so impressed with your insight that they invite you to address their school club. The title for your talk is "The Relationship Fairy Is Dead." What would you tell the audience about increasing relational satisfaction?

NOTES

1. A summary of recent studies concerned with the similarity principle of attraction, what characteristics are perceived as attractive, and the implications of people marrying people with whom they share many similarities, is available in: David M. Buss, "Human Mate Selection," *American Scientist* 73 (January–February 1985): 47–51.

2. For a summary of the research on the effects of physical attractiveness, see: Mark L. Knapp, *Interpersonal Communication and Human Relationships* (Boston: Allyn and Bacon, 1984), pp. 141–44; and H. T. Reis, J. Nexlek, and L. Wheeler, "Physical Attractiveness in Social Interaction," *Journal of Personality and Social Psychology* 38 (1980): 604–17.

3. Buss, p. 48.

4. Jack R. Gibb, "Defensive Communication," *Journal of Communication* 11 (September 1961): 141–48.

5. Kenneth N. L. Cissna and Evelyn Sieburg, "Patterns of Interactional Confirmation and Disconfirmation," in C. Wilder-Mott and J. H. Weakland, eds., *Rigor and Imagination: Essays from the Legacy of Gregory Bateson* (New York: Praeger, 1981), pp. 253–82.

6. Dale G. Leathers, *Successful Nonverbal Communication: Principles and Applications* (New York: Macmillan, 1986), pp. 227–30.

7. Valerian J. Derlega, "Self-Disclosure and Intimate Relationships," in Valerian J. Derlega, ed., *Communication, Intimacy, and Close Relationships* (Orlando, FL: Academic Press, 1984), pp. 1–9.

8. Lawrence B. Rosenfeld and W. Leslie Kendrick, "Choosing to Be Open: Subjective Reasons for Self-Disclosing," *Western Journal of Speech Communication* 48 (1984): 326–43.

9. The Johari Window was developed by Joseph Luft and Harry Ingham. For a detailed explanation, see: Joseph Luft, *Group Processes: An Introduction to Group Dynamics*, 2d ed. (Palo Alto, CA: National Press Books, 1970), pp. 11–20.

10. Lawrence B. Rosenfeld, "Self-Disclosure Avoidance: Why I Am Afraid to Tell You Who I Am," *Communication Monographs* 46 (1979): 63–74.

11. A series of studies concerned with relationship disengagement is summarized in: Leslie A. Baxter, "Accomplishing Relationship Disengagement," in Steve Duck and Daniel Perlman, eds., *Understanding Human Relationships* (Beverly Hills, CA: Sage, 1985), pp. 243–65.

FOR FURTHER INVESTIGATION

Baxter, Leslie A. "Accomplishing Relationship Disengagement." In *Understanding Personal Relationships*, edited by Steve Duck and Daniel Perlman, pp. 243–65. Beverly Hills, CA: Sage, 1985.

Bell, Robert A., and John A. Daly. "The Affinity-Seeking Function of Communication," *Communication Monographs* 51 (1984): 91–114.

Buss, David M. "Human Mate Selection." *American Scientist* 73 (January–February 1985): 47–51.

Chelune, Gordon J., ed. *Self-Disclosure*. San Francisco: Jossey-Bass, 1979.

Derlega, Valerian J., ed. *Communication, Intimacy, and Close Relationships*. Orlando, FL: Academic Press, 1984.

Gibb, Jack R. "Defensive Communication." *Journal of Communication* 11 (September 1961): 141–48.

Glaser, Susan R., and Anna Eblen. *Toward Communication Competency: Developing Interpersonal Skills*, 2d ed. New York: Holt, Rinehart and Winston, 1986.

Jourard, Sidney M. *The Transparent Self*, 2d ed. Princeton, NJ: Van Nostrand, 1971.

Knapp, Mark L. *Interpersonal Communication and Human Relationships*. Boston: Allyn and Bacon, 1984.

Luft, Joseph. *Of Human Interaction*. Palo Alto, CA: National Press Books, 1969.

Petronio, Sandra, Judith Martin, and Robert Littlefield. "Prerequisite Conditions for Self-Disclosing." *Communication Monographs* 51 (1984): 268–73.

Powell, John. *Why Am I Afraid to Tell You Who I Am?* Chicago: Argus Communications, 1969.

Rosenfeld, Lawrence B. "Self-Disclosure Avoidance: Why I Am Afraid to Tell You Who I Am." *Communication Monographs* 46 (1979): 63–74.

Rosenfeld, Lawrence B., and Mary W. Jarrard. "Communication Climate and Coping Mechanisms in the College Classroom." *Communication Education* 32 (1983): 167–74.

Rosenfeld, Lawrence B., and W. Leslie Kendrick. "Choosing to Be Open: Subjective Reasons for Self-Disclosing." *Western Journal of Speech Communication* 48 (1984): 326–43.

Sieberg, Evelyn. "Confirming and Disconfirming Organizational Communication." In *Communication in Organizations*, edited by James L. Owen, Paul Page, and Gordon I. Zimmerman. New York: West, 1976.

CHAPTER 9

▶ # *Managing Relationship Discord*

*This chapter on managing relationship discord will help you practice and develop communication competencies that fall into four broad categories: (1) **communication codes,** which include listening effectively and using verbal and nonverbal cues that are appropriate to a particular situation; (2) **oral message evaluation,** such as distinguishing facts from opinions and recognizing when someone does not understand your message; (3) **basic speech communication skills,** which include expressing ideas clearly and concisely, defending your point of view, and asking questions to obtain information; and (4) **human relations,** including describing another's viewpoint, describing differences in opinion, and expressing your feelings. Specifically, the competencies you will gain will enable you to do the following:*

▶ *Describe the three distinguishing features of conflict situations and use them to analyze your own conflicts.*

▶ *Recognize the sources of your personal view of conflict.*

▶ *Analyze the constructive and destructive consequences of your conflicts.*

▶ *Describe your conflict strategies and style and assess their advantages and disadvantages.*

▶ *Respond assertively in conflict situations.*

▶ *Describe the advantages and disadvantages of win-lose, lose-lose, and win-win approaches to conflict.*

▶ *Apply a win-win conflict management technique.*

▶ *Assess the process and outcomes of a conflict.*

*H*ow many of the following fairy tale endings do you recognize?

She was as good as she was beautiful. She set aside apartments in the palace for her two sisters and married them the very same day to two gentlemen of high rank about the court.

They were all quite happy now. The huntsman skinned the wolf and took the skin home. The grandmother ate the cake and drank the wine that the little girl had brought and she soon felt quite strong. The little girl thought, "I will never again wander off into the forest if my mother forbids it."

There she lay, looking so beautiful he could not take his eyes off her; he bent down and gave her a kiss. As he touched her, she opened her eyes and looked lovingly at him. . . . Then their wedding was celebrated with great splendor, and they lived happily till they died.

Then Jack showed his mother the golden harp, and what with showing that and selling the golden eggs, Jack and his mother became very rich, and he married a great princess, and they lived happily ever after.

The first ending is from "Cinderella," the second from "Little Red Riding Hood," the third from "Sleeping Beauty," and the fourth from "Jack and the Beanstalk." Four different stories, one common outlook: conflicts should end happily.

CONFLICT AND CONFLICT SITUATIONS

You may believe that even better than a conflict that ends happily is no conflict at all. You may wish for, hope for, and even work for peace between nations, between groups within a nation, between individuals, and in your own relationships. How successful are you? Is peace—*real* peace, not merely a cease-fire—possible?

Your own experiences probably confirm that a conflict-free relationship between normal human beings is unlikely. The inevitability of conflict, however, shouldn't disturb you. In fact, conflict can play a positive role in healthy and growing relationships. Conflict may be impossible to eliminate, but it can be managed successfully with appropriate communication skills.

What do you do when you're involved in a conflict? Do you scream, cry, call names, throw things, hit walls or people? Do you stop talking, withdraw, glare at the other person, mutter hostile remarks under your breath? Do you try to reason things out, discuss the problem, seek solutions that satisfy both your needs and the needs of the other person? Do you behave differently in different conflicts?

Although types of conflicts and responses to conflict vary, all share some common characteristics.

A Definition of Conflict

A **conflict** is any situation in which you perceive that another person, with whom you're interdependent, is frustrating or might frustrate the satisfaction of some concern, need, want, or desire of yours. The source of the conflict is your perception of a limited resource, such as not enough money, an individual difference between you and the other person, such as differences in gender, and/or differences in how you and the other person define your relationship, such as "friend" versus "co-worker." Knowledge Checkup 9.1 will help you grasp the basic outline of all conflict situations.

KNOWLEDGE CHECKUP 9.1

Analysis of Relationship Discord

Think of a conflict in which you are currently engaged as you complete the following checkup. (If you are not involved in a conflict at this time, think of your most recent one.) Complete the following.

1. I want *(your concern, need, want)*_____ ,

but *(the other person)*_____

wants *(the other's concern, need, want)*_____ .

2. Describe how you and the other person are interdependent in ways that affect the conflict.

3. Describe the sources of the conflict.

Frustration

Conflict is a process that begins when you perceive that someone else has either frustrated some concern of yours, such as obtaining a goal, or is going to frustrate some concern of yours. Consider the following examples:

> I want *to borrow the car Saturday night,*
> but *my father*
> wants *to use it himself.*

> I want *to switch jobs with a co-worker,*
> but *the supervisor*
> wants *people to stay in the jobs they were hired to do.*

I want *to date different people,*
but *the person I'm dating right now*
wants *us to date only each other.*

If you communicate your concern to the other person, you have an **interpersonal conflict**, a conflict between people: you ask your father for the use of the car, you request the job swap from your supervisor, and you tell your current dating partner that you want to go out with other people.

If you decide to resolve the conflict on your own, you have an **intrapersonal conflict**, a conflict within one person. Without talking to your father, you may decide that he wants to use the car and that you couldn't have it even if you asked. You may decide that the supervisor is too inflexible and that it wouldn't pay to ask him about switching jobs. You may decide to keep your frustration about dating others to yourself because you fear you'll harm your current relationship. However, you are likely to communicate your frustration by being curt with your father, sarcastic with your supervisor, or withdrawn from the person you're dating. Recognizing interdependence, and resolving conflicts interpersonally, may well be less taxing in the long run.

Interdependence

You and the other person in your *I want . . . but . . . wants . . .* example are **interdependent**; that is, you depend on each other and need each other. Parents and children, workers and supervisors, and partners in a dating relationship all depend on each other for something, whether care, affection, goods, or services. Without interdependence, there is no interpersonal conflict.

You and your father together own the problem of who gets the car Saturday night. If you each had a car and if both cars were working and available—if you were not interdependent—there would be no conflict.

You and your supervisor need each other to solve the problem of how you can swap jobs with a co-worker. If you both saw the job change in the same way, there would be no conflict.

You and the person you're dating need each other to solve the problem of how to satisfy your desire to date other people. If you both defined your relationship the same way—as casual and nonexclusive or as serious and exclusive—there would be no conflict.

In what way are you and the other person in Knowledge Checkup 9.1 interdependent?

Sources of Conflict

The frustration that triggers your conflict has a source. Three common sources of conflict are limited resources, individual differences, and differences in defining your relationship.

Limited Resources   Limited resources are a widespread source of conflict. You may feel that any problem could be solved if there were more money, more time, more space, more tools, or more people to help. Because you and your father have only one car to share, the limited resource—the car—becomes a source of conflict.

Individual Differences   Individual differences are probably the most common and least-often acknowledged source of conflict. Each person's perceptions of the world are uniquely her or his own, based on her or his past experiences, her or his background and history, and how she or he interprets and responds to events. No two people view the same object or event in exactly the same way; these perceptual differences may trigger conflicts.

Among the typical sources of frustration are individual differences in gender, attitudes, beliefs, values, experiences, upbringing, and education. For example, your supervisor may believe that not rocking the boat is an important goal and have little experience with training methods that differ from how he or she was trained ("You get a job and stay in it"). You enjoy taking risks and have training in a variety of positions in the organization. The differences may not matter under most circumstances, but when you decide to swap positions with a co-worker, the stage is set for conflict.

Differences in Defining Your Relationship   The third general source of conflict stems from your view of your relationship: you and the other person may define your roles in the relationship differently, or you may define the relationship itself differently. For example, you may want to date other people because you see your current relationship as casual; you view yourselves as steady but not serious long-term partners. The other person may define the relationship as serious, and define your roles as intimate friends and prospective spouses. Under these circumstances, your desire to date other people triggers a conflict, one born of your different definitions of your relationship.

What is the source of the conflict you outlined in Knowledge Checkup 9.1?

PERCEPTIONS OF CONFLICT

Can you think of a situation in which limited resources, individual differences, or differences in definitions of the relationship do *not* exist? Such a situation would require individuals who were identical in their concerns, wants, needs, desires, attitudes, beliefs, values, goals, and perceptions of the other person and the relationship. Even identical twins raised in the same household are not *that* similar.

cathy®   by Cathy Guisewite

CATHY Copyright 1985 Universal Press Syndicate.
Reprinted with permission. All rights reserved.

Given that no two people are identical, it follows that conflict is natural and inevitable. The above comic strip expresses the normality of conflict.[1] The answer to Cathy's question requires a look at three main socializing agents: the family, educational institutions, and television.

Family

Perceptions of conflict are based on your early experiences with your family. How was conflict treated by your parents? Was it something to do openly, in front of you and your siblings, or was it something to be hidden behind closed doors late at night? Was it handled in productive ways so that the outcomes were positive, or were most conflicts screaming bouts followed by periods of cool silence? "Don't fight in front of the children" may be a norm in many families, but the message it communicates is that conflict is wrong, unfit for children.

As conflicts rage around you (whether conducted quietly or not), you're taught: "Don't fight with your brother!" "If you don't have something nice to say, don't say anything at all!" "Don't talk back!" "*Real* friends don't fight!" The intended point of these messages is the same: conflict is unnatural, something that good people who like each other don't do. But these messages are pitted against reality: people who love each other *do* fight, just as siblings and spouses who really care for each other do.

"And they lived happily ever after" is the essence of fairy tales, not *real* relationships between *real* people. Adopting the fairy-tale version of life can create frustration for yourself and your partner. Yet people are inclined to ask "What's wrong with us that we fight?" rather than reject the unrealistic and unattainable fairy-tale ending.

Educational Institutions

The message about conflict that you learn in educational institutions is similar to the one you learn at home: conflict is bad. In lower grades, a fight with a classmate means being sent to the principal and possibly having your parents called in for a conference. Instead of teaching youngsters how to deal constructively with their conflicts—how to define their problems and communicate their feelings and needs to each other to find a mutually satisfactory resolution—our schools punish children for perfectly understandable and predictable behavior.

Because open conflicts between teachers and students are forbidden, more subtle expressions of discord prevail. Teachers and students often exchange bristle statements, comments that each knows will probably trigger the other's anger. For example, a teacher may tell a student, "It's in the book—try reading it," or "No one forced you to take this course," while a student may ask, "Are we doing anything important in class today?" and "Do spelling and grammar count?" Each attacks the other in ways that sidestep the issue. Educational institutions teach students to fight dirty because, in our culture, conflicts are perceived as dirty.

Television

You have probably spent more hours watching television than you have spent in school, and you have probably learned more about day-to-day life from the tube than from your teachers. What are conflicts like in the programs you watch? In half-hour programs, you see complex problems being solved in twenty-four minutes plus commercials. In one-hour programs, even more complex problems get resolved in about fifty minutes plus commercials. But real life is *not* made up of half-hour and one-hour segments.

Your own life is not realistically portrayed on television, so when your conflicts fail to conform to television-style conflicts and resolutions, you probably assume that something is wrong with *you*. "What's wrong with *me*, and what's wrong with *us*, that our conflicts last for a long time, rarely end neatly, and aren't as glamorous or as gloriously dramatic as the conflicts on TV?" Television may embody the modern fairy tale where, in the end, everybody but the bad guy lives happily ever after, but is this reality?

CONSEQUENCES OF CONFLICT

Your early experiences no doubt introduced you to many of the negative consequences of conflict, and they may have persuaded you that conflict is something to be avoided. But conflict may also have positive consequences that benefit your work, your relationships, and you personally.

Effects on Work

Conflict is dysfunctional when it keeps you from doing your work. It takes time and energy to engage in or avoid a conflict. Also, an unresolved conflict requires a great deal of thought about who said what, when, and how, what caused the conflict, and what can be done about it. When you have a conflict on your mind, reading one page of a textbook may take an hour, concentrating on a lecture may be difficult, and dealing with a customer may be almost impossible.

Conflict may also be dysfunctional when it forces conformity. If you fear that open conflict may lead to public ridicule, blame, or harsh punishment, you are likely to accept whatever happens and keep your frustrations to yourself.

In contrast, conflict is functional when it increases your motivation to interact with the person causing your frustration, to discuss the areas of conflict, and to arrive at new and better solutions to the problem. Conflict often yields results when heightened excitement and interaction get channeled into direct confrontations that focus on resolution.

Effects on Relationships

Conflicts are dysfunctional when they threaten the integrity of a relationship. Given that half the marriages in the United States end in divorce, conflicts obviously threaten and destroy relationships.[2] If two persons perceive that an important problem cannot be resolved within the confines of their relationship, they may terminate the relationship.

Conflicts are functional when they promote relationship growth, which can happen in two ways. First, conflicts require negotiation about how to negotiate. How will you and your partner communicate your thoughts and feelings? How will you agree on a solution? As you answer these questions, you develop new strategies for interacting with each other.

Second, conflicts require the exchange of new information about the subject of the dispute. Information about each person's needs, wants, desires, and goals is necessary to generate and select a mutually satisfactory solution to the problem. Acquiring and using new strategies for interacting, plus gaining and using new information, equals relational growth.

Knowledge Checkup 9.2 helps you analyze the messages a television program provides concerning the effect of conflict on relationships.

KNOWLEDGE CHECKUP 9.2

Boob-Tube Battles

Here's your chance to watch television and *admit it*! Choose a program that focuses on personal or family relationships (sitcoms and evening soaps are good sources).

1. Describe the conflicts portrayed in a single episode.

2. Describe the negative consequences of each conflict.

3. Describe the positive consequences.

4. Based on your observations, agree or disagree with these statements:

    a. Conflicts threaten the integrity of relationships.

    b. Conflicts strengthen relationships.

    c. Relationship growth is a consequence of conflict.

Personal Effects

A conflict is dysfunctional when it leaves you feeling foolish, inadequate, or cruel. Insults such as "You're stupid," whether you say them or someone says them to you, are personally destructive. If you say them, they testify to your cruelty; if someone says them to you, they prompt self-doubt and feelings of inadequacy, or possibly fury.

In contrast, functional conflicts increase your self-understanding and feelings of self-worth. You learn about yourself, how you view certain issues, and how strongly you feel about them. You also increase your ability to see life through someone else's eyes, to understand how others think and feel about issues that are important to them.

Knowledge Checkup 9.3 will help you assess whether your conflicts are primarily functional or dysfunctional by focusing on your verbal shooting gallery.

KNOWLEDGE CHECKUP 9.3

Inventory of Your Verbal Shooting Gallery

Think about conflicts you have had with your parents, siblings, and friends. Which of these phrases (or similar ones) did you use? Circle all that are part of your verbal shooting gallery.

"You're stupid!"
"I hate you!"
"You're just like your father/mother/sister/brother!"
"I wish you were dead!"
"If you loved me you wouldn't . . . ."
"You think *that's* a problem? That's *nothing*!"

"If you'd do it *my* way . . . ."
"I told you so!"
"Your problem is easy to trace: poor toilet training!"
"Why do you always . . .?"
"Can't you ever do anything right?"
"For an idiot, that's a good answer!"
"That's *ridiculous*!"
"*You're* ridiculous!"

APPROACHES TO CONFLICT

You learn early in life how to manage conflicts. The particular conflict strategies you use now stem from your interactions with your parents and siblings, teachers and classmates, friends and enemies—and from familiar television programs. Your responses to conflict are probably automatic, which poses a problem: automatic responses are difficult to recognize, yet you must recognize them before change is possible.

Conflict Strategies

When your needs seem incompatible with other people's needs, how do you react? What strategies do you use to resolve your conflicts? Knowledge Checkup 9.4 will help you increase your awareness of the conflict strategies you use.

KNOWLEDGE CHECKUP 9.4

Self-Assessment of Conflict Strategies[3]

Consider situations in which your wishes differ from those of another person. How do you usually respond? Listed below are twenty responses to conflict. As you respond to these items, think of either your *typical* response to most conflicts or your response to conflicts with one *particular* person. Use the following scale to indicate how often you respond in each way:

Write 1 if you never or almost never respond this way (0–10% of the time)
Write 2 if you rarely respond this way (11–30% of the time)
Write 3 if you sometimes respond this way (31–70% of the time)
Write 4 if you usually respond this way (71–90% of the time)
Write 5 if you always or almost always respond this way (91–100% of the time)

_____ **1.** I generally try to satisfy the needs of the other person.
_____ **2.** I attempt to avoid being put on the spot and try to keep my conflict with the other person to myself.
_____ **3.** I try to integrate my ideas with the other person's to come up with a joint decision.
_____ **4.** I usually avoid open discussion of my differences with the other person.
_____ **5.** I usually stick to my solution to a problem.
_____ **6.** I try to find a middle course to resolve an impasse.
_____ **7.** I sometimes help the other person to make a decision in her or his favor.
_____ **8.** I exchange accurate information with the other person so we can solve our problem together.
_____ **9.** I use my influence to get my ideas accepted.
_____ **10.** I try to keep my disagreement with the other person to myself in order to avoid hard feelings.
_____ **11.** I usually propose a middle ground for breaking deadlocks.
_____ **12.** I try to bring all our concerns out in the open so that the issues can be resolved in the best possible way.
_____ **13.** I usually grant concessions to the other person.
_____ **14.** I am generally firm in pursuing my side of the issue.
_____ **15.** I generally avoid an argument with the other person.
_____ **16.** I negotiate with the other person so that a compromise can be reached.
_____ **17.** I try to work with the other person for a proper understanding of the problem.
_____ **18.** I often go along with the suggestions of the other person.
_____ **19.** I sometimes use my power to win a competitive situation with the other person.
_____ **20.** I give some to get some.

Scoring

Avoidance
    Add your responses to items 2, 4, 10, and 15: _____
Smoothing Over
    Add your responses to items 1, 7, 13, and 18: _____
Dominance
    Add your responses to items 5, 9, 14, and 19: _____
Compromise
    Add your responses to items 6, 11, 16, and 20: _____
Integration
    Add your responses to items 3, 8, 12, and 17: _____

On which of the five strategies did you score highest and on which did you score lowest? You may use different strategies in different situations, but the odds are that you have a favorite strategy that you use whether or not it is most appropriate for the situation.

You need to know your typical responses to conflict so that you can examine their appropriateness and make decisions about their use. If you understand which strategy is best for a given conflict, you can increase the range of your responses and, therefore, react more effectively.

Each of the five conflict strategies balances differing amounts of self-satisfaction and concern for the other person. Being too concerned with the other person's welfare may leave your own needs unsatisfied, while concern only for yourself may seem self-aggrandizing, even if you do get what you want. Each strategy has advantages and disadvantages that must be weighed against the demands of the situation:[4] no one strategy suits every situation.

Avoidance

Also called denial or withdrawal, avoidance strategy posits that a conflict will just go away if it is ignored. Only rarely, however, does a conflict permanently go away, so people who use this strategy must worry that their conflict will reoccur.

The biggest problem with avoidance strategy is that neither your needs nor the other person's needs are satisfied. Though you may be able to persuade yourself that your needs are unimportant, you will likely find out differently in time. You can intellectually reject the issue as trivial, but your body may respond with stress-related disorders, such as headaches and ulcers.

Of course, avoidance sometimes is an appropriate response to a conflict. *If* neither the issue nor your relationship with the other person is very important to you, withdrawal may be a reasonable strategy. But don't fool yourself about the true importance of these two variables.

What was your avoidance score on the self-assessment? A score of fourteen or more is higher than most, and a score below eight is lower than most.

Smoothing Over

Also called an obliging or suppression strategy, a **smoothing-over** strategy shows concern for the other person but not for yourself. This strategy aims to satisfy the other person's concerns, to the neglect of your own. It grows out of the notions that "nice people don't fight" and "if you don't have something nice to say, then don't say anything."

Smoothing is often used as a delaying tactic, to keep things peaceful until the conflict goes away. However, because your needs have been subverted, the conflict does not go away. Just like people who avoid open conflict, people who smooth things over must always worry that the problem will recur.

A smoothing strategy does suit some conflicts. *If* your concern is really unimportant to you and *if* maintaining your relationship with the other person is very important, smoothing may be effective. But once again, an honest assessment of the importance of these two factors is crucial.

What was your smoothing-over score on the self-assessment? A score of twelve and above is higher than most, and a score below six is lower than most.

Dominance

Also called power or forcing, **dominance** is the reverse of smoothing over: it focuses on your own needs at the expense of the other person. Your ability to dominate the other person may come from your position (you may be the supervisor, the parent, or the person with the needed information), your physical size or strength, or your control of rewards and punishments. "Do what I want or else!" is a common threat from those who try to use dominance to solve their problems.

The primary problem with this strategy is that, while your own needs may be satisfied, those of the other person remain unsatisfied, which will likely breed resentment, hostility, and a desire for revenge. For example, a father who refuses to give his daughter the car when she needs it may satisfy his need to use the car himself or his need to confirm that he's in charge, but his daughter is likely to retaliate by refusing to cooperate in some other situation.

There are times when a dominating strategy is appropriate. For example, an emergency situation may call for quick and decisive action, and discussion may make matters worse. When a small child runs into a busy street, you must return her to the sidewalk quickly. You and the child may have incompatible goals and both feel frustrated, but the circumstance requires a dominating strategy to avoid disaster.

On the whole, however, a dominating strategy is rarely the best one. It should be used only *if* your goal is very important to you and *if* your relationship with the other person is of little or no importance. Remember that once you create a situation with you as the winner and the other person as the loser, you probably also create an enemy.

What was your dominance score on the self-assessment? A score of fourteen and above is higher than most, and a score below six is lower than most.

Compromise

Also called bargaining or negotiating, **compromise** is a sharing strategy designed to satisfy everyone's concerns to some extent. The aim is to give up something to gain something.

Although compromise seems ideal in theory, in reality it rarely resolves conflicts. Getting your own way at another's expense (dominating), or letting another have her or his way at your expense (smoothing over) may be forestalled by compromise, but compromise usually does not permanently resolve conflicts.

Compromise may be a popular conflict strategy because people generally believe that something is better than nothing. If the odds of getting your needs fully satisfied are slight, or if the end result may be no satisfaction at all, a little satisfaction may seem a worthy goal. The problem with compromise, however, is that people rarely negotiate in good faith. Because they assume that they'll have to give in a little, they inflate their demands. And because they assume that something is better than nothing, they are willing to compromise on matters that are truly important to them and thus should not be conceded. If both persons operate on the assumption that honesty may not be the best policy, they try to deceive each other by arguing for irrelevant issues, which they can later relinquish as bargaining chips. For example, union negotiators often include extraneous items in their list of demands so that they can seem to be giving something up when they withdraw those items from negotiation.

Finally, working out a fair compromise requires communication skills that may be too advanced for many people. For example, you need to communicate exactly what your concerns are and what you are and are not willing to give up. You also need to listen actively to determine how the other person's concerns do and do not conflict with your own.

If your goal and your relationship are both moderately important to you, compromise may be an appropriate conflict strategy, but the importance of these two variables and the level of both individuals' communication skills are crucial determinants.

What was your compromise score on the self-assessment? A score of fifteen and above is higher than most, and a score below eight is lower than most.

Integration

Also referred to as collaboration, problem solving, and confronting, **integration** has as its goal the full satisfaction of your own and the other person's concerns. By definition alone, this strategy may seem to be the best one, but it has limited usefulness. *If* the goal and the relationship are both very important, integration may be the most appropriate strategy to employ. However, in most cases, either the concern or the relationship is not very important or both are of only moderate importance.

Besides taking the most time, an integrating strategy requires the widest range of well-developed communication skills. For example, you must be able to self-disclose openly and honestly about your own needs and to listen actively to the disclosures of the other person. You must be able to see the problem from the other person's perspective and integrate that other person's perspective with your own. You must integrate your needs with the other person's needs to be able to generate creative and mutually satisfying solutions. You must also realize that the issues at stake in the conflict are more important than the contestants' egos.

What was your integration score on the self-assessment? A score of seventeen and above is higher than average, and a score below ten is lower than average.

Conflict Resolution Strategies

To increase your ability to respond to conflicts appropriately you need to recognize the strategies available to you and understand when each is best to use.

1. Avoidance, a strategy of denial or withdrawal based on the belief that if the conflict is ignored it will go away, is appropriate when neither your relationship with the other person nor the conflict issue are important to you.

2. Smoothing over, an obliging strategy that aims to satisfy the other person's needs while denying your own, is appropriate when your relationship with the other person is important to you and the conflict issue is not.

3. Dominance, a power or forcing strategy that aims to satisfy your own needs while ignoring the other person's, is appropriate when your relationship with the other person is unimportant and the conflict issue is very important.

4. Compromise, a bargaining or negotiating strategy that aims to satisfy your own and the other person's needs to some extent, is appropriate when your relationship with the other person and the conflict issue are both of moderate importance to you and full satisfaction of your and your partner's needs seems impossible to attain.

5. Integration, a collaboration or problem-solving strategy that aims to satisfy both your and your partner's needs fully, is appropriate when both your relationship with the other person and the conflict issue are very important to you. This strategy requires highly developed communication skills as well as a great deal of time.

SKILL CHECKUP 9.1

Selecting a Conflict Strategy

Situation 1

1. Describe a conflict that you observed from beginning to end between two people.

2. Identify each person's conflict strategy.

3. Based on the conflict strategies you observed, how important did the conflict issue seem to be to each person? What specific behaviors did the individual display that support your conclusion?

4. Based on the conflict strategies you observed, how important did the relationship seem to be for each person? What specific behaviors did each individual display that support your conclusion?

Situation 2

1. Describe a conflict involving you and one other person.

2. Identify your conflict strategy. What behaviors support your identification?

3. Given the importance of the conflict issue and the relationship, was your strategy appropriate? Why was it appropriate, or why was it not? If it wasn't appropriate, which strategy would have been?

4. Identify the other person's conflict strategy. What behaviors support your identification?

5. Based on the other person's conflict strategy, what is your assessment of the importance of the conflict issue and the relationship for the other person?

Conflict Styles

Although your conflict strategy may vary from situation to situation, your **conflict style**, the characteristic way you express yourself in a conflict, remains fairly stable. The questionnaire in Knowledge Checkup 9.5 should help you determine your personal conflict style.

KNOWLEDGE CHECKUP 9.5

Self-Assessment of Conflict Style[5]

In responding to the following items, think of conflicts you have recently had with others. There are four parts in this questionnaire, each composed of four statements. For each part, divide *ten* points among the four statements to reflect how characteristic each is of your behavior. For example, if one of the four statements is completely characteristic of your behavior and the remaining three are totally uncharacteristic, you may decide to assign all ten points to the applicable statement and no points to each of the others. At the other extreme, if the four statements are almost equally characteristic of your behavior, two may be assigned three points each and two may be assigned two points each. In each part, make sure that points you assign to all four statements total ten.

Part 1

_____ **1a.** I stated my concerns directly and honestly.

_____ **1b.** I either avoided stating my concerns or expressed them in a self-deprecating way.

_____ **1c.** I stated my concerns in a way that either blamed or accused the other person of the problem.

_____ **1d.** I stated my concerns indirectly, hinting at them, even though I was angry.

Part 2

_____ **2a.** I expressed myself in a firm voice.

_____ **2b.** I expressed myself loudly, with a demanding tone.

_____ **2c.** I expressed myself with a weak, hesitant tone of voice.

_____ **2d.** My tone of voice was unrelated to how I really felt (for example, I was angry, but I spoke as if I were sad).

Part 3

_____ **3a.** I looked as though I didn't mean what I said.

_____ **3b.** I made an exaggerated show of strength.

_____ **3c.** I communicated caring and strength and listened attentively.

_____ **3d.** I acted however I felt would get me what I wanted, regardless of how I felt.

Part 4

_____ **4a.** I tried to make sure everyone came out a winner.

_____ **4b.** My concerns went unsatisfied, except in some cases when I was lucky.

_____ **4c.** I tried to beat out the other person to make sure I got my way.

_____ **4d.** I attempted to manipulate the other person to get what I wanted.

Scoring

Nonassertion
Add your responses to 1b, 2c, 3a, and 4b: _____
Indirect Aggression
Add your responses to 1d, 2d, 3d, and 4d: _____
Direct Aggression
Add your responses to 1c, 2b, 3b, and 4c: _____
Assertion
Add your responses to 1a, 2a, 3c, and 4a: _____

Which of your four scores is highest? That one style is probably most typical of how you express yourself during a conflict.

To successfully manage your conflicts requires that the other person be aware of your concerns. Two of the four conflict styles—nonassertion and indirect aggression—fail to directly communicate that there is a problem, and a third—direct aggression—communicates your concerns in a way that is almost guaranteed to raise more problems.[6]

Nonassertion

Reluctance to communicate your feelings and thoughts characterizes **nonassertive behavior** (also called passive behavior). Linked with avoidance strategies, nonassertive behavior virtually ensures that your concerns go unsatisfied, unless you are lucky or the other person takes pity on you. A nonassertive person will fail to take action or take action with someone completely uninvolved in the conflict. For example, you would be nonassertive if you received an incorrect bill from the gas company overcharging you for the month of April; and, instead of demanding a correction, you paid the bill and said nothing or complained to a friend about the unfairness of big business. Neither course informs the gas company that there is a problem.

Nonassertive communicators often defend their behavior by saying, "It wasn't the best time [or place] to talk," "I didn't think the other person was ready to hear what I wanted to say," or "They won't like me if I say what's on my mind." Such excuses have nothing to do with the actual situation; they merely justify avoiding an unpleasant exchange or a possible confrontation.

Several nonverbal cues accompany nonassertiveness, including rapid blinking, avoiding eye contact, squinting, repeated swallowing, throat clearing, tightening or pursing the lips, tensing and wrinkling the forehead, covering the mouth while speaking, shifting weight from foot to foot, and preening behaviors, such as hair smoothing, beard stroking, and fingernail cleaning. Notice whether you employ these behaviors. If you do, assess whether you want to change your conflict style.

Indirect Aggression

Indirect aggression is the expression of concerns in a disguised way. Rather than stating the real issue, you attack in various ways. These include the following:

▶ attacking the other person directly (you receive a D on a paper and, bursting into the professor's office, tell her, "I think you're a lousy teacher!");

▶ attacking the person indirectly ("What was your curve for the grades on the last set of papers?");

▶ lying about your real feelings ("I've thought about the D you gave me, and I really think I deserved it.");

▶ manipulating the situation ("I know you don't believe in extra-credit assignments, but if I do another paper on the same topic, will you read it and give me your comments?");

▶ embarrassing the person ("My lack of ability to write reflects your lack of ability to teach!");

▶ hinting about the problem ("Do you think I can still get an A in your course?");

▶ withholding something from the other person—some service, compliance with a request, or courtesy ("I forgot to pick up the papers that

▶ you wanted to give out in class today.");

inviting the person to feel guilty ("No, no, it's okay if you give me a D and I lose my scholarship."); and

▶ using sarcasm ("You want me to write better papers? Great advice coming from a teacher with ten typos on a five-page exam!").

Indirect aggression is risky for several reasons. First, because you communicate your concerns indirectly, the other person may miss the point. Second, even if the other person understands your message, she or he may decide to ignore it because your indirectness offers a ready excuse: "I didn't know what you wanted!" Third, indirect aggression is risky because people who feel manipulated often respond angrily. Even if the other person does what you want, the relationship may be damaged and future conflicts may be more difficult to resolve.

Direct Aggression

Direct aggression, unlike nonassertiveness and indirect aggression, is easy to recognize. **Direct aggression** is the open expression of feelings, needs, wants, desires, and ideas *at the expense of others*. People who use direct aggression try to dominate and possibly humiliate the other person by acting self-righteously, as if they're superior, certain of themselves, and know what's best for everyone. For example, in response to your request to use the family car, your father may say: "No, I want to use it, and I don't care that you need it to go see your friends. I have to go to the store and that's more important!" In this way, your father clearly expresses that his needs will be satisfied at the expense of yours.

Direct aggression may get you what you want, but the costs are high. Initial hurt and humiliation may fade, but a loser is often left feeling angry, resentful, and vengeful and is apt to retaliate in kind. Direct aggression begets further direct aggression, ensuring continued uncooperativeness and hostility.

Skill Checkup 9.2 provides you with the opportunity to practice nonassertive, indirect aggression, and direct aggression responses. This should help you recognize when you respond in one of these three ways.

SKILL CHECKUP 9.2

Responding to Relationship Discord

Respond to the following situation with a statement or action that represents each conflict style noted below.

> Your supervisor insists that you work overtime on Friday. Ordinarily, you wouldn't mind staying the extra hours, but this Friday you have tickets to a concert.

1. Nonassertion:

2. Indirect aggression:

3. Direct aggression:

Assertion

Assertion is the direct statement of needs and wants. Because it is direct, assertion is more closely related to direct aggression than to either indirect aggression or nonassertiveness. Assertive communication lacks an important element of direct aggression, however: it expresses thoughts and feelings directly and clearly without judging or dictating to others. It is honest and has as its goal the resolution of conflict. Unlike direct aggression, assertiveness does not mean winning at the other person's expense—it attacks the problem, not the person.

An assertive style toward conflicts has several advantages over other styles. It increases the probability that your concerns will be satisfied and that you'll feel good about yourself. In addition, others are more likely to understand your needs and, possibly, work with you in managing the conflict. Relationships are often improved when assertiveness is used because the participants know exactly what they are in conflict about.

Assertive communication is useful in both simple and complex situations. The way you assert yourself will depend on who you are in conflict with and how involved the problem is.

Assertive Skills for Simple Situations A conflict situation is simple when the problem is narrow and well defined and you are not emotionally close to the other person. Such conflicts can be handled by simply stating your perception of the facts. For example, if you receive a bill from your school charging you for a class you did not sign up to take, you could assert yourself in three different ways. You could call the business office and say the following:

1. "Hello, this is _____. I received my tuition bill today and I'm being charged for a class I'm not taking."

2. "Hello, this is _____. I know you're probably not the person who's responsible, but I received my tuition bill today and I'm being charged for a class I'm not taking."

3. "Hello, this is _____. I received my tuition bill today and I'm being charged for a class I'm not taking. I would like the overcharge removed."

All three assertive comments are variations on the same theme—stating your perception of the facts. In the first instance, you simply present the facts with the assumption that once the other person knows them, he or she will resolve the problem. The advantage of this assertion is that it does not accuse the other person of anything, states exactly what's frustrating you, and does not back the other person into a corner.

The second assertion takes into account the role of the other person in the conflict situation. This recognizes his or her needs and softens the impact of the message.

The third assertion goes one step further. You not only state the facts, but you also specify what needs to be done to satisfy your concerns.

In none of these three assertions do you tell the person *how* to do what you feel needs to be done, which forestalls a defensive response. Defensiveness is common when you command someone to do something, when you overstate your case, when you don't clearly state what's wrong, or when you implicitly communicate, "I know more about your job than you do."

●KILL CHECKUP 9.3

Stating Simple Assertions

Your instructor has just handed back your graded test. Your answer to question 6, which was C, was marked wrong. While reviewing the answers, the instructor says, "The answer to question 6 is C." In response, write three statements, each reflecting a different assertion type that may be used in a simple conflict situation.

_____

_____

_____

Assertive Skills for Complex Situations A conflict situation is complex if it has one or more of the following characteristics: it is a long-term dispute, it involves people to whom you're emotionally close, there is a strong possibility of physical or verbal violence, and there are differences in power. Such cases require more detailed assertive responses.

A complex assertive message can be expressed by using the **A*S*S*E*R*T formula**:

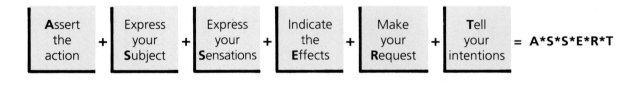

▶ **FIGURE 9.1**   A*S*S*E*R*T Formula

A: Describe the *action* that prompted the need for the assertive message. Your description should be behavioral; that is, it should focus on *who* is involved, the *circumstances* that are relevant, and the *specific behaviors* that are the source of your frustration and that trigger the assertive message. The expression of a descriptive message is clear and objective—for example, "When we discuss a serious matter, you joke around."

S: Express your *subjective interpretation* of the action. Using "I" language, offer your interpretation of the behavior you describe. Separate this subjective interpretation from the objective description. For example, "When you joke around, I think you want to avoid talking about the serious issue under discussion."

S: Express your *sensations* related to the action. Say how you feel about the behavior as precisely as possible even if you are somewhat confused. Try to include the intensity of your feelings. Does the joking make you thoughtful, sad, or grief-stricken? Are you distracted, surprised, or amazed? Are you apprehensive, fearful, or filled with terror? Are you annoyed, angry, or enraged? For example, "I feel angry when you don't stop kidding around. I also feel frustrated because I don't know what to do to get you to take what we're talking about seriously."

E: Indicate the *effects* of the action. Effects can focus on *you* ("I want to avoid discussing serious matters with you because you joke around"), on the *other person* ("I think you're missing out on some good discussions that might improve our relationship"), or on *others* ("I think people misinterpret the importance of our relationship when they see you joke around about serious matters").

R: Make your *request*. Indicate what specific behaviors you want. For example, "When we discuss a serious matter, I want you to stop telling jokes and kidding around." (Note that the request ends with a period, not an exclamation point—it is a statement, not a command.)

   T: *Tell* your intentions: "If we can't resolve this problem, I'll avoid discussing serious issues with you."

SKILL CHECKUP 9.4

A*S*S*E*R*T Yourself

Your roommate studies after you go to bed. The light makes it difficult for you to fall asleep, and you've mentioned this several times before. There has been no behavioral change. Use the A*S*S*E*R*T formula to present your view of the situation to your roommate.

A:

S:

S:

E:

R:

T:

Now that you know the differences among nonassertion, indirect aggression, direct aggression, and assertion styles, put what you know into action!

MANAGING RELATIONSHIP DISCORD

The successful management of relationship discord depends on several prerequisites that have already been discussed: you must be able to analyze the conflict situation, understand your thoughts and feelings about conflict in general, and recognize your usual conflict strategies and styles. You must then determine your goal for who, if anyone, will win and who, if anyone, will lose, choose the most effective approach, and implement the appropriate procedures. There are three general approaches to managing conflict: win-lose, lose-lose, and win-win.

Win-Lose Conflict Management

In the **win-lose** approach to conflict, one person wins and the other loses. If your goal is to win and have the other person lose (the goal of a dominance strategy), or to lose and have the other person win (the goal of a smoothing-over strategy)—regardless of the situation—you are likely to take a win-lose approach.

People often use the win-lose approach to conflict management, even when it isn't necessary. Most of the conflicts you observed or participated in while growing up were probably treated as win-lose. For example, television programs stress good guy–bad guy conflict, with the good guy almost always winning. Sports stress the bottom line: the team that scores the most points wins. Promotions at work may be limited to a select few: some get ahead, some don't. At home, conflicts with siblings and spouses are often win-lose: you get to watch the television program you want and your brother doesn't, you turn down your radio so that your roommate can study, and the last cookie goes to your spouse. Even our political system, majority rule, is a win-lose approach to conflict management. One candidate wins, the other loses; one party comes into power, the other waits in the wings for two or four years.

The unequal power that distinguishes win-lose conflicts tends to damage relationships. Power may take the form of physical force, control over rewards and punishments, or cunning. For example, if you want to study but your roommate wants to watch television, you might threaten physical violence: "Shut that off or you're dead meat"; threaten the loss of a reward: "You're not going to get one of my Mom's cookies when they come in the mail"; threaten a nonphysical punishment: "Shut it off or I'll watch television the next time *you* want to study"; or use cunning to get your way: "It's okay if you watch television while I study—it doesn't distract me *too* much [sigh]."

In some cases—when resources are limited and only one person or group can succeed, for instance—a win-lose approach to managing conflict is appropriate. Most sporting events can be won by only one team or person, most job vacancies can be filled by only one applicant, and promotions often go to only a select few. For each of these situations, the interaction is competitive, not cooperative.

A win-lose approach is also appropriate when the person with whom you're in conflict chooses it. Sometimes another person ignores your repeated invitations to approach a conflict cooperatively and instead insists on being competitive. You must then decide whether to accept the win-lose approach and attempt to win, be the loser, or change the situation so that your needs will be met in another way. For example, when you pull into a gas station, if someone pulls in alongside you and takes the pump you planned on using, you can argue over your right to use the pump because you pulled in first, you can brood while you wait for the latecomer to finish using the pump, or you can use another pump.

Finally, a win-lose approach is appropriate when the other person is clearly behaving improperly. Few would disagree that drunk drivers, people trying to carry weapons aboard planes, and child abusers should all be restrained.

Lose-Lose Conflict Management

In the **lose-lose** approach to conflict, neither your goals nor the other person's goals are fully satisfied. There may be some gain, but something important is also lost. It may seem ridiculous to purposely manage a conflict so that the outcomes are unsatisfactory to everyone, but one of the most popular conflict strategies, compromise, is actually a lose-lose approach.

The lose-lose nature of compromise is evident in its outcomes. No sooner is a labor-management compromise reached than one side or the other complains about what they had to give up and threatens to drive a harder bargain the next time. A couple arguing about whether to dine at a Mexican restaurant or a Chinese one may compromise and eat Italian food, although neither really was in the mood for it. Two nations may compromise by dividing up a disputed territory, but the resulting hard feelings and lost lives are likely to fuel further conflicts.

A lose-lose approach to managing conflict may be appropriate when the odds of fully satisfying your concerns are low or the chances of getting nothing at all are high. In addition, a lose-lose approach can usefully reduce tension in a conflict long enough for a different, more productive and long-lasting approach to be found.

Usual Outcomes of Win-Lose and Lose-Lose Conflicts

Win-lose and lose-lose approaches to managing relationship discord are more common than an approach in which everyone wins. As a result, the outcomes of most conflicts are dysfunctional and negative.

In a typical conflict, *people rarely give in* because their egos are at stake. Rather than admit that the other person may be right, they try to reconceptualize the problem or the issues. By saying, "Oh, *that's* what you mean. Well, that's *different*," people can save face by claiming that there really was no conflict in the first place. In the absence of such face-saving devices, the conflict may rage on indefinitely.

In a typical conflict, *biases are obvious and selfishness predominates.* You see yourself as "good" and the other as "bad," yourself as "trustworthy" and the other as "deceitful," yourself as "open" and the other as "sneaky." Even if one person tries to cooperate (and in almost every conflict, each person makes bids for cooperation), the other person ignores the attempt. Cooperative behavior from a "bad, sneaky, deceitful" adversary is not deemed credible.

In a typical conflict, *tactics become more coercive* as the discord persists. Because you see the other person as bad, your trust decreases and your suspicion increases. You tell yourself, "The only way to deal with this untrustworthy sneak is to force him to do what I want."

In a typical conflict, the *original issue gets lost and the conflict spreads to other issues*. Although the source of the problem gets lost in the struggle, new issues, such as hurt feelings and resentment, arise; the conflict spreads to new areas: "If I can't trust you to wash the car when I ask you to [the original issue], how can I trust you to drive responsibly [a seemingly related issue] or do your homework [an unrelated issue]?"

In a typical conflict, you and the other person *grow apart as human beings*, lose the ability to communicate with each other as individuals, and see each other only as roles or symbols. A police officer who stops you after you go through a red light may change from "Officer Long" (based on a past incident when he came to your house to investigate a break-in), a unique individual; to "officer," a role; to "cop," a negative term for the role; and, finally, to "pig," an animal symbolizing disrespect for law-enforcement officials. Of course, you can't reason with a "pig," so productive communication ceases.

At the end of a typical conflict, neither you nor the other person gets what you want (even though it may seem so in the short run), the possibility for a continuing relationship is damaged, and neither of you has positive self-feelings. A more productive way to manage relationship discord is the win-win approach.

Win-Win Conflict Management

The purpose of **win-win** conflict management is to satisfy everyone's needs. This approach recognizes the importance of both the issue and the participants; neither person gives up something crucial and neither one feels that the relationship was damaged by the conflict management process or its outcomes. Success hinges on dedication to the win-win process and to the other person, mutual respect, and strong communication skills. Although true win-win conflict management is sometimes difficult to carry out, the results justify the effort.

Steps in Win-Win Conflict Management

Step 1. *Define the conflict for yourself before approaching the other person.* This requires some self-analysis: What is your concern? Who or what is frustrating you? What is the source of conflict?

Once you understand the conflict from your perspective, approach the other person and agree on a time to talk. Don't spring the conflict on the other person without warning or bring it up when there isn't enough time to deal with it. If the other person feels attacked, he or she may become defensive, which will make it difficult for you to establish a supportive climate.

Also agree on an appropriate place for your discussion. Certain locations may inhibit open and honest interaction. Attempting to deal with conflict in a public place, such as a restaurant, virtually assures failure.

Step 2. *Communicate your understanding of the problem assertively to the other person.* This includes describing the other person's behaviors, as they affect you, in a direct, clear, nonjudgmental way. You must also communicate your interpretation of the situation and your feelings.

Once your own concerns are clear, invite the other person to express her or his concerns. Listen carefully to the content of the message and try to perceive the feelings that accompany it.

Share your perceptions of the other person's point of view without labels ("That's stupid!") or insults ("You're crazy!"). Be sure you can state your partner's perspective to her or his satisfaction. Then reverse the process and encourage your partner to reiterate your point of view to your satisfaction.

When you complete this step, both you and your partner will have defined the problem specifically; described your feelings; and recounted the actions that led to the conflict and perpetuated it.

Step 3. *Based on your understanding of your own and the other's perspective, arrive at a mutual, shared definition of the problem and a mutual, shared goal.* Consider your areas of agreement and disagreement; figure out how you're dependent on one another. Discuss the consequences of the conflict for each of you.

Step 4. *Communicate your cooperative intentions.* Let your partner know that your aim is to satisfy the needs of *both* of you and to achieve your shared goals, and that you do not want to win by being competitive or combative. If you can (and it may be difficult under stressful conditions), communicate your intention in a calm, firm voice and invite your partner to join you in being cooperative.

Successful conflict resolution is impossible unless both you and your partner are motivated to behave cooperatively. If your partner is reluctant to cooperate, you may want to discuss what each of you gets out of continuing the conflict. Perhaps the conflict gives you something to complain about or an excuse to end the relationship. Or perhaps you feel threatened because a solution to your shared problem will require changes in your behavior. Whatever the reasons, they must be recognized and overcome before you can proceed.

Step 5. *Generate solutions to your shared problem.* Avoid discussing or evaluating each solution as it is generated; instead, generate as many ideas as you can. If you and your partner agree to defer evaluation, the number of possible solutions should be high. Be spontaneous and creative and build on each other's suggestions. Remember that even a foolish-sounding solution may contain a shred of useful information.[7]

Approaches to Managing Conflict

There are three general approaches to managing conflict, each appropriate under different circumstances.

1. Win-lose conflict management, in which one person wins (has her or his needs satisfied) and the other loses (fails to have her or his needs satisfied)—associated with dominance and smoothing-over strategies—is appropriate when limited resources dictate only one person can win, when the other person uses this conflict management approach, and when the other person is behaving in a clearly wrongful and dangerous way.

2. Lose-lose conflict management, in which you and the other person both lose (fail to have your needs satisfied)—associated with a compromise strategy—is appropriate when it's impossible to fully satisfy your needs, when your goal is to reduce tension so that productive communication can begin, and as an intermediate step toward win-win conflict management.

3. Win-win conflict management, in which you and the other person both win (have your needs satisfied)—associated with an integration strategy—is appropriate when there is mutual respect, well-developed communication skills, recognition that it's important to achieve satisfaction of both your needs, and commitment to the win-win conflict process. The win-win process requires sharing individual perceptions of the conflict, arriving at a mutual definition of the problem, generating solutions, evaluating and implementing a solution, checking on whether the solution is successful, and making adaptations if necessary.

Step 6. *After you've suggested all the solutions you can think of, evaluate them and select the best one.* How might each solution satisfy the shared goal? How easy or difficult would each be to implement?

Step 7. *Implement the solution.* First, be sure that you and your partner truly agree on which solution to implement. Make sure that you both agree *fully* and that you're not agreeing because you're tired, because you want to please your partner, or for some other reason that will later undermine the solution.

Second, agree on who does what, when, and how. If you don't specify the particulars, the groundwork may well be laid for the next conflict.

Third, do what needs to be done.

Step 8. *Plan to check on how the solution is working.* You may have to adjust your plan or scrap the solution and generate a new one. The need for modification is a predictable consequence of changes brought on by time and an inability to foresee all possible outcomes during the initial problem-solving stage.

Although this eight-step procedure takes a lot of work, it pays off: in the end, both you and your partner will get what you want, strengthen your relationship, and feel good about yourselves. Furthermore, in the long run, the win-win approach takes less effort than do the other two approaches. Most importantly, the win-win approach lets you productively confront the problem—you don't have to let it fester unresolved. Win-lose and lose-lose approaches require repeated attempts to resolve the problems they themselves create, while the win-win approach usually gets at the problem and eliminates it.

ASSESSING CONFLICT PROCESSES AND OUTCOMES

Assessing the process and outcomes of a conflict can help you understand its constructive and destructive consequences.[8] Are your communication skills effective for managing relationship discord? What can you do to improve your conflict management strategies?

SKILL CHECKUP 9.5

Conflict Process Profile

Think of a recently resolved conflict in which you were involved and circle the word that best describes the process of your conflict.

1. To what extent did each person agree that there was a problem?

| strongly agreed | agreed | disagreed | strongly disagreed |

2. To what extent did each person agree on what the problem was?

| strongly agreed | agreed | disagreed | strongly disagreed |

3. How did each person appear to enter into the discussion?

| cooperatively | somewhat cooperatively | somewhat competitively | competitively |

4. How were possible solutions generated?

cooperatively   somewhat   somewhat   competitively
            cooperatively   competitively

5. How were the possible solutions evaluated?

cooperatively   somewhat   somewhat   competitively
            cooperatively   competitively

6. How committed was each person to the selected solution?

very   committed   somewhat   uncommitted
committed   committed

7. To what extent did each person agree on how to implement the solution?

strongly   agreed   disagreed   disagreed
 agreed   strongly

8. How were feelings and ideas expressed?

openly   somewhat   guardedly   not at all
        openly

9. To what extent did each person perceive the problem from the other's perspective?

totally   moderately   somewhat   hardly at all

After you have completed the questionnaire, join your circled answers with a line going from the first item to the last. This line graphically represents your Conflict Process Profile. If the line stays mainly to the left, your conflict process was *constructive*, but if it stays mainly to the right, your conflict process was probably *dysfunctional*. If your circled answers form a jagged line, you can pinpoint your weak areas by looking at the items for which your responses fell to the right side.

1. What were the constructive aspects of your conflict process?

2. What were the dysfunctional aspects of your conflict process?

3. What did you learn about yourself as a participant in this conflict that you can apply to future conflicts?

The analysis of a conflict has two parts. You have already completed the first part, an assessment of the conflict process. The second part focuses on outcomes.

SKILL CHECKUP 9.6

Conflict Outcomes Profile

Based on the same situation that you used to complete Skill Checkup 9.5, answer the following questions.

1. How effective was the solution in dealing with the problem?

   effective   somewhat   somewhat   ineffective
                          effective   ineffective

2. How did you feel about yourself and your behavior while you were working toward conflict resolution?

   positive   somewhat   somewhat   negative
                         positive   negative

3. How did you feel about the other person and her or his behavior while you were working toward conflict resolution?

   positive   somewhat   somewhat   negative
                         positive   negative

4. How did you feel about the relationship before the conflict?

   positive   somewhat   somewhat   negative
                         positive   negative

5. How did you feel about the relationship after the conflict was resolved?

   positive   somewhat   somewhat   negative
                         positive   negative

Join your circled answers with a line going from the first response to the last. This line graphically represents your Conflict Outcomes Profile. A line that stays predominantly to the left represents a *constructive* conflict, while a line that stays predominantly to the right suggests a *dysfunctional* conflict. Questions for which your circled responses fall to the right indicate your trouble spots.

1. What were the constructive aspects of your conflict outcomes?

2. What were the dysfunctional aspects of your conflict outcomes?

3. What did you learn about yourself as a participant in this conflict that you can apply to future conflicts?

Every conflict has the potential to be constructive—to help you, the other person, and your relationship. Your understanding of conflict and how to manage it can increase your ability to communicate effectively and, therefore, increase the probability of your having constructive conflicts.

Cinderella and her sisters are having a conflict. Cinderella defines the conflict this way: "*I want* to stop being the servant in this house and having to do all the dirty chores, *but* my sisters and mother *want* me to stay in this role." Her sisters define it this way: "*We* want Cinderella to stay in her position as servant, *but* Cinderella *wants* to stop being our servant."

1. Describe the conflict between Cinderella and her sisters with respect to their interdependence and the sources of their conflict.

2. What are the dysfunctional consequences of Cinderella's conflict with her sisters? Consider the effects on Cinderella's work, her relationship with her sisters, and her feelings about herself.

3. What are Cinderella's conflict strategy and conflict style with her sisters? What are the advantages and disadvantages of her strategy and style?

4. Cinderella comes to you for advice. "I want to use an assertive conflict style to solve my problem with my sisters," she tells you. Describe the A*S*S*E*R*T system for her and outline how she might use it.

5. Is Cinderella's conflict with her sisters win-lose or lose-lose? What steps can Cinderella take to use win-win conflict management?

6. Cinderella is enthusiastic about using a win-win conflict management approach with her sisters. "How can I assess what the results of the conflict are?" she asks you. Describe a procedure she can use to assess whether her conflict process was functional or not and another procedure she can use to assess the outcomes.

7. All of your work with Cinderella is for nothing! The prince comes along and saves her before she ever has to confront her sisters. The two, of course, live happily ever after. How realistic is this outcome for *your* life?

NOTES

1. Cathy Guisewite, *Cathy*. Universal Press Syndicate, April 18, 1985.
2. Kathleen M. Galvin and Bernard J. Brommel, *Family Communication: Cohesion and Change*, 2d ed. (Glenview, IL: Scott, Foresman, 1986), pp. 5–6.
3. Adapted from: M. Afzalur Rahim, "A Measure of Styles of Handling Interpersonal Conflict," *Academy of Management Journal* 26 (1983): 368–76.
4. Joyce Hocker and William W. Wilmot, *Interpersonal Conflict*, 2d ed. (Dubuque, IA: Wm. C. Brown, 1985); David W. Johnson, *Human Relations and Your Career*, 2d ed. (Englewood Cliffs, NJ: Prentice-Hall, 1987), chapters 9 and 10.
5. Adapted from: Pamela Cumming, *The Power Handbook* (Boston: CBI Publishing, 1981), pp. 158–80 and 288–305.
6. Ronald B. Adler, *Confidence in Communication: A Guide to Assertive and Social Skills* (New York: Holt, Rinehart and Winston, 1977).
7. Alex F. Osborn, *Applied Imagination*, rev. ed. (New York: Scribner, 1957).
8. Adapted from: Lawrence B. Rosenfeld, *Now That We're All Here . . . Relations in Small Groups* (Columbus, OH: Charles E. Merrill, 1976), pp. 63–65.

FOR FURTHER INVESTIGATION

Bach, George R., and Peter Wyden. *The Intimate Enemy*. New York: Avon, 1968.

Bower, Sharon, and Gordon H. Bower. *Asserting Yourself: A Practical Guide for Positive Change*. Reading, MA: Addison-Wesley, 1976.

Dyer, Wayne. *Pulling Your Own Strings*. New York: Avon, 1977.

Ellis, Donald G., and B. Aubrey Fisher, "Phases of Conflict in Small Group Development." *Human Communication Research* 1 (1975): 195–212.

Fisher, Roger, and William Ury. *Getting to Yes: Negotiating Agreement Without Giving In*. Boston: Houghton-Mifflin, 1981.

Forward, Susan. *Men Who Hate Women and the Women Who Love Them*. New York: Bantam, 1986.

Halpern, Howard. *How to Break Your Addiction to a Person*. New York: Bantam, 1983.

Handly, Robert. *Anxiety and Panic Attacks: Their Cause and Cure*. New York: Rawson and Associates, 1985.

Hocker, Joyce L., and William W. Wilmot. *Interpersonal Conflict*, 2d ed. Dubuque, IA: Wm. C. Brown, 1985.

Johnson, David W., and Frank P. Johnson. *Joining Together*, 3d ed. Englewood Cliffs, NJ: Prentice-Hall, 1987. See chapter 6, "Controversy and Creativity," and chapter 7, "Conflicts of Interests."

_____. *Learning Together and Alone: Cooperative, Competitive, and Individualistic Learning.* Englewood Cliffs, NJ: Prentice-Hall, 1987.

Kline, Nathan. *From Sad to Glad.* New York: Ballantine, 1974.

Rosenfeld, Lawrence B., and Mary W. Jarrard, "Student Coping Mechanisms in Sexist and Nonsexist Professors' Classes." *Communication Education* 35 (1986): 157–62.

Thomas, Kenneth. "Conflict and Conflict Management." In *Handbook of Industrial and Organizational Psychology*, edited by Marvin D. Dunnette, pp. 881–935. Chicago: Rand McNally, 1976.

CHAPTER 10

▶ # *Communication in Small Groups*

*This chapter on communication in small groups will help you to practice and develop communication competencies that fall into two broad areas: (1) **basic speech communication skills,** which include expressing ideas clearly and concisely and asking questions to obtain information, and (2) **human relations,** which include describing differences of opinion and performing such social rituals as introducing yourself and making small talk in small group settings. Specifically, the competencies you will gain will enable you to do the following:*

▶ *Define a small group.*

▶ *Identify several reasons for joining a small group and explain how each reason affects a group member's participation.*

▶ *Help make a group more appealing to its members.*

▶ *Trace the four phases of group development and offer specific strategies for helping a group progress successfully through each phase.*

▶ *Describe the characteristics of a problem best suited to group problem-solving procedures.*

▶ *Outline the six steps of the problem-solving process and cite specific strategies for successfully completing each step.*

▶ *Recognize common obstacles to effective problem solving and suggest methods of overcoming them.*

*T*o which of the following groups do you belong?

In school:
_____ classes
_____ groups within classes
_____ fraternity or sorority
_____ student government
_____ teams (athletic, debate, etc.)
_____ clubs
_____ honorary organizations
_____ others (specify)

Outside of school:
_____ family group
_____ job groups
_____ friendship groups
_____ teams
_____ religious groups
_____ political organizations
_____ social groups

THE IMPORTANCE OF SMALL GROUPS

Each of these broad categories contains many different subgroups. For example, you may belong to several social groups, have many different groups of friends, and belong to a variety of organizations in school. If you take the time to write down *all* the groups you belong to, you may find that the list comes close to defining who you are. Knowing what groups you belong to makes it relatively easy for you or someone else to predict how you spend your time, what you believe, and what your aspirations are.

Your list contains groups to which you belong voluntarily, such as Young Democrats or Young Republicans, and those to which you belong involuntarily, such as your family and age group. It perhaps contains groups to which you aspire: you don't belong to them yet, but you act as if you were a member.[1] These groups provide you with standards for judging your own and others' behavior. For example, you may not be a member of the "in group" in your community, but if you hope to belong to it, you will probably notice how the members dress and behave and attempt to copy what you see. You may even go so far as to adopt their attitudes, liking a particular person because *they* like her and disliking a particular restaurant because *they* dislike it.

A balanced list also contains groups to which you belonged in the past that still affect your behavior. You may no longer see the group of friends you had when you were a child, but the effects of their friendship persist—you may perceive yourself as a good athlete because of the feedback they gave you, or you may have trouble resolving conflicts because they always accused you of clamming up when things got tough. The influence on your current behavior may be more direct: some problem that was unresolved within a past group may linger in your mind. For example, you may find yourself thinking about a fight you started that escalated and ruined a friendship because you were too stubborn to apologize.

WHAT IS A SMALL GROUP?

Think of the groups to which you belong. How do you know you belong?

1. Do you interact more with group members than with people outside the group?
2. Do you and the other group members think of yourselves as a group?
3. Are you and the other members interdependent? That is, do many of the events that affect one of you affect all of you?
4. Do you have shared goals?
5. Do you and the other group members follow certain rules—whether spoken or unspoken—that structure how you interact with each other?
6. Would an objective observer be able to recognize specific patterns of behavior that typify your group members' interactions?
7. Are members of your group able to influence each other?

Each of these questions corresponds to a different way of defining the notion of *group*.[2] For example, you may define your English class as a group because you all follow the same rules for interacting, including "Raise your hand if you want to say something." If someone observed the class, she would notice the pattern and think, "They're a group because they all follow the same hand-raising rule." On the other hand, you may define your band as a group because you have shared goals (to play together on weekends and to earn money) and are interdependent (if one member gets sick, the whole group is affected—whether an engagement must be canceled or a replacement player found).

Once you know what a group is, you need to know whether it qualifies as *small*. One person does not constitute a group and a two-person interaction is technically classified as a *dyad*. Thus, it takes three or more people to make a group. But at what point does a group become too large to be considered *small*?

If group members need to interact a great deal (such as those in a problem-solving group versus those in a group painting a house), the number can't be too large; conversely, as the size of the group grows, the amount any one group member can contribute to the interaction decreases. A group becomes too large when so many people need to contribute that some lose the opportunity. Typically, a small group functions best if it has from three to ten members (or even more, in some cases). Groups with more than seven members tend to break down into subgroups, which makes it hard for each member to have access to all other members.

In short, a **small group** is three or more people, usually not more than ten, who perceive themselves as a group, are interdependent and mutually influential, have patterned interaction, and pursue shared goals.

WHY DO YOU JOIN SPECIFIC GROUPS?

Most of your reasons for joining different groups fall into one of six categories. You may be attracted to the task or to the people (task attraction or people attraction); or you may try to use the group to satisfy some need you have outside the group (outside need attraction). You may also join a group because it satisfies your need to interact with other people (inclusion attraction), to lead or to follow (control attraction), or to be friendly (affection attraction). Knowing your reasons for joining a group can help you develop strategies for increasing your attraction to the group.

Sources of Attraction

You may join a group because you like the task or activity in which the group is engaged—**task attraction**. You may have a problem that is too thorny to solve alone, and a group may offer the resources for tackling it. If you join a group for this reason, you'll probably be extremely task-oriented; that is, you'll keep your talk to matters related to the task and you'll want to finish quickly and efficiently.

A second reason for joining a group is that you like the people—**people attraction**. When a teacher assigns a group project and asks students to form groups, the most common procedure is for class members to seek out friends, regardless of the task's requirements. Whether the friends are good co-workers and whether the talents of the group will suit the task are apparently less important than being with friends and feeling comfortable and safe. If you join a group because of the people in it, you will probably engage in behaviors that are unrelated to the group's task, such as having long and pleasant conversations. Remaining friendly will take priority over accomplishing the task.

A third reason for joining a group is that it satisfies a need you have outside the group—**outside need attraction**. You may have joined a sorority or fraternity not because you need a place to live and eat, nor because of the services the organization performs, but because it was what your parents expected you to do. If you join a group because of some outside need, you will probably behave cautiously, stay to yourself, and avoid doing anything that could risk your membership, such as being uncooperative. You will be *in* the group, but not really a *part* of it.

These three reasons probably explain why you joined a great many of the groups to which you belong.[3] However, three other reasons for joining groups are more closely related to your basic human needs. Did you ever wonder why a hermit is considered odd or why a person who prefers to stay alone is thought peculiar? It may be because such people seem to reject what most psychologists regard as normal: people have needs that can only be satisfied by interacting with others. Three interpersonal needs have been identified.[4]

First, you need to belong, to be included in what others do and to include them in what you do—**inclusion attraction**. Your family group was the first to offer you togetherness. As you grew, you joined other groups and formed some of your own to continue satisfying your need to share activities with other people. The question "Who am I?" is answered, in large part, by your membership in different groups; if you are lonely, detached, and ignored, you are likely to suffer psychologically.

Second, you need to exercise control over others as a leader and to have them exercise control over you as a follower—**control attraction**. Being influential, powerful, achieving, and intellectually superior all satisfy your need to exercise authority over your environment and feel in control of your life. The other side of the coin, being controlled, includes being dependent and cooperative, both of which are essential for decision making. Without group members willing to depend on others and be influenced by others, the group will spend all its time trying to resolve conflicts.

Third, you need to express affection and have it returned to you—**affection attraction**. Liking, loving, and being emotionally close all satisfy your need to both express and receive attention, to share confidences, and to be intimate. Whereas people attraction concerns feeling comfortable and safe, the primary concern of affection attraction is the opportunity to be intimate.

Groups satisfy all three of these basic human needs.

KNOWLEDGE CHECKUP 10.1

Assessment of Group Attraction[5]

What is the basis of your attraction to a group? Select one group to which you belong and keep it in mind as you respond to the statements in this questionnaire. Use the following scale to indicate how true or false each statement is for you:

Write 1 if the statement is definitely false.
Write 2 if the statement is mostly false.
Write 3 if the statement is neither true nor false.
Write 4 if the statement is mostly true.
Write 5 if the statement is definitely true.

_____ **1.** I think members of this group could be friends of mine.
_____ **2.** The group's members are good problem solvers.
_____ **3.** I try to be with members of the group.
_____ **4.** At times I try to be the dominant person in the group.
_____ **5.** Being a member of this group helps me achieve goals I have outside the group.
_____ **6.** I try to have a close relationship with members of the group.
_____ **7.** I like members of the group to invite me to do things with them.
_____ **8.** It's very easy to talk to members of the group about things that are unrelated to the group's goals.
_____ **9.** At times I let other people take charge of the group.
_____ **10.** I behave cautiously as a group member because I don't want to jeopardize my membership.
_____ **11.** I have confidence in the group members' ability to accomplish the group's task.
_____ **12.** I act friendly toward members of the group.
_____ **13.** I have authority in the group.
_____ **14.** I enjoy being with group members when we're not working on the group's task.
_____ **15.** I belong to this group for reasons other than its tasks or goals or how I feel about the other members.
_____ **16.** Members of this group don't goof off.
_____ **17.** My relationship with group members is highly personal.
_____ **18.** I participate fully in the group's activities.

Scoring

Task Attraction
     Add your responses to items 2, 11, and 16: _____
People Attraction
     Add your responses to items 1, 8, and 14: _____
Outside Need Attraction
     Add your responses to items 5, 10, and 15: _____
Inclusion Attraction
     Add your responses to items 3, 7, and 18: _____
Control Attraction
     Add your responses to items 4, 9, and 13: _____
Affection Attraction
     Add your responses to items 6, 12, and 17: _____

A score of twelve or above in any category indicates that that source of attraction is an important reason for your membership in the group; a score of six or below indicates that a source of attraction is unimportant. Which of your six scores is highest? Is your highest score twelve or above? In what ways, if any, is the group attractive for you? For example, a classroom group may be attractive because of the people, the task (assignment), and the opportunity it gives you to lead and exercise some control.

Examine your attraction to several groups and try to determine why you are attracted to them. Your attraction tells a great deal about how you like to interact and how you are likely to behave as a group member.

High Attraction

The more attracted you are to a particular group—the higher your level of attraction and the greater the number of sources of attraction—the more you'll assume the responsibility of membership, be open to influence, accept group standards, and feel calm when interacting with group members.

In addition to the self-knowledge provided by knowing why you join a particular group, knowing why another member is attracted to a group enables you to develop strategies for raising her or his level of attraction. For example, if a person is attracted by control, you can raise her level of attraction to the group by increasing the number of opportunities for her to lead. If her attraction is based on her need to provide affection, you can raise her level of attraction by being more receptive to her self-disclosures.

Even if you don't know exactly what attracts a member to a group, you can still attempt to raise his or her level of attraction by manipulating all six bases for attraction. For example, you can raise a group member's task attraction by successfully accomplishing a group task, people attraction by being friendly, inclusion attraction by assigning him to a subcommittee that is small and interacts a great deal, control attraction by letting him lead a subgroup, and affection attraction by self-disclosing enough to encourage his intimacy with group members.

SKILL CHECKUP 10.1

Raising Group Attractiveness

Your group assignment in a math class is to present ways geometric principles apply to daily living. John has missed some group meetings and, when he attends, seems bored. He's generally active in class, so you assume the problem is his low attraction to the group. Name five ways to raise John's attraction to the group.

1.

2.

3.

4.

5.

GROUP DEVELOPMENT

Groups develop over time: different issues take priority as members become acquainted with each other and their task, resolve conflicts, work on a group problem, and then disband. Because virtually all groups develop in similar ways, knowing the general pattern of group development is useful for both leaders and participants.

First, such knowledge helps you organize your perceptions and make sense out of what you see. Second, it gives you a framework for assessing whether the group is developing normally and for predicting what happens next. The framework, in turn, helps you focus on a larger, more inclusive picture of the group and avoid getting bogged down in details.

Third, and most important, understanding group development lets you know when to speed up, slow down, or even freeze a group's development if doing so is beneficial. For example, group members often start working before they totally understand the problem they are dealing with. Slowing the group down, perhaps by introducing a discussion of the forces that already exist to resolve the problem, can increase the group's effectiveness by preventing action until preparations are complete.

Four relatively distinct stages mark a group's development: the orientation stage; the conflict stage; the balance, or high work, stage; and the disintegration stage. Movement from one stage to another is hardly as orderly as a discussion of them may imply. Although development is generally linear—from orientation to conflict to high work to disintegration—aspects of all four stages may be present at any one time. One stage, however, should predominate. Figure 10.1 on page 240 shows the four phases of group development.

The Orientation Phase

Even before a group's first meeting, things happen that affect the group development process. Group members begin by separating themselves from attachments outside the group. For example, if you know that your group meets on Tuesday evenings, you need to resign yourself to missing your favorite television shows or plan to videotape them for later viewing. You may also need to reschedule your dinner time or a standing commitment. In addition, you may prepare yourself by trying to learn as much as possible about the new situation, the group task, and the people with whom you'll be working.

After this preorientation period, orientation begins. During the **orientation stage**, participants focus on learning about the group task and how it may be accomplished, group rules for behavior (such as meeting times and the sanctions for tardiness or absence), and who the other group members are. This stage usually lasts through four or more sessions, depending on how well group members know each before getting together. Participants are usually hesitant, feel uncertain and anxious about the new situation, and limit their conversation to small talk, such as names, jobs, classes, and interests.

Communication during this phase displays a great deal of agreement and ambiguity, as in any situation in which strangers are brought together. Each person's goal seems to be to present a pleasant image for the other group members and to keep things running smoothly while learning as much as possible.

Uppermost in group members' minds are several key questions: What is this group about? Do I fit in? Do I want to participate in this group? Will the other members include me or ignore me? What is the task? How will we work on it? How close will we be as a group?

As members seek answers to their questions, they usually accomplish little substantive work. To expect the group to be productive at this stage is unrealistic, and any work that is done will probably not be useful when the group settles in.

Whether you're a group leader or a group member, you can do three things to help a group successfully complete the orientation phase:

1. You can help members understand the purpose of the group, including any pressures that might be important: "If we're successful, the organization will set up other groups like ours around the company."

2. You can help group members formulate personal goals and translate them into group goals: "You want top-level management to notice you? OK, if this group accomplishes its task, that might must happen!"

3. You can help group members speak directly to each other and exchange feedback about their observations. For example, designating a specific time when members can share their thoughts about what is happening in the group emphasizes the importance of being open. Such direct communication should help members develop trust, which is crucial if the group is to survive the next phase.

The Conflict Phase

By the end of the first phase, group members often feel swallowed up by the groupness they've created. In response, they assert their individuality, the primary concern of the **conflict phase**. Conflict is normal and predictable, not a sign that something is wrong.

You know that the conflict phase has begun when agreement and ambiguity are replaced by infighting, defensiveness, competition, disunity, tension, and resistance to task demands. Candor decreases, individual identities take precedence over group identity, confusion about the task increases, and group members complain about the work that's required.

The conflict usually revolves around two issues, regardless of what it *sounds* like group members are fighting about: (1) Should we be close to each other or not? and (2) Is the leader a fool or a benevolent genius?

Once you realize that conflict is normal and that it centers on these two issues, you can focus on helping your group resolve its problems. Specifically, you can do the following:

1. work to create a supportive climate by being empathic and nonjudgmental;

2. deal constructively with criticism as it arises (for example, by asking for clarification of the problem);
3. help group members understand their perceptions of the conflict;
4. avoid taking sides.

Like the orientation stage, the conflict stage generates little substantive work.

The Balance, or High Work, Phase

The conflict stage of group development fades as four different kinds of delicate balance occur. Achieving the four kinds of balance is the concern of the **balance, or high work, phase**:

1. Members recognize and start to accept the distinction between the group whole and its individual members.
2. Group goals and individual goals are integrated.
3. Members establish a comfortable level of closeness.
4. The role and authority of the leader are clarified: the leader is recognized as neither a fool nor a genius.

The first part of the balance phase is marked by overcompensation: the group achieves harmony by avoiding conflict. Once overcompensation declines, constructive, substantive conflict occurs. When conflict revolves around the task and not the personalities of the group members, highly productive work finally begins. Getting there may take as many as eight meetings, but then the group quickly and efficiently progresses.

During this phase, the group tends to ignore its social aspects. For example, a problem-solving group will devote its time to clarifying the problem, suggesting solutions, generating criteria for evaluating solutions, and selecting the best solution; in the process, the group avoids nontask interaction. Total exclusion of nontask interaction could lead the group into dysfunctional conflict, so it is crucial to encourage rap sessions, informal lunches, casual get-togethers, and even a party or two.

Once the group's task is completed or its deadline expires, it's time for the last phase of group development.

The Disintegration Phase

Whether the group experience has been painful or pleasant, its members feel anxiety about separating. The **disintegration phase**, which focuses on coping with this anxiety, is at hand when tardiness increases, absences are frequent, members daydream or withdraw in other ways, and discussions are hard to maintain.

Although different people deal with separation anxiety in different ways, two responses are typical: some people deal with their anxiety by making disparaging remarks about the group; others cope by refusing to acknowledge the group's ending. People in the second category collect members' names and addresses, talk about a reunion party, and say "See you soon" instead of "Good-bye."

You can facilitate this phase of development by understanding your own feelings and empathizing with others' feelings. Don't disparage members who plan a party—even if you know the party will never come off—or people who dwell on their negative experiences with the group. Both are doing what they can to cope.

You might want to discuss a way to inform members about the ongoing results of their effort. Feedback is likely to increase positive feelings about the

▶ **F I G U R E   1 0 . 1**   Group Phase Development

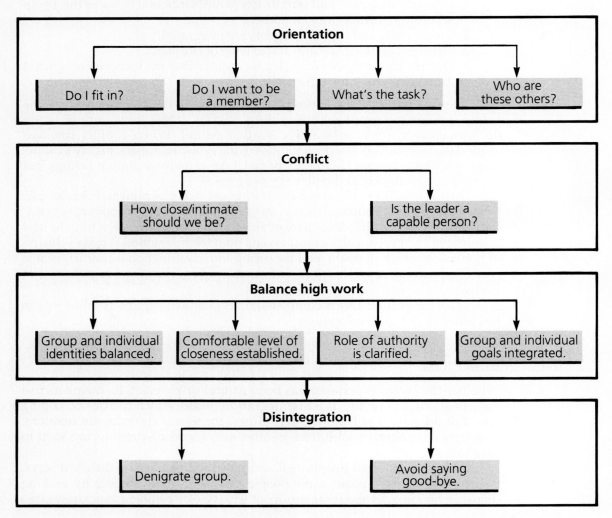

group (even if the feedback is negative), and maintaining some contact facilitates rebanding in the event that another task needs to be handled.

GROUP PROBLEM SOLVING

In addition to the general framework provided by the orientation, conflict, balance, and disintegration stages of group development, several specific frameworks focus on the group processes associated with accomplishing particular tasks. For example, groups may be viewed as problem-solving mechanisms, with the problem-solving process treated as a subdivision of the four phases of group development. Whether the question concerns dropping a bomb on a particular place at a particular time or which movie to see this Saturday night, the problem-solving process is essentially the same.

Preconditions for Problem Solving

Problem solving is the process of making a choice, from the first moments when a problem is defined until the last moments when its solution is evaluated. Not all situations are amenable to group problem solving. What you call a problem may not be considered so by others, and even if a group sees a situation similarly, coping may still best be tackled by an individual.

Problems are caused by gaps between what *is* and what you *would like*. For instance, you may see a gap between what the air quality in your area *should be* and what it *actually is*. From your perspective, industrial pollution is a problem that needs to be solved.

Recognizing a gap is important only if you are motivated to do something about it. There are lots of problems to think about, but only a few may compel your attention sufficiently to move you to act.

In addition to perceiving a problem and being motivated to do something, you must also feel you have the ability to find a solution and get the resources to take the necessary action. The problem you've identified may require money, time, expertise, and other resources that are beyond your grasp.

Should you use a group to solve your problem, or are you better off alone? Several factors can help you decide. A group is more likely to produce better results than will an individual when a problem requires a division of labor. This is especially true of complex problems that are multifaceted or call for a great deal of information. Similarly, problems that demand a variety of perspectives are better suited to groups. Several individuals working together are likely to generate a wider range of solutions, more plans for implementation, and more methods of judging the effectiveness of one solution over another than an individual is.

Nevertheless, a problem that requires a division of labor and a variety of perspectives may still not be suitable to group problem solving. If a problem is highly personal or likely to cause strong disagreement among group members, you may be better off working alone. "Never argue about sex, politics, or religion" is practical advice, given the low probability of a group's ever agreeing on a solution to a problem related to those three topics.

If a problem is too hard or too easy for a group, nontask behavior may result, making individual problem solving more efficient. To avoid feeling frustrated, a group might ignore a task that's too difficult, or it may waste time by exaggerating a problem that's too easy.

Finally, because groups take time to develop, an individual may be able to work more quickly alone.

Being able to assess a problem with regards to its being better suited to an individual or group problem-solving approach is a first step in increasing your efficiency as a problem solver. Skill Checkup 10.2 presents two problems for analysis and requires you to make up one of your own.

SKILL CHECKUP 10.2

Problem Solving Alone or with Others

Decide whether the following two problems should be solved by a group or an individual. Generate and assess a third problem that is clearly suited to either a group or an individual problem-solving procedure.

Problems:

1. Your instructor assigns the following problem to a group of five students. Should they tackle it as a group or not? *What are common obstacles to effective problem solving?*

2. You and several friends are concerned with the following problem. Should you attempt to solve it alone or as a group? *What can be done to persuade a local bakery to package their frankfurter buns in a number equal to the number of frankfurters sold in a package?*

3.

Answer questions a through e for each problem:

a. Does the problem require a division of labor?

b. Does the problem require a variety of perspectives?

c. Is the problem likely to be considered personal?

d. Is the problem too difficult or too easy for the potential group members?

e. Is enough time available to allow for group development, assuming there are seven weeks available in a school semester?

Steps in the Problem-Solving Process

As a group solves a problem, it typically goes through six steps, four of which deal directly with problem solving and two of which focus on what happens after a decision is reached. The problem-solving process consists of (1) defining the problem, (2) generating solutions, (3) setting criteria to evaluate the generated solutions, (4) choosing a solution, (5) implementing the solution, and (6) evaluating the results. Figure 10.2 on page 251 summarizes the process.

Defining the Problem

The definition of a problem requires proof that a problem exists and a discussion of the most important aspects and consequences of the problem. The problem's context—what forces are already operating to relieve the problem and what forces are perpetuating it—must also be specified. For example, environmental groups and certain federal and state laws are already trying to resolve the problem of air pollution, but weak law enforcement and public apathy perpetuate the problem.

Generating Solutions

The goal of the second step is to devise as many potential solutions as possible. Group members should continue to offer suggestions until all possibilities are exhausted. Two useful methods of generating solutions are brainstorming and the nominal group technique.

Brainstorming, an easy and popular approach, stresses the quantity—not the quality—of the solutions a group generates. There are four rules for brainstorming:[6]

1. Express ideas, no matter how wild, without analysis or critical evaluation.
2. Emphasize quantity, not quality.
3. Generate new possibilities by building one idea on top of another (piggybacking).
4. Stick to one task at a time.

It's also a good idea, but not a rule, for one member of the group to write down the ideas as they are expressed so everyone can see them. This helps stimulate piggybacking ideas.

SKILL CHECKUP 10.3

Brainstorming

Form a group with about three other students to work on the following problem. At the same time, a few people should work on the problem alone.

Imagine that your great-aunt Fay has bequeathed you a warehouse filled with bricks. How many uses can you think of for bricks? Spend ten minutes generating ideas. It is important not to evaluate the ideas. Instead, concentrate on suggesting as many uses as possible, no matter how wild or crazy they may seem. Write down the ideas as they are generated.

1. Who produced more ideas, the group or the individuals?

2. Who appeared to be more motivated?

Because it emphasizes quantity and downplays evaluation, brainstorming encourages idea generation. If the results of your brainstorming experiment are typical, you found that the group generated more solutions than did the individuals working alone. You probably also found that working in groups was more motivating because it encouraged creativity and sharing. Even though brainstorming admits silly ideas, it also makes way for an excellent solution that may otherwise have remained hidden.

When a group is too large to use brainstorming, the nominal group technique is useful. Best suited for groups of about twelve or thirteen members, the **nominal group technique** requires that group members generate ideas silently before discussion. This approach avoids many common problems with participation. These problems include when one member dominates and others remain silent, when members hesitate to speak because they are uncertain about the nature of the problem or its solutions, when discussion is cut short due to disagreement, or when individual participation is unbalanced because the group is larger than seven or so members. The first three parts of the nominal group technique relate to idea generation, while the fourth part pertains to selecting the solution:[7]

1. The leader states the problem (often in the form of a question) and each person, working alone, writes down ideas and solutions.

2. The ideas and solutions are collected and read to the group, or members take turns reading one idea at a time from their lists. Each idea is presented without discussion.

3. Group members may ask for clarification of the ideas that have been suggested but may not offer any evaluation.

4. Group members vote for their preferred solutions, the votes are recorded, and the solutions are rank-ordered from most to least favorite. The solution ranked highest is selected. If two or more solutions are tied for first choice, the group discusses and clarifies the options and takes a second vote.

KNOWLEDGE CHECKUP 10.2

Choosing Between Brainstorming and the Nominal Group Technique

Imagine that the president of a local organization has invited you to facilitate idea generation in one of her work groups. What questions would you ask the president about the group and her goals in order to decide on the brainstorming or the nominal group technique?

Setting Criteria

In this step, the group develops guidelines for evaluating the solutions that were proposed during brainstorming or the nominal group technique. They determine what criteria a solution must meet in order to be considered useful or adequate.

The **rational management technique** develops criteria by considering the *musts* and the *wants* of a solution.[8] The **musts** are the things that are required; without them, a solution would not be effective under any circumstances. For example, a workable solution to the problem of storing toxic waste *must* keep the waste from getting into water supplies. The **wants** are the nonessential, desirable characteristics of a proposed solution. For example, the group might *want* companies that contribute to the costs of storing toxic waste to feel good about helping to solve the problem.

SKILL CHECKUP 10.4

Establishing Criteria

Select a problem in your community or school, such as how to handle problems of cheating on exams, and develop a list of musts and wants for any solution. Explain how you would use your list for evaluating proposed solutions.

Problem:

Criteria for any solution:

    Musts:

    Wants:

How the lists of musts and wants will be used to evaluate the proposed solutions:

Choosing a Solution

This is the **decision-making** step, the object of which is to discuss the solutions that meet the must and want criteria and to select the best one. There are seven decision-making methods, each with advantages and disadvantages.[9] Some of the methods require little group interaction, whereas others require a great deal.

Authority Rule without Discussion   In **authority rule without discussion**, the method that requires the least interaction, the leader chooses the solution and communicates it to group members. Although this approach may not produce the best solution if the leader lacks key information and may cause resentment and low commitment among group members, it is useful when a problem is trivial, when there is little time for discussion, or when the leader is expected to dictate a solution. Highly authoritarian systems, such as the army, often use this method. Enlisted personnel do not expect to be asked for opinions because decisions, they are taught, are the exclusive property of the officers in charge.

Expert Opinion   When one person has far greater expertise than other group members, he or she may be expected to use that expert opinion, that knowledge and skill, to the group's advantage. Of course, some members may feel resentment and a lack of commitment to the decision if they do not recognize the expert's special knowledge. Furthermore, unless there is some group interaction, even an expert may lack key information.

Averaging   When commitment is not important and group members cannot easily meet to discuss a solution to a problem, it may be useful to average opinions. In **averaging**, group members rank or rate the proposed solutions, the rankings are added, the sum is divided by the number of respondents, and the solution with the highest number is selected. Unfortunately, the solution derived from such an average may not suit anyone. For example, if a solution receives both high and low ratings, the two extremes may cancel each other out and lead to rejection, even though the solution has strong advocates. As a result, a solution rated neutrally by everyone, without any enthusiastic supporters, may be selected by default.

Authority Rule After Discussion   Unlike authority rule without discussion, **authority rule after discussion** allows group members to exchange thoughts with the leader, who then makes the final decision. If a leader listens to group members and makes a decision that adequately reflects the group's discussion, the approach has few drawbacks. But if a leader does not listen, a great deal of resentment may result.

Majority Rule Under **majority rule**, a solution is chosen if it is preferred by more than half the group members. Although majority rule may leave a resentful minority uncommitted to the chosen solution, this method is useful when discussion time is limited or when an issue is not very important. Of course, the smaller the majority, the more the resentment. For example, a candidate who wins office with 50.1 percent of the vote may have a large hostile minority with which to contend.

Minority Rule Under **minority rule**, a small subgroup of the larger group is given authority to select a solution. In such cases, the problems of majority rule can compound, and the group may be forced to cope with a hostile majority. This method is useful, however, for trivial issues, when commitment is unimportant, or when quick action is necessary.

Consensus Under the **consensus** method of decision making, discussion continues until all group members agree on a solution. This approach produces the highest quality decisions and generates the most commitment because everyone is included in the decision-making process. However, because consensus takes a great deal of time, energy, and interpersonal skill, it is best reserved for problems that are crucial to the group, that are highly complex, and that call for the most creative and innovative solutions.

Comparisons of Decision-Making Methods Members of groups that use consensus to make decisions feel the most understood and listened to, the most influential, the most committed to the solution, and the most satisfied of all group members. The opposite is found in groups that use authority rule without discussion. When consensus is impractical, authority rule with discussion may offer all the same benefits as long as the leader listens to and respects group members' opinions. The remaining decision-making methods—expert opinion, averaging, majority rule, and minority rule—fall between the extremes of consensus and authority rule without discussion, although members seem to be more satisfied by averaging than by either majority or minority rule. In the latter two cases, only members who are part of the decision-making minority or majority express satisfaction with the group and their role in it.

The goal of decision making is to select a solution that has both the *highest quality* possible and the *greatest member acceptance*. Several key questions can help you choose the decision-making method that will yield both in your

Advantages and Disadvantages of Decision-Making Methods

Method	Advantages	Disadvantages
Authority rule without discussion	Useful with knowledgeable leader and when the problem is trivial, time pressure is high, or this approach is expected	Possible resentment and low commitment; does not use information held by others
Expert opinion	Useful when one member has superior expertise and will use it to the group's advantage	Possible resentment and low commitment; does not use information held by others
Averaging	Useful when there is no time for discussion and the task is simple or trivial	Lack of member interaction reduces sharing of information; a mediocre solution may be selected by default; possible low commitment and resentment

particular situation. "Yes" responses indicate support for a consensus-oriented decision-making method, whereas "no" responses suggest that a more authoritarian approach is appropriate.

1. Is it important to produce a high-quality decision? That is, do group members care about the decision and think it is important?
2. Is a great deal of information necessary to make a high-quality decision?
3. Is the problem unstructured or highly complex?
4. Is it important for group members to be committed to the decision in order to implement it?
5. Do group members believe in the group's goals?
6. Is intense conflict among group members unlikely?
7. Do group members expect to participate in the decision-making process?

Method	Advantages	Disadvantages
Authority rule after discussion	Useful when the leader uses the information shared by the members	Possible resentment and low commitment
Majority rule	Useful when there is little time for discussion and the issue is minor or unimportant	May leave a hostile minority; possible low commitment
Minority rule	Useful when not everyone can meet for discussion, the problem is routine or the subgroup possesses all relevant information, and time is short	Resources of many group members are not utilized; possible low commitment and unresolved conflict
Consensus	Useful when the problem is important and there is little time pressure; produces highest levels of commitment and satisfaction	Takes a great deal of time, energy, and interpersonal skill

SKILL CHECKUP 10.5

Selecting a Decision-Making Method

Determine the most appropriate decision-making method for each problem. Justify your selection by referring to the seven key questions listed before this skill checkup.

1. A group composed of student, faculty, and administration representatives is discussing what changes, if any, should be made to the current deadlines for dropping and adding courses.

2. Four college roommates are discussing what meals should be planned for the upcoming week and who should cook them.

Implementing the Solution

At this point, the group determines the tasks that need to be done, how they should be carried out, and who should be responsible for them. In addition, the group needs to determine when results may be expected and what problems may arise that could stand in the way of implementing the solution.

Implementation is different from the four earlier steps in the problem-solving process because it requires the greatest specificity. Unless all group members clearly understand the steps necessary to implement a solution, they will find it difficult to coordinate activities and develop an overall plan. This could result in confusion and the need for emergency meetings to develop new strategies. Similarly, unless all members clearly understand their accountability, they will lack the agreement necessary to ensure that tasks are carried out. If, as a result, steps are skipped or left uncompleted, the implementation could ultimately fail.

Each part of the implementation process could generate new mini-problem-solving sequences of its own. This is highly likely as the group moves from the drawing board to reality.

Evaluating the Results

The object of the last step is to determine how the solution worked and whether modifications are desirable. To assume that a solution is working and will continue to work is to deny the reality of constant change. No solution lasts forever.

To evaluate their solution's effectiveness, a group must assess the extent to which their approach solved the problem; how much the solution cost in terms of time, money, anxiety, and energy; and whether the solution may have caused new problems to emerge. Such information may be obtained through questionnaires, interviews, or direct observation. No matter what procedure the group chooses, they must recognize that their task is not completed until they have evaluated their results.

Overcoming Obstacles to Effective Problem Solving

Although an infinite number of difficulties may interfere with a group's ability to solve problems, several are common enough to deserve special attention. Obstacles may relate to the preconditions for problem solving, to group interaction, and to groupthink.

Obstacles Related to the Preconditions for Problem Solving

Motivation is a precondition to successful problem solving. Unless group members are motivated, they are apt to lose interest in the problem or lack commitment to the solution or its implementation. To counteract this potential problem,

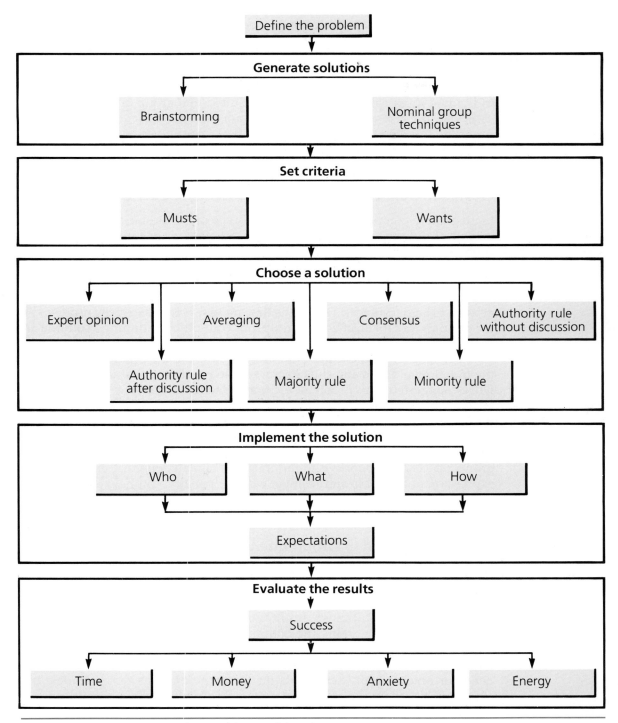

▶ **FIGURE 10.2**   The Problem-Solving Sequence

group members must be persuaded to see the personal relevance of the problem and the importance of finding a solution. Personal goals and group goals must be combined for members to have the highest motivation possible.

Difficulties may also arise if a group problem-solving procedure is used for a problem that could be more easily handled by an individual, or if an individual must solve a problem better suited to a group approach. In either case, the likely results are frustration and wasted resources. To avoid such mistakes, take the time necessary to analyze alternatives and choose the best problem-solving approach.

Obstacles Related to the Problem-Solving Sequence

Inadequately completing any of the six steps of the problem-solving process may destroy any possibility of finding an effective solution. For example, problem-solving groups often fail because they do not take the time to state their problem clearly. They ignore the fact that being able to state a problem clearly goes a long way toward solving it since stating the problem clarifies the important aspects of the problem and its consequences, as well as forces already at work to help resolve it. Taking the time necessary to identify the problem sets the groundwork for an effective group, one committed to finding a solution and implementing it.

Prematurely evaluating solutions is another common problem that blocks the free flow of ideas and thus decreases the possibility that the best solution will be suggested. This problem can be avoided if evaluation is postponed until all available ideas have been presented and criteria for evaluating them have been established.

Phony consensus—agreement for the sake of agreement— guarantees that hidden resentments will undermine the implementation of the solution the group selects. A supportive communication climate, one that encourages the expression of thoughts and feelings without penalty, can help a group avoid phony consensus.

Obstacles Related to Group Interaction

A variety of obstacles may affect a group's interaction. For example, a competitive, hostile communication climate, one in which group members are judgmental, highly evaluative, and have hidden agendas, ensures a long conflict phase. Such a climate also promotes low risk-taking behavior, such as withdrawal, which curtails the communication of creative ideas that could stimulate a productive discussion.

A group that promotes conformity and lacks tolerance for unconventional behavior automatically sets limits on the range of ideas that members may express. This affects the group's ability to produce innovative solutions.

Finally, both inactive and overzealous group members tend to cause problems. Inactive members can be doubly difficult when they refuse to contribute to group deliberations and fail to support the contributing group members. In contrast, overzealous members, because they tend to dominate interaction and consume much of the group's time, often cause resentment and the withdrawal of members who could be strong contributors.

Many obstacles to group interaction can be overcome by developing and maintaining a supportive communication climate. Members' comments should focus on the group's problem rather than individual personalities; they should reflect open-mindedness rather than arrogance and certainty; and they should show trust rather than secretiveness. All members should feel that they are valuable and that the problem-solving process is productive.

Groupthink[10]

Groupthink occurs when group members' desire for uniformity interferes with their willingness to assess alternative solutions to their problem. This overconforming way of thinking, which is especially likely in highly cohesive groups, often leads members to think that they have done a great job when, in actuality, they have not.

There are eight symptoms of groupthink:

1. Group members believe that the group position is shared by everyone.
2. Individual members, assuming that everyone else agrees with the group's solution, ignore their own doubts in order to make agreement unanimous.
3. Members who raise alternative perspectives are pressured into conforming with the group's decision.
4. Group members invent justifications for the actions they plan to undertake.
5. Group members dismiss competitors and potential critics as stupid or weak or too evil to warrant consideration.
6. Members assume the group's actions are ethical and morally justified.
7. Members protect the group from contradictory information by keeping it from their colleagues.
8. Members develop an illusion of invulnerability, which generates unwarranted optimism and excessive risk taking.

Groups can guard against groupthink the following ways:

- ▶ being open-minded and considering all solutions thoroughly before rejecting them;
- ▶ emphasizing the search for information rather than the search for the right solution;
- ▶ reexamining choices made earlier to make sure that ideas were not rejected prematurely;

▶ recognizing that it is easy and comforting—and potentially dangerous—to side with those who agree with the group and reject those who disagree;

▶ being open to criticism from both inside and outside the group;

▶ developing contingency plans in case some unanticipated event or person blocks the implementation of the chosen solution.

Given how much both your happiness and well-being depend on the small groups to which you belong—your classes, teams, clubs, family, job groups, friendship groups, religious groups, political groups, and social groups—it is important to understand why you belong to them, how they develop, how they solve problems, and how to overcome obstacles that may prevent effective problem solving. This information will make you a more competent communicator in the small-group setting and, thus, a better group member and leader.

1. These diners consider themselves a group. What could be their defining characteristics?

2. What seems to be the group's source of attraction for all its members? How does this source of attraction relate to their behavior?

3. If, upon arrival, one member said, "I have other things I should be doing tonight," what techniques could the rest of the members use to increase the group's attraction for him or her?

4. In what phase of development does the group seem to be? If a new person joined the group, how could the other members help her or him complete the orientation stage?

5. The bill arrives and a problem develops. How should the cost be split? Should one person pay the entire amount? Should the total be split evenly or should each person figure out the exact amount she or he owes? In what other ways could the bill be handled? Describe the problem-solving process the group is likely to follow, including the preconditions that exist and the six steps in the problem-solving sequence.

6. Several obstacles interfere with the group's ability to solve its problem with the check: one member keeps saying "I don't care" and is clearly unmotivated;

another seems willing to agree with any solution, although the others sense this is phony; and a third dominates the interaction by continuously yelling "Let's divide the bill evenly!" How can group members overcome their obstacles in order to arrive at an effective solution?

NOTES

1. Referred to as *reference groups*, these groups were first discussed by Thelen. Herbert Thelen, *Dynamics of Groups at Work* (Chicago: University of Chicago Press, 1954).

2. Michael Burgoon, Judee K. Heston, and James C. McCroskey, *Small Group Communication: A Functional Approach* (New York: Holt, Rinehart and Winston, 1974), pp. 2–5; David W. Johnson and Frank P. Johnson, *Joining Together: Group Theory and Group Skills*, 3d ed. (Englewood Cliffs, NJ: Prentice-Hall, 1987), pp. 4–8.

3. According to Quey, task attraction, people attraction, and fulfilling a need outside the group are universal motivations for joining groups. R. L. Quey, "Function and Dynamics of Work Groups," *American Psychologist* 26 (1971):1077–82.

4. William C. Schutz, *The Interpersonal Underworld* (Palo Alto, CA: Science and Behavior Books, 1966).

5. Items for the questionnaire were suggested by those developed by McCroskey and McCain for their *Attraction Questionnaire* and by Schutz for his *FIRO-B* (Fundamental Interpersonal Relations Orientations—Behavior). See: James C. McCroskey and Thomas A. McCain, "The Measurement of Interpersonal Attraction," *Speech Monographs* 41 (1974): 261–66; and Schutz, *The Interpersonal Underworld*.

6. Alex F. Osborn, *Applied Imagination*, rev. ed. (New York: Scribner, 1957).

7. Andre L. Delbecq, A. H. Van de Ven, and D. H. Gustafson, *Group Techniques for Program Planning: A Guide to Nominal Group and Delphi Processes* (Glenview, IL: Scott, Foresman, 1975).

8. C. H. Kepner and B. B. Tregoe, *The Rational Manager: A Systematic Approach to Problem Solving and Decision Making* (New York: McGraw-Hill, 1965).

9. David W. Johnson and Frank P. Johnson, *Joining Together: Group Theory and Group Skills*, 3d ed. (Englewood Cliffs, NJ: Prentice-Hall, 1987), pp. 97–105. The boxed review on pp. 248-249 is adapted from the table on pages 104–5 in Johnson and Johnson, *Joining Together*.

10. *Groupthink* was first explicated by Janis in 1972. Irving L. Janis, *Victims of Groupthink* (Boston: Houghton Mifflin, 1972). An updated analysis with recent cases was published in 1982: Irving L. Janis, *Groupthink: Psychological Studies of Policy Decisions and Fiascoes*, 2d ed. (Boston: Houghton Mifflin, 1982).

FOR FURTHER INVESTIGATION

Bass, Bernard. "Team Productivity and Individual Member Competence." *Small Group Behavior* 11 (1980): 431–504.

Brilhart, John. *Effective Group Discussion,* 5th ed. Dubuque, IA: Wm. C. Brown, 1986.

Carron, Albert V. *Group Dynamics in Sport.* London, Ontario: Spodym Publishers, 1988.

Cragan, John F., and David W. Wright. "Small Group Communication Research of the 1970s: A Synthesis and Critique." *Central States Speech Journal* 31 (1980): 197–213.

Evans, Nancy J., and Paul A. Jarvis. "The Group Attitude Scale: A Measure of Attraction to Group." *Small Group Behavior* 17 (1986): 203–27.

_____"Group Cohesion: A Review and Reevaluation." *Small Group Behavior* 11 (1980): 359–70.

Fisher, B. Aubrey, and Randall K. Stutman. "An Assessment of Group Trajectories: Analyzing Developmental Breakpoints." *Communication Quarterly* 35 (1987): 105–24.

Hirokawa, Randy Y. "Discussion Procedures and Decision-Making Performance: A Test of a Functional Perspective." *Small Group Behavior* 12 (1985): 203–24.

Jablin, Fred. "Cultivating Imagination: Factors that Enhance and Inhibit Creativity in Brainstorming Groups." *Human Communication Research* 7 (1981): 245–58.

Johnson, David W., and Frank P. Johnson. *Joining Together: Group Theory and Group Skills*, 3d ed. Englewood Cliffs, NJ: Prentice-Hall, 1987.

Mudrack, Peter E. "Defining Group Cohesiveness: A Legacy of Confusion?" *Small Group Behavior* 20 (1989): 37–49.

Poole, Marshall Scott, David Seibold, and Robert McPhee. "Group Decision-Making as a Structurational Process." *Quarterly Journal of Speech* 71 (1985): 74–102.

Rosenfeld, Lawrence B. *Now That We're All Here...Relations in Small Groups*. Columbus, OH: Charles E. Merrill, 1976.

Schmuck, Richard A., and Patricia A. Schmuck. *Group Processes in the Classroom*, 5th ed. Dubuque, IA: Wm. C. Brown, 1988.

Schultz, Beatrice G. *Communicating in the Small Group: Theory and Practice*. New York: Harper and Row, 1989.

Shaw, Marvin E. *Group Dynamics: The Psychology of Small Group Behavior*, 3d ed. New York: McGraw-Hill, 1981.

Tuckman, M. "Developmental Sequences in Small Groups." *Psychological Bulletin* 63 (1965): 384–99.

Zander, Alvin. *Making Groups Effective*. San Francisco: Jossey-Bass, 1982.

CHAPTER 11

▶ # *Influence and Participation in Small Groups*

This chapter on influence and participation in small groups will help you to practice and develop communication competencies that fall into three broad categories: (1) **communication codes,** *which include choosing words and grammar that are appropriate to a particular situation and using your voice effectively; (2)* **basic speech communication skills,** *such as expressing ideas clearly and concisely and asking and answering questions; and (3)* **human relations,** *which include expressing feelings and performing social rituals in a group setting. Specifically, the competencies you will gain will enable you to do the following:*

▶ *Describe the characteristics of group norms.*

▶ *Assess the importance of group norms and the consequences of nonconformity.*

▶ *Specify the five determinants of role behavior.*

▶ *Identify three categories of roles specific to classroom and small group settings.*

▶ *Recognize five kinds of conflicts that may arise when roles are enacted: role, role-role, and self-role conflict, and role overload and role ambiguity.*

▶ *Evaluate your sources of power and describe methods of increasing each one.*

▶ *Note the conditions necessary for exercising power.*

▶ *Describe five approaches to the study of leadership.*

▶ *Analyze your group's situation and determine the best leadership for the circumstances.*

Wandering through Wonderland, Alice is confronted by a rabbit with a pocket watch, a cat who can both talk and disappear, the celebration of *un*-birthdays, and a tea party during which seats are changed every few minutes. She is confused and can only utter "Dear me!" as she tries to learn the standards of behavior. Alice just didn't understand the norms of the situation.

NORMS AND CONFORMITY

The rules of conduct that group members agree are important and use to regulate their behavior are called **norms**. Classes often seem like Wonderland for the first few sessions, but then, as norms are established, things seem to settle down. What are some of the norms in your class?

- ▶ Do people seem to take the same (or nearby) seats each class period?
- ▶ Does the class begin and end at set times (which may or may not coincide with the official beginning and ending times)?
- ▶ What are the rules for gaining recognition? Do you have to raise your hand to be recognized?
- ▶ Is it clear who's in charge? What rules help to keep this person in charge?

Norms regulate a group's performance by specifying what behaviors are appropriate and allowed—what should and should not be done by particular members at particular times. Norms emerge in a group's development because members sense that the group will not achieve its goals without some form of coordination.

Three areas of group life are regulated by norms. Norms govern information—what information is considered important and what information is ignored. Norms regulate procedures—how a task should be divided, how issues should be discussed, and how decisions should be made. Norms also dictate interpersonal relations—how intimate members should be, how nontask behaviors should be dealt with, and how conflict should be handled.

Sometimes a norm created to help the group achieve its goal has just the opposite effect. For example, a common norm is "There will be no conflict among group members"; however, that rule may well prevent members from ever progressing through the conflict phase of group development.

Norms differ along a number of dimensions.[1] For example, some norms are more important than others ("Eat everything on your plate" is usually less important than "Don't take the family car without permission"); some are highly specific while others are broad ("Being on time for a group meeting means being no more than five minutes late" is more specific than "Our group presentation should include charts"); and some are clearer and better understood by group members than others ("Meetings are serious business" may be ambiguous enough that some members interpret it as "No joking around" and others think it means "Everything is important").

Group members adhere to a norm for various reasons: some may follow a rule so that other members will like them; some may follow it to avoid punishment; some may follow it as an affirmation of their loyalty to the group, even when they don't think much of the rule itself; and some may follow it because they think the norm is a good idea. For example, a rule in some organizations is "Men wear ties." Some workers wear ties so others will think they're "part of the team," some wear them to avoid being fired, others wear ties to affirm that they belong to the organization, and yet others actually think that ties are good to wear.

Recognizing and analyzing a group's norms equips you to understand how your groups function. However, your close involvement in a particular situation may hinder you from recognizing particular norms. You need to distance yourself from the situation and look at it as an outsider would. One way to do this is to purposely violate what you think is a norm and see what happens.

KNOWLEDGE CHECKUP 11.1

The Role of Norms

A good way to learn about norms is to challenge them momentarily. The object of this exercise is to break a norm and observe the verbal and nonverbal consequences.

1. Identify a norm governing face-to-face interaction in a public place, such as a supermarket, office, corridor, classroom, bus stop, or bank. For example, speaking in hushed tones is the norm in a library, just as avoiding eye contact is the norm in an elevator.

2. Break the norm without being self-conscious. *Do not break the law or hurtfully shock or disturb people.*

3. Observe people's verbal and nonverbal responses and write down the results.

4. Analyze the results you obtained:
   a. How important is the norm you broke? (How intense were the responses you observed?)

   b. Does the norm relate to a specific behavior or to a range of behaviors?

   c. How clear and well understood is the norm? (Did people recognize that you were breaking a norm?)

   d. Why do you think people conform to or accept the norm?

   e. What value does the norm have or what function does it serve?

Conformity—acting in accordance with group norms—is highest when you want to be a member of the group, you perceive the group as cohesive (members want to stay in the group), communication is personal, members seem committed to the group, and you feel your position in the group is important. Conformity is also likely if sanctions are imposed for breaking the norm. When you did your norm-breaking exercise, how did people encourage you to change your behavior back to "normal"? Did they yell at you or tell you to stop? Sanctions in schools often include fines, ridicule, suspension, and restrictions on the activities in which you participate.

When someone in a group breaks a norm, the response is predictable. First, the group steps up its interaction with the violator, both to find out why the norm is being broken and to persuade the norm-breaker to stop. If their goals are met, the group resumes its standard behavior. If the violation continues, what happens next depends on who broke the norm. If the violator is a valued group member, the nonconformity may be ignored; however, if the violator is not a valued member, she or he may be dismissed from the group, or the group may show open hostility and exclude her or him.

If you're dissatisfied with a norm in your group, you can change it, but doing so is hard work—forces to change a norm will be met by counterforces to maintain it. Changing a norm is easier if you have high status—others will listen to you. You may also enlist the help of a subgroup of new members—the larger the subgroup, the better—who are as yet uncommitted to established norms. Or you may use outside consultants; if the group perceives them as objective, members might listen to their suggestions.

GROUP ROLES

Although norms govern the behavior of all group members, not all members of the group behave in the same way. Group members display their individuality in much the same way that characters in a play act and speak in specified ways. A **role** is a pattern of behaviors that signals a predictable way of acting. Group members come to anticipate this pattern, which may mark a position in the group. You can identify group members as "leaders" or "followers," "troublemakers" or "cooperators," based on their patterns of behaviors.

How Roles Are Determined

At least five factors determine the role you play in a group: who you are, where you are, whom you're with, what you want from others, and what others want from you.

Who You Are

The first and most important determinant of your role is *you*. Who you think you are and what you think you want, need, and like all determine how you behave.

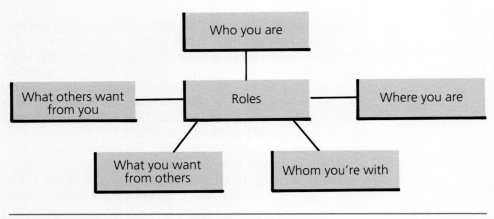

▶ **FIGURE 11.1**   Determinants of Roles

Knowledge Checkup 11.2 will help you uncover what your motivations are when you participate in a group. Do you desire to be successful, influence others, or enjoy the interaction?

KNOWLEDGE CHECKUP 11.2

Motivation Questionnaire

For each set of three statements, give a 3 to the choice that most accurately describes you, a 1 to the choice that least accurately describes you, and a 2 to the choice that falls in between. Even if all three choices seem to apply equally, assign only one 3, one 2, and one 1.

_____ **1a.** When doing a job, I seek feedback.
_____ **1b.** I prefer to work alone and enjoy being my own boss.
_____ **1c.** I tend to be uncomfortable when forced to work alone.

_____ **2a.** I go out of my way to make friends with new people.
_____ **2b.** I enjoy a good argument.
_____ **2c.** After starting a task, I am not comfortable until it is completed.

_____ **3a.** Status symbols are important to me.
_____ **3b.** I am always getting involved in group projects.
_____ **3c.** I work better when there is a deadline.

_____ **4a.** I work better when I feel challenged.
_____ **4b.** I would rather give orders than take them.
_____ **4c.** I am sensitive to others, especially when they are angry.

_____ **5a.** I am eager to be my own boss.
_____ **5b.** I accept responsibility eagerly.
_____ **5c.** I try to get personally involved with my group members.

_____ **6a.** I am very concerned about my reputation or position.
_____ **6b.** I want to outperform others.
_____ **6c.** I want to be liked and respected.

_____ **7a.** I enjoy and seek warm, friendly relationships.
_____ **7b.** I try to be completely involved in a project.
_____ **7c.** I want my ideas to predominate.

_____ **8a.** I want to make unique accomplishments.
_____ **8b.** I think about counseling and helping others.
_____ **8c.** I have a need to influence others.

_____ **9a.** I think a lot about my feelings and the feelings of others.
_____ **9b.** I am verbally fluent.
_____ **9c.** I am restless and innovative.

Scoring

Achievement Motivation
   Add your responses to items 1a + 2c + 3c + 4a + 5b + 6b + 7b + 8a + 9c: _____
Power Motivation
   Add your responses to items 1b + 2b + 3a + 4b + 5a + 6a + 7c + 8c + 9b: _____
Affiliation Motivation
   Add your responses to items 1c + 2a + 3b + 4c + 5c + 6c + 7a + 8b + 9a: _____

   The range of possible scores for each type of motivation is from 9 to 27, with lower scores indicating low motivation and higher scores indicating high motivation. Are you motivated more by achievement, power, or affiliation? Your source of motivation influences the role you take in a group.

   If you are **achievement motivated**, your aim is to succeed in situations that require excellence. You focus on goals and how to obtain them and on obstacles and how to overcome them. You seek tasks that allow you to be innovative, that challenge you, and that provide clear feedback about your performance.
   If you are **power motivated**, your aim is to control or influence events. You're concerned with your reputation, your status, and how to control other

group members. You seek tasks that allow you to assume leadership and that require interaction between yourself and others in authority.

If you are **affiliation motivated**, your aim is to be with others and enjoy mutual friendships. You're concerned with being liked, with your own as well as others' feelings, and with helping group members. You seek tasks that require cooperation and allow time for casual, nontask interaction.

If you find yourself in the role of leader and are predominantly achievement motivated, you are likely to behave in an egalitarian, democratic way, stressing the equality of group members' contributions. If you're power motivated, you will probably be more authoritarian, stressing your own importance. And if you're affiliation motivated, you might be a permissive leader, letting group members do as they please in an effort to keep their friendship.

If you are in the role of subordinate and are predominantly achievement motivated, you are likely to behave cooperatively. If you're power motivated, you are more likely to rebel. If you're affiliation motivated, you will probably try to ingratiate yourself with other group members, perhaps by doing them favors.

Other aspects of who you are, such as your gender, age, physical characteristics, abilities, and personality characteristics, all affect how you behave in a group. For example, males tend to initiate activity while females tend to act in the role of respondent; males have a greater tendency than females to assume task-oriented roles; and, while females tend to assume cooperative roles, males tend to assume competitive ones. Also, women are more likely than men to assume roles that encourage all group members to participate.[2]

Older group members seem to interact more than younger ones and tend to be selected more often for a leadership role.[3] Leaders also tend to be taller and in better physical condition than other members. Abilities that influence what roles a member enacts include intelligence (more intelligent group members are less likely to be manipulated by the group) and task ability (the greater a member's ability to perform a group's task, the more likely she or he will be to enact task-oriented roles and to influence the group). Personality variables that relate to particular roles include authoritarianism (in the role of follower, authoritarians are compliant and submissive with the leader, and in the role of leader, they are demanding and controlling with subordinates), empathy (members with greater empathy make more bids for leadership and participate more), and independence (independent members tend to be less friendly and interact less than more dependent members).

Where You Are

Whether a role is appropriate or inappropriate depends on the setting in which it is enacted. For example, playing the role of "comic" and telling jokes would be inappropriate in a group of mourners at a funeral, but not with a group of friends at a casual get-together. If you assume a role that is inappropriate for the situation, you will draw negative attention to yourself. Sanctions will follow, often in the form of reminders about the requirements of the situation, such as, "This is a business meeting, not a picnic. Put that sandwich away!"

Whom You're With

Just as where you are affects how you behave, so do the people with whom you're interacting. Fifth-grade teachers don't behave the same as college teachers mostly because their students are different. Doctors act as doctors only when they're with their patients, just as baseball pitchers can assume the role of pitcher only when other team members are around. Pitchers can *be* pitchers without the other players, but they can *act* like pitchers only when they're with specific people.

What You Want from Others

You behave in ways that you believe will help you achieve your goals. Given who you are, where you are, and the people you're with, you'll choose behavior that you think will get you what you want. If you want to be liked, you'll be cooperative and friendly. If you want to take charge, you'll volunteer to coordinate an aspect of your group's project.

What Others Want from You

Other group members may ask you—either implicitly or explicitly—to take on a particular role and to behave in particular ways. For example, if you have information your group needs, you may be cast in the role of information giver, whether or not it's a role you want to enact.

Specific Roles

Because the environment determines what roles are appropriate, particular roles are identified with particular meetings.

The Small Group Setting

Specific roles may be identified in any small group, whether a PTA meeting, a support group, a classroom, or a group of students working on a class project. The classroom is often a setting for an intricate play between teacher roles and student roles. Among the most common student roles are the compliant student, who is conventional, trusting, and wants to absorb what the teacher says without much independent thinking; the anxious student, who worries about his or her abilities and what the teacher thinks; the discouraged worker student, who tends to be intelligent and hard working, but depressed and distant from other class members; the independent student, who is self-confident and interested; and the sharpshooting student, who attacks the teacher with loaded questions or requests for details she or he thinks the teacher doesn't know.[4]

The variety of roles teachers assume demonstrates the complexity of their position. At one time or another, most teachers are judge (grade-giver), resource (knowledge source), guidance counselor, referee, detective (seeker of rule-breakers), stereotypical father (task-oriented and unsentimental), stereotypical mother (kindly and emotion-oriented), older sibling (guide and instructor of students), favorite uncle (lively, interesting, and well liked), target for hostilities, friend, confidant, and ego-supporter.

Despite the multiplicity of roles, they may all be divided into three categories: task roles, social roles, and self-centered roles.[5]

Task Roles   **Task roles** are sets of behaviors that help the group accomplish its goals. Any member may enact one or several of these roles:

> initiator—proposing ideas and making suggestions;
>
> information seeker—asking for ideas, clarifications, and suggestions, and identifying what information is needed;
>
> information giver—offering facts and personal experiences;
>
> opinion seeker—drawing out convictions and feelings from others;
>
> opinion giver—offering opinions and personal feelings;
>
> orienter—summarizing what's been said and combining points into broader themes to help the group stay on track;
>
> evaluator—applying standards and checking for agreement; and
>
> recorder—taking notes and checking on the group's progress.

Social Roles   Group tasks cannot be accomplished at the expense of social needs, such as your need to be comfortable when interacting with other members, your need to feel as if you're an important member of the group, and your need to get along with other members. Groups that ignore social needs may never accomplish their tasks because the level of conflict is high or the level of interest and motivation is low. Patterns of behavior that help satisfy social needs and build feelings of groupness are **social roles**:

> encourager—praising, agreeing, and making offers of solidarity;
>
> harmonizer—reconciling disagreements and reducing tensions;
>
> compromiser—offering to admit personal errors and cooperate in compromises that maintain group cohesion;
>
> gatekeeper—encouraging participation from all group members;
>
> follower—accepting others' ideas and serving as an audience; and
>
> standard setter—expressing the group's standards.

Roles in the Small Group Setting

Task Role	Objectives
Initiator	Stimulate group activity and thinking
Information Seeker	Gather information for group consideration; clarify information; identify needed information
Information Giver	Provide information for group consideration and increased understanding
Opinion Seeker	Gather opinions for group consideration; clarify opinions; identify needed opinions
Opinion Giver	Provide opinions for group consideration and increased understanding
Orienter	Check understanding
Evaluator	Check agreement
Recorder	Keep a record of the group's progress and assess that progress

Social Role	Objectives
Encourager	Promote interaction
Harmonizer	Reduce tension and hostility
Compromiser	Resolve conflict and increase cohesion
Gatekeeper	Increase participation; equalize participation
Follower	Increase morale and cohesion
Standard Setter	Regulate the group's behavior

Self-Centered Role	Objectives
Blocker	
Dominator	Satisfy personal goals; resolve personal problems;
Cut-Up	fulfill personal needs and desires
Confessor	
Point-Picker	
Special-Interest Pleader	

Self-Centered Roles   Although most members are interested in group goals and group accomplishment, some individuals focus mainly on themselves. They enact **self-centered roles**, which are designed to satisfy personal rather than group needs. Members who assume self-centered roles try to solve their own problems at the expense of the group. Typical self-centered roles include the following:

blocker—refusing to cooperate;

dominator—dictating demands to the group and speaking sarcastically;

cut-up—refusing to take anything seriously;

confessor—engaging in inappropriate self-disclosure and using the group for personal therapy;

point-picker—taking apart every idea; and

special-interest pleader—representing the interests of another group.

Understanding small group processes requires the ability to recognize the variety of roles that members play. Skill Checkup 11.1 will give you practice in identifying roles.

SKILL CHECKUP 11.1

Observing Roles

1. Observe a meeting of a group with between four and seven members (preferably a group you don't belong to). Among the possibilities are the meeting of a class group, a staff meeting, or the meeting of a community group. If you cannot observe such a group firsthand, select a group from a movie or a television program. Which of the following roles are enacted by members of the group? (If possible, do this activity with another person and compare your perceptions.)

Task Roles   **Group Member(s)**

a. Initiator   _____

b. Information Seeker   _____

c. Information Giver   _____

d. Opinion Seeker   _____

e. Opinion Giver   _____

f. Orienter   _____

g. Evaluator   _____

h. Recorder   _____

Social Roles

i. Encourager   _____

j. Harmonizer   _____

k. Compromiser   _____

l. Gatekeeper   _____

m. Follower   _____

n. Standard Setter   _____

Self-Centered Roles

o. Blocker   _____

p. Dominator   _____

q. Cut-Up   _____

r. Confessor   _____

s. Point-Picker   _____

t. Special-Interest Pleader   _____

2. Which roles were enacted by several members?

3. Which roles were not enacted at all?

4. Did task roles dominate the interaction, or did social roles? Were the two balanced?

5. To what degree were self-centered roles enacted?

6. If the group hired you to increase its efficiency, what recommendations would you make about its role behavior?

Problems with Roles

Roles are not simple, neat categories of behavior. So many factors determine which roles are appropriate and how particular roles should be enacted that complications are almost inevitable. Five of the most common problems are role conflict, role-role conflict, self-role conflict, role overload, and role ambiguity.

Role conflict occurs when two or more incompatible expectations or definitions exist for the same role. Have you ever been in a situation where you defined your role one way and another member of the group defined it another? A problem would arise, for example, if your boss thought your role was to stack cartons and clean up, and you, defining your role differently, tried to help a customer.

Role-role conflict arises when you're called on to assume two contradictory roles at the same time. This problem is so common and often severe that organizations create rules to prevent its occurrence. For example, most schools implicitly forbid teachers to date their students, which avoids the conflict that would arise if a teacher had to choose between acting as a teacher and acting as a friend. Similarly, in the armed services, enlisted personnel and officers are not allowed to fraternize; and in the business world, managers and line workers often have separate work areas, lunchrooms, and other facilities that prevent much interpersonal contact.

Self-role conflict occurs when you enact a role that doesn't fit your view of yourself. For example, you may see yourself as a compromiser, yet your co-workers may nominate you to aggressively represent their interests to your manager. The greater the disparity between a role and your view of yourself, the greater the self-role conflict. If the conflict becomes too great, you will probably distance—or totally dissociate—yourself from the role. Thus, you might tell your manager, "Although I would like to compromise, my co-workers expect me to make sure their interests are heard." The implicit message is clear: "It's not *me* behaving this way, it's my *role*."

Role overload means that your own or others' expectations for your behavior call for performing several roles simultaneously. The roles may not be incompatible, which would give rise to role-role conflict, but they require more skill, time, or energy than you have. For example, during the 1980s several demanding roles were combined under the general title "superwoman." Women felt expected to assume the roles of mother, wife, and general manager and caretaker for the home, while simultaneously assuming the roles of full-time worker outside the home and co-producer of money. The results of such role overload was severe stress.

The four conflicts discussed so far assume that roles are concisely defined. In contrast, a fifth problem, **role ambiguity**, arises when the expectations for a role are not communicated clearly enough to enable full understanding of the role's requirements. For example, the role of a good group member may be to "contribute to the group's progress." Does this mean "participate," and, if so, how often? Perhaps it means "provide information," but if it does, how much and when? Such lack of clarity is bound to cause problems for group members who are attempting to coordinate their behavior.

The many roles you enact virtually ensure that problems with roles are the rule and not the exception in your life. But you are able to overcome these conflicts because of the chameleon-like skills that all social beings develop. Automatically and spontaneously, you shift from role to role in a process so natural that you hardly notice it's happening.

POWER AND THE POTENTIAL FOR LEADERSHIP

People who study group processes focus much of their attention on leadership. But before you can understand leadership, you must understand power. Power is the *potential* for influence, while leadership is the *actual* influence, or the *exer*cise of power.

Power is the ability to bring about something that you want to happen, or, conversely, to block the occurrence of something that you don't want to happen. Put simply, power is the ability to choose. Any good thesaurus lists the following synonyms for *powerful*: *potent, capable, strong, competent, energetic, influential,* and *productive.* In contrast, the synonyms for *powerless* are *impotent, incapable, weak,* and *incompetent.* Power is hardly a problem—but powerlessness is!

People who feel powerless rarely contribute to their groups and often behave in ways that increase their feelings of powerlessness. For example, if you feel powerless, you may accept the role you enact in your group as the best that you can do, thereby becoming complacent, lethargic, and perhaps resentful. You may project your hostilities onto other group members, perhaps those you perceive as less powerful than yourself or, in some cases, on those you perceive as more powerful, which is likely to decrease everyone's performance. You may form a "failure support group," a subgroup of all who feel powerless, in an effort to reduce your feelings of frustration. Such subgroups typically complain and blame others for their inability to influence the group, which guarantees that they will remain powerless. Or you may refuse to participate or stop attending group meetings, which is sure to increase your feelings of powerlessness and to reduce your potential for influence. Group members who isolate themselves by not interacting rarely get the chance to influence the group.

Knowledge Checkup 11.3 will help you assess your own feelings of powerfulness.

KNOWLEDGE CHECKUP 11.3

How Powerful Do You Feel?[6]

Think of one group in which you value your membership and keep it in mind as you complete the following questionnaire. Each item has two alternatives. Your task is to divide ten points between the two alternatives according to how well each describes you. You may give all ten points to one alternative and none to the other, split the points evenly (five and five), or assign any other combination of ten points that seems appropriate.

1. When someone in the group says something with which I disagree, I
_____ **a.** assume my position is correct.
_____ **b.** assume what the other person says is correct.

2. When I get angry at another group member, I
_____ **a.** ask the other person to stop the behavior that offends me.
_____ **b.** say little, not knowing quite what to do.

3. When something goes wrong in the group, I

_____ **a.** try to solve the problem.

_____ **b.** try to find out who's at fault.

4. When I participate in a group activity, it is important that I

_____ **a.** live up to my own expectations.

_____ **b.** live up to the expectations of the other group members.

5. I try to surround myself with group members

_____ **a.** whom I respect.

_____ **b.** who respect me.

Scoring

Add all of your **a** responses: _____
Add all of your **b** responses: _____

The two totals, **a** and **b**, indicate how powerful you feel in the group you chose. The total number of points is fifty, so one score could be fifty and the other zero, although that is unlikely. If your **b** score is greater than your **a** score by ten or more points, you probably feel somewhat powerless in your group because you see others' choices as more important than your own. If your two scores are within ten points of each other, you are probably unsure of your own power and your potential to influence others. If your **a** score is greater than your **b** score by ten or more points, you most likely feel quite powerful and in control of the choices you make as a group member.

Power Bases

There are five different power bases, or sources of power. Two relate to **informal power**, perceptions of your abilities, qualities, and traits, and three pertain to **formal power**, your position in the group. Knowledge Checkup 11.4 will help you assess your sources of power—an important step in the process of increasing your feeling powerful.

K N O W L E D G E   C H E C K U P   1 1 . 4

Power Questionnaire[7]

With your experience as a member of one particular group in mind, indicate the extent to which each statement is true of you.

Write 5 if the statement is true.
Write 4 if the statement is sometimes true.
Write 3 if the statement is neither true nor false.
Write 2 if the statement is sometimes false.
Write 1 if the statement is false.

_____ **1.** I try to set a good example for the other group members.
_____ **2.** The other members in this group consider me an expert.
_____ **3.** My position in this group gives me a great deal of authority.
_____ **4.** I can reward other group members.
_____ **5.** Group members see me as having a lot in common with them.
_____ **6.** Members know I have no trouble doing my work in the group.
_____ **7.** I get to review the work of others in this group.
_____ **8.** I can keep other group members from achieving their goals or satisfying their wants.
_____ **9.** I have something that the other members want or value, and I can make it available to them.
_____ **10.** I get along well with other members of this group.
_____ **11.** My previous experience prepared me to work well in this group.
_____ **12.** My work checks the work of other group members.
_____ **13.** I can help group members achieve their goals.
_____ **14.** Group members respect my authority.
_____ **15.** My diligence reduces error in the group.

Scoring

Expert Power
   Add your responses to items 2, 6, and 11:   _____
Referent Power
   Add your responses to items 1, 5, and 10:   _____
Reward Power
   Add your responses to items 4, 9, and 13:   _____
Coercive Power
   Add your responses to items 8, 12, and 15:   _____
Legitimate Power
   Add your responses to items 3, 7, and 14:   _____

Which of the five power bases is your strongest?
   Do you need to increase one or more of your power bases to be a more effective group member?

Expert Power

Expert power is your capacity to influence other group members because of the knowledge and skills they presume you have. Note that *being* an expert and being *perceived* as an expert are two different things; you may have expertise, but to use it you must be perceived as an expert. To build expert power, you need to communicate your expertise to the rest of the group. You can do this by mentioning your background and training, demonstrating that you are well informed on topics important to the group, and accomplishing tasks competently and *noticeably*. In other words, you need to call attention to yourself. For example, telling members of your class group that (1) you had the professor for another course and therefore understand her assignments and (2) that you have experience in analyzing group behavior—the focus of your group project—should help gain you expert power.

Referent Power

Referent power is based on loyalty, friendship, affection, and admiration, traits that rely on your perceived personal characteristics. The key to securing this power base is demonstrating your friendliness and trustworthiness. For example, emphasize the similarities between yourself and other group members, such as background, goals, attitudes, and values. The more similarities the better, because they show that you're "one of the gang" and a "regular person." It also helps to communicate your support for other members, give others the benefit of the doubt, and create symbols that bind you together, such as in-jokes and special language. If you smile frequently, encourage others when their ideas are good, and share secret nods when something happens that only members of your group would consider significant, you will increase your chances of having referent power in your group.

Reward Power

Whereas expert and referent power are based on your perceived abilities and traits, reward, coercive, and legitimate power are based on your position in the group. **Reward power** requires that you be perceived as the best or only source of desired rewards. To have reward power, you must (1) know what others want, (2) amass the objects of desire, and (3) let others know that you have the desired objects and tell them what to do to get them. For example, you know that group members want a place to hold an end-of-project party and you have access to a private cabin. You communicate that the cabin is yours to give, and then you spell out what group members need to do to get it.

Be careful! If the reward is deemed a bribe, you're likely to meet resistance.

Coercive Power

In contrast to reward power, which is based on positive outcomes, **coercive power** is based on negative outcomes, wielded as weapons. To exercise coercive power, you need to (1) know what weapons group members fear most, (2) acquire them, (3) communicate that you have them, and (4) persuade others that you're

Informal and Formal Power Bases

Informal Power Base	Source of Power
Expert Power	Group member is perceived as having knowledge and skills relevant to the group task
Referent Power	Group member is perceived as loyal, friendly, and trustworthy

Formal Power Base	Source of Power
Reward Power	Group member is perceived as the best or only source of an object of desire
Coercive Power	Group member is perceived as able to produce a negative outcome
Legitimate Power	Member is perceived as having the authority to grant certain rights and privileges

willing to use them. For example, you know that being able to force someone to work the weekend shift is a powerful weapon because everyone wants the weekend off. To acquire this weapon, you get yourself into the management position that controls scheduling. You make sure everyone knows you have the authority to make people work weekends. And you make it clear that if subordinates do not comply with your requests, you will not hesitate to assign them to weekend hours.

Because people tend to resist coercive power, whether by punching the power broker in the nose or by slowing withdrawing from the group, avoid its overuse. If you do use it, however, be calm and reasonable, and act only *after* you are convinced that it's the most effective power base at your disposal. The goal is to be perceived as fair—even if you must use a displeasing source of power.

Legitimate Power

Legitimate power stems from group members' belief that they should do what someone requests because of the position that person occupies. For example, parents have the right to make requests of their children, generals have the right to make requests of lieutenants, and bosses have the right to make requests of their workers. To increase your legitimate power, you must either move into a new position with more authority or persuade others that you have more authority by changing their expectations of the position you're in. Call yourself the "primary researcher" instead of "the one who gets the references from the library" and others' view of your job may change!

Choosing Your Power Base

Which power base should you use?[8] The answer depends in part on whether you want commitment or compliance from group members. When group members are committed to a request, they feel enthusiastic about it, agree that it's a good idea, and believe that it's the right thing to do. When they merely comply with a request, they obey reluctantly, without believing in the rightness of the idea.

The choice of power base also depends on how much time you have: some sources of power get quicker action than others. If you want to get things done quickly, with little or no discussion, and if group members need not feel committed to your request, you may find that reward and coercive power work best. But both sources of power have drawbacks.

If you plan to use coercive power, you must expect to be disliked. In addition, the more you use coercive power, the less effective it tends to become, so your threats must escalate. For example, to get children to eat their vegetables, parents may first threaten them with no dessert, then with no television, and ultimately with grounding for longer and longer periods of time. Finally, because coercive power causes so much resentment, you'll have to develop a strategy for ensuring that your demand is obeyed. Watch outcomes carefully! (A child can devise a hundred ways to make it *seem* as if the vegetables were eaten.)

Reward power raises some of the same problems. For example, a reward needs to be increased regularly to maintain the same effect. After a few years, a consistent annual salary raise of 5 percent ceases to be a reward and anything less than 7 percent begins to look like punishment. Also, when you use reward power routinely, you're likely to get results only if you keep an eye on group members to ensure the work is *really* done as opposed to *looking as if* it's done, which may be seen as an alternative if the only goal is to get the reward.

Using legitimate power in combination with small doses of reward and coercive power can be effective, but, unlike reward and coercive power used alone, the best you can hope for is compliance without enthusiastic support. Group members will do what you ask because you ask them to, not because they want to. "The boss told me to do this job" may be the only explanation a worker offers for doing it.

If your request is very important and if you want commitment, expert and referent power are the most productive power bases. A perceived expert who communicates a request without arrogance or insult is likely to command commitment instead of merely compliance. Of course, such commitment is limited to the particular task in the area of expertise the expert is perceived to possess.

Because referent power can compel commitment on the widest range of requests, it is perhaps the most useful source of power. Unlike expert power, which inspires commitment to the *request*, referent power inspires commitment to *you*. An expert can only make requests that relate to her or his perceived area of expertise, but someone with referent power can make requests in any area.

The primary drawback of referent power is that it takes a great deal of time to develop. Relationships need to move from the stranger stage through the acquaintance stage before a low level of friendship is established and referent power can begin to gain strength.

LEADERSHIP

Regardless of your source of power, certain conditions must exist before you can show **leadership**—the exercise of power. If you hope to influence a group, you must know both what the group needs and when it is safe to make your request. Someone who is insecure or lacks self-confidence is unlikely to exercise power.

To influence group members, a leader must be perceived to have a source of power, to be committed to his or her request, and to be able to determine whether the request was fulfilled. If someone in your group asks you to drop by the copy center and pick up the handouts for the next group meeting, you ask yourself: "Why should I? Can this person reward me if I do or punish me if I don't? Does this person have the authority to make the request? Should I obey because this person knows what's best for the group or because this person is my friend?" Once you've answered those questions, you may wonder, "Does this person *really* want me to pick up the material, or is the request only a suggestion?" Finally, you would ask yourself, "Will this person know if I don't pick up the material?"

Approaches to Leadership

Leadership may be examined from five perspectives:

1. personal traits;
2. forms of behavior;
3. the style with which the behaviors are performed;
4. the aspects of a situation that determine which personal traits, behaviors, and style will be most effective; and
5. how group members are transformed or changed by the leader's actions.

The first perspective is called the trait approach, the second the function approach, the third the style approach, the fourth the situational approach, and the fifth the transformational approach.

The Trait Approach

A short story by James Thurber, "The Owl Who Was God," describes how some animals choose an owl as their leader because of the traits the bird possesses. He can see at night, seems to be able to answer any question, walks with great dignity, and, even when leading his group down the middle of a highway toward an oncoming truck, appears unafraid. "He's God," the animals scream just before all of them, including the owl, are killed.

By selecting their leader based solely on his traits, the animals proved what a lot of researchers have since verified: it's not healthy! The **trait approach** to leadership assumes that people possess certain characteristics that make them leaders. Although research does not support this assumption, the *feeling* persists that traits can define leadership and should determine who leads. For example, people may decide that they want a leader who is bold, confident, and articulate. But when they select such a leader, they may fail to consider other crucial criteria, such as whether this person understands the group's needs.

Every researcher who sets out to identify leadership traits typically comes up with her or his own favorite list, which usually bears little resemblance to lists generated by other researchers. Nonetheless, a few traits seem to emerge with some regularity,[9] but even these are not necessarily a sound basis for leader selection. They are merely the traits that people *think* leaders should possess. Among these traits are high self-assurance and low nervous tension, dominance, perceived intelligence, higher status than other group members, alertness, willingness to tolerate frustration, sensitivity and emotional maturity, and greater persuasiveness than average.

If your group is task-oriented, intelligence and organizational ability are important traits to look for; if your group has a social orientation, attractiveness and team spirit rise to the top of your list. If your group is both task- and social-oriented, you want someone who possesses all these traits, as well as the ability to leap tall buildings in a single bound and change the course of mighty rivers.

The Function Approach

The **function approach** evaluates leadership by behavior rather than traits. From this perspective, everyone in the group can be the leader, at least at a particular time.

Two broad categories of functions need to be performed in any group: **task functions**, which are behaviors that help a group get its job done, and **social functions**, which are behaviors that help group members get along with each other. Common task functions include defining the problem, setting an agenda, clarifying ideas and positions, keeping the discussion moving, making sure that everyone who wishes to participate has the opportunity, and summarizing key points. Common social functions include encouraging participation, creating a warm and supportive communication climate, giving feedback, controlling members who dominate the discussion, and resolving interpersonal conflicts.

The same individual rarely provides both task and social leadership because task behaviors often create resentment whereas social behaviors usually lead to liking. Instead, two leaders generally emerge, one who concentrates on tasks and one who focuses on the group's process and relationships. Only a few historical figures, such as Franklin D. Roosevelt and Mahatma Gandhi, provided both task and social leadership.

The only way to discover which functions are called for is to carefully analyze your group's needs. For example, when the work is boring and tedious, *consideration* is needed; when group members lack self-confidence, *praise* is required; when the task requires members to work together, *coordination* is necessary; and when group members compete with each other for status, *conflict management* is needed.

The Style Approach

According to the **style approach**, leadership is not related to personal characteristics or to particular functions, but to the overall pattern that emerges from a leader's interaction with group members. For example, a leader who uses a *controlling style* talks but does not listen, sends directive and demanding messages, and uses manipulation to gain compliance. A leader with a *dynamic style* communicates in brief, frank, and direct messages that are pragmatic and action-oriented. A leader with a *withdrawal style* avoids communication altogether, gives others' thoughts and ideas more weight than his or her own, and shifts leadership responsibility to the other members of the group.

Leaders are often classified as exhibiting a style along a continuum, as shown in figure 11.2, with autocratic leadership at one end and laissez-faire leadership at the other. These endpoints of the continuum represent extreme

▶ **FIGURE 11.2**   Leadership Style Continuum

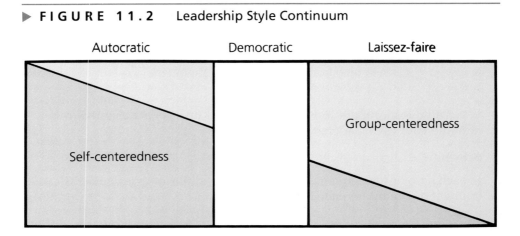

differences in self-versus group-centeredness. A leader who displays an **autocratic leadership style** tends to focus on his or her own needs, wishes, thoughts, ideas, and concerns and thus tries to control group members. A leader with a **laissez-faire leadership style** focuses on the group's wishes, thoughts, ideas, and concerns and thus adopts a hands-off policy with members. In fact, an observer would have a hard time determining who the leader is in a group led by someone using this style. And between these two extremes is the **democratic leadership style**, which is characterized by both self- and group-centeredness. A democratic leader works to make sure the group members are involved in and contribute to the group task *and*, as one of the members, she or he also communicates her or his own ideas, thoughts, and feelings.

KNOWLEDGE CHECKUP 11.5

Assessing Your Leadership Style[10]

Picture yourself leading a group discussion. Then, for each pair of statements, check the one that you believe is of greater importance. Do not check both items.

When leading a discussion, I think it is more important

1. _____ To give everyone a chance to express her or his opinion.
_____ To know what the group and its members are doing.

2. _____ To assign members to tasks so more can be accomplished.
_____ To let members reach decisions all by themselves.

3. _____ To assist the group in getting along well together.
_____ To point the group toward what I think is the best answer.

4. _____ To get the job done.
_____ To let members reach decisions all by themselves.

5. _____ To help members see how the discussion is related to the group's purposes.
_____ To assign members to tasks so more can be accomplished.

6. _____ To ask questions that will cause members to do more thinking.
_____ To get the job done.

The questionnaire in Knowledge Checkup 11.5 is designed to help you examine your own leadership style.

Scoring

In each pair, one statement is autocratic (A) and the other is democratic (D). Give yourself one point for each D response.

1. D	2. A	3. D	4. A	5. D	6. D
A	D	A	D	A	A

If your score is five or six, you would probably be a democratic leader, and if your score is zero or one, you would probably be an autocratic leader. Scores of two through four indicate that you could adopt either leadership style.

Highly autocratic leaders make decisions for the group, ask few questions and answer only those that arise, disagree with and often antagonize other group members, and rarely encourage participation.[11] Such leaders focus on themselves—they want to get their own way. Although the autocratic style sounds less than desirable, some circumstances call for it—for example, when there is an emergency or when group members need to accomplish their task quickly.

In contrast, democratic leaders talk less and listen more, ask questions to find out members' views, and encourage participation by releasing tension and offering positive feedback. They care about the group and achieving *its* objective. But just as the autocratic style is not always bad, the democratic style is not always good: in some situations, for instance, group members expect the leader to behave autocratically; if the leader uses a democratic style, it will not be effective.

Figure 11.2 shows a wide shaded area for democratic leadership because within the general style labeled "democratic" are many variations in the balance between self- and group-centeredness. For example, although both male and female democratic leaders may be democratic, they go about the business of leading in different ways.[12] A female democratic leader's style appears to be more group-centered, whereas the male's appears to be more self-centered. The female democratic leader's communication is more likely to be friendly and contain a great deal of agreement, whereas the male's communication behavior is more likely to contain a great many suggestions for group members to consider.

The Situation Approach

The **situation approach to leadership** involves considering individual circumstances to determine what style of leadership is best. No single style is always superior to the others, although one will be better than another in a specific situation.

Consider what it would be like if, all of a sudden, you fell to the ground, ill, and a group of doctors and nurses surrounded you. How would you feel if they took a democratic approach to your treatment, openly discussing what to do and giving long consideration to each person's thoughts and feelings about the possible courses of action? Clearly, in an emergency, autocratic leadership is often necessary.

Other circumstances also influence the choice of leadership style. Is there little time to complete the task? Do group members expect the leader to be autocratic? Does the leader have the sole responsibility for the group's outcomes? Do members lack the knowledge and/or skills to perform the group's task? Do group members refuse to do the required work? If the answer is yes to one or more of these questions, an autocratic, controlling leadership style may be appropriate. Conversely, when there is plenty of time, members expect democratic leadership, and so on, a democratic, flexible style is called for.

What about leadership functions? Under what circumstances should a leader perform task functions? When are social functions a better choice? And when are both necessary? Knowledge Checkup 11.6 should help you evaluate these factors.

KNOWLEDGE CHECKUP 11.6

Assessment of Leadership Adaptability

Assume that you are the leader of the group described for each situation. What would you do to solve the problem?

1. You are a friendly leader, concerned for the welfare of your group members. Your group has been assigned a new job and work is at a standstill.

2. Up to now, the group you lead has been pretty good at solving its problems. Relationships have also been good. A new problem, however, seems too difficult for the members to resolve by themselves. Two attempted resolutions have failed.

3. Your group is working well: the task is getting done and members seem to be getting along. Nonetheless, you are not sure that your hands-off approach to group leadership is getting the best possible results.

4. Your group is beginning to work hard at its task. All members seem to understand their jobs and the standards for quality. The work has just begun, however, and the task won't be successfully completed for quite some time. You are unsure what to do.

Each situation calls for a different response from you as leader. In the first case, you would do best to assume a high task and a low social style, emphasizing what needs to be done and how to do it while downplaying your friendliness. This should encourage the group to assume a task orientation and begin work on the new job.

The second situation calls for an opposite style: low task and high social. The members of the group, who have proved their competence in the past, need your encouragement to help them tackle the new, difficult problem. If you jump in to rescue them too soon, they may resent your intrusion and lack of faith in them.

In the third case, the real problem is your own insecurity. Don't make your problem into the group's problem. Instead, since everything is going well, continue your hands-off policy. Use a low task and low social style. If you feel the need to do *something*, try a high social and low task style—for example, encourage group members to have a party after work or go to lunch together, which should ensure that social needs are met without interfering with high performance.

The fourth situation requires the most from you as leader: your style should have both high task and high social components. The group needs to be kept on track to ensure that members can put their knowledge into action. At the same time, members need to develop the kinds of relationships that will enhance group cohesiveness. High group cohesiveness decreases the chances that arguments arising from the frustration of coping with a long-term schedule will result in extended conflicts or in members leaving the group.

The most important attributes for a leader to possess may well be *insight* and *flexibility*: the insight to stand apart from the group and determine what needs to be done and the flexibility to respond to a wide variety of demands and challenges. The most effective leaders have a large repertoire of behaviors that enable them to adapt quickly and easily to a group's changing circumstances.

The Transformational Approach

A new approach to leadership that considers a leader's traits, behaviors, and style as well as situational conditions is called **transformational leadership**. A transformational leader motivates group members to achieve more than they originally expected by changing—*transforming*—their attitudes and values toward both the group task and themselves.[13] Such a leader is typically trusted and admired by the group, accepted unquestioningly as the leader, and seen as a role model. This leader is self-confident, willing to take risks, and an effective communicator.

To change a group,[14] a transformational leader does the following:

1. recognizes the need for change and communicates this recognition to group members without making them feel that they are the source of the problem;
2. creates a new vision by painting an appealing picture of what the future can be like based on a new mission or purpose; and

3. institutionalizes the change by getting others to support the vision and help to develop implementation strategies.

By behaving in a group-centered way, the leader obtains members' commitment to his or her vision and the group's plan for implementation. In the process, the group members are transformed: they see the problem from a new perspective, are motivated to do something about it, share a new vision with other group members, and feel powerful and capable of meeting the high expectations established by the leader.

We observed an example of transformational leadership in a student-run television studio. There was little equipment, few workers, and limited understanding of what needed to be done. In fact, the group actually expected to fail in their attempt to produce programs for the local cable station. A leader emerged who presented the group with a vision of what they could be—what they could produce, the influence they could have, the groundwork they could lay for an important student-controlled production studio. Because the leader expressed his vision clearly and with great enthusiasm, he motivated the group to see things as he saw them. He also communicated his expectations for what each person could do and persuaded them they had the skills and knowledge to act appropriately. Beliefs and attitudes changed dramatically: the belief that failure was at hand was replaced with a vision of success, and the negative attitudes about the equipment—that it was bad because it was old and inadequate—became positive as they saw new ways to use what they had. A highly cohesive, well-functioning group developed plans, implemented them, and produced shows for the cable company. Beyond a doubt, the leader was the sole force responsible for the transformation.

Whether viewed from the trait, behavior, style, situation, or transformational approach, a leader's effectiveness is measured by the group's outcomes:

▶ whether the group obtains its goals;
▶ whether group members are satisfied with their outcomes and the process used to obtain them; and
▶ whether group members are committed to their goals, outcomes, and each other's well-being.

1. What norms that are typical for this kind of situation are being violated by group members?

2. What task, social, and self-centered roles are being enacted by the students?

3. The teacher looks confused and bewildered. Is the problem role conflict, role-role conflict, or self-role conflict? What information do you need to be sure?

4. For the students who are paying attention, what sources of power does the teacher likely have? For the students who are not paying attention, what are the teacher's most likely sources of power?

5. What recommendations could you make to this teacher to enhance her sources of power?

6. Discuss the teacher in terms of the five approaches to leadership: the trait, function, style, situation, and transformational approaches.

7. What recommendations could you make to this teacher to increase her effectiveness as a leader?

NOTES

1. Based on a system developed by J. M. Jackson. Jackson, "Structural Characteristics of Norms," in *The Role Orientation: Readings in Theory and Application*, ed. R. J. Thomas and B. J. Biddle (New York: John Wiley, 1966).

2. John E. Baird, Jr., "Sex Differences in Group Communication: A Review of Relevant Research," *Quarterly Journal of Speech* 62 (1976): 179-92; Judy Cornelia Pearson, *Gender and Communication* (Dubuque, IA: Wm. C. Brown, 1985), pp. 316–24.

3. Marvin E. Shaw, *Group Dynamics: The Psychology of Small Group Behavior*, 3d ed. (New York: McGraw-Hill, 1981).

4. Barbara Ringwald, Richard D. Mann, Robert Rosenwein, and Wilbert J. Mc-Keachie, "Conflict and Style in the College Classroom," *Psychology Today* 4 (1971): 45–47, 76, 78–79.

5. Based on a system developed by Kenneth D. Benne and Paul Sheats, "Functions and Roles of Group Members," *Journal of Social Issues* 4 (1948): 41–49. For a discussion of how these roles apply specifically to leadership, see: Gary A Yukl, *Leadership in Organizations* 2d ed. (Englewood Cliffs, NJ: Prentice Hall, 1989), pp. 237–41.

6. Adapted from: Pamela Cuming, "Empowerment Profile," *The Power Handbook* (Boston: CBI, 1981), pp. 2–5.

7. Adapted from: Pamela Cuming, "Determining Your Power Bases," *The Power Handbook* (Boston: CBI, 1981), pp. 57–59; and D. L. Dieterly and B. Schneider, "The Effect of Organizational Environment on Perceived Climate and Power," *Organizational Behavior and Human Performance* 11 (1974): 334–35.

8. Yukl, *Leadership in Organizations*, pp. 43–49.

9. M. W. McCall and M. M. Lombardo, *Off The Track: Why and How Successful Executives Get Derailed*, Technical Report No. 21 (Greensboro, NC: Center for Creative Leadership, 1983); Ralph M. Stogdill, *Handbook of Leadership: A Survey of Theory and Research* (New York: Free Press, 1974), pp. 72–82.

10. Adapted from: James F. Sargent and Gerald R. Miller, "Some Differences in Certain Communication Behaviors of Autocratic and Democratic Group Leaders," *Journal of Communication* 21 (1971): 233–52.

11. Descriptions of communication behaviors of autocratic and democratic leaders come from: Sargent and Miller, "Some Differences"; and Lawrence B. Rosenfeld and Timothy G. Plax, "Personality Determinants of Autocratic and Democratic Leadership," *Speech Monographs* 42 (1975): 203–8.

12. Gene D. Fowler and Lawrence B. Rosenfeld, "Sex Differences and Democratic Leadership Behavior," *Southern Speech Communication Journal* 45 (1979): 69–78.

13. Bernard M. Bass, *Leadership and Performance Beyond Expectation* (New York: Free Press, 1985).

14. Noel M. Tichy and Mary Ann Devanna, *The Transformational Leader* (New York: John Wiley, 1986).

FOR FURTHER INVESTIGATION

Asch, Solomon. "Effects of Group Pressure Upon the Modification and Distortion of Judgments." In *Groups, Leadership and Men*, edited by Harold Guetzkow, pp. 177–90. Pittsburgh: Carnegie Press, 1951.

Baird, John E., Jr. "Sex Differences in Group Communication: A Review of Relevant Research." *Quarterly Journal of Speech* 62 (1976): 179–92.

Benne, Kenneth D., and Paul Sheats. "Functional Roles of Group Members." *Journal of Social Issues* (1948): 41–49.

Conrad, Charles. "Communication, Power and Politics in Organizations." In *Strategic Organizational Communication*, pp. 177–99. New York: Holt, Rinehart and Winston, 1985.

Cuming, Pamela. *The Power Handbook: A Strategic Guide to Organizational and Personal Effectiveness*. Boston: CBI, 1981.

Dieterly, D. L., and B. Schneider, "The Effect of Organizational Environment on Perceived Power and Climate: A Laboratory Study." *Organizational Behavior and Human Performance* 11 (1974): 334–35.

Fisher, B. Aubrey. "Leadership: When Does the Difference Make a Difference?" In *Communication and Group Decision Making*, edited by Marshall Scott Poole and Randy Y. Hirokawa, pp. 197–215. Beverly Hills, CA: Sage, 1986.

_____. "Leadership as Medium: Treating Complexity in Group Communication Research." *Small Group Behavior* 16 (1985): 167–96.

Fowler, Gene D., and Lawrence B. Rosenfeld. "Sex Differences and Democratic Leadership Behavior." *Southern Speech Communication Journal* 45 (1979): 69–78.

French, John, R. P., Jr., and Bertram Raven. "The Bases of Social Power." In *Studies in Social Power*, edited by Dorwin Cartwright. Ann Arbor, MI: Institute for Social Research, 1959.

Hersey, Paul, and Kenneth H. Blanchard. *Management of Organizational Behavior: Utilizing Human Resources.* Englewood Cliffs, NJ: Prentice-Hall, 1977.

Jablin, Fred. "Cultivating Imagination: Factors that Enhance and Inhibit Creativity in Brainstorming Groups." *Human Communication Research* 7 (1981): 245–58.

Johnson, David W. "Cooperating and Leading." In *Human Relations and Your Career*, 2d ed., pp. 65–104. Englewood Cliffs, NJ: Prentice-Hall, 1987.

Johnson, David W., and Frank P. Johnson. *Joining Together: Group Theory and Group Skills*, 3d ed. Englewood Cliffs, NJ: Prentice-Hall, 1987.

Kelman, H. "Compliance, Identification, and Internalization." *Journal of Conflict Resolution* 2 (1958): 51–60.

Rosenfeld, Lawrence B. *Now That We're All Here . . . Relations in Small Groups.* Columbus, OH: Charles E. Merrill, 1976.

Sargent, James F., and Gerald R. Miller. "Some Differences in Certain Communication Behaviors of Autocratic and Democratic Group Leaders." *Journal of Communication* 21 (1971): 233–52.

Shaw, Marvin E. *Group Dynamics: The Psychology of Small Group Behavior*, 3d ed. New York: McGraw-Hill, 1981.

Stodgill, B. *Handbook of Leadership: A Survey of Theory and Research.* New York: Free Press, 1974.

Yukl, Gary A. *Leadership in Organizations*, 2d ed. Englewood Cliffs, NJ: Prentice-Hall, 1989.

CHAPTER 12

▶ *Public Speaking:
The Groundwork*

COMMUNICATION COMPETENCIES

*This chapter on public speaking will help you practice and develop communication competencies that fall into three broad categories: (1) **communication codes,** which include choosing words that are appropriate to your audience and your situation; (2) **oral message evaluation,** such as identifying main ideas and distinguishing messages with different purposes; and (3) **basic speech communication skills,** which include expressing ideas clearly and concisely, organizing your messages so others can understand them, and asking questions to obtain information. Specifically, the competencies you will gain will enable you to do the following:*

▶ *Summarize the "Five-P Process for Speeches."*
▶ *Describe the benefits of presenting messages to audiences.*
▶ *Assess yourself, your audience, and the speech setting to prepare for public speaking.*
▶ *Use the information gathered in your assessment of yourself, your audience, and the setting to develop a statement of purpose.*

Your instructor has just announced that your course's first public speaking assignment is due next week. **Public speaking** is a form of communication in which a speaker addresses a relatively large audience with a prepared message.

What do you do?
Where do you begin?

PUBLIC SPEAKING AND YOU

Speakers typically complete five tasks to prepare for a speech. Those tasks are listed here in random order. Rearrange them in the order that you would tackle them.

_____ Research the topic
_____ Develop a statement of purpose
_____ Assess the audience
_____ Select a topic
_____ Organize the structure of the main points

These five tasks are integral to planning and preparing a speech. Their preferred sequence is as follows:

__1__ Assess the audience
__2__ Select a topic
__3__ Develop a statement of purpose
__4__ Research the topic
__5__ Organize the structure of the main points

The Five-P Process for Speeches

The five tasks you just ordered make up the first two steps in the Five-P Process for Speeches.

P-1: **Plan.** *Assess yourself, the audience, and the setting; select the topic; and develop a statement of purpose.* This chapter presents methods for assessing the public speaking situation—including yourself, the audience, and the setting—as well as the steps necessary for selecting a topic and developing a statement of purpose.

P-2: **Prepare.** *Research your topic and develop the structure for your presentation.* Chapter 13 covers the different types of information you may present to support your ideas and suggests resources for researching information. Chapter 14 presents a variety of ways you can structure your speech, starting with methods for beginning your talk and finishing with ways to drive your point home.

In the remaining three steps, you determine the best way of presenting your speech, making the presentation, and wrapping up the speaking event:

P-3: **Practice.** *Develop a presentation strategy for your speech.* Chapter 15 deals specifically with methods of presentation, such as impromptu speaking, extemporaneous speaking, and speaking from a manuscript. It also covers auxiliary materials and how to select the best ones for your speech, audience, and setting.

P-4: **Present.** *Overcome obstacles to effective presentations and give your speech.* Chapters 15 and 16 both consider how to manage the speaking event. Chapter 15 tells how to introduce yourself to the audience or have someone else introduce you, while Chapter 16 explains how to deal with the fears associated with public speaking and describes verbal and nonverbal delivery techniques.

P-5: **Probe.** *Answer audience and personal questions; evaluate your speech and your performance.* Chapter 15 suggests how to prepare for and handle questions from the audience. The end of Chapter 16 summarizes the discussion of public speaking in Chapters 12 through 16 by presenting a checklist for evaluating your speech and your performance as a speaker.

Figure 12.1 shows the Five-P Process for Speeches. By using the process, you can see both similarities and differences between public speaking and everyday conversation. For example, both public speaking and conversation require that you plan what you're going to say, but public speaking usually involves more thought and less spontaneity. Assessing your audience and selecting a topic are important for both conversation and public speaking— adapting what you say to your audience, whether one person or many, is characteristic of all competent communication in all situations. Similarly, conversation and public speaking both require that you organize your thoughts and communicate them logically, although for public speaking the organization is likely to be more structured and take into account extra factors, such as time limits, that are not normally imposed on conversations.

Being responsive to feedback—which may come in the form of audience questions, nods of understanding, smiles of enjoyment or approval, and frowns of disagreement or incomprehension—is also important in both conversation and public speaking. In both cases, you must be aware of others' reactions in order to adapt how you present your ideas.

On the other hand, practice rarely precedes conversation, except when you want to deliver your message in a particular way without leaving anything out. This is often the case in stressful situations, as when asking for a raise. Conversation and public speaking also differ in terms of presentation. In public speaking, language is usually more formal and the speaker goes on without interruption for a longer period of time. The public speaker must also worry about visual aids, microphones, room size, audience size, and other details that would rarely occur to a conversationalist.

Above all, public speaking is not merely conversation with a great many as opposed to one or several other people. More requirements must be considered and more work must be put into developing and presenting an effective

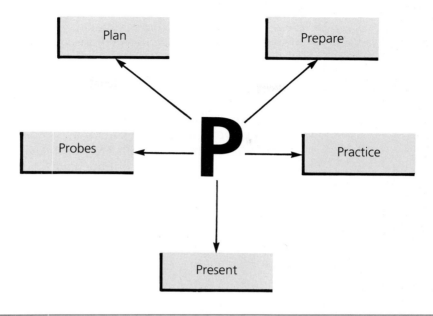

▶ **FIGURE 12.1** The Five-P Process for Speeches

public speech than into carrying on an effective conversation. But the extra work is worth the effort: there are many benefits to learning how to prepare and deliver public speeches and to gaining practice in this important form of communication.

The Benefits of Learning Public Speaking

Are you uneasy at the thought of giving a speech? If so, you are not alone: public speaking is not just *your* fear, it's the foremost fear of most Americans. In a recent national survey, 61 percent of the respondents said that speaking before a group was their greatest fear.[1] What is more, the fear of speaking before a group outranked fear of heights, insects, financial problems, and sickness. Ironically, based on these statistics, a case could be made for the proposition that the *real* crazies are the people who aren't afraid of speaking in public.

Despite the widespread negative feelings about public speaking, people continue to give speeches and to seek out courses that will help them acquire and polish public speaking skills. The reasons are many. In the process of learning about and becoming an effective public speaker, the following benefits are yours:

▶ Acquire the ability to formulate ideas clearly.
▶ Develop confidence and gain pride in the fact that you can do something that most people are afraid to do.

▶ Open alternatives for yourself that are closed to people who are afraid to speak in public. You will feel more comfortable answering questions in class, taking courses that require oral presentations, applying for jobs that require the ability to express yourself, and presenting your views in public meetings, such as the student senate, fraternity or sorority sessions, the PTA, and open meetings of your city government.

▶ Improve your credibility and reputation through the presentation and defense of your ideas, whether in an academic or business setting. Because public speaking skills are a basic requirement for upper-level managers, your ability to communicate with co-workers will signal your readiness for advancement. Corporate speechmaking is an indispensable weapon in the communication arsenal.

▶ Improve your ability to handle interviews and media appearances, and equip yourself to enter any occupation that requires interacting with people, such as law, medicine, teaching, business, and social work.

GATHERING INFORMATION: ASSESSING THE SITUATION

Giving a speech isn't so difficult if you start at the beginning and proceed systematically. You will rarely be expected to just stand up and start talking. Instead, you will usually have ample time to prepare.

The initial step in the public speaking process is P-1: Plan. You need to develop a systematic way to assess the communication situation—yourself, the audience, and the setting. Although your first impulse may be to try to select a topic, this approach often results in wasted time and effort. Knowing something first about yourself, your audience, and the occasion or purpose for your speaking will help you to choose the best topic for each unique circumstance.

Assessing Yourself

First, let's assess your attitude toward yourself as a public speaker. Complete the self-examination in Knowledge Checkup 12.1.

KNOWLEDGE CHECKUP 12.1

Personal Report of Public Speaking Anxiety (PRPSA)[2]

This questionnaire explores your feelings about communicating with other people. Indicate the degree to which each statement applies to you. Work quickly—just record your first impressions.

Write 1 if you strongly agree that the statement applies to you.
Write 2 if you agree.
Write 3 if you are undecided.
Write 4 if you disagree.
Write 5 if you strongly disagree.

_____ 1. I feel tense and nervous while preparing for a speech.
_____ 2. I feel tense when I see the words *speech* and *public speaking* on a class outline or in a course catalog.
_____ 3. My thoughts become confused and jumbled when I am giving a speech.
_____ 4. Right after giving a speech I feel that I had a pleasant experience.
_____ 5. I get anxious when I think about a speech coming up.
_____ 6. I have no fear of giving a speech.
_____ 7. Although I am nervous just before starting a speech, I settle down soon after starting and feel calm and comfortable.
_____ 8. I look forward to giving a speech.
_____ 9. When the instructor announces a speaking assignment in class, I feel myself getting tense.
_____ 10. My hands tremble when I am giving a speech.
_____ 11. I feel relaxed while giving a speech.
_____ 12. I enjoy preparing for a speech.
_____ 13. I am in constant fear of forgetting what I prepared to say.
_____ 14. I get anxious if someone asks me something that I do not know about my speech topic.
_____ 15. I face the prospect of giving a speech with confidence.
_____ 16. I feel that I am in complete control of myself while giving a speech.
_____ 17. My mind is clear when I am giving a speech.
_____ 18. I do not dread giving a speech.
_____ 19. I perspire just before starting a speech.
_____ 20. My heart beats very fast just as I start a speech.
_____ 21. I experience considerable anxiety while sitting in the room just before my speech starts.
_____ 22. Certain parts of my body feel very tense and rigid while I am giving a speech.
_____ 23. Realizing that I have only a little time left to finish a speech makes me very tense and anxious.
_____ 24. I know I can control my feelings of tension and stress while giving a speech.
_____ 25. I breathe faster just before starting a speech.
_____ 26. I feel comfortable and relaxed in the hour or so just before giving a speech.
_____ 27. I give speeches poorly because I am anxious.
_____ 28. I feel anxious when the teacher announces the date of a speaking assignment.
_____ 29. When I make a mistake while I am giving a speech, I find it hard to concentrate on the parts that follow.

    30. During an important speech, I feel helplessness building up inside me.

    31. I have trouble falling asleep the night before a speech.

    32. My heart beats very fast while I give my speech.

    33. I feel anxious while waiting to give my speech.

    34. I get so nervous while giving a speech that I forget facts I know well.

To determine your score on the PRPSA, complete the following steps:

1. Add the scores for items 1, 2, 3, 5, 9, 10, 13, 14, 19, 20, 21, 22, 23, 25, 27, 28, 29, 30, 31, 32, 33, 34.
Total A = _____

2. Add the scores for items 4, 6, 7, 8, 11, 12, 15, 16, 17, 18, 24, 26.
Total B = _____

3. Complete the formula:
(132 - Total A _____) + Total B _____ = _____

Your score, which should range between 34 and 170 (if it doesn't, you need to recalculate), indicates how you view yourself as a public speaker *at this time*. Check your score against the following interpretations:

34–84	Minimal anxiety about public speaking
85–92	Low level of anxiety about public speaking
93–110	Moderate anxiety in most public speaking situations
111–119	High anxiety about public speaking
120–170	Extremely high anxiety about public speaking

Whatever you scored on the PRPSA, keep in mind that learning how to present effective public communications should reduce your anxiety. Most people are afraid of the unknown—and public speaking is most likely an unknown to you right now because you have had little training in it. Once you learn how to select an appropriate topic, prepare an interesting and well-developed speech, and present your material in a way that holds audience attention, you will probably find that many of your fears decrease.

A starting point for most speakers is an assessment of their personal resources for selecting a topic. You will sometimes be told what to talk about, but often you will have to choose your speech topic yourself. If you develop an inventory of speaking topics, you will be better able to choose appropriate topics when you must. The same inventory can help when you are assigned a topic: it may provide you with background about the assigned topic, understanding of your attitude toward the topic, or specific information that can be incorporated into your presentation. Knowledge Checkup 12.2 is a good starting-point for your inventory.

KNOWLEDGE CHECKUP 12.2

Self-Inventory

Supply detailed information about yourself in the following areas.

1. Special interests and hobbies

2. Places traveled

3. Special skills (such as sports, sewing, computers, carpentry, cooking, electronics)

4. Work experiences

5. Funny experiences

6. Favorite books, movies, TV shows, and music

7. People I admire

8. Strong beliefs I hold

9. Important attitudes that help define who I am

Assessing the Audience

You may have discovered from your self-inventory that you already have a number of potential topics about which you can talk. Speaking about something you are interested in or know about is a good starting point. However, because people like to listen to speeches that have interest and value for them, you need to make sure that the subject you favor suits your audience. This means that you must learn about the audience in order to select a topic that will be appropriate for both you *and* them. You also need to develop preparation and presentation strategies that are appropriate to your audience. For instance, matching your language level, examples, and background information to your audience increases the probability that you will achieve your goals for giving your speech.

Assessing your audience is probably the most important aspect of analyzing the communication situation. It makes little sense to give a speech if no one is going to listen to you or understand what you say.

You can gather information about your audience in several ways. First of all, if you are contacted by a representative of an organization that would like you to speak, you can ask specific questions about the audience's basic characteristics, attitudes, beliefs, and values, as well as why they will be in attendance. Questions that probe for such information are: "What is the age range of the members?" "What are their interests?" "Do they hold any strong political views?" "Do the members have a particular religious affiliation?"

Another way of gathering useful information is to observe the group firsthand. For example, it is fairly easy to learn about the members of your speech class by observing them. The same holds true for the people with whom you work. Questions about such traits as gender, age, and race may be quickly answered through direct observation.

A third method of assessment is to interview members of the potential audience. Formal inquiries are rarely necessary; casual conversations will suffice. Of course, you can use this approach only if you know or can make contact with audience members.

Still another way of learning about an audience is through library research. For example, if you plan to speak to the local Kiwanis Club, you can check back issues of newspapers for articles about the group's social service activities and look up information about the national organization's projects and membership. Such basic information should help you understand the type of audience you are likely to encounter.

To assess an audience, you must consider several different kinds of information about members, including their demographics, predispositions, and reasons for attending the speech.

Demographics

Demographics is vital information about such characteristics as age, gender, education, religion, race, occupation, socioeconomic status, group memberships, and home region.

Your choice of topic, purpose, and examples will all be directly affected by who the audience members are and what they already know. For example, a group of auto mechanics would have little interest in a talk about how to change a car's oil, unless you were proposing some novel method. Similarly, if you incorrectly assume that audience members already understand the specialized vocabulary you plan to use, you may choose inappropriately difficult language and confuse your listeners.

Predispositions

Just as important as knowing your audience's demographics is knowing their **predispositions**—their attitudes, beliefs, and values about key issues. Such information will help you select a topic and purpose, and guide you in your preparation.

Attitudes reflect an audience member's likes and dislikes. For each of your possible topics, your audience may be hostile, neutral, or supportive. Knowing their general attitude enables you to adapt your material to ensure your desired effect.

Awareness of audience members' **beliefs**—their convictions, or what they understand and hold to be true about the world—also equips you to adjust your communication appropriately. Audience members may believe that people are basically good, or they may believe that war is a natural and inevitable consequence of the human condition. If your audience is composed of liberal Democrats, you can make certain assumptions about their beliefs concerning what's good and what's bad for the country. Imagine that the purpose of your speech is to persuade the members of such a group to vote for your favorite conservative Republican candidate: Some of the beliefs that you are going to talk about will be in conflict with those of your audience, and you will need to adjust. One way you can do this is to find areas of similarity between your candidate's beliefs and those of your audience.

A **value** is a belief about the inherent worth or worthiness of different ways of behaving and of different goals. Values fall into two categories, end-state values and instrumental values.[3] **End-state values** relate to desired ultimate goals, such as a world at peace, a secure family, or a loving relationship. **Instrumental values**, which are associated with desired ways of behaving, include being honest, being free, being reasonable, or being fair. If your audience is composed primarily of Americans, you can make certain assumptions about their values concerning work and honesty. In general, this is a work-oriented culture that respects the notion that "honesty is the best policy."

Figure 12.2 illustrates how values, beliefs, and attitudes relate to each other. Values form the point of the inverted triangle. You have fewer values than you do beliefs or attitudes.

Your beliefs grow out of and are connected to your values. For example, if you value honesty, you may believe that it is important not to lie, that you should return money received by mistake, and that you must live up to your agreements.

Attitudes form the top of the inverted triangle: you have more attitudes than beliefs or values, and your attitudes grow out of and are connected to your beliefs. For example, if you believe it is important not to lie, you may dislike liars; if you believe it is important to return money received by mistake, you may compliment a friend who tells a waiter that he returned too much change; and if you believe that you should live up to your agreements, you may be angry with a work partner who doesn't complete her research by the deadline that you both set.

Reasons for the Encounter

The final aspect of your analysis is to assess audience members' reasons for coming to hear you and their understanding of your role in the situation. For example, if audience members are required to attend your speech, you would plan differently than if they attend because they are interested in you or your topic. Similarly, you know that your attitudes toward a required course outside your major area are often very different from your attitudes toward a course that you selected yourself in your field of interest. Teachers who know this

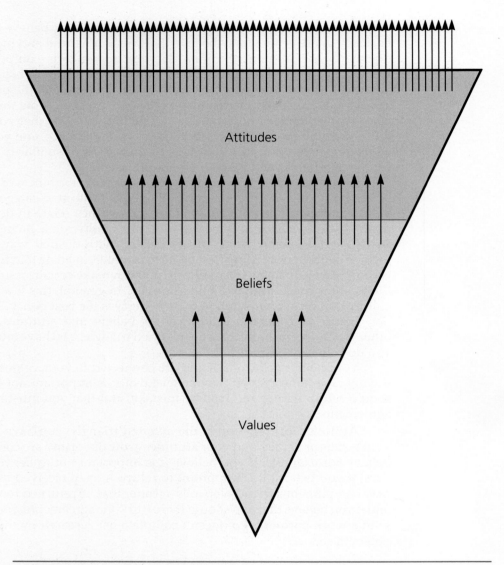

Attitudes

Beliefs

Values

▶ **FIGURE 12.2**   Values, Beliefs, and Attitudes

adjust their instruction accordingly. They may spend more time explaining the value of a course that is a general requirement than they would for a course that students have chosen.

The audience's understanding of their relationship to you and your role in the speaking event can further affect how you perform. If you are the senior manager speaking to assembly-line workers, the situation is quite different than it would be if you were a senior manager speaking to other senior managers. As a senior manager speaking to assembly-line workers, you have high status and your listeners depend on you for rewards, such as pay increases, and for inside information about the organization. Knowing this, you can assume that the workers are willing to listen to you and that you already have their attention. On the other hand, you cannot assume that a group of managers on your own level will be as ready or as willing to hear what you have to say. Because they may not be as dependent on you as the assembly-line workers are, you will need to gain their attention and hold it by persuading them of the importance of your message.

Your audience's understanding of the purpose of your speech is also important. Do they expect a factual report? Do they expect a proposal? Do they expect you to defend a policy? Do they expect to be entertained? Do they expect to hear your reasons for a belief? Do they expect you to attempt to change their minds about a particular issue? If your purpose and the audience's purpose are not in harmony, you are unlikely to succeed, and they are unlikely to think positively of you for wasting their time.

When you combine your findings about demographics, predispositions, and audience members' reasons for attendance, you should arrive at a fairly accurate audience assessment. For example, imagine that you are giving a speech on economics to two different groups. Your assessment of the first group shows that they are retired senior citizens, that most have college degrees and fixed incomes, that they want to hear you to learn about how to best invest their money, and that they are wary about losing their life savings. Your assessment of the second group suggests that they are middle-class, college-bound high-school seniors who are taking an economics class, that they have little personal financial means, and that they are worried about how to pay for their college educations. To adjust your speeches, you need to consider what topics are suitable for one of the audiences but not the other, and what topics are suitable for both. Whereas the senior citizens would probably want to know about how the newly proposed federal budget will affect their social security payments, the high-school seniors would probably be more interested in learning how to finance a college education. At the same time, both might be interested in low-cost, safe, short-term investments.

Sometimes you are asked or required to speak to an audience you have addressed before, such as when you address your communication class for the second time. Speaking before such a group makes it even more vital to consider audience members' expectations. If you first speech was a success, you can use the same audience assessment to guide your second speech. But if your original audience assessment led to errors, such as choosing an inappropriate topic, you can learn from your mistakes by altering your analysis or how you use the information.

SKILL CHECKUP 12.1

Audience Assessment

Assume that you are going to give a speech to your communication class. Assess the audience using the following questions:

1. What are the relevant demographic characteristics of your audience? Consider age, gender, educational level, religion, race, occupations, socioeconomic levels, group memberships, and home regions.

2. What are the relevant predispositions of your audience? Consider attitudes, beliefs, and values.

3. What are the reasons for the encounter? Consider why the audience is assembled. What is your relationship to the audience? What do audience members expect of you?

Assessing the Setting

You must also analyze the context in which you and the audience come together. Consider at least these three factors:

1. Where will the speech be given? The physical setting includes where the speech will take place, when the speech is scheduled, the size of the room, the seating arrangement, the seating capacity, how many people are expected, and heating and lighting considerations. You also need to find out whether the room can be darkened for a slide or film presentation.

2. What equipment is available? You may want to ask whether a lectern, easel for displaying charts or posters, slide projector, overhead projector, microphone, video playback unit, and screen are available.

3. What are your constraints? Time limits are common. Audience members have only so much time to devote to your speech—their attention spans have limits—and external factors may further limit your speaking time. For example, in your communication class, the instructor must be certain that each student gets a chance to speak. Time limits will therefore be placed on each speaker to ensure that everyone gets a turn.

The number of speakers on the agenda and the format for the presentation are additional constraints. For example, is your speech part of a ceremony that includes awards and a banquet? If so, when is your speech scheduled and what will precede and follow you? If other speakers are scheduled, the issue is even more complex. You must find out what the others will be speaking about, where you fit in the program, and how your purpose jibes with theirs. Repeating the same ideas as another speaker, using the same approach, or even speaking about the same topic may bore the audience and lead to negative reactions.

⬤SKILL CHECKUP 12.2

Assessing the Setting

Assume that you are going to give a speech to your communication class. Assess the situation by answering the following questions.

1. What is the room size?

2. What is the seating arrangement?

3. Will there be other speeches given on the day you speak?

4. What equipment is available?

The size of the room where you will speak is important for planning the size of your visual aids (graphs, drawings, pictures). In a small room with a small audience, you may be able to use actual objects to help clarify or demonstrate what you say. For example, to demonstrate the focusing element on a camera, you could walk around while you speak and show audience members exactly what you mean. In a large room, with a big audience, however, you would have to prepare drawings or slides to ensure that everyone sees the controls.

The seating arrangement may also be important. If you want to have people physically participate in an activity such as aerobics but the seats are bolted to the floor, you will need to reconsider your plans.

USING THE INFORMATION: SELECTING A TOPIC AND DEVELOPING A PURPOSE

The information you gathered in your assessment of the audience and the situation is useful for selecting your topic and deciding the purpose of your speech.

Selecting a Topic

Your topic needs to suit you, the audience, and the situation. To select a topic, begin with your responses to the self-inventory you completed in Knowledge Checkup 12.2. List subjects that you are interested in, that you can knowledgeably speak about, and that fit your specific assignment. Narrow the list by identifying the topics that most interest you. Based on your audience analysis, further condense the list by determining whether the topics suit your specific audience. Finish narrowing the list of topics by

Step 1
Topic: Theater
  Subtopics:
    History
    Types
    Performers

Step 2
Topic: Types of Theater
  Subtopics
    Drama
    Musicals
    Comedy
    Farce
    Melodrama
    Tragedy

Step 3
Topic: Musicals
  Subtopics:
    Writers
    Types
    Sources

Step 4
Topic: Writers
  Subtopics:
    Rogers and Hammerstein
    Lerner and Loewe
    Sondheim
    Berlin

Step 5
Topic: Lerner and Loewe
  Subtopics:
    Plays
    Philosophy
    Financial success
    Writing techniques

Step 6
Topic: Philosophy
  Subtopic:
    The perfect time, the perfect place, the perfect love story

Step 7
Topic: How Lerner and Loewe's musicals portray their search for the perfect time, the perfect place, and the perfect love story

---

▶ **FIGURE 12.3**   Narrowing a Speech Topic

considering any constraints imposed by the setting for the speech. For example, if your topic requires showing a videotape and no equipment is available, you must move to a new topic.

Narrowing Your Topic

Once you have selected a general topic, you must often narrow it, or make it more specific. The process of narrowing requires that you divide your general topic into related subtopics. From that list, you select a single entry and narrow further by dividing the new topic into subtopics. You continue the process until you arrive at a topic that is specific and limited enough to fit your time limit. Figure 12.3 illustrates the narrowing process.

As you narrow your topic, keep your audience's interests in mind. For example, you would like to tell your communication class something about your summer employment with McDonald's. Your audience assessment shows that most of your classmates eat at fast-food restaurants, know of the advertising competition among fast-food chains through watching television, and have read newspaper stories about McDonald's campaign to stop rumors that unapproved substances are being added to their hamburgers.

You reason that the class would probably be bored by a topic such as "How I Prepared Hamburgers" or "How the Milk Shake Machine Really Works," so, based on your audience analysis and your self-assessment, you may narrow your speech topic to "The Strategies McDonald's Has Used to Counter the Burger King Media Assault" or "How Workers Are Trained to Handle an Angry Customer at McDonalds."

SKILL CHECKUP 12.3

Selecting a Topic

Assume that you must give a five-minute speech to your communication class on a topic of your choice. You will be the first of five speakers giving their presentations that day in your communication classroom. You are going to choose a topic based on your responses to the Self-Inventory and your assessments of audience and setting covered earlier in this chapter.

Answer the following questions using your responses to the Self-Inventory:

1. On which five topics from your list would you like to speak?

2. Which of the five topics interests you the most as the subject for a speech? Which is your second choice?

Answer the following questions using your responses to the audience assessment:

3. Based on your analysis of the audience, is the topic you picked as your first choice in question 2 suitable for your audience? Is your second choice better? What in your audience assessment leads you to these conclusions?

4. Which of your two potential subjects is likely to be more interesting to your audience? What in your audience assessment leads you to this conclusion?

5. Would any of the remaining three topics be more suitable *and* more interesting? What in your audience assessment leads you to this conclusion?

Answer the following questions using your responses to the setting assessment:

6. Do the size of the room, seating arrangement, and seating capacity pose any problems? Does any potential problem affect your choice of topic? If so, how? If the problem is insurmountable, choose another topic by starting over at question 5.

7. Will any special equipment be necessary for your presentation? How does this affect your choice of topic? If the equipment is not available and cannot be obtained, go back to your original topics and, starting with question 5, repeat the topic selection process.

8. Is the topic narrow enough to fit the time limit?

Most speakers choose a topic without careful attention to the kinds of information you generated when you completed the topic inventory, audience assessment, and setting assessment in this chapter. If you prepare a topic inventory, audience assessment, and setting assessment whenever you are going to give a speech, you should be able to select a subject that interests you, matches the particular audience, and fits the specific setting. A flowchart of the process for selecting a topic is diagrammed in figure 12.4.

You have just completed the first step in the public speaking process. Armed with a topic that suits you, your audience, and the setting, you are ready to proceed to the second step: developing a statement of purpose.

Developing a Statement of Purpose

Unless you have a clear notion of exactly what you want to accomplish, your speech may go off in a direction that neither you nor your audience wants or expects. If you speak without a clear-cut purpose, you are likely to wander off your topic, fail to impress your audience, and feel frustrated because you've

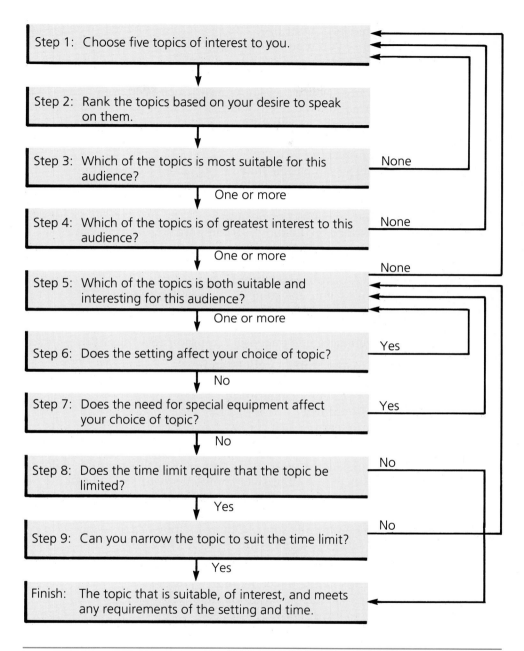

FIGURE 12.4 Flowchart for Choosing a Topic

wasted both your time and the audience's time. You'll also feel more anxious because you won't know exactly where you're headed.

The lack of a purpose also makes it virtually impossible to prepare your speech adequately, which will leave you feeling confused, frustrated, and insecure. You won't know how much preparation time to allow, what kind of information you need, where to look for it, what your goal is, how to structure your speech, or what kinds of examples and appeals are most suitable. You wind up "spinning your wheels" and getting nowhere, wasting time and accomplishing little.

The same topic may be presented from a number of different angles. For example, if you select the soap opera "Days of Our Lives" as your topic, you may decide to (1) tell the audience the history of the show, (2) describe the various sets used in the taping, (3) discuss various relationships that have been developed on the show, (4) compare "Days of Our Lives" to "General Hospital," or (5) demonstrate how the producers of the show can increase their audience size. When you choose a purpose, you clarify exactly which angle you'll take.

A **purpose statement** is a declaration of what you want from the audience and how you are going to go about getting it. A useful technique for stating your purpose is to follow the pattern of "To . . . of/that/how/about . . . by . . . ."

The **to** part of your statement identifies your goal, aim, or objective. Every speech has some purpose. Common speech purposes include the following:

> **to** develop an understanding
> **to** change the belief
> **to** develop an attitude
> **to** inform
> **to** learn
> **to** persuade

Select the words that best answer the question "What do I want from my audience?" Your answer completes your "to" part of the process.

The **of** part of your statement specifically identifies the topic of your speech. The word *of* is only an example of the kind of word that can be used to help identify the topic. Others include *that, how,* and *about*. Using the terms *of, that, how,* and *about* is illustrated as follows:

> **to** develop an understanding **of . . . by . . . .**
> **to** change the belief **that . . . by . . . .**
> **to** develop an attitude **that . . . by . . . .**
> **to** inform **how . . . by . . . .**
> **to** learn **about . . . by . . . .**
> **to** persuade **that . . . by . . . .**

The **by** part of your statement identifies your method of accomplishing your *to*. Every speech is developed using some method of organization. Words used to indicate organizational schemes include the following:

to develop an understanding of . . . **by** listing the steps of . . . .

to change the belief that . . . **by** explaining the causes of . . . which resulted in . . . .

to develop an attitude that . . . **by** comparing . . . to . . . .

to inform how . . . **by** the contrasting of . . . with . . . .

to learn about . . . **by** comparing and contrasting . . . and . . . .

to persuade that . . . **by** stating the problem of . . . and proposing . . . as solutions . . . .

The selection of your organizational scheme completes the *by* part of your statement. Examples of purpose statements are

To develop an understanding **of** how to build a Chinese kite **by** listing the steps of designing, obtaining the materials and constructing it.

To change the belief **that** sidestream smoke is harmless **by** explaining the causes of cancer as reported in a series of studies proving the toxic effect of smoking on nonsmokers.

To develop the attitude that community colleges are an effective educational source **by** comparing the exit test results of community college sophomores to sophomores at four-year state schools.

To inform **how** the greenhouse effect is spreading **by** contrasting atmospheric data of 1950 with 1990 data.

To learn about **how** the United States is losing its industrial competitive edge **by** comparing and contrasting post-Korean War and current U.S. and Japanese industrial production statistics.

To persuade **that** our present plan of public school funding is inadequate **by** stating the problem of school indebtedness and proposing three possible solutions.

Note that once the **by** part is added, each statement of purpose is complete.

SKILL CHECKUP 12.4

Assembling Your Statement of Purpose

Using the speech topic you selected in Skill Checkup 12.3, write a statement of purpose by taking the following steps:

1. Determine the **to** part of your purpose statement. What do you want from your audience? What information from your audience assessment shows that your purpose is suited to your listeners?

2. Determine the **of**. What is the clearest way to inform your audience of your topic?

3. Determine the **by**. What method of presentation best suits both the topic and your audience? What information from your audience assessment suggests that your choice is appropriate?

4. Write your statement of purpose. Then rewrite it as many times as necessary to ensure the greatest clarity. Do you feel you will make a positive impression on your audience and not waste your time or theirs?

By assessing yourself, your audience, and the setting, and by selecting a topic and writing a statement of purpose, you complete the groundwork for developing an effective public presentation, the first step in the Five-P Process for Speeches.

COMMUNICATION COMPETENCY CHECKUP

The student in the photo is clearly distressed about having to give a public speech.

1. What would this student gain from learning how to communicate effectively in a public setting?

2. The student in the photo is expressing fright. She doesn't know where to begin. She tells you, "I don't know anything that I can talk about." What recommendations can you make to help her develop a topic inventory?

3. She develops a list of topics but doesn't know which one to select. She asks you, "How do I know what topic would be appropriate for the students in my class?" What recommendations can you make for helping her assess her audience?

4. She has completed the audience assessment. "I think," she tells you, "I'll demonstrate how to twirl a flaming baton." It occurs to you that she is unaware of the need to assess the setting in which the speech will be given. What recommendations can you make to help him assess the setting?

5. "Okay," she tells you, "I developed a list of topics, I analyzed the audience, I assessed the setting. Now, how do I put it all together and select a topic?" What questions could guide her topic selection?

6. Now that she has selected a topic, she looks a lot calmer. "There is one more thing to do," you tell her. "You need to determine precisely what you want from your audience and plan how to accomplish it." What advice can you give her about developing a statement of purpose?

NOTES

1. Tony Rodriguez, "Update of the Bruskin Study" (Unpublished paper, Cerritos College, CA, 1985).

2. Adapted from the PRPSA presented in Virginia P. Richmond and James C. McCroskey, *Communication: Apprehension, Avoidance, and Effectiveness* (Scottsdale, AZ: Gorsuch, 1985).

3. For a discussion of values see: Milton Rokeach, *Understanding Human Values* (New York: Free Press, 1979), and Milton Rokeach and Sandra J. Ball-Rokeach, "Stability and Change in American Value Priorities, 1968–1981," *American Psychologist* 44 (1989): 775–84.

FOR FURTHER INVESTIGATION

DeVito, Joseph A. *The Elements of Public Speaking*, 2d ed. New York: Harper and Row, 1984.

Ehninger, Douglas, Bruce E. Gronbeck, Ray E. McKerrow, and Alan H. Monroe. *Principles and Types of Speech Communication*, 10th ed. Glenview, IL: Scott, Foresman/Little, Brown, 1988.

Kelly, Lynne, and Arden K. Watson. *Speaking with Confidence and Skill*. New York: Harper and Row, 1986.

Lucas, Stephen E. *The Art of Public Speaking*, 3d ed. New York: Random House, 1989.

Richmond, Virginia P., and James C. McCroskey. *Communication: Apprehension, Avoidance, and Effectiveness*. Scottsdale, AZ: Gorsuch, 1985.

Rokeach, Milton. *Understanding Human Values*. New York: Free Press, 1979.

Rokeach, Milton, and Sandra Ball-Rokeach. "Stability and Change in American Value Priorities, 1968–1981." *American Psychologist* 44 (1989): 775–84.

Sprague, Jo, and Douglas Stuart. *The Speaker's Handbook*. San Diego, CA: Harcourt Brace Jovanovich, 1984.

Taylor, Anita. *Speaking in Public*, 2d ed. Englewood Cliffs, NJ: Prentice-Hall, 1984.

CHAPTER 13

▶ # *Public Speaking: Information Strategies*

COMMUNICATION COMPETENCIES

*This chapter on information strategies will help you practice and develop communication competencies that fall into two broad categories: (1) **communication codes,** which include using words that are appropriate to a particular situation, and (2) **basic speech communication skills,** which include expressing ideas clearly and concisely and defending your point of view with evidence. Specifically, the competencies you will gain will enable you to do the following:*

▶ *Assess whether your speech is audience-centered.*

▶ *Evaluate and develop audience members' perceptions of your competency, trustworthiness, and goodwill.*

▶ *Distinguish types of logical appeals and determine when each type would be most useful.*

▶ *Use emotional appeals to support and reinforce your contentions.*

▶ *Recognize resources for developing logical and emotional appeals.*

▶ *Consider the ethical dimensions of your public communication.*

Assume that the following paragraphs appeared in two different speeches on the same topic:

> Speech 1: According to the Center for Disease Control, 12,000 to 27,000 people die each year in hospitals. Each is a potential organ donor, yet only 15 percent donate their vital parts. As many as 20,000 people die yearly— people you may know and care about—because they can't get needed organs.

> Speech 2: There's a problem in this country when a friend of mine dies because he couldn't get a kidney he needed for a kidney transplant. There must be lots of people who could have donated one to him. How many people die each year because they can't get an organ they need? It must be a lot!

If you listened to these two speeches, which speaker would you have more confidence in? Which speaker seems more trustworthy, more competent, and better prepared? Which one provides stronger proof of the problems caused by a lack of organ donors?

PREPREPARATION

The first speaker shows that she is audience-centered by referring to "people you [audience members] may know and care about." In contrast, the second speaker is self-centered: by talking only about "a friend of mine," he misses the chance to involve his audience directly in his speech. Audience-centered speakers seem more trustworthy and gain audience members' attention more often than do speakers who are self-centered.

After his personal example, the second speaker asks a rhetorical question: "How many people die each year…?" Although such a question may get the audience thinking, it does little to show that the speaker is competent or well prepared. In contrast, the first speaker appeals to audience members' logic and demonstrates her knowledge by presenting a list of facts. The facts she has chosen also stimulate an emotional response because they are interesting and attention-getting. By appealing to logic, the first speaker seems more competent and well prepared than the second speaker. Such logical appeals also build stronger support for the problem caused by the shortage of organ donors than do the solely emotional appeals relied on by the second speaker.

The first speaker's strong opening paragraph suggests that she will present an effectively prepared speech. Such a speech is both audience-centered and speaker-centered. It presents information that supports the speaker's intention, offers logical and emotional supporting arguments, and establishes the speaker as a credible and ethical source. It has a plan—an outline or a blueprint of major and minor points. And it is the result of the speaker's careful analysis of the best and most effective channels for presenting the message.

AUDIENCE-CENTERED AND SPEECH-CENTERED COMMUNICATIONS

All public communication takes place in the mind of the listener; it is thus an audience-centered art. Your job as speaker is to rouse a response from your audience. You seek to persuade your listeners to behave in accordance with your speech's purpose. If you're presenting information, you want audience members to believe what you're saying. If your goal is to get audience members to do something, such as buy your services, you want them to believe that your services will satisfy some need they have. If your aim is to entertain the audience, you want to persuade them that what you have to say is funny.

Persuasion is at the heart of the public communication process; all persuasion takes place within the audience members. The challenge is to determine what will best inspire the audience to learn, believe, enjoy, or whatever else you want them to do.

The audience may be your first consideration, but you too are important. A student, after finishing a classroom speech, might say: "Well, it would have been better if I had chosen a topic I was interested in," or "If I had had another week to prepare, I could have found *something* interesting to say." Both reactions point to typical problems: speakers often choose a topic, or accept an assigned topic, that does not interest them, or they lack the information they need to present an interesting, well-developed message. Even the most skilled speakers cannot speak well on every topic. Picture yourself in the following situation: After you have made a highly successful presentation to the local PTA on "A College Freshman's View of How to Adjust to College," a member of the audience, impressed with your speech, invites you to address the local Knights of the Nights on the topic of "Jousting and the Use of the Iron Maiden." You protest: "I'm not interested in that topic and I don't know anything about it." But he insists, "Oh, come on! You're a terrific speaker—you could talk about anything!" You're too smart to fall for that line—you know that without interest or information (even if you could do some fast research), the chances of developing a successful presentation are small. *Just* being interested or *just* having some information isn't enough. You have to *care* about the topic and be *comfortable* with what you're talking about.

INFORMATIONAL SUPPORT

Speakers use three broad categories of support to underscore their ideas. As first identified several thousand years ago by the Greek philosopher Aristotle, they are speaker credibility (*ethos*), logical appeals (*logos*), and emotional appeals (*pathos*). These categories of support are as useful today as they were when Aristotle first presented them.

Speaker Credibility

The first category of support is **speaker credibility**—audience members' perceptions of the speaker's competency, trustworthiness, and goodwill. An audience will not even begin to listen to your ideas unless they perceive you as credible—that is, unless they see you as competent to talk about your subject, recognize you as someone they can trust to be truthful, and believe you have their best interests at heart. If you seem too weak, too aggressive, too unprepared, or too manipulative, your audience will ignore your message, no matter how qualified you may be to present it.

In our society, the effectiveness of what is said depends in large part on who says it. People are willing to purchase life insurance from Art Linkletter, take hints on solving their plumbing problems from Josephine, let Bill Cosby influence which gelatin they buy, and trust Meredith Baxter-Birney to tell them which hair coloring is best. The power of individual influence extends beyond product buying. Robert Young, for example, developed high credibility over many years. He started out as the conscientious father on Father Knows Best and ended his career as the dedicated doctor, Marcus Welby. In all his acting roles, he seemed to have everyone's benefit at heart. As a result, his credibility was so high that at one time he held a lucrative contract to promote decaffeinated coffee and still received over 5,000 letters a week asking for medical advice. While you may not want to sell your audience decaffeinated coffee or give medical advice, your credibility will determine how successful you are, whatever your goal.

A speaker's level of credibility is not constant; it varies over time. Even before you begin to speak, your audience is likely to have already begun forming an opinion of you. Their impressions of your **initial credibility** may be based on interactions with them prior to your speech (for example, you may be in the same class), things other people have said about you (for example, the remarks of the person who introduces you to the audience), and your clothing and physical appearance. As you interact with your audience, your credibility develops further. This **process credibility** is affected by what you say and how you say it. For example, giving audience members facts they understand and accept as true, and presenting them confidently, increases your credibility, whereas relying exclusively on personal examples and presenting them uncertainly undermines your credibility.

Initial credibility combines with process credibility to form **terminal credibility**. Few speakers are consistently strong throughout an entire speech. They may rely too heavily on quoted material at one point and offer a brilliant example at another. They may hesitate and grope for words at one moment and speak assertively and clearly at another. Terminal credibility is the final and overall perception of a speaker's credibility when the speech is completed. The level of your terminal credibility is a strong indication of how effective you were as a speaker.

Knowledge Checkup 13.1 will help you measure your perceptions of how an audience is likely to perceive your credibility. How competent, trustworthy, and goodwilled do you think they perceive you?

KNOWLEDGE CHECKUP 13.1

Assessing Your Credibility

Credibility is not something you possess, but something you earn from your audience. The audience has the power to perceive you as credible or not, regardless of who you actually are. Circle the number on each scale that represents how you think your audience (your communication class members) is likely to perceive you when you give your first speech.

Competence

expert	7	6	5	4	3	2	1	inexpert
educated	7	6	5	4	3	2	1	uneducated
intellectual	7	6	5	4	3	2	1	unintellectual
intelligent	7	6	5	4	3	2	1	unintelligent
qualified	7	6	5	4	3	2	1	unqualified

Trustworthiness

honest	7	6	5	4	3	2	1	dishonest
opinions similar to theirs	7	6	5	4	3	2	1	opinions dissimilar to theirs
dependable	7	6	5	4	3	2	1	undependable
open-minded	7	6	5	4	3	2	1	closed-minded

Goodwill

concerned	7	6	5	4	3	2	1	unconcerned
interested in them	7	6	5	4	3	2	1	not interested in them
humorous	7	6	5	4	3	2	1	humorless

Scoring

Add your circled responses to the scales in each area:

Competency = _____
Trustworthiness = _____
Goodwill = _____

Your scores suggest which areas of your credibility need development. If your score for competency is thirty or above, you believe that your audience will perceive you as highly competent; if it is ten or below, you believe that they will perceive you as highly incompetent; and if it is between eleven and twenty-nine, you believe that your audience will perceive you as neither highly competent nor highly incompetent. If your score for trustworthiness is twenty-four or above, you believe that your audience will perceive you as highly trustworthy; if it is eight or below, you believe that they will perceive you as highly untrustworthy; and if it is between nine and twenty-three, you believe that your audience will perceive you as neither highly trustworthy nor highly untrustworthy. If your score for goodwill is eighteen or above, you believe that your audience will perceive you as having a great deal of goodwill; if it is six or below, you believe that they will perceive you as lacking goodwill; and if it is between seven and seventeen, you believe that your audience will perceive you as neither overflowing with goodwill nor lacking it completely.

You can gain even greater insight into your estimated credibility by examining each scale individually. For example, even though your total score for competency may be thirty, you may have given yourself a low rating on the item *expert-inexpert*. Once you recognize that you feel weak in this area, you can take steps to make yourself feel and appear better informed.

Increasing Perceptions of Your Competency

There are five methods of increasing listeners' perceptions of your competency. Each helps you demonstrate your knowledge of your subject matter or your familiarity or association with people whom your listeners perceive as competent.

▶ Associate yourself with other credible sources. If you are not knowledgeable on your speech topic, you have several ways of gaining credibility through association. If you personally know experts, you can mention your relationship. For example, during a demonstration speech on tennis, you could mention that you are a friend and former student of the pro at the local tennis club, whom audience members know and respect. If you don't personally know any experts, you can conduct interviews and library research to find credible experts whose ideas match your own.

▶ Use examples to demonstrate your personal acquaintance with your topic. For instance, you may not be a tennis pro, but you can point out experience you've gained by playing tennis or watching professional matches.

▶ Demonstrate your familiarity with the vocabulary of your topic. Use words that are specific to your subject matter and show that you know what you're talking about (and be sure you pronounce the words correctly!). At the same time, be careful not to confuse your audience by using, but failing to define, terms that they don't understand.

▶ Be well organized. A well-ordered speech makes it easy for your audience to follow your ideas and enhances the impression that you know what you're talking about. Even the most knowledgeable person can seem uninformed if he or she is disorganized.

▶ Be well prepared. Audience members will perceive that you know what you're talking about if your speech itself doesn't exhaust the breadth of your knowledge. The extent of your knowledge becomes obvious during question-and-answer periods. If you can't answer what audience members perceive to be simple questions, you look incompetent.

Increasing Perceptions of Your Trustworthiness

You can use four methods to increase listeners' perceptions of your trustworthiness. Each demonstrates your willingness to be open and forthright or shows that your background and attitudes are similar to those of your audience.

▶ Be as explicit as possible about your purpose. Stating your purpose early in your speech demonstrates that you are willing to be open about what you want from your audience. You may choose, on certain occasions, to conceal your true purpose so that it doesn't alienate audience members, but such an approach may be risky. Your audience, in addition to feeling manipulated, may view your lack of forthrightness as unethical. For example, a speaker who is in favor of banning the construction of nuclear energy plants may usually state as his central idea, "Nuclear waste is a problem in this country. I believe that building more nuclear energy plants escalates the problem." However, if he is speaking before what he perceives to be a hostile audience because they favor the building of nuclear plants, he might state, "Nuclear waste is a problem in this country. Let's investigate some of the options for decreasing the waste." Later in the speech, when the real goal of stimulating opposition to new nuclear power plants is revealed, the audience may react with hostility. If the speaker ever appears before that audience again, members probably will not trust him.

▶ Communicate that you are similar to audience members. People tend to trust those who are like themselves, who share their attitudes, beliefs, opinions, and background. Through audience assessment you can discover commonalities to mention during your presentation. For instance, if you go back to your high school to talk to graduating seniors about applying to college, you can mention how uncertain you felt when you were in their place.

▶ Don't contradict something you said in a previous speech, unless that is your explicit purpose. Politicians often get into trouble when they present opposing ideas on the same topic to different audiences. For example, during the 1988 presidential campaign, candidate Michael Dukakis was accused of alternately refusing and accepting the summary label of "liberal." Some perceived him as untrustworthy because they thought he was more interested in manipulating the audience than in really stating his beliefs as reflected in his voting record as governor of Massachusetts.

▶ Disassociate yourself from ideas, people, groups, and organizations that audience members do not trust. Just as associating yourself with respected sources builds your credibility, associating yourself with questionable sources will undermine it. Although it would be unethical to lie directly or by omission about associations that are relevant to your topic, there are times when not mentioning an association has no real bearing on your presentation. For example, a recovering alcoholic speaking about making wise financial investments, need not mention her drinking problem; but if she is speaking to a group about the need for changing the state's drinking age, it would be unethical for her not to mention her addiction.

Increasing Perceptions of Your Goodwill

Three methods can help increase listeners' perceptions of your goodwill. Each allows you to demonstrate that you care about your audience members and have their best interests at heart.

▶ Show a sense of humor. Humor is often an excellent way to gain and hold an audience's attention. In addition, it communicates that you care enough about your listeners to go out of your way to make your speech appealing to them. Avoid derogatory humor, however, unless you have a good, specific reason for using it.

▶ Explain how your message is relevant, important, or beneficial to your audience. Good speakers give the impression that they have their audience's best interests at heart and that their message is based on an assessment of their listeners' needs. Tell the audience how they will benefit from what you are discussing and how their lives will be improved. You can often communicate this directly by saying, for example, "Following my plan to protest the building of a nuclear power plant near here will ensure that your children grow up in a safe area with low levels of radiation. It will also ensure that the value of your real estate will not drop."

▶ Communicate interest and affection. If audience members see that you are interested in them and that you feel warmly toward them, they will believe in your goodwill. To demonstrate goodwill, use supportive and confirming behaviors, such as praising the audience's accomplishments, thanking them for having you as a speaker, and complimenting either the arrangements or some other aspect of the setting. Be sincere! If you are perceived as patronizing—complimenting without really meaning it—you are likely to provoke hostility instead of gaining goodwill.

Skill Checkup 13.1 will help you practice developing strategies for enhancing your credibility.

●SKILL CHECKUP 13.1

Increasing Perceptions of Your Credibility

For each situation, suggest one way to increase perceptions of your competency, one way to increase perceptions of your trustworthiness, and one way to increase perceptions of your goodwill. Make up details as you need them. For instance, when speaking on the subject of the pass-fail grading system to your communication class, you could say, "I have worked with the university's Committee on Grading Policy for the past year" to increase perceptions of your competency, "I am a student just like you—one concerned about making sure the grading policy in our university is fair" to increase perceptions of your trustworthiness, and "The pass-fail grading system, once in place, will help you get the most out of your college education" to increase perceptions of your goodwill.

Situation 1: Speaking to a parent group, you are advocating the opening of a coeducational dormitory.

Situation 2: Speaking to a group of college students, you are trying to persuade them to donate their time to help run the campus Special Olympics.

Logical Appeals

Logical appeals are the arguments and information a speaker uses to support or prove a point or proposal. The effectiveness of a logical appeal depends on how the audience reacts to it. The key to success is to present information that listeners consider appropriate and acceptable and to draw conclusions that they find both expected and acceptable.

Listeners must believe that your supporting information is appropriate for your topic. Information is appropriate when audience members think, "Yes, that's the kind of background data I'd expect for that argument." For example, if your goal is to inform your audience about the relationship between self-esteem and success in school, they would logically expect you to cite scientifically conducted experiments that support your point, as well as the opinions of experts in education and psychology.

Listeners must also find your supporting information acceptable based on who said it, where it came from, whether it's up-to-date, and how it was collected. For example, telling your audience that your conclusion is based on a study conducted in 1989 by the Institute for Research in the Social Sciences at the University of North Carolina at Chapel Hill, using a sample of schools across the United States and a research design that controlled for many of the possible errors associated with research techniques, is more convincing than saying, "The people I know who think well of themselves get good grades." Both may be correct, but audience members who think about what you say will find the scientific study more convincing than your personal observation.

Finally, your supporting information must lead to a conclusion that is both expected and acceptable. You need to give your listeners enough acceptable information to lead them to say, "Yes, that conclusion makes sense—it's just what I expected." For example, if you cite several research studies that all argue for a direct relationship between self-esteem and academic success, you are likely to get a response such as, "A lot of evidence seems to support what the speaker is talking about. I can buy the conclusion."

For a conclusion to be acceptable, it must accord with listeners' personal experiences. Audience members who have or know others who have positive self-images and success in school are likely to accept your conclusion about the correlation between self-esteem and education. Listeners who have no personal experience with what you're talking about may or may not find your conclusion acceptable for themselves, although they may admit its possibility after hearing your evidence. But listeners whose experiences contradict yours are likely to reject your point, concluding, "It may be true for you, but it's not for me."

You may not always be able to present information and conclusions that the entire audience finds both expected and acceptable. Sometimes you may be able to convince only a few, but that is a worthy goal in some situations. For example, if you are arguing for a Republican candidate before the Democrats for a Better Government, your chances of total success are slim; however, one or two people may alter their thinking after hearing you, or several may postpone a final decision until they have more information. *Failure* and *success* are relative terms—in some cases, getting just one person to agree with you may be a great success.

The specific criteria each listener uses to judge whether an appeal is logical come from her or his upbringing. Some people will accept your information and arguments and others will not. This raises a problem for you as a public speaker. To make sure that you reach as many listeners as possible, you must try to use a variety of logical appeals.

You can use several types of information to give logical support to the thesis of your speech. These include examples, facts, testimony, and analogies and contrasts.

Examples

An **example** clarifies or expands on an idea by citing a specific instance, which is brief, or an illustration, which is long. There are three types of examples: quantitative, real, and hypothetical.

Quantitative examples are information in numerical form. For example, you can make the statement "This coffee is caffeine-free" more specific by providing numerical information, such as, "This coffee is 99.7 percent caffeine-free." Numerical examples add specificity and thus lend credibility to your support.

Quantitative examples can be extremely persuasive, but be careful how you use them. Not everyone is comfortable with math terminology and the techniques used to gather and interpret numerical data. Furthermore, expressing something in numerical form doesn't necessarily make that something accurate or true. You have to consider the credibility of your source when choosing quantitative examples. You must also seek out numerical examples that are current, well explained, and logical.

To make the most of your numerical examples, remember that people are easily confused by both complex numbers and too many numbers. Help your listeners understand by giving them adequate background information and presenting your numbers as simply as possible. Round numbers off whenever you can. Cite the source for your numbers. For example, consider these two examples:

> According to the Ohio Department of Safety's *1985 Annual Report and Accident Fact Book,* over a ten-year period there were 28,574 deaths when the speed limit was 70 miles per hour, while during the ten-year period when the speed limit was 55 miles per hour, there were 22,146 deaths. That is 6,428 lives saved in ten years, which is 643 lives each year.

> According to the Ohio Department of Safety's *1985 Annual Report and Accident Fact Book,* the change in highway driving speeds from 70 to 55 miles per hour resulted in 6,400 fewer deaths over a ten-year period. The change dropped the number of deaths from approximately 28,000 to 22,000.

Real and hypothetical examples also can give logical support to your presentation. **Real examples** are actual events drawn from your own life or from someone else's—for example, "When I first came to this campus, I was so lost I couldn't find the Student Union Building for two weeks." Or you could say, "When a friend of mine first came to this campus, he was so lost he couldn't find the Student Union Building for two weeks—even with help!"

Hypothetical examples are made-up instances or stories that help to clarify or expand an idea. Because you create the hypothetical examples, you can make them as pointed and specific as necessary. You aren't compelled to "stick to the facts," as you are with real examples. For instance, a speaker's experience with trout fishing may not have been particularly exciting or interesting, but a hypothetical example could make it both for an audience:

> Picture a fisherman out in the middle of a clear, swift-flowing stream, away from the noise and pollution of the city, surrounded by tall trees and a blue sky. Water rushes over jutting rocks. This is trout fishing at its best—whether you catch a fish or not!

When deciding whether to use a real example or a hypothetical one, remember that real examples are usually better at connecting the audience to you as a speaker because they are personal. For instance, a speaker's account of her own experiences with skin grafting after she was burned in a fire would be far more interesting than any story she could make up.

Facts

Facts are statements based on observations; they relate directly to what you see, hear, touch, taste, or smell. When used to support a statement, facts are meant to prove rather than just to amplify or clarify. Three facts are, "Columbus discovered America in 1492," "Two parts of hydrogen and one part of oxygen combine to form water," and "Whales are mammals."

Make sure that the facts you use are accurate and relevant to your topic. To be accurate, a fact should be up-to-date and true for the context in which you use it. "The earth is round" is a fact that meets the accuracy requirement and would be appropriate to use in a speech about the orbiting pattern of satellites.

Audience members can't easily disagree with proven facts. Nonetheless, your presentation of facts does not guarantee a listener's acceptance of your point of view. Presenting facts merely means that you have done your best to provide the information necessary for agreement. For example, the conclusion that the earth is flat is neither up-to-date nor true, in light of current research. A group called the Flat Earth Society, however, has yet to accept modern thought on the subject. When they give speeches, they still argue that no proven information refutes their theory. You must always be ready for the possibility that one speaker's facts are one audience member's fiction.

In presenting facts, be sure to give enough background information to establish credibility and equip audience members to understand. Cite your source, explain how you know the material is factual, or summarize the studies that led to the fact. In addition, be aware that listeners often think facts are dull. You might want to present your facts with other forms of support, such as examples:

> Sex education reduces cases of venereal disease. According to the Sex Information and Educational Council of the United States, in Los Angeles County, after the introduction of sex education in the schools, there was an 84 percent drop in venereal disease cases in four years.

Testimony

Testimony is the quoting or paraphrasing of someone else's opinions, beliefs, predictions, or statements as a way of supporting your own ideas. Because the person a speaker chooses to quote or paraphrase is usually an expert, listeners often presume that testimony is true. To ensure the reliability of any testimony you plan to use, make sure that the person you are quoting or paraphrasing has the necessary education, training, or experience to be considered knowledgeable in the field and that his or her conclusions are unbiased, open-minded, and without ulterior motive.

Unless you are an expert on the topic of your speech, audience members may question your authority. However, because people are used to accepting the opinions and advice of experts—doctors, lawyers, mechanics—using testimony usually works to your advantage. For example, if you simply state that people in the United States stand farther away from each other during conversation than do people in the Middle East, your audience may question your claim. But if you quote Edward T. Hall, a noted anthropologist who has done extensive research on spatial relationships, you will immediately become more believable.

In using testimony, cite your source as well as the qualifications of your expert, try to choose experts that your audience already accepts as credible, be sure that the testimony is relevant to the idea you are trying to support, and make sure that you present the testimony accurately. For example, in a speech advocating sex education, the following testimony may constitute a logical appeal for the audience:

> James Collier, an expert who published a book for the Sex Information and Education Council of the United States, stated in his article "Sex Education is Desperately Needed" that a comprehensive nationwide program both in home and in school, including information on contraceptives, is drastically needed.

Analogies and Contrasts

An **analogy** points out the similarity between two or more things, whereas a **contrast** points out differences between two or more things. Both analogies and contrasts can help clarify ideas your audience is unfamiliar with. For example, in explaining the function of the human kidney, a speaker could compare the organ to the filtering system in a swimming pool (analogy) and then point out that, unlike a swimming pool filter, a damaged kidney cannot be repaired but can only be replaced (contrast).

When you use analogies and contrasts, make sure that your audience understands exactly what the similarities and differences are. You can usually accomplish this by keeping analogies and contrasts very simple.

Emotional Appeals

Whereas logical appeals are used to support or prove a speaker's ideas, **emotional appeals** are used to evoke strong emotions in listeners, such as sadness, anger, happiness, sympathy, or fear. Audiences often tune out speakers who do not touch them emotionally. It would be nice to assume that logic alone could win over your audience, but that is not usually the case. Audiences are affected by a wide range of emotions, and logic and emotion combine to determine reactions. For example, you buy toothpaste because advertisers have proven to you that using toothpaste reduces cavities, but you buy a particular brand of toothpaste because the advertiser's emotional appeal—promises of sex appeal, good taste, and social acceptability—touch you.

When you speak, no matter how expected and acceptable your information or conclusions are, and no matter how trustworthy and competent you seem to be, if you do not give your audience an emotional reason to accept what you say, you are likely to fail to achieve your goal.

One way of appealing to your audience's emotions is to relate what you say to their needs. Thus, you may focus on physiological needs (such as the need for food), security needs (feeling safe), needs for affection (being liked or loved), needs for recognition (gaining praise, awards, or promotions), and needs for belonging (being a member of a group). You may also touch emotions by appealing to what audience members value, such as fairness, peace, independence, honesty, friendship, and equality.

Your audience assessment should point out the needs and values that are important to your listeners and thus suggest which emotional appeals would be most motivational. For example, if you know that your audience values a world at peace, you could emphasize how your proposal would increase the chances for a peaceful world. Or if you know that your audience values honesty, you could avoid making suggestions that seem dishonest, such as proposing that one way to get an idea for a term paper is to use ideas from old papers written for other teachers.

Among the techniques that encourage people to become emotionally involved are giving vivid descriptions of moving situations, using words or referring to events that provoke a predictable emotional reaction, using propaganda, and showing personal involvement.

Vivid Descriptions

People tend to respond strongly when they hear descriptions or see pictures of touching situations. That is why charities seeking donations often show pictures or tell stories about an abused child or an elderly person in a wheelchair. The pity, anger, or sympathy that people feel increases the probability of their donating.

Emotionally Charged Words or Events

Words like *abortion, puppy, snake, communist, birthday, love,* and *Christmas* typically stimulate emotional reactions. Associating your ideas with words that evoke positive or negative emotions can stir up your audience. For example, to recruit students to protest the actions of a faculty member to the dean, a student activist might call the faculty member "a Hitler who uses concentration-camp tactics to control the students."

Propaganda

Propaganda is the use of facts, ideas, or allegations to get listeners to respond emotionally. Although propaganda may be ethically questionable, some speakers employ it masterfully. A common propaganda technique is the **glittering generality,** in which the speaker relies on a vague and highly attractive idea to gain listener support. Glittering generalities include "the American way," "common sense," and "middle America." None of these can be concisely defined, but audiences tend to respond to them very positively.

Another common propaganda technique, called **plain folks,** associates an idea with the typical or average person. This approach aims to make listeners feel that, because the average person goes along with the speaker's message, they must be out of step with the mainstream if they do not agree. Plain folks appeals usually begin with such phrases as "Everybody agrees that…," and "Most Americans.…"

A third common propaganda technique is **name calling**, or guilt by association. In this case, the speaker associates something or someone she or he wants the audience to reject with something or someone perceived in an unflattering way. A political candidate who calls another candidate "a pawn of special interests" or "anti-American" hopes to get the audience to reject his opponent. Notice that the speaker offers no evidence for his claim; he merely seeks an emotional response.

A fourth common propaganda technique, **card stacking,** occurs when a speaker presents only the arguments and evidence that support his or her points—even if they have to be distorted—and deliberately ignores contradictory arguments and evidence. The speech is presented as fair and unbiased when, in fact, it is neither. For example, saying that a proposition passed a student government vote "with a clear majority" while neglecting to mention that the vote was nine to eight in favor—and that a minority opinion was filed with the proposition—creates a false impression.

Personal Involvement

Listeners take many of their cues about how to feel from their perceptions of the speaker's feelings. A speaker who uses vivid adjectives and adverbs shows her own excitement and, in turn, excites her audience. Speakers who use words such as *dynamic, exciting, explosive,* and *electrifying* are apt to create strong emotions themselves as well as in their audience. Unless you are being sarcastic, it is difficult to communicate boredom when you call someone "an exciting, dynamic, explosive, and electrifying speaker."

Developing skill in identifying the various logical and emotional appeals—the focus of Skill Checkup 13.2—is the first step in using them effectively in your own speeches.

SKILL CHECKUP 13.2

Identifying Logical and Emotional Appeals

Tell whether each of the following statements is an example (E), a fact (F), testimony (T), an analogy (A), a contrast (C), a vivid description (V), an emotionally charged word or event (EC), propaganda (P), or a display of personal involvement (PI).

1. The party was like a Fourth of July celebration!
2. Atomic energy will be the death of us all!
3. According to the book *Phobias: The Facts,* almost all agoraphobics are women.
4. I have had personal experience with group homes. My son, David, lived with us until 1981. Then he moved into a group home.
5. According to Arthur Caplan, a medical ethicist in New York's Hastings Center, "We cannot tolerate giving people the right to hurry death; the opportunity for abuse is too huge."
6. A computer is not like a traditional typewriter: it can store and retrieve information, whereas a typewriter cannot.
7. Ten-year-old Meday went out with her family for a Mexican dinner. A half-hour after they finished their meal, Meday, an asthmatic, complained that she was sick. Shortly afterward, she suffered severe brain damage and died as a result of sulfites.
8. It was the most thrilling time of my life, filled with more wonder and excitement than I could ever imagine!
9. Just about everyone today owns a video cassette recorder.

The first statement is an analogy because it offers a comparison. The second statement is emotionally charged because it alludes to a common fear, death. The third statement is a fact, while the fourth is a personal example based on the speaker's own experience. The fifth statement offers the testimony of an expert, and the sixth is a contrast because it focuses on differences. The seventh statement is a real example. The eighth statement illustrates personal involvement, and the last statement is the propaganda technique of plain folks.

RESOURCES FOR LOGICAL AND EMOTIONAL APPEALS

After yourself, your most valuable resource for a speech is other people. You can gain access to other people in one of two ways: you can communicate with them directly by interviewing them face-to-face, by telephone, or by letter, and you can familiarize yourself with their thoughts and work through books, articles, films, and examination of their inventions. Your main resource for studying other people's thoughts and work is the library, but it is only one of many available resources. For example, logical and emotional appeals in support of a speech on organ transplants could be developed using the following methods:

Interviewing a local doctor who performs transplants or is knowledgeable about them

Visiting libraries to examine books, magazine articles, videotapes, newspaper accounts, and scholarly medical articles about transplants

Contacting medical associations, pharmaceutical companies, and religious and social service organizations for material they have produced about transplants

Conducting Interviews

The first step in conducting an interview is to determine specifically what you need to know. What you need to know depends on your statement of purpose and the person you will interview. Obviously, different people can provide different kinds of information that you can use for different purposes. For example, a surgeon who performs transplant operations will know about the technical aspects of the procedure, while a social worker who counsels preoperative patients will know about patients' psychological state.

The second step is to make a list of questions, one leading to another, so that they guide the interview logically. Depending on how the interview progresses, you may not ask all of your questions, or you may develop new questions as you go along. Just be careful that you don't lose track of your purpose and leave the interview with important questions unanswered.

Depending on the information you want, you may plan to use three kinds of questions: closed, open, and probe.

If you want a direct, tightly focused answer, use a closed question. A **closed question** is worded so that the interviewee responds in a few words, such as by saying yes or no, or by giving a statistic. Examples of closed questions are: "How many transplants have you performed?" and "Is pretransplant counseling required by state law?"

If you want to let your interviewee give a more detailed response, use an open-ended question. An **open-ended question** suggests a topic and encourages the interviewee to elaborate. Examples of open-ended questions are: "What procedure do you use in performing a transplant operation?" and "What are the most common fears that clients express to you about transplants?"

Sometimes you want the person being interviewed to expand on the answer to a closed or open-ended question. In such cases you use a **probe**, a question that calls for additional information about something that was just said. For example, if the surgeon's response to the closed question about the number of transplants was, "I've done 24 transplants," your probe might be, "Was the procedure for each similar?" If the social worker's response to the open-ended question about fears was, "They talk about their fear of dying and they also mention their relatives' concern for them," an appropriate probe might be, "How do you encourage them to face the possibility that they may die?"

Probes that may be useful regardless of an interviewee's specific response are: "Can you tell me more?" "Is there anything you want to add?" "Can you give me an example?" and "Anything else?" Sometimes by pausing or saying "Uh-huh" or "I see," you encourage the interviewee to elaborate.

After determining what you need to know and developing your questions, you need to contact the person you will interview and set up an appointment to either meet face-to-face or talk later on the telephone. Don't assume that you will be able to conduct your interview when you first call. Tell the interviewee who you are, the reason for your call, the topic of your interview, and approximately how long the interview will take. Then request a time to call back or to meet.

The fourth step is to conduct the interview. Whether you call back your interviewee or meet face-to-face, begin by restating who you are, what your purpose is, the topic of the interview, and how long the interview should take. Then ask your questions as you wrote them out (to ensure that you don't skip any) and probe for clarification and elaboration as needed. Make your notes as detailed as you can during the interview, and don't be embarrassed to ask the interviewee to slow down, repeat something, or wait a moment while you write. Most interviewees understand that note taking is difficult during an interview.

When you have either asked all your questions or used up the time allotted for your interview, the fifth step is to thank the person for the information and ask for a follow-up interview, if necessary. A follow-up interview may be desirable if time ran out before you could ask all your questions, if the interviewee had to stop the interview, or if you thought of new questions that you wanted to develop before you asked them.

The last step is to review the information you received and complete your notes. This should be done immediately after the interview, while the experience is still fresh in your mind. Write out your notes in complete sentences and add comments about the interviewee's emotions, if they are relevant. Be sure that your notes are thorough so that you will be able to reconstruct the interviewee's responses when you are ready to use them in your speech.

●KILL CHECKUP 13.3

Developing Interview Questions

You are developing a speech about the complexities of writing a communication textbook and decide to interview one of the authors of this text.

1. Prepare a closed question about how long it took to write the book.

2. Based on the interviewee's answer, prepare an open-ended question you can use as a follow-up.

3. When you ask, "Why are the chapters presented in the order they are?" the author answers, "The publisher's survey indicated that this order is consistent with how most classes are taught." What probe question could you ask next?

Library Resources

To find information on your topic, you must be familiar with the resources your library offers. Small local facilities may offer only a limited number of books, magazines, and recent newspapers, while large university libraries typically offer sophisticated computer searches of indexes to a vast array of sources.

Although people often regard library research with dread, it need not be a painful experience. You can facilitate your search for the materials you need by taking two steps. First, if you are not already familiar with your library, take an orientation tour and read through the pamphlets that describe its layout. Second, recognize that there are three important resources in the library: the librarian, the card catalogue, and the reference section.

The Librarian

The librarian is an expert who knows what the library contains and how to find material. The librarian can help you determine what resources would be best for you to consult, how to locate particular sources, and how to find specific pieces of information.

The Card Catalogue

The card catalogue lists the library's print and nonprint materials. The cards are organized three ways: by author, by title, and by subject. Each can be extremely helpful, depending on your needs.

▶ Author cards are arranged alphabetically by author. These cards list an author's name, the title of her or his book, the call number that corresponds to its location in the library, and a list of topics to help you find more books on the same subject.

▶ Title cards are similar to author cards, except that they are arranged alphabetically according to the title of the book.

▶ Subject cards are arranged alphabetically by subject headings. Each card has the subject at the top, followed by the same information found on the author card.

The card catalogue also contains cards for periodicals. The information on each card includes the title of the periodical, such as *Time*, its call number, the issues the library contains, and the location of the issues. For example, current issues are commonly place in an open reading room and older issues are usually bound and shelved.

The Reference Section

To review the sources pertaining to your topic in depth, you need to be familiar with the reference section in your library. References can provide specific pieces of information or tell where information may be located. For example, periodical indexes indicate where articles—on a particular topic, or by a particular author, or with a particular title—can be found. Among the useful resources you may find in your library's reference section are: the following:

▶ General information sources—dictionaries (such as the *Dictionary of American Biography)*, atlases (such as the *Guide to Atlases: World, Regional, National, Thematic*), handbooks (such as the *Complete Book of the American Musical Theatre*), encyclopedias (such as the *Encyclopedia Britannica*), almanacs (such as the *Information Please Almanac*), directories (such as the telephone book), and yearbooks (such as *Facts on File*).

▶ Periodical indexes, such as the *Reader's Guide to Periodical Literature, Psychological Abstracts, Sociological Abstracts, Chemical Abstracts, Business Periodicals Index,* and *Education Index.*

▶ Bibliographies—general bibliographies (such as the *Bibliographic Index*), selective bibliographies (such as the *Reader's Adviser and Bookmen's Manual*), and trade bibliographies (such as the *Cumulative Book Index*).

▶ Government publications—guides (such as the *Guide to Information from Government Sources*), U.S. publications (such as the *Index to U.S. Government Periodicals*), United Nations publications (such as the *United Nations Documents Index*), and publications about government and elected officials (such as the *Municipal Yearbook: An Authoritative Resume of Activities and Statistical Data of American Cities*).

ETHICS AND PUBLIC SPEAKING

As they create and present speeches, speakers must often consider ethics, or the rules for conduct that distinguish right from wrong. Speakers' ethics may be judged in two ways: according to the ends they seek and according to the means they use. When it comes to ends, such lofty goals as "world peace," "ridding the world of hunger," and "finding a cure for cancer" are bound to be perceived as ethical. In contrast, goals such as "world domination," "profits at any price," and "ridding the world of inferior people" can be rejected outright as unethical.

The ethics of a speaker's means are not always so clear-cut. You may believe that a speech is unethical because it is filled with error or deception or because the speaker purposely tries to mislead the audience through propaganda, but the speaker may argue that the goal is so noble that any means are justified to achieve it.

Although a speaker who purposely deceives an audience clearly demonstrates unethical behavior, the problem is more subtle when a speaker uses white lies, lies by omission, or evades the facts. Nonetheless, small lies, leaving out information that doesn't support the message, and refusing to confront relevant issues all mislead the audience and are all unethical.

Considering the end and the means together creates further complications. If a speaker's goal, for example, is to persuade children to refuse to take car rides with strangers—a good and just goal—does it matter whether the speaker uses terrifying but true stories to demonstrate what happens to children who accept such rides? Anything less dramatic may not get the desired result. On the other hand, scaring children can have consequences far beyond teaching them to refuse to ride with strangers. Does the end justify the means? Are the means ethical?

Knowledge Checkup 13.2 will help you find out your own ethical inclinations.

KNOWLEDGE CHECKUP 13.2

Examining Your Ethics

Respond to the situation by answering yes or no to the questions that follow. Your answers should reflect what you would *actually* do, not what you think you *should* do.

A local river is being polluted. Your company has been dumping waste into the stream. You are asked to speak to the local city council about your company and its impact on the environment.

1. Do you mention the polluted river in your speech?

Yes   No

2. Do you mention that your company's philosophy is, "The cheapest method of getting rid of our waste is the best method"?

Yes   No

3. When asked if your company is depositing waste products into the river, do you admit it?

Yes   No

4. When asked if your company is depositing waste products into the river, do you refer the questioner to the company's public relations director?

Yes   No

5. Knowing you will get fired if the public finds out about your company's waste-dumping policy, when asked if your company is depositing waste products in the river, do you say no?

Yes   No

6. Look back at your responses to questions 1 through 5. Did you answer all of them honestly?

Yes   No

If you circled no to question 1, you have committed a lie by omission. A no response to question 2 indicates that you are willing to mislead your audience by not revealing your company's philosophy. A no answer to question 3 and a yes answer to question 5 indicate you are willing to lie. A yes answer to question 4 shows your willingness to evade telling the truth. And question 6 raises some interesting possibilities. If you responded no, you were honest in this one response but indicated your willingness to lie in your other answers. If you responded yes to question 6 and answered no to any of questions 1, 2, or 3 and/or yes to questions 4 or 5, then not only are you willing to lie to protect your company and yourself, but you are willing to lie about your lying! If you answered yes to questions 1, 2, 3, and 6 and no to questions 4 and 5, you are consistently ethical.

The person in the picture is preparing a speech. How would you respond to the following questions?

1. What specific things can I do to make sure that my speech is audience-centered?

2. I'm going to be talking to my communication class about the 1988 presidential election. What can I do to establish my credibility with the audience?

3. I know that I need to include logical appeals in my speech. What kinds of appeals would work best with this topic and where can I find the necessary information?

4. To make sure that my audience responds positively to my speech, I want to include appropriate emotional appeals. What kinds of emotional appeals are there and how will I know which ones to use?

5. What questions can I ask myself to ensure that I am an ethical speaker?

FOR FURTHER INVESTIGATION

Ehninger, Douglas, Bruce E. Gronbeck, Ray E. McKerrow, and Alan H. Monroe. *Principles and Types of Communication*, 10th ed. Glenview, IL: Scott, Foresman/Little Brown, 1988.

Hart, Roderick P., Gustav W. Friedrich, and Barry Brummett. *Public Communication*, 2d ed. New York: Harper and Row, 1983.

Huff, Darrell. *How to Lie with Statistics*. New York: W. W. Norton, 1954.

Kahane, Howard. *Logic and Contemporary Rhetoric: The Use of Reason in Everyday Life*, 4th ed. Belmont, CA: Wadsworth, 1984.

McCroskey, James C., and Thomas J. Young. "Ethos and Credibility: The Construct and Its Measurement After Three Decades." *Central States Speech Journal* 32 (1981): 24–34.

Minnick, Wayne C. *The Art of Persuasion*, 2d ed. Boston: Houghton Mifflin, 1968.

Rubin, Rebecca B., Alan M. Rubin, and Linda J. Piele. *Communication Research: Strategies and Resources*. Belmont, CA: Wadsworth, 1986.

CHAPTER 14

▶ *Public Speaking: Developing the Speech*

This chapter on developing public communication will help you practice and develop communication competencies that fall into two broad categories: (1) **oral message evaluation**, which includes identifying main ideas, and (2) **basic speech communication skills**, which include expressing ideas clearly and concisely, organizing messages so that others can understand them, and summarizing messages. Specifically, the competencies you will gain will enable you to do the following:

▶ Identify the six parts of a public speech.
▶ Gain an audience's attention.
▶ Choose the background material necessary to help an audience understand and appreciate your message.
▶ State the purpose of your speech.
▶ Arrange the information in your speech to ensure that the audience comprehends it.
▶ Summarize the key points of your speech.
▶ Drive home the points of your message.

*B*ased on your own listening experience, rank order the following eight statements. Rank as 1 the statement that best helped you understand and pay attention to the speech. Rank the second most helpful 2, and so on through 8.

_____ **a.** The speech starts with something that really gets my attention.

_____ **b.** The speaker defines the words and concepts I need for understanding the material.

_____ **c.** The speaker provides a context for the speech by giving necessary background.

_____ **d.** The speaker gives personal background that relates him or her to the topic.

_____ **e.** The speaker clearly states the purpose for the speech.

_____ **f.** The speaker organizes information in a way that is easy to follow.

_____ **g.** At the end of the speech, the speaker repeats the main points that I should remember.

_____ **h.** The speaker concludes with something memorable.

As you have probably guessed, each item is necessary to the creation of an effective speech. Each may help a member of the audience understand what a speaker is saying and stay attentive to the message. Which are most important, however, differs from listener to listener, as you will discover if you and your classmates compare your rankings. To make sure that you reach *all* your listeners, you need to include all these elements in your speech.

The eight elements are incorporated in a speech at different times: item a is used at the beginning of a speech, items b, c, and d are used during the early part of a speech to create a foundation, item e is used after the foundation is presented and before the main points are discussed, item f is used when the main points are introduced, and items g and h are used at the end.

THE PARTS OF A SPEECH

Although a speech can be divided into as many parts as you wish—some people like to think of speeches as having three parts, including a beginning, a middle, and an end—dividing a speech into six equally important parts makes a lot of sense. Doing so makes it clear that you need to "grab" your audience and give them the background they'll need to understand what you have to say, to let them know what your speech is about, to present and summarize your information, and to persuasively, forcefully recap your main points. Figure 14.1 shows the six parts of a speech and summarizes the main point each part should express.

Any speech is only as strong as its weakest link. Although some people may argue that the discussion section of a speech, when the main body of information is presented, is the most important part, if a speaker lacks an attention-getting opener, the audience will not pay attention long enough to hear the discussion. In

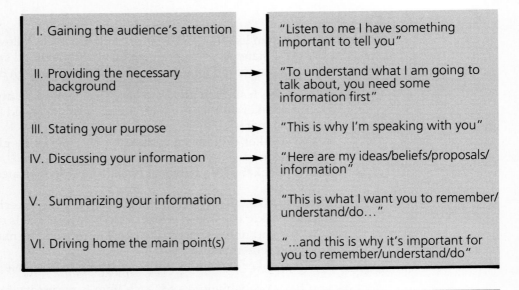

▶ FIGURE 14.1   The Six Parts of a Speech

this sense, the short introduction is as important as the long discussion. The six equally important parts of a speech we consider here are as follows:

    I. Gaining the audience's attention
   II. Providing necessary background
  III. Stating your purpose
  IV. Discussing your information
   V. Summarizing your information
  VI. Driving home the main point(s)

GAINING THE AUDIENCE'S ATTENTION

The first challenge a speaker faces is gaining the audience's attention. Unless an audience's curiosity is immediately piqued, their minds will wander and they'll miss even the most brilliant material.

Among the surest methods of gaining attention are telling a joke or an interesting story, posing a real or rhetorical question, presenting a highly dramatic piece of information, reading a captivating quote, and referring to the occasion or audience. Of course, the joke, story, question, information, quote, and reference must have some connection to your speech. If you open with an irrelevant remark, you'll probably confuse your audience rather than impress them. Furthermore, the goal of your opening remark is to gain attention, not to show how clever or glib you are.

Tell a Joke

Audiences appreciate a speaker with a sense of humor. They tend to relax when they hear a light introduction and to feel that the speech is going to be enjoyable. Jokes based on personal experiences are perhaps the most attention-getting and amusing. They also show that you trust your audience because you are willing to share something personal.

Be careful not to offend your audience by using sexist, racist, or any other "-ist" humor, unless you intend to use the slur to make a point. A speech arguing against sexist humor may begin with a sexist joke and then go on to show why such humor is objectionable.

Tell a Story

For whatever reason—and it probably goes back to bedtime reading in childhood—audiences enjoy hearing a good story. A personal story that relates to your topic communicates your involvement. A dramatic story stimulates the emotions. A story with a moral previews the point of your speech and suggests the response you want from your listeners. For example, you might begin a speech on training air traffic controllers by saying: "I was sitting in the plane, minding my own business, when I looked out the window and saw another plane coming toward us. It seemed close enough to touch, although it couldn't have been. Our plane dove suddenly, trays went flying, coffee cups overturned, and shrieks filled the cabin. It was like a scene from the movie *Airplane*, but nobody was laughing."

Make sure that the story you tell is short enough to hold interest, that its point is clear, and that its theme fits the subject of your speech. Also be sure that it will evoke the emotional reaction you want.

Pose a Question

Speakers commonly ask two types of questions to start a speech: one that requires an answer and one that doesn't. Asking a question stimulates the audience to think about your topic. If the question is nonthreatening and easy to answer, you may solicit responses from audience members. It is then *essential* to use their responses in your presentation. Otherwise, audience members may feel that you manipulated them into revealing something for no purpose. Whether you ask for answers or not, you must tie the question to the rest of the speech. The following introduction, which requires audience participation, could serve as an attention-getting device for a speech on television violence:

> How many of you watch TV during the prime-time hours of eight to ten at least two nights a week? [*The speaker waits for a response, such as a show of hands or head nods before continuing.*] Do you know how many shootings, stabbings, rapes, and other violent crimes you witness during those hours?

An example of a question that would not require a response would be, "Have you ever walked into a room filled with strangers and thought that you'd like to fade into the wallpaper?" Such a rhetorical question could serve as an introduction to a speech about shyness.

Give a Highly Dramatic Piece of Information

An unusual attention-getting device is to present a piece of information that is shocking, mind-boggling, or odd. The desired response from the audience may be, "Oh!" "I didn't know that!" or even "Wow!"

"In the United States nearly three thousand different substances are intentionally added to foods during processing." This startling fact from a National Research Council report could stimulate your listeners to pay close attention to a speech about why additives should not be used in food processing.

Attention-grabbing statements should always be well documented. If an audience suspects that they have been tricked by phony information, they will become hostile.

Use a Quote

Quote for color, quote for interest, or quote because an authority stated the point better than you could or has the credentials to state what you don't know about. A quote may be a joke, a story, a question, or a dramatic piece of information, but it may also present information or state a point of view without being dramatic.

If you were presenting a speech on the role of testing in education, you might begin with this paraphrase from Andrew Strenio's *The Testing Trap*:

> According to Andrew Strenio in his book *The Testing Trap*, "Tests shape rather than serve education whenever high scores are viewed as ends in themselves. Standardized achievement tests have strangled the creative talents of many of our best teachers, who are forced to 'teach to the test.' "

Make a Reference to the Occasion or the Audience

A common and effective way to gain an audience's attention is to comment on why they are assembled, why you are there, your relationship with them, or some aspect of their identity—their jobs, their role in life, where they come from, and so on. This approach helps to link the audience, the speaker, and the occasion. For example, a student speaking to a group of other students about the need to change the college's grading system could state, "We are here to discuss a problem we have in common: the grading system at our school." This introduction mentions the occasion and builds a bridge between the audience and the speaker.

SKILL CHECKUP 14.1

Preparing an Introduction

For one of your speaking assignments you want to explain to your communication class why it is important to have a drug-free campus.

1. Write two introductions for your speech, using a different attention-getting device in each.

2. What attention-getting device would not be appropriate for this speech?

PROVIDING NECESSARY BACKGROUND

The kind and amount of background information you will need to present varies from topic to topic and from audience to audience. The more your audience knows about your topic, the less you'll need to prepare them. Two general questions to ask yourself are as follows as follows:

What must my audience know in order to understand my entire speech?
What does my audience already know?

The difference between what your audience needs to know and what they already know is the kind and amount of background you must provide.

To determine what you need to provide, use the following questions:

What specialized terms must I use that my listeners may not recognize?

What background—historical, legal, theoretical, practical—do they need to understand and appreciate the information I am going to present?

What does the audience need to know about me—about my background, attitudes, and beliefs—to understand and appreciate my speech?

You can find the answers to all these questions through an audience assessment and an analysis of what *you* needed to learn about your subject when you first approached it. What terms were unfamiliar to you? What background did you have to acquire? Chances are your audience will need just as much basic preparation, or more.

SKILL CHECKUP 14.2

Providing Necessary Background

What background material do you need to present to your (communication class) audience for your speech explaining why it is important to have a drug-free campus?

What words probably need to be defined?

What history needs to be presented?

What information about you may help the audience understand your interest in the topic?

STATING YOUR PURPOSE

Your statement of purpose has several functions. It lets your audience know your goal for your speech. In many cases, it tells them what you expect from them. Finally, it reminds you why you are speaking and how you are going to present your information.

"Today, I'd like to explain to you the early, middle, and late phases of alcoholism and the symptoms that are typical of each phase." This statement of purpose tells the audience the speaker's goal—to explain the phases and the typical symptoms of alcoholism. If this statement follows a reference to the speaker's own experiences as a recovering alcoholic, it also shows her willingness to be open with her audience. This statement of purpose also specifies how the speech will proceed—the speaker will trace the three phases of alcoholism, stressing their characteristic symptoms.

Not all speakers are so open about their personal background. In some cases, the speaker may not have any related experience (she may not be a recovering alcoholic, but may have picked the topic simply because it was interesting). Or the speaker may choose not to reveal related personal information, perhaps because it is too self-threatening.

Similarly, not all speakers are open about their goal. For example, if a speaker intends to ask audience members to support the development of a local chapter of Alcoholics Anonymous, she may at first withhold her intent if she thinks listeners will reject the idea and stop listening before they have enough information to make an intelligent decision.

If your audience assessment suggests that your listeners may for some reason be against your proposal, you may not want to reveal your goal too early. For example, if you plan to encourage a predominantly environmentalist audience to support road construction in a designated wilderness area, you can assume a hostile audience. Revealing your intentions early in the speech would probably alienate your listeners and leave you with little opportunity to accomplish your goal.

DISCUSSING YOUR INFORMATION

The information in your speech must be presented logically if your audience is to understand it. Using a standard pattern of organization enables your audience to know where you are in your presentation and where you are going, freeing them to concentrate on absorbing the information you are presenting. Audience members also tend to feel more secure when they can follow the structure of a speech.

The discussion section of a speech is commonly organized in one of six ways. Because most audience members are familiar with these six patterns, they can quickly adapt their thinking to the method you choose. The usual patterns of organization are: topical, sequential, spatial, causal, problem-solution, and comparison and/or contrast, as shown in figure 14.2.

Topical Arrangement

In a **topical arrangement** the points of the discussion are organized as subdivisions of the same subject. For example, a speaker whose purpose is to inform his audience about the units included in a course in interpersonal communication would divide his information into seven topics: self-concept, perception, listening, relationship development, verbal language, nonverbal language, and conflict. These are all subdivisions of the broad subject of interpersonal communication; they could be discussed in any order.

A topical outline of the discussion section of a speech on the units in a course on interpersonal communication would look like this:

IV. Units included in a course on interpersonal communication
    A. Self-Concept
    B. Perception
    C. Listening
    D. Relationship development
    E. Verbal language
    F. Nonverbal language
    G. Conflict

Sequence Arrangement

A **sequence arrangement** presents information in a logical order. Many of the things you might discuss in a speech follow a sequence—they happen in a series or they are done in a specific order. If the sequential nature of your topic is important, choose this type of arrangement. For example, speeches about historical topics often use this arrangement. A speech whose purpose is to describe the progression of World War I from June 28, 1914, when it began, until June 28, 1919, when it ended, lends itself to a sequence arrangement.

Demonstration speeches and how-to speeches also often employ a sequence arrangement. Consider a speech on baking a cake that begins with mixing the batter, then specifies the oven temperature, then lists the ingredients, and finishes by describing how to grease the pan. Confusing? Of course!

A sequence outline for the discussion section of a speech that describes the history of human biological transplants would be the following:

IV. Highlights of the history of human biological transplants
  A. 2000 B.C.: grafts of skin from the neck or cheek used to repair a mutilated nose, lip, or ear
  B. 1954: transplant of a kidney from one twin to his brother
  C. 1967: first heart transplant performed by Dr. Christian Barnard

Spatial Arrangement

A **spatial arrangement** organizes information according to physical or geographical layout. Items are discussed in terms of their relationship in space. Thus, the speaker may progress through the items from top to bottom, bottom to top, left to right, right to left, center to periphery, periphery to center, north to south, south to north, and so on.

Although certain topics, such as geography, naturally lend themselves to this kind of arrangement, creative thinking may reveal others. For example, a company's organizational chart may depict personnel from the top down, starting with the president and flowing to the assembly-line workers, or it may show the president as the hub of a wheel, with the spokes standing for divisions by product and the rim representing the assembly-line workers.

Assume that a speaker's purpose is to inform the audience of the corn, hay, and oat production of the Midwest on a state-by-state basis. If she uses an east-to-west spatial arrangement for the five Midwestern states, her outline might be as follows:

IV. Midwest states and their production of corn, hay, and oats
  A. Ohio
  B. Michigan
  C. Indiana
  D. Illinois
  E. Wisconsin

Causal Arrangement

A **causal arrangement** organizes material in either a cause(s)-to-effect pattern or an effect-from-cause(s) pattern. In each case you discuss contributing events and consequences, but the order in which you present them depends on the subject and your goal. For example, if you want to stress consequences, you may prefer an effect-from-cause pattern, starting with the outcome and then working backwards by describing the sequence of causes. After the Chernobyl nuclear reactor disaster in the Soviet Union, the first reports simply announced that there had been a nuclear accident. Then, one-by-one, the events that brought it about were revealed. News reports often use the effect-from-cause sequence—mentioning noteworthy consequences first heightens drama.

If your goal is to stress the circumstances that led up to something, you would do better to use a cause-to-effect pattern. For example, a speech whose purpose is to inform the audience of the actions that led to a school bond's adoption in the last election could trace the series of events that brought about the favorable vote.

Here is a causal outline for the discussion section of a speech whose purpose is to describe the effects of putting certain additives in food products:

IV. Why additives are used in food products
  A. Cause: Using additives in food products
  B. Effects of using additives in food products
      1. Preserves the product
      2. Improves the texture
      3. Improves flavor, taste, or appearance
      4. Minimizes loss of quality during processing

Problem-Solution Arrangement

One of the most common patterns speakers use when their goal is to change listeners' attitudes or behavior is the problem-solution arrangement. In the **problem-solution arrangement**, the speaker identifies what is wrong and then suggests a way of setting things right. Two variations on this approach are (1) to state the problem, analyze possible solutions, and recommend the best solution; and (2) to state the problem, discuss the reasons for its existence, and recommend a solution that attacks the reasons.

The following is a problem-solution outline for the discussion section of a speech whose purpose is to explain why the best way to reduce the death rate of young Americans between the ages of sixteen and twenty-one is to raise the drinking age to twenty-one:

IV. Drunk driving and the legal drinking age
  A. Problem: Drunk driving is the leading cause of death for young Americans between the ages of sixteen and twenty-one
      1. Every year, 25,000 sixteen- to twenty-one-year-olds die due to drunk driving
      2. Every hour of every day three Americans are killed and eighty are injured by drunk drivers
  B. Solution: Raise the national drinking age to twenty-one
      1. There is a direct correlation between the minimum drinking age and alcohol-related accidents (Presidential Commission on Drunk Driving)

2. Raising the drinking age to twenty-one resulted in a 28 percent reduction in nighttime fatal accidents involving eighteen- to twenty-one-year-old drivers (Presidential Commission on Drunk Driving)

Comparison and/or Contrast Arrangements

You can organize the information in the discussion section of your speech by using a **comparison arrangement**, in which you describe similarities, a **contrast arrangement**, in which you describe differences, or a **comparison and contrast arrangement**, in which you describe both similarities and differences. Such arrangements lend themselves to speeches in which your purpose is to show how things are alike, different, or both.

There are two ways to use these arrangements. If the purpose of your speech is to inform the audience of the similarities and differences between a two-year and a four-year college, you may either speak about the similarities and then the differences between the two types of colleges, or you may examine each characteristic separately and compare and contrast how the two types of schools display it. The main points for the discussion using the first approach would be as follows:

IV. Two-year versus four-year colleges
    A. Similarities between two-year and four-year schools
        1. Both are schools of higher education
        2. Both need accreditation
        3. Both offer a wide variety of programs
    B. Differences between two-year and four-year schools
        1. Orientation toward research and teaching
        2. Differences in degrees

The main points for the discussion of the second approach would be as follows:

IV. Characteristics of two-year and four-year colleges
    A. Student population
        1. Similarities
        2. Differences
    B. Faculty
        1. Similarities
        2. Differences

Knowledge Checkup 14.1 provides you with some experience selecting the most appropriate organizational pattern for different topics.

KNOWLEDGE CHECKUP 14.1

Selecting an Arrangement for Your Information

What method of arrangement would you use for each of the following speech purposes?

1. To propose a plan of action for dealing with smoking in public places

2. To discuss the temperaments of five different breeds of dogs

3. To explain the relationship between the use of seat belts and the decrease in the number of traffic deaths

4. To explain the similarities and differences between the flute and the clarinet

5. To explain the westward movement of the pioneers by discussing their activities in each state as they traveled on the Oregon Trail

6. To describe the events that led to the establishment of the United States

The first topic is best handled with a problem-solution arrangement, first describing the problem caused by smoking in public places and then presenting a solution.

The second is best handled with a topical arrangement in which the order of the discussion of the five breeds is arbitrary.

The third is best handled with a causal arrangement, first discussing the effect—a decrease in the number of traffic deaths—and then the cause—wearing seat belts, or first discussing the cause and then the effect.

The fourth is best handled with a comparison-contrast arrangement, first explaining how the flute and clarinet are similar and then how they are different, or first how they are different and then how they are similar.

The fifth is best handled with a spatial arrangement, beginning with a description of the pioneers' activities in Independence, Missouri, the eastern end of the Oregon Trail, and then following them through Kansas, Nebraska, Wyoming, Idaho, and into Oregon, the western end of the trail.

The sixth is best handled with a sequence arrangement, beginning with the French and Indian War (1754–1763) and then discussing, in order, the Stamp Act (1765), The Townshend Act (1766), the Boston Massacre (1770), the Boston Tea Party and the Intolerable Acts (1774), and Battles of Lexington and Concord (1775), the Revolutionary War (1775–1783), and, finally, the Declaration of Independence (1776).

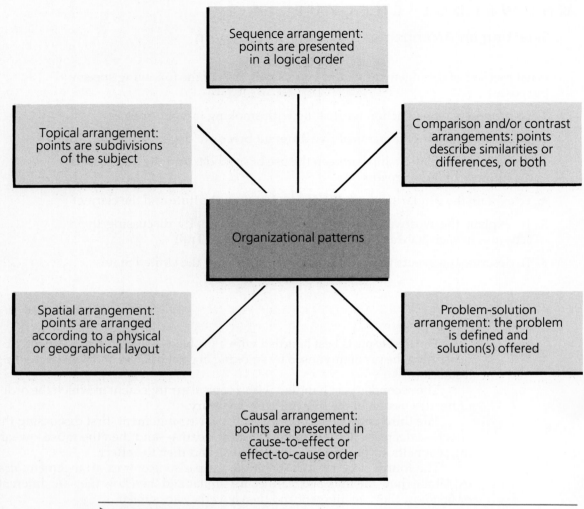

▶ **FIGURE 14.2** Organizational Patterns

SUMMARIZING YOUR INFORMATION

Once you have presented all the information in your discussion section, you will be ready to conclude your speech. The first requirement of an effective conclusion is that you reinforce your main points by summarizing them as simply and clearly as possible. One of the best ways to do this is to repeat the main headings of your discussion section.

This is your last opportunity to help the audience understand the details of your message, so you may want to use one of two techniques to make this section as memorable as you can. One approach is to use a mnemonic device. A **mnemonic device** helps your audience remember your speech by associating each of its main points with a letter of the alphabet, so that when the letters are combined they form a meaningful word or a letter combination that is easy to remember. Say, for example, that in a speech whose purpose is to describe assertiveness for complex situations, the main heads of the discussion were the following:

A. Describe the action
B. Express your subjective interpretation of the action
C. Express your sensations related to the action
D. Indicate the effects of the action
E. Make your request
F. Tell your intentions

By taking the first letter of each key word in the assertiveness process, you can spell out the mnemonic device ASSERT.

A mnemonic device may also be a phrase in which the first letter of each word stands for a main heading. For example, if you presented a spatially arranged speech designed to help people remember the order of the planets from the sun outward, you could summarize your information with the mnemonic device, "Mary's violet eyes make John stay up nights, period" (Mercury, Venus, Earth, Mars, Jupiter, Saturn, Uranus, Neptune, Pluto).

Another way of making your summary more interesting is to use a visual aid, such as a chart listing your main points. As you review the chart with your audience, you reinforce your key headings both orally and visually.

SKILL CHECKUP 14.3

Developing a Mnemonic Device

Develop a mnemonic device for each of the following:

1. To remember the south-to-north order of the three states bordering the Pacific Ocean.

2. To remember the six parts of a speech outline.

A mnemonic device for remembering the order of the states could be COW (California, Oregon, Washington). One for remembering the six parts of a speech outline could be Anything Brilliant Provides Inventive Speech Delivery (attention getting, background, purpose, information, summarization, drive home the points).

DRIVING HOME YOUR POINT

You can *drive home the point* of your speech by using the same techniques that you used to gain your audience's attention. You may emphasize your point by telling a joke or a story, by posing or answering a question, by presenting a quote or a highly dramatic piece of information, or by referring to the audience or the occasion. You may also drive home your point by creatively restating your theme.

At this stage, do not add any ideas that you have not already discussed, because doing so will confuse the audience. Also, make sure that your closing technique does not distract from the rest of the speech by being *too* dramatic or drawing *too* much attention to itself. In such cases, the audience might remember the clever device you used to end your speech, but have a hard time remembering what the speech was about or why you gave it.

A speech advocating the abolition of IQ tests could end with this restatement of its theme: "Thousands of children are in classes for the mentally retarded today who do not belong there. Often their futures are shattered because an IQ score has become the all-important educational evaluation."

A speaker whose purpose is to inform the audience of the arguments against a constitutional amendment calling for prayer in the public schools could end by paraphrasing a group of rabbis representing the Jewish Theological Seminary:

> Rabbis representing the Jewish Theological Seminary remind us that, although a school prayer amendment to the Constitution may appear to enhance religious liberty, in reality it exerts undue pressure to conform in terms of what is prayed, how it is prayed, when it is prayed, and for how long it is prayed. Under such circumstances, *true* prayer cannot be expressed.

ANALYZING A MODEL SPEECH

By examining the structure of a speech you can gain familiarity with the form and flow of speech organization. The following speech illustrates the six-stage approach to speech development.

Self-Knowledge and Student Mental Health: A Case for Both[1]

For those of you who wonder why you're in college, well, you don't have to wonder anymore. A *Newsweek* story on education came up with the

The opening humor should increase perceptions of goodwill and, therefore, enhance the speaker's credibility.

answers. You are probably here because your friends went to college and it seemed like the right thing to do, or because your parents expected you to go, or because your parents didn't want you to go and you decided that you'd show them who's boss. And, *Newsweek* tells us, you are most likely here because you expect a college education to help you get a better job after graduation. And then the article spells out—in horrible, gruesome detail—how this last reason is a hoax and you'd better run from the ivy-covered walls if that's your reason for clinging to them in the first place.

> Direct reference to the needs and interests of audience members should increase their interest in the speech topic.

Another reason was given, but little was made of it and it was relegated to near the end of the list. Some people go to college to "find themselves." This is mentioned and then ignored. Yet I believe it is one of the few valid reasons for being here: *self-knowledge* should be the name of the game played in college—and my point is to show you why it should be *your* reason for being here.

> Because of their vividness, words such as *horrible* and *gruesome* appeal to listeners' emotions.

It feels good addressing a group like you—members of the National Freshman Honorary. You have the distinction of being successful in college, which probably means you learned to play the academic game well enough to get a high grade-point average. You can probably read and absorb large amounts of material quickly and remember more than enough to pass tests and write papers.

> Explicit statement of purpose should increase perceptions of the speaker's trustworthiness. The statement of purpose lets audience members know the speaker's goal as well as his expectations for their response.

But I have a fear: I fear that in your quest for academic success you might have either given up "finding yourself," or, worse, never started the trip.

> Reference to the audience and occasion gains listeners' attention and links the speaker, the audience, and the occasion.

> Complimenting audience members should increase perceptions of the speaker's goodwill.

> The speaker's indication that he has audience members' best interests at heart should increase perceptions of his goodwill.

Your high grade-point average may well be hazardous to your health.

I'll begin at the beginning and explain why I believe that knowing yourself is probably one of the most important life tasks you can undertake—and probably the most important reason for being in college. Then we'll look at some of the disadvantages of a lack of self-knowledge. And, finally, we'll look at some ways you can solve the problem of gaining self-knowledge *and* a college education at the same time.

Did you ever ask yourself, "Who am I? How do I feel about me?"

There are a great many advantages to asking and answering these questions because a high degree of self-knowledge leads to self-acceptance, and self-acceptance promotes a positive self-concept. The more you know about yourself, the more you'll accept who you are and the more you'll like who you are. *It all begins with self-knowledge, with knowing who you are.*

Here are only a small fraction of the advantages— summarized by Morris Rosenberg in his book, *Conceiving the Self.*

First of all, you'll be independent of the roles you enact. You'll see yourself as more than *just* a student, a daughter, or a son. You'll have a more realistic view of the totality of all the separate roles that you play.

Second, you'll be secure enough to change your ideas and opinions easily and gracefully, and accept ideas from others without becoming defensive. Secure people are relatively immune to the judgments of

Humor should increase audience members' attention and interest. Also, the speaker explains why the speech is relevant to this particular audience. This should increase interest as well as perceptions of his goodwill.

Preview of the organization of the speech helps orient the listeners. The discussion section develops using a problem-solution arrangement (advantages of self-knowledge, problems associated with a lack of self-knowledge, and solutions to the problems). Each main portion of the discussion is supported by four subpoints.

Reference to the source of information increases the probability that it will be accepted by audience members.

Advantages one through four are facts that support the main point that having self-knowledge is desirable. Audience analysis indicated these four advantages were of particular interest and concern for this group.

others but open to what others have to say. For example, I know from my experiences with students in my classes that some parents want their children to major in certain areas of study and not others. And I know that the secure students are less upset by the advice they receive.

Third, you are apt to be more effective interpersonally—better able and more willing to reach out to others and to make others feel welcome and at ease. You tend to be more accepting, warm, and involved with the people around you.

And by the way, this fourth advantage should interest you: you also do better in school. According to a 1987 study by educational psychologist Ernest Pascarella and his colleagues, published in the *American Educational Research Journal*, a positive self-concept is a good predictor of success in college—perhaps better than intelligence.

A dramatic illustration of the effect of self-concept comes from a comparison of kindergarten children, some with positive self-concepts and some with negative ones. Those with positive self-concepts enter new situations less fearfully, make friends more easily, trust their teachers more, and are more creative and more willing to share. Most important of all, they are happier.

Research with older children and adults supports these findings with five-year-olds. Who do you think is going to have a richer, fuller, happier life—

Personal reference indicates both involvement with the topic and acquaintance with examples involving students similar to members of the audience. This increases perceptions of the speaker's competency and goodwill.

Audience analysis indicated that these students value doing well in school—that perhaps it is their most important value. This advantage is emotionally appealing because it directly concerns audience members' value of success in school.

Reference to recent research increases the speaker's being perceived as competent to talk about self-concept.

An example supports the importance of a positive self-concept.

▶ the person who thinks well of others or disapproves of others?

▶ the person who expects to be accepted by others or who expects to be rejected?

▶ the person whose self-evaluations are positive or whose self-evaluations are negative?

▶ the person who feels comfortable with higher-status people or who feels threatened by them?

▶ the person who is able to defend herself or himself against negative comments or the one who has difficulty and is easily influenced?

The person with a positive self-concept is clearly at an advantage—and the basis for a positive self-concept is self-knowledge.

What are the disadvantages of a lack of self-knowledge and a negative self-concept? Besides those already implied, such as feeling insecure and not being effective in your interactions with others, there are four others worth mentioning.

First, people with negative self-concepts have feelings of inferiority. Second, they are unable to "read" or "hook into" others. Third, they believe that failure is the rule for their lives and not the exception.

The fourth consequence, a very important one, is called *self-alienation*. Sidney Jourard, one of the most prominent psychologists doing research on self-concept and intimate communication, has the following to say about it:

> Alienation from one's real self not only arrests one's growth as a person, it also tends to make a

---

The series of contrasts builds a logical appeal that dramatically presents the advantages of a positive self-concept.

The rhetorical question serves as a transition to the next main point: the disadvantages of a lack of self-knowledge and a negative self-concept.

Disadvantages one through four are facts that support the main point that having little self-knowledge is undesirable. Audience analysis indicated these four disadvantages were of particular concern for this group.

The use of the term *self-alienation* indicates the speaker's familiarity with the vocabulary of the speech topic, which increases the probability that he will be perceived as competent.
The credibility of the source is established in an effort to increase audience acceptance.

farce out of one's relations with people. . . . A self-alienated person . . . can never love another person nor can he be loved by another person. Effective loving calls for knowledge of the object. . . . How can I love a person I do not know? How can he love me if he does not know me?

Sounds hideous, doesn't it? Self-alienation doesn't sound like the kind of thing that can sell breakfast cereals, but it is sold through the educational process. Studies done during the 1960s found that students from the third through the eleventh grades experienced a drop in positive self-concept. The pattern was like this: there was a decrease from September to June, then a rise during the summer months, and so on through the years. Unfortunately, the rise during the summer never fully compensated for the drop during the school year. I hate to think about what was happening to those students who went to summer school! And, it seems, 44 percent of the eleventh graders studied wished they were someone else.

Replications have found similar results, including this interesting one: Pescarella, in his 1987 study, found that majoring in a scientific or technical field during college has a negative effect on self-concept for white male students.

Consider that classrooms are places where book learning predominates over self-learning and where the primary measures of success are high grades on tests and quick and correct answers during class discussions—not the kinds of places where learning about yourself is either planned or encouraged.

Testimony is used as a logical appeal to support the problems associated with self-alienation. The quote presents a colorful and dramatic depiction of the problem.

The emotionally charged word *hideous* appeals to listeners' personal feelings. It also communicates the speaker's personal involvement with the topic of the speech.

The use of a quantitative example provides a more precise indication of the problem.

The speaker communicates his familiarity with the research and presents a fact that is interesting for this group, given that audience analysis had revealed that many of them were majoring in a scientific or technological area.

So, what can be done about the situation? How can you take the opportunity to gain self-knowledge while you're here? There are four things you can do without changing too much of what you do already:

First, take courses that expose you to new thoughts and ideas—thoughts and ideas that will stretch your ways of looking at the world and at yourself.

The rhetorical question serves as a transition to the third and final main point: solutions to the problems associated with a lack of self-knowledge.

Second, take courses that focus on you, the student, as well as on texts and tests. There are courses in almost every department that offer the opportunity for self-learning, and you need to find out which ones they are and take advantage of them. Whether it's the course in interpersonal communication in the Communication Department, or ethics in the Philosophy Department, or race relations in the Sociology Department, the point is the same: you have the opportunity to learn something about who you are.

The speaker acknowledges that members of the audience are busy individuals and that he is adapting solutions to their needs. This increases the probability of his being perceived as having goodwill.

Third, in every course you take, translate the material into something personal. Keep asking yourself, "What does this course have to do with who I am? How does this lecture, book, article, discussion—whatever—relate to me?" You can supplement a focus on the texts and tests with a focus on yourself.

Fourth, talk to people about yourself. One of the quickest ways to gain self-knowledge is to let others know who you are. Avoid hiding from yourself by burying your head in books and assigned readings. Hiding might seem easier, but only for a short time. The poet Rod McKuen tells us, "Maybe when I've done

The quote from poet Rod McKuen increases interest and relates the notion of hiding to the popular notion of seeing all there is to see.

it all, seen all there is to see, I'll find out I still cannot run away from me."

Start your trip toward self-discovery here and now. The advantages are worth the effort—including independence from your roles, feelings of security and reduced defensiveness, more effective interpersonal behaviors, and greater success in school. The bottom line is this: a happier life. The disadvantages likely to result if you put off the trip include feelings of inferiority, decreased effectiveness in your relationships, the expectation that failure, and not success, is your lot in life, and self-alienation.

The conclusion of the speech begins with a summary of the main points. This reinforces audience members' understanding.

Start the trip now! Experiment and take courses in new areas, sign up for courses with a focus on who you are, and make your courses personal by forcing yourself to ask, "What does this information have to do with *me*?" And, finally, talk to others and let them know who you are. Hiding may be safe, but it's the same as condemning yourself to little self-knowledge.

Leo Buscaglia—the child psychologist, world-renowned speaker, and best-selling author—dedicated his book, *Personhood*, this way:

> This book is dedicated to those who are eager to encounter themselves before their death; therefore, it is dedicated to LIFE and those HUMAN BEINGS who strive to give it their special meaning.

The use of testimony from a source that has credibility for this audience drives home the point of the speech. The appeal is novel in that self-knowledge—an encounter with yourself—is the only learning equivalent to life.

Make this your dedication for your years in college. Commit yourself to an encounter with yourself—the only learning that is equivalent to life. Give your life that special meaning.

COMMUNICATION COMPETENCY CHECKUP

1. What kind of attention-getting device is the speaker in the cartoon using?

2. Assume that the speaker is addressing your communication class. If she continued her speech by indicating that she was going to explain how college students can use various banking services, what would you expect her to include in each of the following sections of her presentation?

    a. Necessary background
    b. Statement of purpose
    c. Discussion of information
    d. Summary of information
    e. Driving home her point

NOTE

1. A version of this speech was originally given [by one of the authors of this text] to members of Phi Eta Sigma National Freshman Honorary at the University of New Mexico, Albuquerque, on October 17, 1976.

FOR FURTHER INVESTIGATION

Haynes, Judy L. *Organizing a Speech: A Programmed Guide*, 2d ed. Englewood Cliffs, NJ: Prentice Hall, 1981.

Phillips, Gerald M., and J. Jerome Zolten. *Structuring the Speech: A How-to-Do-It Book About Public Speaking*. Indianapolis: Bobbs-Merrill, 1976.

Sprague, Jo, and Douglas Stuart. *The Speaker's Handbook*. San Diego, CA: Harcourt Brace Jovanovich, 1984.

Zolten, J. Jerome, and Gerald M. Phillips. *Speaking to an Audience: A Practical Method of Preparing and Performing*. Indianapolis: Bobbs-Merrill, 1985.

CHAPTER 15

► # *Public Speaking: Methods of Presentation*

COMMUNICATION COMPETENCIES

*This chapter on methods of presentation will help you practice and develop communication competencies that fall into three broad categories: (1) **communication codes,** which include using works and grammar that are appropriate to a particular situation; (2) **oral message evaluation,** which includes identifying main ideas in messages, distinguishing between informative and persuasive messages, and recognizing when someone does not understand your message; and (3) **basic speech communication skills,** which include expressing ideas clearly and concisely, organizing messages so others can understand them, answering questions effectively, and summarizing messages. Specifically, the competencies you will gain will enable you to do the following:*

- ▶ *Decide how much preparation to do for a speech presentation.*
- ▶ *Develop an impromptu speech.*
- ▶ *Develop an extemporaneous speech.*
- ▶ *Prepare a scratch outline, a working outline, and a presentational outline.*
- ▶ *Develop a manuscript speech.*
- ▶ *Select and create appropriate auxiliary materials.*
- ▶ *Develop a speech of introduction.*
- ▶ *Respond to audience members' questions.*

You have been asked to give a speech. You have completed the groundwork by assessing yourself, your audience, and the setting. You have selected a topic and developed a statement of purpose. You have done your research and collected the material you need. You have given some thought to how to develop the speech. Now, what do you do?

> Do you just get up and talk?
> Do you create an outline and use it as the basis for your speech?
> Do you write out the whole speech, word for word?

HOW DO YOU PREPARE?

This chapter will help you answer these and other questions that often arise when planning and preparing a speech. Other questions include: Should I prepare my speech prior to delivery or speak without preparation? Should I speak with or without notes, with a word-for-word written-out speech, or from an outline? Should I use audio, visual, or audiovisual aids during the presentation? If there will be a question-and-answer session following the presentation, how can I prepare for it?

TO PREPARE OR NOT TO PREPARE

You can choose to prepare or not to prepare for a speech. Not preparing for a speech could mean you are willing to face your audience without any formal notes or research. You may decide that you have enough personal information and are capable of presenting that material without formal preparation. Or you may decide that you don't have enough time to prepare and that you are willing to suffer the consequences. Not preparing for a speech could also mean that you do all the research necessary to prepare yourself, but stop short of actually putting the material together. You do not plan your information strategies, develop your logical and emotional appeals, organize your material, or practice. You may make this decision because you feel that having the information is enough to ensure success, or that preparing too much will destroy the spontaneity of your presentation.

In contrast, you may choose to make formal preparations. Most speakers choose this option because of its many benefits. These include feeling more secure, comfortable, and relaxed because you know the material; having greater familiarity with the ideas; and exercising stronger control because you can time the speech, select the words that best represent your ideas, and test the validity of your logical and emotional appeals.

There are three ways to present a speech: *impromptu*, *extemporaneous*, and *manuscript*. Each requires a different kind and amount of preparation. An impromptu speech is delivered without any formal development. An extemporaneous speech is delivered from a flexible outline or set of notes that guides the speaker through the speech without dictating the exact words that are used. A manuscript speech is completely written out and delivered exactly as it is written.

The Impromptu Speech

Whether you choose to develop your speech formally or not, you need never feel totally unprepared when you present a speech. If you are familiar with speech preparation techniques, you can format a presentation *as you speak*. Even an **impromptu speech**, one for which there is no formal development prior to delivery, should not be totally unprepared.

Although few people would choose to deliver a speech without formal preparation, a situation sometimes requires it. For example, you may be called on to toast someone at a dinner party, endorse a candidate with a short introduction, or present some information in class. Although you may not have realized it, you have delivered impromptu speeches in almost every conversation you've ever had—every time you've spoken for more than a minute, you were delivering a short, unprepared speech.

Every speech must include gaining the audience's attention, providing necessary background, stating your purpose, discussing your information, summarizing your key thoughts, and driving home your point. When you know this, you can enter any speaking situation with a mental outline that you can fill in as you proceed.

When giving an impromptu speech, you can use one of several simple formats during the "discussing your information" section. For instance, if you intend to present a pro-and-con speech, you can present all the arguments for an idea and then all the arguments against it. Your goal should be to avoid mixing the pros and cons because a mixture tends to confuse listeners and makes it difficult for you to remember where you are. For example, compare the following sequences for the topic of wearing seat belts:

Sequence 1

Arguments for wearing seat belts
    Saves lives
    Reduces severity of injuries
    Controls children's actions in moving car

Arguments against wearing seat belts
    Violates individual rights
    Raises cost of car
    Restricts ability to make quick exit from car

Sequence 2

Arguments for and against wearing seat belts
> Saves lives
> Reduces severity of injuries
> Violates individual rights
> Controls children's actions in moving car
> Raises cost of car
> Restricts ability to make quick exit from car

The first sequence clearly separates the arguments by placing them in pro and con categories that will help the audience to understand and retain the information. In the second sequence, because the pros and cons are scrambled, audience members will probably have a hard time telling which arguments are pro and which are con.

If you intend to present a problem and propose a solution, you can first define the problem, then present your solution, and finally explain why your solution is the best choice:

Problem: How to reduce air pollution

Solution: Fine companies that pollute

Advantages: Forces polluters to pay to clear the air they have dirtied
> Increases awareness of the problem
> Makes the public aware of who pollutes

Best solution: Those who pollute should pay to have the air cleaned

This format can be expanded to include several solutions. If you intend to describe how something is done or the order in which a series of events took place, you can present events in chronological order:

Topic: How to cook french fries

> First: Peel the potato.
> Second: Slice the potato into thin strips.
> Third: Place the strips in hot oil.
> Fourth: Remove the strips from the oil when they are lightly browned.

If you intend to present points of view, it is best to explain first why the topic is important to the audience, then discuss others' points of view, and finally present your ideas:

Topic: Standardized intelligence tests

> Why the issue of the validity of intelligence tests is important to the audience:
> > An individual's score on an intelligence test may have a profound influence on his or her life, but the tests are not always valid.

Others' points of view:
1. IQ tests measure only what a child has learned and not native intelligence.
2. The best teachers have their creative talents strangled by standardized achievement tests.

My point of view:
The evidence shows that intelligence tests are a tool of discrimination, are culturally biased, and are misused.

●KILL CHECKUP 15.1

Developing an Impromptu Speech

Prepare an outline for an impromptu speech. Set a timer or use your watch. In three minutes, prepare an outline for a speech on the topic "How to Develop an Outline for an Impromptu Speech."

The Extemporaneous Speech

If you decide to prepare your speech, and not make it impromptu, you might select the extemporaneous method. An **extemporaneous speech** is one in which a thorough but flexible outline or a set of notes guides the speaker through an oral presentation.

The chief advantage of an extemporaneous format is that you have a road map to follow as you travel through the speech. You know what is coming next and can use the information you have prepared to guide you to your goal.

Another advantage is the flexibility provided by the outline or notes. You can adapt your presentation to feedback by adding examples if the audience seems confused, reducing the length of time on a topic or the overall speech if the audience appears bored, or expanding areas in which the audience seems interested.

There are also disadvantages to the extemporaneous format. Because the words are not all written out, you may lose track of your ideas and grope for words. You may also wander from the outline and not find your way back. Finally, if you fear losing your place, nervousness may cause you to do just that.

Outlining the Extemporaneous Speech

An **outline** is a plan for a speech, developed in a standardized format of heads and subheads, that details the most significant features of a presentation.

Although usually done in sentences, some outlines are created using single words or short phrases.

Typically, an outline is constructed using a standard set of symbols, with main points represented by Roman numerals, major headings by capital letters, and minor headings by arabic numerals. Although further subdivisions in an outline often indicate a speech that is too detailed, points under minor headings are represented by lower-case letters.

An outline on the topic outlining looks like this:

I. This is the first main point.
   A. This is a major heading supporting the main point.
   B. This is another major heading supporting the main point.
      1. This is a minor heading support point B.
         a. This is a supporting example.
         b. This is another supporting example.
      2. This is another minor heading supporting point B.
      3. This is another minor heading supporting point B.
II. This is the second main point.

KNOWLEDGE CHECKUP 15.1

Unscrambling an Outline

Place the following information for a speech on fruits and vegetables into the outline form provided:

| apples | lettuce | McIntosh | Yellow Delicious | Red Delicious |
| vegetables | radishes | pears | fruits | cucumbers |

I.

  A.

    1.

    2.

    3.

  B.

II.

  A.

  B.

  C.

The outline for an extemporaneous speech may go through three stages of development, *scratch*, *working*, and *presentational*. The **scratch outline** is a rough indication of the material to be included in each of the six parts of the speech (gaining the audience's attention, providing necessary background, stating your purpose, discussing your information, summarizing your key ideas, and driving home the point). The following is an example of a scratch outline.

Topic: The need for kelp farms
I. List products that contain kelp.
II. Define kelp and where it is found.
III. Indicate why farms should be used to grow kelp.
IV. Explain what kelp is used for, how kelp is gathered, why kelp farms should be encouraged.
V. Repeat major points.
VI. Restate uses of kelp and why it should be farmed.

The **working outline** is an expanded version of the scratch outline. It contains the details—the logical and emotional support— for each main point of the discussion section of the speech, as well as expanded versions of the attention-getting background, purpose, summary, and final point sections. The following is an example of a working outline:

I. Products that contain kelp
   A. Marshmallows, syrup, candy, cream cheese, fruit fillings, pudding, milk shakes, and soft drinks
   B. All contain kelp
II. Kelp
   A. A species of brown seaweed
   B. Found in seacoasts around the world
   C. U.S. industries use kelp in various products
III. Why I feel farms should be used to grow kelp
   A. Makes harvests easier since they can be controlled
   B. Saves many fish and sea animals who need kelp in the ocean to survive
IV. Major points
   A. Kelp is used in many products
      1. To stop frost and ice particles from forming on several products
         a. In ice cream
         b. In popsicles
      2. To thicken texture
   B. How kelp is gathered
      1. Harvested by divers
      2. Processed in a way that is time-consuming and expensive
   C. Need for kelp farms
      1. Controlling environment ensures crop productivity

       2. Creating job opportunities
         a. Robert D. Wildman, Director of Project Support Programs of NOAA: "Owing to the changing of political climates, import of seaweed from other countries is not always dependable"
         b. Sixty percent of all kelp is imported
       3. Kelp farms would create jobs
       4. Farming kelp leaves natural kelp as a source of food and protection for fish and sea animals
  V. Kelp should be farmed
     A. Controlling growth environment ensures crop productivity
     B. Farming creates job opportunities
     C. Farming kelp leaves natural kelp as a source of food and protection for fish and sea animals
  VI. We need kelp farms now
     A. When people brush teeth or eat popsicles they consume kelp
     B. Better for nature and our economy if we farm kelp

    A **presentational outline** is the completed form from which a speaker gives a speech. It is a working outline modified during practice. Sometimes the working outline and the presentational outline are identical if no changes are found necessary during rehearsal. The speech on kelp was modified for the presentational outline by deleting the material that is crossed out and adding the material that is <u>underlined</u>.

    I. Products that contain kelp
     A. <u>Believe it or not</u>, marshmallows, syrup, candy, cream cheese, fruit fillings, pudding, milk shakes, and soft drinks <u>all have one thing in common</u>
     B. All contain kelp
   II. Kelp
     A. A species of brown seaweed
     B. Found in seacoasts around the world
     C. <u>Forms under sea forest to a height of 100 feet</u>
     D. U.S. industries use kelp in various products
  III. Why I feel farms should be used to grow kelp
     A. Makes harvests easier ~~since they can be controlled~~
     B. Saves many fish and sea animals who need kelp in the ocean to survive
  IV. ~~Major points~~ <u>Uses of kelp, harvesting kelp, and reasons to farm kelp</u>
     A. <u>How</u> kelp is used in ~~many~~ products
       1. To stop frost and ice particles from forming ~~on several products~~
         a. In ice cream
         b. In popsicles
       2. To thicken texture
         <u>a. Toothpaste</u>

          b. Shaving cream
          c. Hand lotion
    B. How kelp is gathered
      1. Harvested by divers
          a. On ocean floor
          b. Stalks cut manually
          c. Pulled aboard ships
          d. Dried
      2. Processed in a way that is time-consuming and expensive
    C. ~~Need for~~ Why kelp farms ~~are needed~~
      1. Controlling environment ensures crop productivity
      2. ~~Creating job opportunities~~ Farming ensures a steady supply
          a. Robert D. Wildman, Director of Project Support Programs of
             NOAA: "Owing to the changing of political climates, import
             of seaweed from other countries is not always dependable"
          b. Sixty percent of all kelp is imported
      3. Kelp farms would create jobs
      ~~4. Farming kelp leaves natural kelp as a source of food and protection for fish and sea animals~~
  V. Kelp should be farmed
    A. Controlling growth environment ensures crop productivity
    B. Farming creates job opportunities
    C. Farming kelp leaves natural kelp as a source of food and protection
       for fish and sea animals
  VI. We need kelp farms now
    A. When people brush teeth or eat popsicles they consume kelp
    B. It is better for nature and our economy if we farm kelp

SKILL CHECKUP 15.2

Correcting an Outline

Evaluate the following presentational outline on anorexia nervosa by considering its structure and the development of ideas: the background material presented, the clarity of the statement of purpose, the thoroughness of the support for the main points, and the repetition of the main ideas.

Topic: Anorexia nervosa

  I. Many of us have felt the need for attention from parents, family, and friends
    A. Act crazy
    B. Wear outlandish clothing
    C. Cut or color hair in bizarre ways

II. Anorexia nervosa

III. Discuss how anorexia nervosa affects people

IV. Causes of anorexia nervosa
    A. Need for control
    B. Striving for perfection—according to Dr. Raymond Vath, quoted in former anorexic Cherry Boone O'Neill's *Starving for Attention*
      1. Product of strict, middle-class background
        a. Demand for good grades
        b. Want child to achieve in everything
      2. Family weight-consciousness
        a. Being thin is desirable and praised
        b. Any weight gain is ridiculed
          (1) Anorexic perceives ridicule as criticism
          (2) Anorexics are very sensitive to criticism

V. Says psychoanalyst Barbara Kinoy, "Hopefully, some day these young women will feel worthy beyond appearance"

You may have noticed a great deal wrong with this outline. Did you note the following problems?

1. There was no definition of anorexia nervosa.
2. No background is provided in part II.
3. The statement of purpose does not present a specific goal; it indicates the general topic—anorexia nervosa.
4. Part IV A would have benefitted from the inclusion of examples.
5. There is no restatement of the main points of the speech (what is usually Part V).

The Manuscript Speech

A **manuscript speech** is completely written out and used as the basis for a presentation. The primary benefit of using a manuscript speech is the security that comes from spelling out all the words that will be used for the presentation. Another advantage is that if the way an idea is expressed is crucial (as in a political speech, where misinterpretation could be fatal to a career), reading from a manuscript ensures that the best wording will be used. A manuscript speech can be planned to make sure that the speaker stays within a prescribed time limit. In addition, in some instances, such as in corporate and governmental policy declarations, copies of a scripted speech can be distributed to media representatives to guarantee correct quoting.

There are four primary drawbacks to a manuscript speech:

1. Because written and spoken language are different, a written speech tends to sound awkward and stilted. For example, because contractions and slang are usual components of spoken language and not written language, they tend to be omitted from manuscript speeches, which makes them sound unnatural.

2. A speaker reading from a manuscript tends to use a flat, uninteresting tone of voice. This detracts from the speech because it draws attention to the presentation and away from the material being presented.

3. Manuscript readers tend to avoid making eye contact in order to keep their place in the script. This reduces the speaker's ability to receive audience feedback. Also, audience members may lose interest if they perceive that the speaker is not interested in them.

4. Finally, ironically, although a speaker may write out a speech in order to feel more secure, being dependent on the manuscript increases the fear of getting lost.

If you decide to use a manuscript speech, the most important thing you can do to make your talk more audience-centered is to write the manuscript the way you speak. Because you speak more casually than you write, you want to make sure that the audience hears your speaking style and not your more formal and complex writing style. For example, in *From Sad to Glad*, Nathan S. Kline writes, "If we can demonstrate that a specific medical condition arises from a particular cause—and only that cause—then we think we know with what we are dealing" (p. 43). Read the sentence aloud. Notice that it is too long, too complex, and, though grammatically correct, stilted sounding. A spoken version could be, "We know what medical condition we're dealing with if we know its cause."

When **talk-writing**, that is, creating your manuscript in an oral style, do the following:

> Use contractions (*it's* rather than *it is*).
> Use short sentences (usually no more than ten words).
> Leave out the word *that* whenever possible.
> Do not use *you* when referring to yourself.

●KILL CHECKUP 15.3

Converting a Manuscript from Written Style to Oral Style

Edit the following paragraph so that it is in clear oral style:

> Somebody has said that words are a lot like inflated money. That is, the
>
> more of them that you use, the less each one of them is worth. Right on.
>
> The rule you should follow is: Go through your entire speech as many

times as it is necessary. It is necessary to search out and annihilate all

unnecessary words and sentences—even entire paragraphs.

The edited version might read:

> Somebody said that words are like inflated money—the more you use, the less each one is worth. Go through the entire speech as many times as necessary. Take out all unnecessary words, sentences, and even paragraphs.

Guideposts for the Audience

Any speech, whether impromptu, extemporaneous, or manuscript, needs guideposts to help the audience follow what you're saying, understand your points, and remember what you want them to remember. Redundancy and pointers guide listeners to the points you want them to grasp. Using oral rather than written grammar rules will help keep your speech from sounding stilted. When presenting complex figures, keep in mind that round numbers are easier for your audience to understand and remember.

Build in redundancy by repeating ideas several different ways and by giving your audience some examples to clarify your point. Remember that a reader can go back and reread ideas until they are clear, but a listener only has one chance to grasp the material. For example, to make sure listeners understand, you might say, "Remember, you communicate more about your emotions with your face than with any other part of your body. Your eyes, eyebrows, forehead, lips, chin, mouth, and even the way you wrinkle your nose—all parts of your face—communicate."

Include a great many listening aids, such as pointers. **Pointers** are clues to the audience that something important is going to be said or was just said. The three most common pointers are previews, internal summaries, and final summaries.

Previews are statements that tell the audience what is going to come, such as, "There are three points to consider when we discuss how to use a word processor."

Internal summaries are condensed reviews that highlight what has just been said. A typical internal summary would be, "Therefore, the first point to remember in using a word processor is to familiarize yourself with the manual."

Final summaries are condensed reviews that repeat all the main points of a speech, such as, "The three main points to consider when using a word processor are: familiarize yourself with the manual, use the tutorial materials to learn the different functions of the program, and practice what you have learned."

SKILL CHECKUP 15.4

Previews and Summaries

Complete the body of the following speech by supplying an appropriate preview, internal summary, and final summary.

(Preview)

The first technique is to use contractions freely. Use *don't, it's, haven't,* and *there's* instead of *do not, it is, have not,* and *there is.*

(Internal summary)

The second technique is to use short words. Long, pompous words are a curse. What would Shakespeare have sounded like if he had written "All is well that terminates well"? Replace *locate* with *find, prior to* with *before,* and *sufficient* with *enough.*

(Internal summary)

(Final summary)

A preview statement could be: There are two techniques to "talking on paper."

The first internal summary could be: Use contractions.

The second internal summary could be: Use short words.

The final summary could be: Two techniques for "talking on paper" are use contractions and use short words.

Use oral grammar rules rather than written grammar rules. These more relaxed rules allow the use of sentence fragments and some slang. Of course, you still should not use substandard English, such as double negatives ("I ain't got no money"); include slang that is offensive to your listeners; or break grammar rules in ways that confuse listeners or draw attention to your poor language skills ("I goes down the street and said to him").

Round off numbers to help listeners understand complex figures. "There were 77.326 percent, or 987,346, positive responses," would be better expressed as "There were approximately 80 percent, or one million, positive responses."

AUXILIARY MATERIALS

Different people gain information in different ways. Some are best at grasping ideas presented orally. Others need visual stimulation. And others need a combination of oral and visual input. Although smell, touch, and taste are also senses through which information is gathered, they play a smaller role in public speaking (unless, of course, your speech is about the difference between men's and women's colognes, how to give a massage, or wine tasting).

Some speech topics or parts of a speech are best communicated using **auxiliary materials**—audio, visual, and audiovisual devices that clarify or illustrate your spoken message. A speech about twentieth-century architecture would be confusing and incomplete without pictures of the buildings designed by such architects as Edward Stone and Frank Lloyd Wright. Descriptions of their works would not communicate what the buildings look like as clearly or vividly as drawings or photographs. In addition, the use of pictures eliminates the need for wordy descriptions.

Types of Auxiliary Materials

Auxiliary materials fall into three broad categories—visual aids, audio aids, and audiovisual aids.

Visual Aids

Visual aids are auxiliary materials that depend on the sense of sight. The three primary types of visual aids are objects, representations of objects, and charts.

Objects   **Objects** are the actual items referred to in a speech, such as a tennis racquet used to demonstrate a backhand stroke or a floppy disk used to show how to care for computer equipment.

Representations of Objects   **Representations of objects** are likenesses, images, or other reproductions. A likeness of an object is often presented as a model, such as a miniature Statue of Liberty in a speech on how the statue was refurbished in the mid-1980s. Models have several advantages over real objects: they can be smaller, larger, or less complex. For example, it would obviously be impossible to bring the real Statue of Liberty to a classroom speech. A live fruit fly is too small to show to a large audience, but an enlarged representation would be a practical substitute. And a model of the brain that can be disassembled to show the various parts is easier to work with and generally more acceptable to an audience than an actual brain.

Images, such as pictures and diagrams, can also be used in place of real objects. Photographs, paintings, drawings, and sketches can be used to help listeners visualize objects, places, and events referred to in your speech. Instead of bringing in a combustion engine for a speech on how pistons

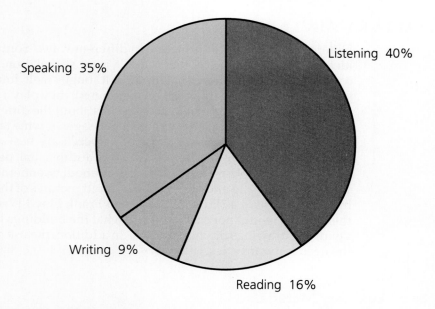

Listening 40%

Speaking 35%

Writing 9%

Reading 16%

▶ **FIGURE 15.1** Pie Graph—Percentage of Time Spent in Various Communication Activities

work, a drawing or sketch would suffice. A series of photographs showing the Great Wall of China clarify what the structure looks like. And a speech on abstract and cubist art would be virtually meaningless without reproductions of paintings in those styles.

Charts **Charts** can be maps or graphs. A **map** is a representation of the surface of the earth or any part of it, or of the universe or any part of it. A speech about Australia would be greatly helped by a map showing its geographical features and its location in relationship to the United States.

A **graph** is a pictorial representation of numbers or the relationship of numbers to each other. There are three kinds of graphs: pie graphs, bar graphs, and line graphs. A **pie graph** is used to illustrate the division of a whole (100 percent) into parts. It consists of a circle divided into parts that each symbolize a percentage of a whole. It looks much like a whole apple pie that has been sliced into pieces of varying sizes. For example, the pie graph in figure 15.1 shows the percentages of time people spend in various communication activities.[1]

A **bar graph** uses columns of various heights to display numbers. They are often used to compare and contrast numbers. For example, the bar graph

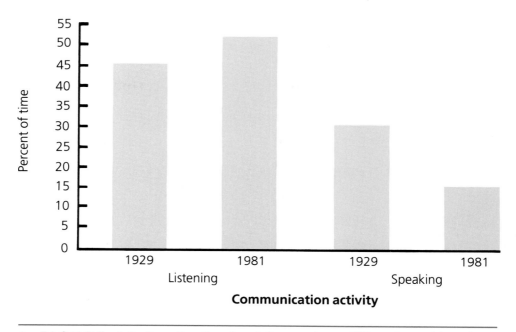

▶ **FIGURE 15.2** Bar Graph—A Comparison of Time Spent Listening and Speaking in 1929 and 1981

in figure 15.2 compares the results from two different studies of how much time people spend listening and speaking.[2]

If you connected the midpoints of the tops of each of the bars in a bar graph with a series of lines, you would have a **line graph**. Line graphs are particularly useful for showing trends. For example, the line graph in figure 15.3 shows the pattern in the number of applications to the University of North Carolina at Chapel Hill Law School from 1984 through 1989.[3]

Audio and Audiovisual Aids

Audio aids are auxiliary materials that depend on the sense of hearing. The two most common audio aids are records and audiotapes. For example, to illustrate how the human voice communicates emotion, a tape recording of the radio announcer reporting the explosion of the Hindenberg zeppelin could be used.

Audiovisual aids are auxiliary materials that depend on both sight and hearing. They include such devices as videotapes, films, and tape-slide presentations. A videotape of testimony during a Senate hearing could be used to clarify the role of questions in government proceedings.

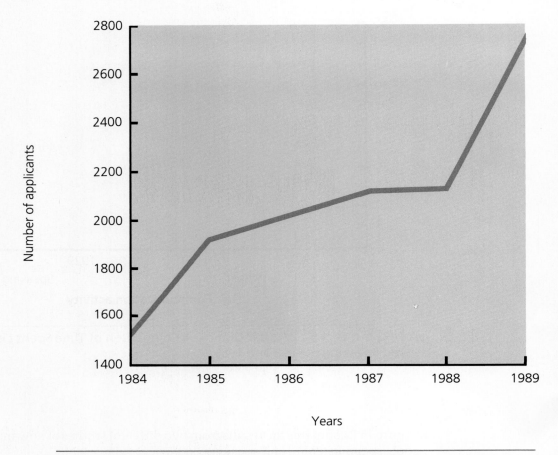

▶ **FIGURE 15.3** Line Graph—Number of Applications to the University of North Carolina at Chapel Hill Law School from 1984 through 1989

SKILL CHECKUP 15.5

Choosing Auxiliary Materials

What types of auxiliary material would you use for each of the following topics?

1. A speech about the musical sound of the Beatles
2. A comparison of the art of Van Gogh and Renoir
3. A demonstration of Chinese wok cooking

4. A speech contrasting the population growth of three countries

5. A speech demonstrating the set design for the play *My Fair Lady* in which you show how the pieces of the set will actually be moved during the performance

6. A speech to a planning commission illustrating the site for a new housing development and how the buildings will be arranged

7. A speech contrasting the verbal and nonverbal comedic styles of Billy Crystal and George Carlin

Although responses may vary, one possibility for each speech topic is as follows:

1. Play a record or an audiotape of a Beatles song
2. Display reproductions of the works of Van Gogh and Renoir
3. Bring an actual wok to the presentation and show how it is used
4. Use a bar or line graph to compare the growth patterns
5. Demonstrate the movements of the set by using a model with adjustable parts
6. Illustrate the construction with a map of the land
7. Play videotapes of Billy Crystal and George Carlin in performance to illustrate their differences in style

Guidelines for Selecting Auxiliary Materials

For some speeches the use of auxiliary materials is an absolute necessity, as in the speech about the backhand stroke in tennis. Other speeches would benefit from the use of auxiliary materials, but their use is optional, as in the speech about computer equipment. In each case, the question that needs to be answered is, "Will my speech be more successful—will the audience members have a better understanding of what I'm saying—if I use an auxiliary aid?" If the answer is yes, use it.

Choose and develop your auxiliary materials with a specific purpose in mind. Decide exactly what you want your audience to gain from your auxiliary material. If you lack a clear purpose, you risk confusing the audience rather than helping them. Auxiliary materials should never be mere decorations, with only a passing relationship to your speech.

Ask yourself if the auxiliary materials you have selected will accomplish your goal. To work well the materials must suit both the audience and the setting for the speech. An aid will be suitable for your listeners if, based on your audience analysis:

▶ It reflects their level of understanding (A cartoon-style drawing of a combustion engine may be appropriate for a beginning driver's education class but it would probably not appeal to a group of experienced auto mechanics.)

▶ It fits their needs (Showing a group of students enrolled in their first art appreciation class a cubist painting is necessary for their understanding, but such an example would not be needed when speaking about cubism to art historians.)

▶ It satisfies their expectations for the speech (A presentation on how to play a twelve-string guitar that does not include a guitar performance would probably frustrate the audience.)

▶ It reflects the desired tone of the speech (Humorous speeches require humorous materials, such as cartoons or caricatures, while speeches on serious topics call for materials that are straightforward and meaningful, such as statistical graphs.)

An aid is suitable for the environment if, based on your analysis of the setting:

▶ The equipment necessary to present your auxiliary materials is available (such as a projector, screen, flip chart, easel, audio speakers, record player, videotape recorder, or television screen)

▶ The material is in a form that can be seen or heard easily from all parts of the room (for example, lines on graphs are bold, drawings are uncluttered, and audio material is static-free)

SKILL CHECKUP 15.6

Assessing Auxiliary Materials

Imagine that you are preparing the following speech.

Statement of purpose: To inform the audience how the Statue of Liberty was refurbished by illustrating the process that was used.
Audience: Your communication classmates
Setting: Your communication classroom

1. What auxiliary materials would you use?

2. To determine whether the auxiliary materials you selected suit your audience, answer the following questions:
   a. Do the materials reflect the audience members' understanding of the topic?
   b. Do the materials fit their needs and help them understand what you are saying?
   c. Do the materials satisfy their expectations for the speech?
   d. Do the materials reflect your desired tone?

3. To determine whether the auxiliary materials you selected suit the setting for the speech, answer the following questions:
   a. Do you have the necessary equipment to present your auxiliary materials?
   b. Given the characteristics of the setting in which you will speak, will the auxiliary materials be easily seen and/or heard by all members of the audience?

MANAGING THE SPEAKING EVENT

Many speakers assume that their sole responsibility is to present their planned speech. While this may be true for many situations, it is not always the case. You must be prepared to take care of certain things before and after your formal presentation.

Before the Speech

Except in classroom situations, where speakers are not usually introduced, both speakers and audiences expect that an introduction will be given. It may be a simple statement, such as "Louise is going to speak next" or "Louise is going to tell us about her plan for the upcoming election." Or it may include pertinent biographical information, such as "Our next speaker, Louise Roberts, a graduate of our state university, has served as mayor for three terms and is now undertaking a race for the state senate. She will talk to us today about her plan for tax revisions."

If someone is going to introduce you, you should be ready to suggest information you would like included or excluded and to recommend the emotional tone that would be appropriate to set. You should provide your name as you want it presented; relevant background, such as education and work experience, as well as your qualifications to speak about your topic; and any information or story that will let audience members know you a bit more personally.

If someone else does not introduce you, it is your obligation to introduce yourself. One method is to begin with several remarks about who you are and why you are speaking to this particular group, on this particular occasion, about this particular topic. For example, if Mayor Roberts weren't introduced by someone else, she could say, "With the state senate elections coming up, I am very happy to be speaking to you about my plan for tax revision because I feel this will be an important issue in this election. My years as mayor of your city and my economics degree from our state university have given me the experience and background to discuss financial matters with you."

A second method is to incorporate relevant information into your speech at the appropriate time.   Thus, when Mayor Roberts talks about financial reform, she can mention her degree in economics.   And when she discusses political procedures, she can mention her experience as mayor.

SKILL CHECKUP 15.7

Writing an Introduction

You have been asked to speak about how to prepare a speech to a group of high school students who have come to your campus to learn about college courses. Write two introductions: (1) the one you would want someone else to give in presenting you to the audience, and (2) the one you would give for yourself if no one introduced you.

After the Speech

Although you may not be called upon to respond to questions from the audience, you should prepare your talk as if there will be questions. This means that you need to have more material at your command than you plan to present in your prepared talk. If the depth of your knowledge is limited to what you say in your speech, you are probably asking for trouble.

People ask questions after a speech for five different reasons:

1. They are confused by what you said and would like clarification.
2. They understood what you said, but want more in-depth information.
3. They are interested in what you had to say and would like you to continue speaking.
4. They want verification of points you made in your speech.
5. They want the opportunity either to express what they are thinking or to launch into a counter-speech.

In each case, with the exception of audience members who want to give their own speeches, there is a format for answering that you can develop as you speak. Your answer is nothing more than an impromptu speech with a beginning, middle, and end.

1. *Repeat the question* in your own words. This ensures that all audience members know what has been asked. It also allows you to check your comprehension of the question and shows the questioner that you understand. Such repetition serves as the introduction to your answer.

2. *Answer the question by relating it to something you presented in the speech.* Expand, if necessary, by defining unclear or misunderstood terms, giving examples, and/or paraphrasing your original comments. Keep your answer short and to the point.

3. *Summarize the key idea of your answer and ask the questioner if your response was adequate and clear.* If the questioner accepts the answer, move on to the next question without additional comments. For example, if a questioner asks, "What did you mean when you said communication is proactive?" you could respond, "You wish to know what I meant by proactive. Proactive means responding to a message in a way that reflects your unique background and experiences. For instance, as you listened to my speech, you responded based on your family background and your religious and political beliefs. Others may have responded differently from you because they have different backgrounds and experiences. You and they were both responding proactively." Look for feedback, such as a head nod, that indicates you were understood. If there isn't any clear indication, ask, "Okay?" or "Does that clarify what *proactive* means?"

4. *If the answer was inadequate or unclear, start the process over* by asking the audience member to rephrase the question so it specifically emphasizes what was not covered in your answer.

5. In answering, *stay focused on the person who asked the question.* Maintain eye contact, watch for feedback that indicates understanding, such as head nods, and do not become distracted by others who want to ask questions or are not interested in the particular line of questioning.

6. *If you are unsure of an answer, say so* and, if you like, offer to find out the information and contact the audience member later. It is never wise to fake your way through a response. If audience members perceive you are faking, you will lose credibility and destroy whatever effect you could have had.

It is not uncommon for a questioner to ask more than one question at a time. In answering, separate the questions and deal with them individually, unless it is possible to join them in a single coherent response.

When people want to give their own speeches or argue with what you had to say, you have two options: Either you can let them speak or you can stop them from speaking. You may choose to keep someone from giving a counter-speech because the audience isn't interested, because there isn't enough time, because you believe nothing can be gained, because a number of other people have questions, or because it would be embarrassing to you or to members of the audience. In such cases, it is important to stop the person as soon as possible by saying something like, "Thank you very much for your comments, but we have questions that we need to handle at this time," or "Thank you for bringing up an alternative viewpoint, but right now what we need to do is clarify what we have been talking about."

Because it is difficult to satisfy a person who is intent on giving a counter speech, you should not even try. It is more productive to spend your energy on accomplishing your purpose for giving your speech.

⬤KILL CHECKUP 15.8

Responding to Questions

You have just completed your presentation on how to prepare a speech, and one of the high school students says, "I don't understand the distinction between impromptu and extemporaneous speaking."

1. What do you say?

2. Evaluate you answer by responding to the following three questions.
   a. Did you paraphrase the question at the beginning of your response?
   b. Did you answer the question by relating it to something you stated in your speech?
   c. Did you summarize your answer and ask if it was satisfactory?

COMMUNICATION COMPETENCY CHECKUP

The student in the drawing is confused. He needs to make several presentational choices about his speech.

1. What three methods of presentation are available to him? What are the advantages and disadvantages of each method?

2. Your discussion of methods of presentation persuades him to use the extemporaneous form. Describe how to move from a scratch outline to a working outline to a presentational outline.

3. He tells you that his speech topic is the history of baseball's American League. He wants to know what auxiliary material he could use in the section on the various types of bats. He worries that listeners will need clarification of his explanation of the configurations of the various stadiums. And he is also thinking of demonstrating three songs that are traditionally identified with baseball. What advice do you have for him?

4. You have given him so much help with his speech that he wants you to introduce him. What information do you need from him in order to prepare a speech of introduction?

5. He is terrified that after his speech someone will ask a question that he won't know how to handle. Calm him down by describing the procedure he can use for answering questions.

NOTES

1. Paul Rankin, "Listening Ability," in *Proceedings of the Ohio State Educational Conference's Ninth Annual Session*, 1929.

2. These results compare Rankin's 1929 study with a study by Larry Barker, R. Edwards, C. Gaines, K. Gladney, and F. Holley, "An Investigation of Proportional Time Spent in Various Communication Activities by College Students," *Journal of Applied Communication Research* 8 (1981): 101–9.

3. *Chapel Hill Herald*, February 20, 1989, p. 1.

FOR FURTHER INVESTIGATION

Carlile, Clark S., and Arlie V. Daniel, Jr. *Project Text for Public Speaking*, 5th ed. New York: Harper and Row, 1987.

Fisher, Tom, and Tracey L. Smith. *Icebreaker: A Manual for Public Speaking*. Prospect Heights, IL: Waveland Press, 1985.

Fletcher, Leon. *How to Design & Deliver a Speech*, 3d ed. New York: Harper and Row, 1985.

Gregory, Hamilton. *Public Speaking for College and Career*. New York: Random House, 1987.

Haskins, William A., and Joseph M. Staudacher. *Successful Public Speaking: A Practical Guide*. Glenview, IL: Scott, Foresman, 1987.

LeRoux, Paul. "Mastering the Art of the Winning Presentation." *Working Woman* (February 1985): 84–86.

O'Malley, Christopher. "Making Quick Presentations: How to Get Better Visuals in Minutes." *Personal Computing* (December 1985): 76–83.

Rodman, George. *Public Speaking*, 3d ed. New York: Holt, Rinehart and Winston, 1986.

Samavor, Larry A., and Jack Mills. *Oral Communication: Message and Response*, 6th ed. Dubuque, IA: Wm. C. Brown, 1986.

Welsh, James J. *The Speechwriting Guide*. Florida: Krieger Publishing, 1979.

Zeuschner, Raymond Bud. *Building Clear Communication*. Glenview, IL: Scott, Foresman, 1985.

CHAPTER 16

▶ # *Public Speaking: Presenting the Speech*

*This chapter on speech presentation will help you practice and develop communication competencies that fall into two broad categories: (1) **communication codes**, which include using words, pronunciation, and grammar that are appropriate to a particular situation; using appropriate nonverbal signs; and using your voice effectively; and (2) **oral message evaluation**, which includes recognizing when a member of your audience does not understand your message and whether an oral presentation accomplishes its goals. Specifically, the competencies you will gain will enable you to do the following:*

▶ *Identify common behaviors associated with speechophobia.*
▶ *Cite some common causes of speechophobia.*
▶ *Deal with speechophobia.*
▶ *Recognize and avoid common verbal delivery distractors in public speaking situations.*
▶ *Recognize and avoid common nonverbal delivery distractors in public speaking situations.*
▶ *Evaluate your own public speaking presentations.*

*H*ere are some common causes of anxiety associated with public speaking. Check the ones that affect you as a public speaker.

_____ I feel the audience is more important than I am.

_____ A very important person is in the audience.

_____ People I don't know are in the audience.

_____ People I know well are in the audience.

_____ I'm unsure whether I'm well prepared.

_____ I feel pressured because there is a time limit.

_____ I don't know enough about the topic.

_____ I'm nervous because the speech will be graded/evaluated/reviewed.

_____ My voice will sound funny because I have to use a microphone.

_____ I'll sound or look ridiculous because the speech will be tape recorded or videotaped.

_____ I'm not going to be entertaining.

_____ I might say something offensive to others.

_____ I'll look silly because I don't know what to do with my hands.

_____ I'll look nervous because I tend to walk around a lot when I speak.

_____ I'll look nervous because my voice trembles/knees knock hands shake/face gets red.

_____ I'm afraid I'll lose my place in my notes.

_____ I'll drop my notes as I speak and I'll make a fool of myself.

_____ The audience won't understand me and I'll make a fool of myself.

_____ What I have to say isn't important and I'll make a fool of myself.

_____ The audience won't like me.

_____ My topic is dull/stupid/boring and people won't pay attention.

SPEECHOPHOBIA[1]

No matter how many items you check, you can overcome your public speaking anxiety. Nothing inherent in any of the situations in the checklist creates anxiety—*your* perceptions are what lead to difficulty. An important person *may* be in the audience, people you don't know *may* be present, or you may say something that offends someone; but none of these is automatically a problem. You have a problem only when you allow one of these factors to interfere with your performance or to set the stage for panic.

Consider this: Your speech is prepared. You are ready to stand up and share your ideas. Despite all the well-laid plans you developed and carried out in your preparation, however, you still have one more hurdle to jump—presenting your speech. But if you have some knowledge of the oral and physical components of speech presentation, you can take this hurdle in stride.

Speechophobia is the anxiety associated with public speaking. Some of the common signs of speechophobia include thinking obsessively about giving the speech or, conversely, purposely putting off preparation; being unable to concentrate on anything, including the speech; manifesting physical signs of anxiety, such as a pounding heart, nausea, headache, and sweating palms, when thinking about giving the speech; and visualizing impending disaster.

Speechophobia has two components: anxiety that arises before giving a speech and anxiety that arises while giving a speech. You may have heard friends say, "I was a nervous wreck for days before I had to give my speech, but it really wasn't so bad once I started speaking," or, "I felt fine until I stood up and saw all those eyes staring at me." Of course, you may be the kind of person who experiences neither type of anxiety, but you likely feel some discomfort. A moderate amount of anxiety should be expected and accepted—it may even prove beneficial. Physically, anxiety increases the flow of adrenaline, which heightens your senses. This heightened awareness allows many people to be more alert, animated, and responsive to the audience. Nevertheless, if you think your anxiety is too high, you need to take steps to reduce it.

If you are the kind of person who solves problems by thinking them through and understanding their causes, knowing what leads to your speechophobia should allow you to control it. You can then rationally analyze the situation and come up with a logical solution—very much like *Star Trek's* Mr. Spock does. If you are the kind of person who solves problems more intuitively, knowing their causes may not be very helpful. Instead, you can tackle your fear by learning stress-reducing methods of relaxation. No matter how you prefer to tackle problems, there are a range of techniques you can use to reduce and manage any anxiety you might feel.

Dealing with Speechophobia

The four basic ways of controlling or overcoming speechophobia are to adopt appropriate attitudes, prepare, rehearse, and relax.

Appropriate Attitudes

Three attitudes that are appropriate for public speakers and help deal with speechophobia are, "I don't have to be perfect," "I don't have to please everyone," and "The audience members want me to succeed."[2]

There is no such thing as perfection. No one has ever given a speech that is perfect or that is perfectly awful. Most speeches have both strengths and weaknesses, and every speech could benefit from a little more work and some alteration of oral and nonverbal presentation. You should strive for your very best performance, but don't feel you have to be perfect!

Go back and reread the items you checked in the questionnaire at the beginning of the chapter, adding the phrase "and I have to be perfect" to each one. Say, for example, "A very important person is in the audience *and I have to be perfect.*" Then reread the items you checked and add the phrase "and no one will like me." For example, say, "My voice will sound funny if I have to use a microphone *and no one will like me.*" Your drives to be perfect and to be liked by everyone may be the roots for much of your public speaking anxiety.

You can adopt an attitude only if you actually *believe* it. Therefore, the next time you hear your internal voice say, "Be *perfect!*" counter with "I can be myself," "I can be human," "I can make mistakes," and, perhaps most difficult of all, "I can accept failure." And the next time you hear your internal voice say, "Every audience member must like my speech," counter with "My audience analysis indicates my topic and material are appropriate—and it's OK if some people don't like it." If your self-talk doesn't work, recall Mark Twain's advice to a speechophobic friend, "Just remember, they don't expect much."

In most cases audience members want you to succeed. They are there to learn from you, to hear new points of view, and even to be amused, not to judge your speechophobia or your ability to cope under pressure. Most audience members will know less than you do about your topic, so you need not fear that they'll challenge everything you say. Above all, the audience wants you to succeed because they don't want to waste their time.

Of course, accepting being less than perfect and accepting that not everyone will be pleased by what you have to say does not mean that you shouldn't strive for excellence through good audience analysis, preparation, and rehearsal.

Preparation

If you have the opportunity to prepare and don't, you are inviting speechophobia. Few people can effectively ad-lib a speech; fortunately, even fewer situations demand an ad-libbed speech. Your fear of making a bad impression because you haven't adequately prepared places additional stress on you. Thus, the obvious solution is to prepare.

Did you check the fifth, sixth or seventh items in the speechophobia questionnaire? Those items most clearly relate to preparing your speech, and your checking them indicates that your feelings of speechophobia fall in that area.

A key to preparation is managing your time effectively. With the time constraints of work, school, relationships, and other responsibilities in mind, you need to allow yourself enough time to prepare your speech. Not all people need the same amount of preparation time. You need to assess your familiarity with the topic, your experience in speech preparation and presentation, and the amount of time you will need simply to consider and reconsider what you will say. An honest assessment should yield a good estimate of the amount of time you need to schedule for preparation.

In deciding how much preparation you need, your minimum goal should be to gather enough information to create your speech and have some left over to answer basic questions from the audience afterward. You will probably sense when you have reached your comfort level with the amount of material you have gathered. As you gain more experience in preparing speeches, you will find it easier and easier to recognize when enough is enough.

Rehearsal

Rehearsing your presentation serves a number of purposes, all of which also help you feel more comfortable as you deliver your speech. Rehearsal will help you with the following points:

- ▶ Gain familiarity with your material
- ▶ Discover which parts of your talk may be hard to understand and thus need to be changed
- ▶ Find out how long your speech lasts
- ▶ Identify and practice the pronunciation of unfamiliar words
- ▶ Develop oral transitions that smoothly connect one part of your speech to another
- ▶ Practice using supplementary materials, such as charts, graphs, and slides
- ▶ Try out different ways of saying your ideas

Begin by practicing informally. Deliver your speech to yourself, making adjustments as you proceed. Don't worry about timing. Instead, look for illogical structure, lack of clarifying materials, words that are difficult to pronounce, sections that are too long or too short, and parts that make you feel uncomfortable for any reason whatsoever.

Once you've worked out the major problems through informal practice, you can begin formal rehearsals. There are a variety of formal rehearsal techniques that you may use either alone or in combination. Perhaps the easiest one is to deliver your speech in an empty room, visualizing an audience. If you know your audience and your setting, as you know the members of your class and your classroom, you can picture them specifically. Deliver your speech as if the actual event were happening: stand, maintain eye contact with your "audience members," use your notes and supplementary materials, and present the entire speech so that you can estimate your delivery time.

Use this first formal rehearsal to make any necessary changes. For example, expand or shorten supporting material, reorganize sections for clarity, or alter the introduction or conclusion.

Then continue to practice until you feel comfortable with your material and are sure that it will fulfill your purpose. You may try practicing in front of a mirror, audio- or videotaping your performance, or asking a group of friends or family members to listen to you. Just remember that feedback from friends and family members may or may not be useful, depending on their understanding of the requirements for an effective speech and their own biases.

As you rehearse, you may discover that you need to add both specific and general hints to your notes to make your presentation more effective. For example, you may want to write out the pronunciations of difficult words, mark places you want to pause, identify sections that should be presented quickly or slowly, or remind yourself where and how you want to use supplementary aids. You may also want to highlight important ideas, words, or transitions.

The night before you give your speech, rehearse using visualization. In **visualization**, you imagine yourself actually going through the experience of giving a successful speech.[3] Do the following:

1. Close your eyes and imagine yourself in the speech setting.
2. Feel sure of your material and your ability to present your speech forcefully and convincingly.
3. See yourself get up from your chair, walk to the front of the room, and arrange your notes and supplementary materials.
4. See yourself pause, look at the audience, and present the introduction. You feel good about this presentation.
5. See members of the audience paying attention and nodding affirmatively.
6. Picture one or more members of the audience, whom you know, smiling at you.
7. Continue through the presentation, imagining positive feedback from the audience members.
8. Find yourself paying attention to the head nodders while making sure that your eye contact covers the entire audience.
9. Feel very good that you have practiced and developed an effective speech. It is going even better than you expected.
10. Conclude the presentation and hear applause from the audience.
11. Feel full of energy and have a sense of general well-being.
12. Return to your seat feeling good about what you have done. You have given a successful speech! Congratulate yourself!

Repeat that visual sequence over and over until you believe you can and will be successful. This is self-fulfilling prophecy in action. You are likely to do well because you have prepared and expect to do well.

Relaxation

Your body responds to speechophobia with muscle tension. Body relaxation techniques can relieve these feelings.

Autogenic relaxation, using verbal instructions to teach your mind and body to relax, creates a state very much like a hypnotic trance by inducing warmth and calmness. When you feel stress about giving a speech, you can try the following autogenic technique:

Step 1. Sit comfortably in a chair or on a stool, with your arms resting on your thighs and one hand forming a relaxed fist.

Step 2. Locate a spot on the ceiling or wall.

Step 3. Concentrate on the spot. Within a few moments it should begin to blur.

Step 4. Slowly close your eyes.

Step 5. Imagine a tranquil scene that includes some kind of flowing motion, such as waves breaking on the shore, floating clouds, or a kite in flight.

Step 6. Become aware of your breathing. Synchronize your breathing with the flow of motion that you are picturing. Breathe in through your nose, slowly bringing the warm air up the front of your head, over your skull, down the entire length of your body to your heels, across the soles of your feet, up the front of your body, and out your mouth.

Step 7. Repeat the process until your tension is gone.

Step 8. When all your tension has been released, slowly open your eyes. If you find it difficult to open your eyes, slowly unfold your fingers one at a time.

Another approach to relaxation, **progressive relaxation**, employs deep muscle techniques that do not require imagination. The following exercise, designed for a quick release of tension, would be appropriate just before you deliver your speech.

Step 1. While either sitting or standing, drop both hands to your sides. Raise the stronger of your two hands to the front of your stomach and turn your palm up to face the ceiling. Place your other hand, palm down, on top of the first hand. Clasp hands. Be sure that your elbows are not touching your body or resting on the arms of your chair.

Step 2. Force your bottom hand upward while forcing your top hand downward. Place enough pressure on your hands to cause your arms to quiver. Continue this isometric action until your arms are tired.

Step 3. Drop your hands to your sides. You should feel the release of tension in your body. If you do not, you may not have forced your hands together hard enough or long enough.

DELIVERY

An effective speech depends not only on what you say, but on how you say it. Your verbal and nonverbal presentation may either enhance your material or distract from it. In presenting material, you must remove as many distractions as possible.

KNOWLEDGE CHECKUP 16.1

Distracting Speaking Behaviors

When you are in an audience, what do speakers do that distracts your attention from the message being presented?

_____ 1. Use empty words or phrases such as "you know," "stuff like that," "well, uh," and "um, uh."

_____ 2. Present supplementary aids without explaining their purpose.

_____ 3. Present supplementary aids and either not explaining them enough or providing too much detail.

_____ 4. Use incorrect grammar.

_____ 5. Use "you" instead of "I" when talking about personal experiences (for example, saying, "When you work in a fast-food restaurant" instead of "In my work in a fast-food restaurant").

_____ 6. Use excessive slang.

_____ 7. Swear.

_____ 8. Use nonexistent words, such as "irregardless" and "alls."

_____ 9. Mispronounce words.

_____ 10. Shuffle feet.

_____ 11. Lean on the podium.

_____ 12. Not maintain eye contact.

_____ 13. Avoid the audience by looking at the lectern, ceiling, floor, or back wall.

_____ 14. Play with a supplementary aid (toss chalk in the air and catch it or tap the pointer on the desk, for instance).

_____ 15. Talk to a supplementary aid instead of to the audience.

_____ 16. Use a supplementary aid at the wrong time.

_____ 17. Fidget and drum fingers.

_____ 18. Unnecessarily shuffle or flip note cards or script pages.

_____ 19. Speak too fast or too slow.

_____ 20. Speak in a monotone.

_____ 21. Use inappropriate gestures, such as stilted, overly rehearsed movements or lack of body motion.

_____ 22. Show uncoordinated verbal and nonverbal behavior, such as using words that indicate excitement while speaking slowly and without facial expression.

Verbal Presentation

The twenty-two items in Knowledge Checkup 16.1 are common roadblocks to effective verbal and nonverbal presentation of a speech. The first nine describe problems that may turn up in your verbal presentation, while the last thirteen pertain to nonverbal presentation. All should be avoided.

As you plan what you'll say during your speech, try to avoid empty words and phrases. Comments like "you know" and "stuff like that" add nothing to your message and may confuse or sidetrack your audience. Audience members may try to figure out whether they really do "know" and determine what other "stuff" is "like that."

Your goal in using visual, audiovisual, or audio aids is to help the audience understand. If you don't explain why the aid is being used, fail to offer enough detail to make the aid understandable, or give so much detail that the aid becomes either confusing or irrelevant, you defeat your purpose.

The words you choose and how you use them reflect on your character as a speaker. Audiences place little faith in speakers who have weak oral language skills, including the following:

- Poor grammar (changing tenses, making incorrect subject-verb agreements, using sentence fragments)
- Using too many "he's," "she's," and "it's" without clear references
- Coining words (making up words that don't actually exist but sound as if they do)
- Using slang and swearing that are inappropriate for the audience
- Mispronunciations

The appropriateness of slang varies with the setting. Your audience analysis should indicate whether your listeners' background and experience will equip them to understand your slang. Swearing, on the other hand, is always a risk. If your goal is to provoke your audience, swearing may be an effective tool. It may also work if you are trying to emphasize an idea. However, many people find swearing so offensive that they will reject everything you have to say because of one objectionable word.

Although pronunciation varies from community to community and from culture to culture, most words have standard pronunciations. If you mispronounce too many words, your audience may decide that you are ill-informed or have not taken the time to find out correct pronunciations.

SKILL CHECKUP 16.1

Commonly Mispronounced Words[4]

Here is a list of commonly mispronounced words. Cover the columns marked *Wrong Pronunciation* and *Right Pronunciation* and go through the first column, saying each word aloud and then checking your pronunciation. Practice any word you pronounce incorrectly.

Correct Spelling	Wrong Pronunciation	Right Pronunciation
across	akrawst	akraws
acts	aks	akts
actually	ak shuh lee	ak choo u lee
all	awls	awl
any	inny	enny
asked	axed	askt
because	becuz	becawz
catch	kech	kach
doing	dewin	dewing
etcetera	ek set er uh	et set er uh
facts	faks	fakts
familiar	familuyuh	fa mi lyur
february	feb yu ay ree	feb roo ay ree
fifth	fith or fif	fifth
friendly	frenly	frend lee
genuine	jen yu wine	jen yu in
going	gowin	gowing
horror	hawr	hawr or
hundred	hun dert	hun dred
introduce	innerdoos	in tro dyoos
just	jist	juhst
library	lie berry	lie brear ee
next	nex	next
nuclear	nookouluhr	noo klee uhr
particular	paticula	per tik you luhr
picture	pi chur	pik chur
prescription	per skrip shun	pri skrip shun
probably	prah blee	prah buh blee
recognized	rekunized	re kug nizd
sandwich	sam wich	sand wich
saw	sawr	saw
stole	stold	stole
terrorists	terr is	ter or ists
washington	warsh in ton or wash in ton	waw shing ton
with	wif	with

Nonverbal Presentation

No matter why a speaker exhibits distracting nonverbal behaviors, whether from nervousness, habit, or fatigue, their effect is the same—they draw attention to themselves and away from what is being said. Perhaps you may have had an instructor whose mannerisms became more important than what he or she was saying. For example, an instructor who constantly uses his glasses to emphasize key ideas may cause class members to place bets on how many times he'll take off his spectacles during a single class period. The students will then concentrate on counting eyeglass removals instead of the topic being discussed.

Effective nonverbal delivery often begins with good eye contact. Good eye contact serves several functions. For example, members of an audience feel included when a speaker looks at them. Eye contact also lets the speaker receive feedback and make appropriate adjustments. You can be fairly certain that listeners are interested and understand when they nod their heads, lean forward, maintain eye contact, take notes, or smile. But feedback needn't be complimentary to be useful. For example, an audience member who seems to be disagreeing most is probably listening the closest, signaling interest in your message. The important thing is to be constantly aware of your audience's reaction, and you can do this by maintaining eye contact.

The lectern, ceiling, floor, back wall, and notes won't give you the feedback you need during a speech and surely won't give you applause afterwards. To avoid giving listeners the feeling that you are "reading at" them and not "talking to" them, pay less attention to your notes and surroundings and more attention to your audience.

Effective nonverbal presentation also is characterized by good vocal delivery. A speaker whose delivery is flat and droning is inevitably boring. People often ignore the message when the presentation is dull. If you want to keep your audience's attention, vary the rate, pitch, and volume of your delivery.

Speakers usually have the greatest problems with nonverbal delivery when they are using a manuscript or reading quotations. They have a tendency to "read" rather than to "speak" when material is printed or written out word-for-word. To avoid this pitfall, if you think that quoted material is important enough to include in your speech, plan to communicate it in a way that the audience will find interesting and meaningful.

Use your body and your voice as naturally as possible, and make sure that one does not contradict the other. When verbal and nonverbal behaviors are mismatched, a speaker may look comical or confused. For example, comic Pat Paulsen gains much comic effect by telling audience members how excited and happy he is to be speaking to them—in a monotone voice, with no body movements, facial gestures, hand gestures, or eye contact. His words express one message and his actions express the opposite.

KNOWLEDGE CHECKUP 16.2

Speaker Dynamism and Sociability

Think of a speaker you have heard—an instructor, a politician, a religious leader—who had an excellent presentational style. With that speaker in mind, complete the following scale using a **B** ("best") to indicate the extent to which that person displayed each characteristic. Then think of a speaker you have heard who had an ineffective presentational style. Complete the scale with this speaker in mind, using a **W** ("worst") to indicate the extent to which this person displayed each characteristic. For example, if your excellent speaker was highly animated (the first scale) you might place a **B** over the 7. If your ineffective speaker was slightly boring, you might place a **W** over the 4.

When you are finished, for each section, add the numbers marked with a **B** and place the sums in the total spaces. Then follow the same procedure for numbers marked with a **W**.

Dynamism

Boring	1	2	3	4	5	6	7	Animated
Passive	1	2	3	4	5	6	7	Energetic
Meek	1	2	3	4	5	6	7	Assertive
Uninvolved	1	2	3	4	5	6	7	Involved

B Total _____
W Total _____

Sociability

Gloomy	1	2	3	4	5	6	7	Cheerful
Irritable	1	2	3	4	5	6	7	Good Natured
Unpleasant	1	2	3	4	5	6	7	Pleasant
Cold	1	2	3	4	5	6	7	Warm

B Total _____
W Total _____

The two presentational characteristics assessed by the questionnaire—dynamism and sociability—separate the best presenters from the worst. Speakers who are dynamic (scores of approximately 22 and higher) and sociable (scores of 22 and higher) are viewed as interesting, forceful, appealing, and friendly, which helps them achieve their communication goals. The least dynamic (scores below 10) and sociable (scores below 10) speakers are not likely to achieve their communication goals.

1. People are usually perceived as interesting and vibrant—dynamic—if they are animated, energetic, assertive, and involved—without being overbearing. The **B** total for dynamism for your best speaker should be higher than the **W** for your worst speaker. How do your two speakers compare?

2. People are usually perceived as appealing and congenial—sociable—if they are cheerful, good natured, pleasant, and warm. The **B** total for sociability for your best speaker should be higher than the **W** for your worst speaker. How do your two speakers compare?

POSTPERFORMANCE EVALUATION

After you have presented a speech, you should have some idea of your strengths and weaknesses. The questionnaire in Skill Checkup 16.2 will help you evaluate specific aspects of your performance. It will also help you focus on key elements of public speaking as you plan a speech.

SKILL CHECKUP 16.2

Postperformance Evaluation

Use the scale below to record your perceptions of how your audience reacted to you, to your message, and to your delivery. If you have trouble responding to a statement, reconsider the audience feedback you observed during your speech, your feelings during and immediately after your presentation, and any verbal and nonverbal reactions you received form audience members when you were finished.

Write 4 if you strongly agree.
Write 3 if you agree.
Write 2 if you disagree.
Write 1 if you strongly disagree.

_____ 1. My topic suited the audience.
_____ 2. My speech suited the setting.
_____ 3. Introductory remarks, by me or by someone else, helped establish my credibility.
_____ 4. The audience thought I was competent, trustworthy, and had good-will.
_____ 5. My speech was ethical.

_____ **6.** I gained the audience's attention with my introduction.

_____ **7.** I provided the audience with necessary basic information.

_____ **8.** I provided a clear statement of purpose.

_____ **9.** I used a clear pattern of organization for the discussion section of my speech.

_____ **10.** My logical appeals were expected by and acceptable to the audience.

_____ **11.** My logical appeals were well supported.

_____ **12.** I used vivid descriptions, emotionally charged words, and statements of personal involvement as emotional appeals.

_____ **13.** I began the conclusion by summarizing the information I presented during the discussion.

_____ **14.** I concluded the speech by driving home my key point(s).

_____ **15a.** (Impromptu Speech) I effectively selected material and structured it.

_____ **15b.** (Extemporaneous Speech) My presentational outline was clear and enabled me to speak spontaneously.

_____ **15c.** (Manuscript Speech) My material was written in an oral style.

_____ **16.** My speech was enhanced by my selection of appropriate supplementary aids.

_____ **17.** My speech was enhanced by the method I used to present my supplementary aids.

_____ **18.** My delivery contained very few verbal distractors.

_____ **19.** My delivery contained very few nonverbal distractors.

_____ **20.** My grammar was appropriate to the audience, the purpose, and the setting.

_____ **21.** My choice of words was appropriate to the audience, the purpose, and the setting.

_____ **22.** My physical movements contributed to my being perceived as dynamic and sociable.

_____ **23.** My vocal variety contributed to my being perceived as dynamic and sociable.

_____ **24.** My eye contact was direct and consistent.

_____ **25.** I achieved the objectives of my presentation.

_____ **Total**

Your total reflects your perceptions of your success as a public speaker in a particular instance. With a possible range from 25 to 100, scores of approximately 75 and above indicate a positive evaluation, and those below 50 indicate a negative evaluation. Regardless of your total score, the items you gave a rating of 1 or 2 suggest your greatest trouble spots, while the items you rated 3 or 4 indicate areas of strength on which you can build. Like most other competencies, competency in public speaking develops as you apply your knowledge and skill.

The speaker in the cartoon is suffering from speechophobia.

1. What are some common fears the speaker might have that are causing his speechophobia?

2. "I'll fail!" he tells you, adding "They'll hate me!" What messages can he substitute for these negative ones?

3. If the speaker in the cartoon came to you a few days before delivering his speech and said, "I'm so nervous for this speech that I can hardly concentrate," what specific recommendations about preparing and rehearsing would you make to help him deal with his speechophobia?

4. The night before his speech, the speaker in the cartoon says, "I've prepared and rehearsed my speech, but I still don't feel ready. What else can I do to get in the right frame of mind for tomorrow?" Explain what else he can do.

5. The speaker says, "I know we talked about visualization in class, but I don't understand how to do it." Demonstrate it for him.

6. Right before his speech, the speaker grabs your arm and says, "I'm more nervous than I thought I'd be—help!" Lead him through an autogenic or progressive relaxation exercise.

7. His turn comes and he delivers his speech. Although he begins by clutching his notes and shaking from head to toe, by the end you would evaluate his dynamism at 24 and his sociability as 22. Describe his verbal and nonverbal delivery patterns. What problems did he avoid in order to receive such a high evaluation?

8. Excited by his success, he completes a postperformance evaluation. He rates himself with an overall total of 70. Items 18 through 24 all received scores of 1 or 2. What questions would you ask him to help him assess what went wrong and to help him begin to develop strategies for improvement?

NOTES

1. Lynda Gorov, "Speechless Over Speech? Relax," *Chronicle Telegram* (April 17, 1983), E–1.

2. Ayres found that students with high speechophobia have more negative thoughts about the speaking event than those with low speechophobia. See Joe Ayres, "Coping with Speech Anxiety: The Power of Positive Thinking," *Communication Education* 37 (1988): 289–96.

3. For a discussion of the use of visualization in reducing communication apprehension in public speaking, see Joe Ayres and Theodore S. Hopf, "Visualization: Is It More than Extra-Attention?", *Communication Education* 38 (1989): 1–5.

4. Roy M. Berko, Fran Bostwick, and Maria Miller. *Basic-ly Communicating: An Activity Approach*, 2d ed. Dubuque, IA: Wm. C. Brown, 1988.

FOR FURTHER INVESTIGATION

Allen, Mike, John E. Hunter, and William A. Donohue. "Meta-Analysis of Self-Report Data on the Effectiveness of Pubic Speaking Anxiety Treatment Techniques." *Communication Education* 38 (1989): 54–76.

Ayres, Joe, and Theodore S. Hopf "Visualization: Is It More than Extra-Attention?" *Communication Education* 38 (1989): 1–5.

Brownell, Winifred W., and Richard A. Katula. "The Communication Anxiety Graph: A Classroom Tool for Managing Speech Anxiety." *Communication Quarterly* 32 (1984): 243–49.

Callahan, Roger. *How Executives Overcome Public Speaking and Other Phobias*. Wilmington, DE: Enterprise Publishing, 1986.

Cathcart, Jim, and Tony Allesandra. "When In Rome." *Training and Development Journal* (June 1985): 22–24.

Gootnick, David E. *Even You Can Give A Talk*. East Elmhurst, NY: Communications Dynamics Press, 1975.

Kelly, Lynne, and Arden K. Watson. *Speaking With Confidence and Skill*. New York: Harper and Row, 1986.

Marken, G. A. "Presentations With Punch." *Management World* (March 1986): 14–15.

Phillips, Gerald M. *Help For Shy People*. Englewood Cliffs, NJ: Prentice-Hall, 1981.

Richmond, Virginia P., and James C. McCroskey. *Communication: Apprehension, Avoidance, and Effectiveness*. Scottsdale, AZ: Gorsuch, 1985.

Wiegand, Richard. "It Doesn't Need to Be Dull to Be Good: How to Improve Staff Presentations." *Business Horizons* (July-August 1985): 35–41.

GLOSSARY

abstract symbol a general representation that may refer to many things (Chapter 2)

achievement motivation the desire to succeed in situations that require excellence (Chapter 11)

adaptor nonverbal behavior that is seldom intentional; body movement performed by habit (Chapter 3)

affect displays body movements that express emotions; most commonly associated with the face (Chapter 3)

affection attraction the need to express affection and have it experienced in return (Chapter 10)

affiliation motivation the desire to be with others and enjoy mutual friendships (Chapter 11)

allness the assumption that when a communicator says something, she or he has said all there is to say on the subject (Chapter 2)

analogy a type of support in which the similarity between two or more things is discussed (Chapter 13)

approachability cues indications that the other person is available for conversation (Chapter 8)

arena (open area) in a Johari Window, information about a person that is known to himself or herself and known to others (Chapter 8)

assertion a conflict style characterized by the direct statement of needs and wants (Chapter 9)

attacking response a response that criticizes or censures (Chapter 8)

attitudes likes and dislikes (Chapter 12)

attractiveness the quality of being good-looking or appealing (Chapter 8)

audio aid an auxiliary material that depends on the sense of hearing (Chapter 15)

audiovisual aid an auxiliary material that depends on both sight and hearing (Chapter 15)

authority rule after discussion a method of decision making in which group members exchange thoughts with the leader, who then makes the final decision (Chapter 10)

authority rule without discussion a method of decision making in which the group leader chooses the solution and communicates it to group members (Chapter 10)

autocratic leader a leader who tends to focus on his or her own needs, wishes, thoughts, ideas, and concerns and thus tries to control group members (Chapter 11)

autogenic relaxation the use of verbal instructions to teach one's mind and body to relax; creates a state very much like a hypnotic trance by inducing warmth and calmness (Chapter 16)

auxiliary material an audio, visual, or audiovisual device that clarifies or illustrates a spoken message (Chapter 15)

averaging a method of decision making in which group members rank or rate the proposed solutions, the rankings are added, the sum is divided by the number of respondents, and the solution with the highest number is selected (Chapter 10)

avoidance a conflict resolution strategy based on the belief that a conflict will go away if it is ignored (Chapter 9)

balance, or high work, phase in a group's life cycle, the time when group members recognize and start to accept the distinction between the whole group and its individual members (Chapter 10)

bar graph a graph in which columns of various heights compare or contrast numbers (Chapter 15)

beliefs convictions, or what one understands and holds to be true about the world (Chapter 12)

blind area in a Johari Window, information about a person that is unknown to herself or himself but known to others (Chapter 8)

body movements motions such as gestures; head, arm, finger, leg, and toe movements; and changes in posture or trunk position (Chapter 3)

brainstorming a process that stresses the quantity—not the quality—of the solutions a group generates (Chapter 10)

bypassing the result of an individual incorrectly assuming that her or his meaning for her or his words is the same as another person's (Chapter 2)

card stacking a propaganda technique in which only the arguments and evidence that supports a speaker's points are presented, even if they have to be distorted; the speaker deliberately ignores contradictory arguments and evidence (Chapter 13)

causal arrangement a way of organizing a discussion so that material is presented in either a cause(s)-to-effect pattern or an effect-from-cause(s) pattern (Chapter 14)

chart a map or graph used in a speech (Chapter 15)

chunking grouping of bits of information according to a mutual relationship (Chapter 6)

cliché a trite expression that conveys a common or popular thought (Chapter 2)

closed question a question worded so that an interviewee responds in a few words, such as by saying yes or no, or by giving a statistic (Chapter 13)

coercive power based on negative outcomes wielded as weapons (Chapter 11)

commitment pledge to the continuation of a relationship (Chapter 7)

communication the process of sending and receiving messages (Chapter 1)

communication anxiety the fear of engaging in communication interactions (Chapter 5)

communication apprehension emotionally based communication anxiety (Chapter 5)

communication competency sufficient knowledge, skills, and motivation for an individual to achieve her or his communication goals (Chapter 1)

comparison and contrast arrangement a method of organizing a discussion in which a speaker describes both similarities and differences between or among people, ideas, objects, or events (Chapter 14)

comparison arrangement a method of organizing a discussion in which a speaker describes similarities between or among people, ideas, objects, or events (Chapter 14)

complementarity the attraction of opposites (Chapter 8)

complementary relationship a relationship structure in which each partner's behavior complements or completes the other's—the behaviors seem to go together. The relationship is based on differences which, when they come together, form a stable relationship. (Chapter 7)

compromise a conflict resolution strategy designed to satisfy everyone's concerns to some extent (Chapter 9)

concrete symbol a highly specific representation that refers to one thing (Chapter 2)

confirming response a response that indicates a person is acknowledged, understood, and accepted (Chapter 8)

conflict any situation in which a person perceives that another person, with whom she or he is interdependent, is frustrating or might frustrate the satisfaction of some concern, need, want, or desire of hers or his (Chapter 9)

conflict phase in a group's life cycle, the time when group members assert their individuality, leading to conflict; the conflict usually revolves around two issues: (1) Should we be close to each other or not? and (2) Is the leader a fool or a benevolent genius? (Chapter 10)

conflict style characteristic way a person expresses herself or himself in a conflict (Chapter 9)

conformity acting in accordance with group norms (Chapter 11)

connotation the secondary personal associations for a symbol, in addition to its explicit associations; a symbol's connotations are not necessarily shared by every member of a language community. See *denotation*. (Chapter 2)

consensus a method of decision making in which discussion continues until all group members agree on a solution (Chapter 10)

context the environment in which communication takes place, made up of such characteristics as the physical surroundings and the other people present (Chapter 1)

contrast a type of support in which the differences between two or more things are discussed (Chapter 13)

contrast arrangement a method of organizing a discussion in which a speaker describes differences between or among people, ideas, objects, or events (Chapter 14)

control attraction the need to exercise control over others (e.g., as a leader) and to be controlled (e.g., as a follower) (Chapter 10)

cultural roadblock an obstacle to effective communication resulting from people's differences in background and experience (Chapter 1)

daydreaming being lost in one's own thoughts, a common barrier to effective listening (Chapter 6)

decision making a step in the problem-solving process during which solutions are discussed and one is selected (Chapter 10)

democratic leader leader behaviors characterized by both self- and group-centeredness (Chapter 11)

demographics vital information about such characteristics as age, gender, education, religion, race, occupation, socioeconomic status, group memberships, and home region (Chapter 12)

denotation the usual explicit associations that members of a particular language community have for a symbol. See *connotation*. (Chapter 2)

direct aggression a conflict style characterized by the open expression of feelings, needs, wants, desires, and ideas at the expense of others (Chapter 9)

disclaimer an expression that excuses what a communicator is saying or asks another person to bear with him or her while he or she makes a point (Chapter 2)

disconfirming response a response that indicates the person is not valued, i.e., considered important (Chapter 8)

disintegration phase in a group's life cycle, the time when group members separate (Chapter 10)

dominance a conflict resolution strategy that focuses on a person's own needs at the expense of the other's (Chapter 9)

ectomorph a person with a thin body shape who is frail-looking (Chapter 3)

ego-extension an environmental element that a person experiences as part of herself or himself, that is, the person refers to it as *my* or *mine*, feels pride or shame for it, and accepts praise or blame for it (Chapter 4)

egospeaking when an individual jumps into a communicative transaction because he or she has something he or she wants to say, or because he or she feels that what he or she has to say is more important or more interesting than what the other person is saying (Chapter 6)

emblem a movement that has a direct verbal translation (Chapter 3)

emotional appeal an argument or information a speaker uses to evoke strong emotions in listeners, such as sadness, anger, happiness, sympathy, or fear (Chapter 13)

emotive words words that seem to be descriptive but actually communicate an attitude toward something or someone (Chapter 2)

empathic listening listening to understand another person's message from her or his point of view (Chapter 6)

empathy the capacity to see things from another person's point of view (Chapter 1; Chapter 5; Chapter 6)

end-state values desired ultimate goals (Chapter 12)

endomorph a person with a fat and round body shape (Chapter 3)

environmental roadblock an obstacle to effective communication caused by something in the physical environment (Chapter 1)

ethics rules for conduct that distinguish right from wrong (Chapter 1; Chapter 13)

euphemism inoffensive language substituted for possibly offensive language (Chapter 2)

example a specific instance, which is brief, or an illustration, which is long, that clarifies or expands on an idea (Chapter 13)

expert opinion a method of decision making in which one person with greater expertise than other group members in some special area chooses the solution (Chapter 10)

expert power the capacity to influence other group members because of the knowledge and skills they presume a person has (Chapter 11)

extemporaneous speech a talk in which a thorough but flexible outline or a set of notes guides the speaker through the oral presentation (Chapter 15)

external distraction person, object, or event in the environment that diverts attention (Chapter 6)

fact a statement based on observation; it relates directly to what can be seen, heard, touched, tasted, or smelled (Chapter 2; Chapter 13)

fact-inference confusion the tendency to respond to something as if it had been observed when, in reality, it had been merely suggested by observation (Chapter 2)

falsify (expression of emotion) to show an emotion when none is felt, to evince little or no facial expression when a particular feeling is experienced, or to cover a true emotion by displaying a false one (Chapter 3)

feedback information about the effect of a message fed back to the message source (Chapter 1)

final summary condensed review that repeats all the main points of a speech (Chapter 15)

flexibility skills skills that enhance an individual's versatility and resourcefulness in communication (Chapter 1)

formal power power based on an individual's position in the group (Chapter 11)

free information elaborations not specifically requested by a question (Chapter 8)

function approach to leadership view of leadership as the performance of task and social group functions. See *task function* and *social function*. (Chapter 11)

generalized others an individual's thoughts about what people in general consider correct or proper (Chapter 4)

gesture a movement made by a particular part of the body, such as the hands (Chapter 3)

glittering generality a propaganda technique in which a vague and highly attractive idea is associated with something the speaker wants the audience to support, e.g., "the American way" (Chapter 13)

goal outcome that an individual wishes to achieve (Chapter 7)

graph pictorial representation of numbers or the relationship of numbers to each other (Chapter 15)

green flag word word or phrase that evokes strong positive emotions and interferes with a person's willingness and ability to listen (Chapter 6)

groupthink an obstacle to group problem solving that occurs when group members' desire for uniformity interferes with their willingness to assess alternative solutions to their problem (Chapter 10)

hedges words that limit a communicator's responsibility for what he or she says (Chapter 2)

hesitations utterances or pauses which indicate that a communicator is unsure of herself or himself (Chapter 2)

hidden area in a Johari Window, information about a person that is known to herself or himself and unknown to others (Chapter 8)

hypothetical example a made-up instance or story that helps to clarify or expand an idea (Chapter 13)

idealized self a person's concept of what he or she would be if he or she were perfect (Chapter 4)

illustrator nonverbal behavior used intentionally to add to or support what is said (Chapter 3)

impromptu speech a talk for which there is no formal development prior to delivery (Chapter 15)

inclusion attraction the need to belong, to be included in what others do and to include others in what one does (Chapter 10)

indirect aggression a conflict style characterized by the expression of concerns in a disguised way. Rather than stating the real issue, a person attacks in various ways, for example, by attacking the other person directly, attacking the person indirectly, lying about his or her real feelings, manipulating the situation, embarrassing the person, hinting about the problem, withholding something from the other person, inviting the person to feel guilty, or using sarcasm. (Chapter 9)

indiscrimination the failure to see things as unique and individual (Chapter 2)

inference a conclusion that is suggested by observations but not based on them (Chapter 2)

informal power power based on perceptions of a person's abilities, qualities, and traits (Chapter 11)

initial credibility audience members' opinions of a speaker prior to his or her speech. See *speaker credibility*. (Chapter 13)

instrumental values desired ways of behaving (Chapter 12)

integration a conflict resolution strategy designed to achieve full satisfaction of the concerns of all those engaged in a conflict (Chapter 9)

interdependent a state in which two or more people depend on and need each other (Chapter 9)

internal distractor something within the communicator that diverts her or his attention (Chapter 6)

internal summary condensed review that highlights what has just been said in a speech (Chapter 15)

interpersonal conflict a conflict between people (Chapter 9)

intimacy quality of a relationship based on detailed knowledge and deep understanding of the other person (Chapter 7)

intimate distance from touching to eighteen inches (Chapter 3)

intimate experience a moment of important personal sharing (Chapter 7)

intimate relationship a relationship characterized by partners' detailed knowledge and deep understanding of each other and in which there is the expectation for continued intimate experiences. See *intimacy* and *intimate experience*. (Chapter 7)

intrapersonal conflict a conflict within one person (Chapter 9)

Johari Window model that illustrates how an individual's willingness to self-disclose and receive feedback operate in a relationship (Chapter 8)

laissez-faire leader a leader who focuses on the group's wishes, thoughts, ideas, and concerns and thus adopts a hands-off policy with members (Chapter 11)

language roadblock an obstacle to effective communication caused by people giving different meanings to words and organizing words in different ways (Chapter 1)

leadership the exercise of power (Chapter 11)

legitimate power group members' belief that they should do what someone requests because of the position that person occupies (Chapter 11)

line graph a graph in which the midpoints of the tops of each of the bars in a bar graph are connected by a series of lines (Chapter 15)

listening active process of receiving, attending to, and assigning meaning to sounds (Chapter 6)

logical appeal an argument or information a speaker uses to support or prove a point or proposal (Chapter 13)

lose-lose an approach to managing conflict whereby neither persons' goals are fully satisfied (Chapter 9)

majority rule a method of decision making in which a solution is chosen if it is preferred by more than half the group members (Chapter 10)

manuscript speech the written version of a speech, used as the basis for a presentation (Chapter 15)

map a representation of the surface of the earth or any part of it, or of the universe or any part of it (Chapter 15)

mere exposure principle the tendency for increases in exposure to increase liking (Chapter 8)

mesomorph a person with a muscular and well-proportioned body shape (Chapter 3)

message the information that a sender devises for a receiver (Chapter 1)

minority rule a method of decision making in which a small subgroup of the larger group is given authority to select a solution (Chapter 10)

mnemonic device a technique a speaker uses for helping his or her audience remember a speech by associating each of the speech's main points with a letter of the alphabet, so that when the letters are combined they form a meaningful word or a letter combination that is easy to remember (Chapter 14)

modulate (expression of emotion) to communicate feelings stronger or weaker than are actually experienced (Chapter 3)

musts required characteristics of a solution (Chapter 10)

name calling a propaganda technique in which something or someone a speaker wants the audience to reject is associated with something or someone perceived in an unflattering way (Chapter 13)

nominal group technique a method of problem solving that requires that group members generate ideas silently before discussion (Chapter 10)

nonassertive behavior a conflict style characterized by a reluctance to communicate feelings and thoughts (Chapter 9)

nonemotive words words that describe something or someone without communicating an attitude (Chapter 2)

nonfluencies vocal behaviors that interrupt or disturb the flow of messages, such as "ah," "you know," and "stuff like that," unnecessary repetition of words, stuttering, incomplete sentences, and corrections (Chapter 3)

nonverbal communication actions and attributes of people other than words that convey meaning (Chapter 3)

norms rules of conduct that group members use to regulate their behavior (Chapter 11)

object the actual item referred to in a speech (Chapter 15)

open-ended question a question that suggests a topic and encourages an interviewee to elaborate (Chapter 13)

ordering arranging of bits of information into a systematic sequence (Chapter 6)

orientation stage in a group's life cycle, the time when participants focus on learning about the group task and how it may be accomplished, group rules for behavior, and who the other group members are (Chapter 10)

outline a plan for a speech, developed in a standardized format of heads and subheads, that details the most significant features of a presentation (Chapter 15)

outside need attraction the appeal of a group that satisfies a need a person has outside the group, e.g., to please her or his parents (Chapter 10)

overloading the feeling a person has when he or she already has too much information to retain (Chapter 6)

oxymoron a self-contradictory phrase (Chapter 2)

parallel relationship hybrid form of relationship structure in which complementary and symmetrical aspects are combined. See *complementary relationship* and *symmetrical relationship*. (Chapter 7)

paraphrasing restating a speaker's message in one's own words (Chapter 6)

people attraction the appeal of a group whose members a person likes (Chapter 10)

perception the process of becoming aware of objects and events, including self (Chapter 5)

personal distance from eighteen inches to four feet (Chapter 3)

personal roadblock an obstacle to effective communication caused by a person's attitudes, values, and beliefs getting in the way of his or her listening (Chapter 1)

personal space an invisible bubble of space surrounding an individual as a body buffer zone. It is larger in front than in the back, and varies in overall size depending on the communicators and the environment (Chapter 3)

personality characteristics the qualities that constitute a person's character and make him or her distinctive (Chapter 4)

physical characteristics body traits, such as height, weight, and eye color (Chapter 4)

physical context objects and their arrangement in the environment (Chapter 3)

pie graph a circle divided into parts, each of which symbolizes a percentage of a whole (Chapter 15)

plain folks a propaganda technique in which an idea is associated with the typical or average person (Chapter 13)

pointers a speaker's clues to an audience that something important is about to be said or was just said (Chapter 15)

polarization the tendency to describe people, ideas, and events in either-or terms (Chapter 2)

posture a movement that involves the whole body; useful for communicating general attitudes (Chapter 3)

power the ability to bring about something that a person wants to happen, or conversely, to block the occurrence of something that a person does not want to happen. Power is the ability to choose. (Chapter 11)

power motivation the desire to control or influence events (Chapter 11)

powerful language language that creates an impression of strength, capability, and control (Chapter 2)

predispositions attitudes, beliefs, and values about key issues. See *attitudes*, *beliefs*, and *values*. (Chapter 12)

presentational outline the completed form from which a speaker gives a speech. It is a working outline modified during practice. (Chapter 15)

preview a statement that tells the audience what is going to come in a speech (Chapter 15)

private language language whose meanings are agreed upon by one segment of a larger language community (Chapter 2)

proactive characteristic of communication; a communicator's response to a message is based on her or his total history or background (Chapter 1)

probe a question that calls for additional information about something that was just said (Chapter 13)

problem solving the process of analyzing a problem; generating, selecting, and implementing appropriate solutions; and evaluating the results (Chapter 1; Chapter 10)

problem-solution arrangement a method of organizing a discussion in which the speaker identifies a problem and then suggests a solution (Chapter 14)

process credibility audience members' perceptions of a speaker based on what she or he says and how she or he says it. See *speaker credibility*. (Chapter 13)

progressive relaxation a deep muscle relaxation technique that does not require imagination (Chapter 16)

propaganda the use of facts, ideas, or allega-

tions to get listeners to respond to a message purely emotionally (Chapter 13)

proximity nearness or distance between communicators (Chapter 8)

psychological context a person's thoughts and feelings toward aspects of the physical context. See *territoriality* and *personal space*. (Chapter 3)

public distance beyond twelve feet (Chapter 3)

public speaking a form of communication in which a speaker addresses a relatively large audience with a prepared message (Chapter 12)

purpose the goal of the communication (Chapter 1)

purpose statement a declaration of what a speaker wants from the audience and how he or she is going to go about getting it. A useful technique for stating a purpose is to follow the pattern of "To... of/that/how/about...by...." (Chapter 12)

qualifiers words that modify what a communicator says (Chapter 2)

qualify (facial expression) to add a second facial expression to change the impact of a first one (Chapter 3)

quantitative example information presented in numerical form (Chapter 13)

racist language language that conveys stereotyped racial attitudes or suggests the superiority of one race over another (Chapter 2)

rational management technique a method of problem solving that considers the *musts* and the *wants* of a solution. See *musts* and *wants*. (Chapter 10)

real example an actual event drawn from a speaker's or someone else's life (Chapter 13)

receiver a person who takes in the message (Chapter 1)

red flag word word or phrase that evokes strong negative emotions and interferes with a person's willingness and ability to listen (Chapter 6)

referent power based on personal loyalty, friendship, affection, and admiration (Chapter 11)

reflected appraisal a person's view of herself or himself consistent with the view others hold of her or him and formed because of the views of others (Chapter 4)

regulator nonverbal behavior used intentionally to influence who talks, when, and for how long (Chapter 3)

relational roadblock an obstacle to effective communication resulting from differences in status and power, differences in the way people define their roles in a relationship, and differences in the way people perceive their relationships (Chapter 1)

relationship an emotional or other connection between people. Synonyms include *dependence, affinity, concern, alliance, affiliation, association,* and *tie.* (Chapter 7)

relative words words that gain their meaning by comparison (Chapter 2)

reordering changing an existing system of organizing information so that a new or different sequence is developed (Chapter 6)

representation of an object likeness, image, or other reproduction of an item referred to in a speech (Chapter 15)

residual message the information that a receiver remembers (Chapter 2)

reticence communication anxiety caused by a perceived lack of skills (Chapter 5)

reward power granted a person perceived as the best or only source of desired rewards (Chapter 11)

roadblock an obstacle that keeps an individual from accomplishing her or his communication goal (Chapter 1)

role a pattern of behaviors that signals a predictable way of acting (Chapter 11)

role ambiguity when expectations for a role are not communicated clearly enough to enable full understanding of the role's requirements (Chapter 11)

role conflict when two or more incompatible expectations or definitions exist for the same role (Chapter 11)

role overload when expectations for an individual's behavior call for him or her to perform several roles simultaneously. The roles may not be incompatible, which would give rise to role-role conflict, but they require more skill, time, or energy than the individual has. (Chapter 11)

role taking engaging in behaviors that fit a situation and do not conflict with an individual's sense of self (Chapter 1)

role-role conflict when two contradictory roles are assumed at the same time (Chapter 11)

rule a regulation that governs actions. Rules are necessary to make predictions about another person's behavior. (Chapter 7)

Sapir-Whorf hypothesis a proposition that language shapes ideas and guides how people see and interpret their environment. (Chapter 2)

scratch outline a rough indication of the material to be included in each of the six parts of a speech (gaining the audience's attention, providing necessary background, statement of purpose, discussion of information, summary of key ideas, and driving home the point(s)) (Chapter 15)

selective interpretation the process of choosing how to explain information selectively perceived and organized (Chapter 5)

selective organization the process of fitting together information selectively perceived in an effort to form a whole (Chapter 5)

selective perception the process of choosing what to focus attention on (Chapter 5)

self-centered role a pattern of behavior

designed to satisfy personal rather than group needs (Chapter 11)

self-concept the totality of a person's thoughts about self, i.e., a person's self-perception. See *self-esteem*. (Chapter 4)

self-disclosure intentionally exposing self to another person by honestly communicating self-revealing information (Chapter 8)

self-esteem the totality of a person's feelings about self. See *self-concept*. (Chapter 4)

self-fulfilling prophecy the tendency of a person's beliefs about self and others to come true (Chapter 5)

self-role conflict when an individual enacts a role that does not fit his or her self-image (Chapter 11)

semantic differential a tool that measures a person's reactions to an object or concept by marking spaces between a pair of adjectives, one positive and one negative, with each space representing an attitude position (Chapter 2)

sender a person who devises a message (Chapter 1)

sequence arrangement a way of organizing a discussion so that information is presented in a logical order (Chapter 14)

serious self a realistic concept of self which conforms to a person's capabilities and the restrictions of her or his environment (Chapter 4)

sexist language language that conveys stereotyped sexual attitudes or suggests the superiority of one gender over another (Chapter 2)

shared language language whose meanings are agreed upon by all members of a language community (Chapter 2)

should self a concept of self that contains all the "oughts" and "shoulds" that serve as the person's moral guideposts (Chapter 4)

shyness a term applied to those who are fearful about communicating and believe they lack communication skills (Chapter 5)

significant other someone whose opinion matters or whose judgment is trusted (Chapter 4)

silence not speaking or making nonverbal vocal sounds, such as "um" (Chapter 3)

similarity having characteristics in com- mon, whether looks, attitudes, opinions, values, beliefs, experiences, or ideas (Chapter 8)

situation approach to leadership involves considering individual circumstances to determine what style of leadership is best (Chapter 11)

small group three or more people, usually not more than ten, who perceive themselves as a group, are interdependent and mutually influential, have patterned interaction, and pursue shared goals (Chapter 10)

smoothing-over a conflict resolution strategy that has as its goal the satisfaction of another person's concerns to the neglect of an individual's own (Chapter 9)

social comparison comparing self to others to evaluate self by the standards set by those others (Chapter 4)

social distance from four to twelve feet (Chapter 3)

social function behavior that helps group members get along with each other (Chapter 11)

social identity the groups or categories to which an individual is socially recognized as belonging and/or with which he or she identifies himself or herself (Chapter 4)

social role a pattern of behavior that helps a group satisfy social needs and build feelings of groupness (Chapter 11)

spatial arrangement a way of organizing a discussion so that information is presented according to a physical or geographical layout (Chapter 14)

speaker credibility audience members' perceptions of a speaker's competency, trustworthiness, and goodwill (Chapter 13)

speechophobia the anxiety associated with public speaking (Chapter 16)

static evaluation the inability of the English language to account for constant change; the tendency to retain perceptions based on prior observations while the reality to which the observations refer is constantly changing (Chapter 2)

stereotype an oversimplified conventional notion of a thing, person, or idea, based on its similarities with other things, persons, or ideas (Chapter 2)

stress the feeling of strain or pressure that arises from any event perceived as interfering with what is considered normal (Chapter 5)

structure how talk is organized and coordinated (Chapter 7)

style approach to leadership overall pattern that emerges from a leader's interactions with group members (Chapter 11)

supportive response a response that gives approval or help (Chapter 8)

symbolic representational. In language, for instance, words have no meaning in themselves but are arbitrary letter combinations that stand for or represent something (Chapter 2)

symmetrical relationship a relationship structure in which each partner contributes equally to the relationship while maintaining her or his individual identity (Chapter 7)

tag question an unnecessary question added to a statement (Chapter 2)

talk-writing creating a manuscript in an oral style (Chapter 15)

task attraction the appeal of a group perceived as able to solve a problem thought to be too difficult to solve alone (Chapter 10)

task function behavior that helps a group get its job done (Chapter 11)

task role a pattern of behavior that helps a group accomplish its goals (Chapter 11)

terminal credibility final and overall perception of a speaker's credibility when the speech is completed. See *speaker credibility*. (Chapter 13)

territoriality a feeling of ownership toward some fixed area (Chapter 3)

testimony quoting or paraphrasing of someone else's opinions, beliefs, predictions, or statements as a way of supporting a speaker's own ideas (Chapter 13)

topical arrangement a way of organizing a discussion so that points of the discussion are organized as subdivisions of the same subject (Chapter 14)

trait approach to leadership assumption that people possess certain characteristics that make them leaders (Chapter 11)

transformational leader leader motivates group members to achieve more than they originally expected by changing—transforming—their attitudes and values towards both the group task and themselves (Chapter 11)

unknown area in a Johari Window, information about a person that is unknown both to himself or herself and others (Chapter 8)

value a belief about the inherent worth or worthiness of different ways of behaving and of different goals (Chapter 4; Chapter 12)

verbal language the ability to communicate orally using words (Chapter 2)

visual aid an auxiliary material that depends on the sense of sight (Chapter 15)

visualization the imagining of oneself performing some action successfully in a carefully guided exercise, e.g., going through the experience of giving a successful speech (Chapter 16)

wants nonessential but desirable characteristics of a solution (Chapter 10)

win-lose an approach to managing conflict whereby one person wins and the other loses (Chapter 9)

win-win an approach to managing conflict whereby everyone's needs are satisfied (Chapter 9)

working outline an expanded version of the scratch outline. It contains the details—the logical and emotional support—for each main point of the discussion section of the speech, as well as expanded versions of the attention-getting, background, purpose, summary, and final point sections. (Chapter 15)

INDEX

Entries in bold are from tables, figures, and other non-text material.

Achievement motivation, 263
Adaptors, 74
Affect displays, 73
Affection, 169
Affiliation motivation, 264
Aggression
  direct, 214–215, **215**
  indirect, 213–214, **215**
Allness, 34, **37**
Analogies, 322
Approachability cues, 177
Arena, 185
A*S*S*E*R*T Formula, 217, **217**, **218**
Assertive behavior
  complex situations, skills for, **217**, 217–218, **218**
  definition, 215
  simple situations, skills for, 215–216, **216**
Attacking behaviors, 181–182, **182–183**
Attitudes, 296
Attraction factors
  attractiveness, 174–175
  complementarity, 176
  personal rewards, 175–176
  proximity, 175
  similarity, 176
Attractiveness, 174–175. *See also* Body image; Body shape
Audience-centered communications, 312
Authority rule after discussion, 246–247
Authority rule without discussion, 246
Autocratic leadership style, **279**, 280
Auxiliary materials
  assessing, **376–377**
  audio aids, 373
  audiovisual aids, 373
  choosing, **374–375**, 375–376
  visual aids, 371–372
Averaging, 246
Avoidance, 207, **210**

Balance phase, group development, 239
Bargaining. *See* Compromise
Bar graphs, 372, **373**
Beliefs, 296–297

Blind area, 185
Body image, 52–53, **53–54**
Body language. *See* Nonverbal communication
Body movements
  categories, 72–74
  perceptual differences, **75–76**
  uses of, 74–76
Body shape, 51, **51–52**
Brainstorming, 243–244, **243–244**
Bypassing, 35–36, **37**

Card stacking, 324
Causal arrangement, 342–343
Charts, **372**, 372–373, **373**, **374**
Chunking, 144
Clichés, 38, **41**
Closed question, 326
Clothing, 54, **55**
Coercive power, 274–275
Collaboration. *See* Integration
Commitment, **166–167**, 167
Communication
  characteristics, 4–6, **6–7**
  components of competency, 7–12, **8**, **9–11**
  definition, 3
  elements, 3, **6–7**
  nonverbal, 48–81
  proactive process, 5
  and stress, 120–128
  verbal, 20–47
Communication anxiety
  apprehension, 123
  causes, 125
  definition, 122, **123**
  effects, 125–126
  methods for handling, 126
  reticence, 123
  shyness, 124–125
Communication competency
  checkups, **9–11**, **18**, **46**, **78–79**, **103**, **127–128**, **152**, **170**, **194**, **227–228**, **255–256**, **285**, **308–309**, **332–333**, **356–357**, **380–381**, **396–397**
  communicators, qualities of competent, 13–17
  functions, 12–13

knowledge, 8
motivation, 11–12
skills, 8, **9–11**, 14
Comparison and contrast arrangement, 344, **345**
Comparison and/or contrast arrangements, 344
Comparison arrangement, 344, **345**
Competency, public speaking, 315–316
Complementarity, 176
Complementary relationship, 160
Compromise, 208–209, **210**
Confirming behaviors, 181–182, **182–183**
Conflict
definition, 198
frustration, 198–199
group development phase, 238–239
interdependence, 199
management approaches, 218–224, **223**
perceptions of, 200–202
personal effects, 204, **204–205**
processes and outcomes, assessing, **224–226**
relationships, effects on, 203
role, 269
role-role, 269–270
self-role, 270
sources, 199–200
strategies, **205–206**, 205–211, **210, 210–211**
styles, **211–212**, 211–218, **215, 216, 217, 218**
work, effects on, 203
Conflict phase, group development, 238–239
Conformity, 261
Confronting. *See* Integration
Connotations, 26–27
Consensus, 247
Contrast arrangement, 344, **345**
Contrasts, 322
Control attraction, 234
Cosmetics, 54
Cultural roadblocks, 15

Daydreaming, 141–142
Deception
nonverbal clues, 76
Decision-making methods
comparisons, 247–248, **248–249**
definitions, 246–247
selecting, **249**
Democratic leadership style, **279**, 280
Demographics, 296
Denial. *See* Avoidance
Denotations, 26

Desired self-concept
idealized self, 93–94
serious self, 94
should self, 94
Disclaimer, 44
Disconfirming behaviors, 181–182, **182–183**
Discord. *See* Conflict
Disengagement process. *See also* Relational
development; Relationships
direct and indirect strategies, 190–192, **191**
reasons for, 190
Disintegration phase, 239–240
Distortions, 39, **41**
Dominance, 208, **210**
Dominance/submission in relationships, 158–164

Ectomorphic body shape, 51–52
Educational institutions, conflict management
messages in, 202
Ego-extensions, 89
Egospeaking, 141
Emblems, 72
Emotional appeals
emotionally charged words or events, 324
personal involvement, 324–325
propaganda, 324
vivid descriptions, 323
Emotionally charged words, 138–139, **139–140**,
324
Emotive words, 38–39, **41**
Empathic listening
assessing, **148–150**
definition, 147
response styles, 150–151
Empathy, 118–119, **119**, 136. *See also* Empathic
listening
Endomorphic body shape, 51–52
End-state values, 297
Environmental roadblocks, 15
Esteem, 169
Euphemisms, 37–38, **41**
Examples, 320–321
Expert opinion, 246
Expert power, 273–274
Extemporaneous speeches, 362–367, **363–367**
External distraction, 140–141
Eye behavior, 57
Eye contact, 392

Facial expressions, 56–57, **58**

Fact-inference confusion, 32–33, **33–34**, **37**
Facts, 32, 321
Falsification, facial, 56
Families, conflict management messages in, 201
Favorable impression
    characteristics, 179–180
    creating, 179
Feedback, 3, 146, **146**, **147**, **184–185**, 185–190
    from public speaking, 392
Feeling and behavior, 77, **77**
Final summaries, 369, **370**
Flexibility skills, 14
Forcing. *See* Dominance
Formal power, 272, **275**
Free information, relational, 178–179, **178–179**
Function approach to leadership, 278–279

Generalized others, 91
Gestures, 75
Glittering generality, 324
Goodwill, 317–318
Green flag word, 138
Group development
    balance, or high work, phase, 239
    conflict phase, 238–239
    disintegration phase, 239–240
    orientation phase, 237–238
    phase development, **240**
Group problem solving
    decision-making, 246–249, **248–249**
    defining the problem, 243
    evaluating results, 250
    generating solutions, 243–244, **243–244**
    implementing the solution, 250
    overcoming obstacles, 250, 252–254
    preconditions, 241–242, **242**
    sequence diagram, **251**
    setting criteria, 245, **245**
Groupthink, 253–254

Hairstyle, 54
Hedges, 44
Hesitations, 44
Hidden area, 185
High attraction, 236
High work phase. *See* Balance phase
Hypothetical examples, 320–321

Idealized self, 93–94
Illustrators, 72

Impromptu speeches, 360–362, **362**
Inclusion attraction, 234
Indiscrimination, 31–32, **32**, **37**
Inferences, 32, **37**
Informal power, 272, **275**
Initial credibility, 313
Initiating contact, steps, 177–178, **178–179**
Instrumental values, 297
Integration, 14, 209, **210**
Interdependence, 199
Internal distractor, 141
Internal summaries, 369, **370**
Interpersonal conflict, 199
Interviews, conducting, 326–327, **328**
Intimacy, 158, 168–169
Intimate distance, 63
Intimate experience, 168
Intrapersonal conflict, 199
Introductions to speeches, 378–379, **379**

Jargon. *See* Private language
Jewelry, 54, 55
Johari Window, 185–188, **186**, **187**, **188**

Knowledge checkups
    body image, **53**
    body shape self-analysis, **51–52**
    brainstorming and nominal group
      techniques, **245**
    clothing, **55**
    commitment, **166–167**
    communication anxiety, **123**
    conflicts, personal effects of, **204–205**
    conflict strategies, **205–206**
    conflict style, **211–212**
    credibility assessment, **314–315**
    disclosure and feedback, **184–185**
    distracting speech behaviors, **389**
    elements and characteristics of
      communication, **6–7**
    emotional triggers, **139–140**
    empathic listening, **148–150**
    ethics, **330–331**
    fact-inference confusion, **33–34**
    group attraction, **234–235**
    information arrangement for speeches, **345**
    ladder of abstraction, **25**
    leadership adaptability, **282**
    leadership style, **280–281**
    listening self-evaluation, **131–132**

mate preferences, **177**
motivation questionnaire, **262–263**
nonlistening signals, **137**
norms, role of, **260**
outlines, **363**
perception process, **112–113**
personal space, **64**
physical environment, **60**
power, personal, **271–272**
power questionnaire, **272–273**
public speaking anxiety, **292–294**
relationship dimensions, **155–156**
relationship discord, **198**
relationship rules, analysis, **165**
self-concept, **84, 85, 87**
self-inventory, **295**
self-perception, **124**
speaker dynamism and sociability, **393–394**
specialized language, **29**
stress and communication, **121**
structure of relationships, **161–162**
television, conflicts on, **203–204**
territory, **61**
touch, **67**
unclear language, **40**
vocal cues, **70–72**

Ladder of abstraction, 23–25, **25**
Laissez-faire leadership style, **279**, 280
Language. *See also* Verbal communication
    abstract and concrete symbols, 23–25, **25**
    barriers, 29–36, **31, 32, 33–34, 35, 37**
    definition, 22–23
    denotation and connotation, 26–27
    effective use, 36–46
    powerless, **44, 44–45, 45**
    private, 27–28, **29**
    racist, 43, **44**
    roadblocks, 15–16
    sexist, 40–42, **42–43, 44**
    shared, 28
    supportive, 181
    unclear, 36–40, **40, 41**
Language roadblock, 15
Leadership
    approaches, 277–284, **279, 280–281, 282**
    definition, 277
Legitimate power, 275–276
Library resources, 328–329
Line graphs, 373, **374**

Listening
    barriers, 137–142
    definition, 133
    effective, techniques, 142–147
    empathic skills, developing, 147–151
    importance as communication skill, 136–137
    levels, 134–135, **135**
    nonlistening cues, 138–142
    patterns, **131–132**, 131–135, **135**
    stages, 133–134
Listening techniques
    organizing material, 144–145, **145**
    paraphrasing, 142–143
    physically paying attention, 143–144
    providing feedback, 146, **146, 147**
    repeating, 143
    taking notes, 143
Logical appeals
    analogies and contrasts, 322
    definition, 318
    examples, 320–321
    facts, 321
    testimony, 322
Lose-lose conflict management, 220–221, **223**
Love/hostility in relationships, 158–164
Lying. *See* Deception

Majority rule, 247
Manuscript speech, 367–368, **368–369**
Maps, 372
Mere exposure principle, 175
Mesomorphic body shape, 51–52
Message, 3
Minority rule, 247
Mnemonic devices, 347, **347**
Model speech, analyzing, 348–355
Modulation, facial, 56
Musts, 245, **245**

Name calling, 324
Negotiating. *See* Compromise
Nominal group technique, 244
Nonassertive behavior, 213, **215**
Nonemotive words, 38
Nonfluencies, 68
Nonlistening cues. *See also* Listening; Listening techniques
    arguing with speaker, 138
    emotionally loaded words, responding to, 138–139, **139–140**

external distractions, 140–141
failing to receive the whole message, 140
internal distractors, 141–142
overloading, 138
Nonverbal communication
body movements, 72–75, **75–76**, **77**
competency checkup, **78–79**
deception, 76
face and eyes, 56–57, **58**
functions, 49–50
physical appearance, **51–52**, 51–55, **53**, **55**
physical environment, 59–60, **60**
psychological environment, 60–64, **61**, **64**
in relational development, 182
speeches, presenting, 392, **393**
touch, 64–66, **67**
voice, 68–69, **68–69**, **70–73**
Norms, 259–260, **260**
Note-taking, 143

Objects, 371
Obliging strategy. *See* Smoothing over
Open-ended question, 326–327
Open-mindedness, 117–118, **118**
Ordering, 144–145
Orientation stage, group development, 237–238
Outlines
correcting, **366–367**
stages, 364–366
unscrambling, **363**
Outside need attraction, 233
Overloading, 138
Oxymorons, 39, **41**

Parallel relationship, 161
Paraphrasing, 142–143
People attraction, 233
Perception
of conflict, 200–202
of others, organizing, 110–111
perceptual accuracy, 114–120
selective, 107–108, **112–113**
selective interpretation, 111–113
selective organization, 108–110
self-fulfilling prophecy, 113–114
Perceptual accuracy
empathy, 118–119, **119**
open-mindedness, 117–118, **118**
sense awareness and imagination, 114,
115–116

Personal distance, 63
Personality characteristics, **85**, 85–87
Personal rewards, 175–176
Personal space
definition, 61–62
purpose of, 62
zones, 63, **64**
Physical characteristics, 89
Physical environment
elements, 59–60, **60**
Pie graphs, 372, **372**
Plain folks, 324
Pointers, 369
Polarization, 29–30, **31**, **37**
Postures, 75
Power. *See also* Dominance
bases, 272–277
definition, 271
personal, questionnaire, **271–272**, **272–273**
Powerless language, **44**, 44–45, **45**
Powerlessness
body movements, 75
language, **44**, 44–45, **45**
Power motivation, 263–264
Predispositions, 296–297, **298**
Presentational outlines, 365–366
Previews, 369, **370**
Private language, 27–28, **29**
Probe, 327
Problem-solution arrangement, 343–344
Problem solving, 14. *See* also Group problem
solving; Integration
Process credibility, 313
Propaganda, 324
Proximity, 175
Psychological environment
personal space, 61–63, **64**
territoriality, 60–61, **61**
Public distance, 63
Public speaking
audience assessment, 295–300, **300**
audience-centered and speech-centered
communications, 312
benefits of learning, 291–292
emotional appeals, 323–325, **325**
ethics, 330, **330–331**
Five-P Process, 289–291, **291**
interviews, conducting, 326–327, **328**
library resources, 328–329
logical appeals, 318–322, **325**

prepreparation, 311
self-assessment, 292, **292–294**, 294, **295**
setting assessment, 300–301, **301**
speaker credibility, 313, **314–315**, **318**
speechophobia, 383–388
statement of purpose, developing, 304, 306–307, **307–308**
topic selection, 301, **302**, 303, **303–304**, **305**
Purpose statement, 304, 306–307, **307–308**, 340–341
Put-downs, avoiding, 100–101, **101**

Qualifiers, 44
Quantitative examples, 320
Questions, responding to, 378–379, **380**
Quotations, reading, 392

Racist language, 43, **44**
Rational management technique, 245
Real examples, 320
Receiver, 3
Red flag words, 138
Referent power, 274
Reflected appraisal
generalized others, 91
significant others, 90, **90–91**
Regulators, 73
Rehearsal, 386–387
Rejection, fear of, 189–190
Relational development
attraction factors, 174–177, **177**
disengagement strategies, 190–192
favorable impression, creating, 179–180
initiating contact and gathering information, 177–179
self-disclosure and feedback, 183–190
supportiveness and confirmation, 181–182
Relational roadblocks, 15
Relationships. *See also* Relational development
analyzing structure of, 161–163
beginning, 173–180
commitment role, 166–167, **166–167**
complementary, 160
conflict, managing, 197–228
definition, 156–157
dimensions of, **155–156**
ending, 190–192
father-son example, 162–163
goals, 157–158, 177–180
increasing satisfaction with, 192–193
intimacy, 158, 168–169

maintaining, 180–190
parallel, 161
resources, 169
rules for, 164–165, **165**
satisfying, achieving, 192–193
structure, 158–163, **159**, **161–162**, **163**
symmetrical, 160–161
time, effect of, 169
Relative words, 36–37, **41**
Relaxation
autogenic, 387–388
progressive, 388
Reordering, 145
Repeating, 143
Representations of objects, 371–372
Residual message, 39
Reward-cost balance, 175–176
Reward power, 274
Roadblocks
definition, 14
to effective speech presentation, **389**, 389–390
types, 15–16
Role ambiguity, 270
Role conflict, 269
Role overload, 270
Role-role conflict, 269–270
Role taking, 14

Sapir-Whorf hypothesis, 22
Schools. *See* Educational institutions
Scratch outlines, 364
Selective interpretation, 111
Selective perception
determinants, 107–108
organization of perceptual information, 108–111
Self-centered roles, **267**, 267–268
Self-concept. *See also* Desired self-concept; Self-esteem
ideal, 93–94
organizing the elements, 92–93, **93**
real content of, 84–93, **85**, **87**, **90**, **91**, **93**
self presented to others, 94–97
sources, 89–92
Self-disclosure
fear of rejection, 189–190
increasing, **188–189**
Johari Window, 185–188, **186**, **187**, **188**
relationship functions, 183–184

Self-esteem
    analyzing, **97**, 97–98
    improving, **99**, 99–103, **100**, **101–102**
    low, sources, 99–102
Self-fulfilling prophecy, 113–114
Self-perception
    as competent communicator, 17–18
Self presented to others
    expectations of others, 95–96
    objectives of, 96–97
    perceived requirements of a situation, 95
Self-role conflict, 270
Semantic differential, 27
Sender, 3
Sense awareness, 114, **115–116**
Sequence arrangement, 341–342
Serious self, 94
Sexist language, 40–42, **42–43**, **44**
"Should" messages, 94, 99, **99**
Should self, 94
Shyness
    public and private, 124–125
    situational, 125
Significant others, 90, **90–91**
Silence, 68
Similarity, 176
Situation approach to leadership, 281–282
Skill checkups
    A*S*S*E*R*T Formula, **218**
    associations, **116–117**
    audience assessment, **300**
    auxiliary materials, **374–375**, **376–377**
    body movements, **75–76**
    brainstorming, **243–244**
    commonly mispronounced words, **390–391**
    conflict outcomes, **226**
    conflict process, **224–225**
    conflict strategy, **210–211**
    credibility, perceptions of, **318**
    decision-making methods, **249**
    empathy assessment, **119**
    expressing emotions, **68–69**
    facial expressions, **58**
    feedback, **146**, **147**
    feeling and behavior, **77**
    group attraction, **236**
    impromptu speeches, **362**
    information probe, **178–179**
    interview questions, **328**
    introductions, writing, **378**

    logical and emotional appeals, **325**
    manuscript speeches, **368–369**
    mnemonic devices, **347**
    open-mindedness, **118**
    organizing material, **145–146**
    outlines, correcting, **366–367**
    polarization, **31**
    postperformance evaluation, **394–395**
    powerless language, **45**
    previews and summaries, **370**
    problem solving, **242**
    purpose statement, **307–308**
    relationship discord, **215**
    responding to questions, **380**
    role observance, **268–269**
    self-concept, **90**, **91**
    self-disclosure, **188–189**
    self-esteem, **99**, **100**, **101–102**
    sense awareness and imagination, **115**
    setting assessment, **301**
    sexist language, **42–43**
    simple assertions, **216**
    solution criteria, **245**
    speeches, **331**, **340**
    static evaluation, **35**
    stereotypes, **32**
    supportive and confirming responses,
        182–183
    topic selection, **303–304**
Small groups. *See also* Group development;
  Group problem solving
    definition, 232–233
    importance of, 231–232
    role determination, 261–265, **262–263**
    role problems, 269–270
    rules of conduct, 259–261, **260**
    sources of attraction to, 233–236, **234–235**
    specific roles, 265–269, **267**, **268–269**
Smoothing over, 207–208, **210**
Social comparison, 91, **91–92**
Social distance, 63
Social identity, 84–85
Social roles, 266, **267**
Spatial arrangement, 342
Speaker credibility
    competency, 315–316
    goodwill, 317–318
    trustworthiness, 316–317
Speech-centered communications, 312

Speeches. *See also* Public speaking
  attention-getting techniques, 335–339, **339**
  auxiliary materials, 371–377, **372, 373, 374–375, 376–377**
  causal arrangement, 342–343
  comparison and/or contrast arrangements, 344–345
  extemporaneous, 362–367, **363–367**
  guideposts for the audience, 369–371, **370**
  impromptu, 360–362, **362**
  introductions, 377–378, **378**
  manuscript, 367–369
  mnemonic devices, 347, **347**
  model, analysis of, 348–355
  nonverbal presentation, 392, **393**
  point–making strategies, 348
  postperformance evaluation, **394–395**
  problem-solution arrangement, 343–344
  providing background, 339, **340**
  purpose statement, 340–341
  question and answer period, 378–379, **380**
  sequence arrangement, 341–342
  spatial arrangement, 342
  speechophobia, 383–384
  topical arrangement, 341
  verbal presentation, 389–390, **390–391**
  visual aids, 347
Speechophobia
  appropriate attitudes, 384–385
  components, 383–384
  preparation, 385–386
  rehearsal, 386–387
  relaxation, 387–388
Static evaluation, 34–35, **35, 37**
Stereotypes, 31
Stress
  communication anxiety, 122–126, **123, 124**
  communication indicators, 120–121, **121**
Style approach to leadership, **279**, 279–280
Supportive behaviors, 181–182, **182–183**
Suppression strategy. *See* Smoothing over
Symbols
  abstract and concrete, 23–25, **25**
Symmetrical relationship, 160–161

Tag question, 44
Task attraction, 233

Task roles, 266, **267**
Television, conflicts on, 202, **203–204**
Terminal credibility, 313
Territoriality, 60–61, **61**
Testimony, 322
Topical arrangement, 341
Topics for speeches
  narrowing, **302**, 303
  selecting, 301, **302**, 303, **303–304, 305**
Touch
  expectations for, 66
  responses to, **67**
  uses of, 65–66
Trait approach to leadership, 278
Transformational approach to leadership, 283–284
Trustworthiness, 316–317

Unknown area, 185

Values, 87, **87–88**, 297
Verbal communication
  effective language, 36–46
  importance, 21–22
  language, 22–29
  language barriers, 29–36, **31, 32, 33–34, 35, 37**
  in relational development, 181–182
  speeches, presenting, 389–390, **390–391**
Visual aids, 347, 371–372
Visualization, 387
Vocal behaviors
  good vocal delivery of speeches, 392
  nonfluencies, 68
  silence, 68
  use in expressing emotions, **68–69**
  vocal cues, 69, **70–72**
Vocal cues, 69, **70–72**

Wants, 245, **245**
Win-lose conflict management, 219–221, **223**
Win-win conflict management
  purpose, 221
  steps, 221–224, **223**
Withdrawal. *See* Avoidance
Working outlines, 364–365